Gendering Legislative Behavior

In democracies, power is obtained via competition. Yet, as women gain access to parliaments in record numbers worldwide, collaboration appears to be on the rise. This is puzzling: Why, if politicians can secure power through competition, would we observe collaboration in congresses? Using evidence from 200 interviews with politicians from Argentina and a novel data set from twenty-three Argentine legislative chambers over an eighteen-year period, *Gendering Legislative Behavior* reexamines traditional notions of competitive democracy by evaluating patterns of collaboration among legislators. Although only the majority can secure power via competition, all legislators – particularly those who do not have power – can influence the policy-making process through collaboration. Tiffany D. Barnes argues that as women have limited access to formal and informal political power, they collaborate more than men to influence policy making. Despite the benefits of collaboration, patterns of collaboration vary among women because different legislative contexts either facilitate or constrain women's collaboration.

Tiffany D. Barnes is an assistant professor at the University of Kentucky. With the support of the National Science Foundation and the Ora N. Arnold Fellowship, she conducted extensive fieldwork in Argentina, visiting nineteen of the country's twenty-four provinces, collecting a large data set of legislative activity, and conducting more than 200 interviews with legislators and elite political observers. In 2013 she was a visiting fellow at the Kellogg Institute for International Studies at the University of Notre Dame. Her articles appear in journals such as *Journal of Politics*, *Comparative Political Studies*, *Politics & Gender*, the *Election Law Journal*, and the *Journal of Women, Politics & Policy*.

Gendering Legislative Behavior

Institutional Constraints and Collaboration

TIFFANY D. BARNES

University of Kentucky

CAMBRIDGE
UNIVERSITY PRESS

CAMBRIDGE
UNIVERSITY PRESS

One Liberty Plaza, 20th Floor, New York, NY 10006, USA

Cambridge University Press is part of the University of Cambridge.

It furthers the University's mission by disseminating knowledge in the pursuit of education, learning, and research at the highest international levels of excellence.

www.cambridge.org
Information on this title: www.cambridge.org/9781316507650

First published 2016

Printed in the United States of America by Sheridan Books, Inc.

A catalogue record for this publication is available from the British Library.

Library of Congress Cataloging in Publication Data
Names: Barnes, Tiffany.
Title: Gendering legislative behavior: institutional constraints and collaboration /
Tiffany D. Barnes, University of Kentucky.
Description: New York: Cambridge University Press, [2016] |
Includes bibliographical references and index.
Identifiers: LCCN 2015051004| ISBN 9781107143197 (hardback) |
ISBN 9781316507650 (pbk.)
Subjects: LCSH: Women legislators – Cross-cultural studies. |
Women – Political activity – Cross-cultural studies.
Classification: LCC HQ1236.B264 2016 | DDC 320.082–dc23
LC record available at https://lccn.loc.gov/2015051004

ISBN 978-1-107-14319-7 Hardback
ISBN 978-1-316-50765-0 Paperback

To my family,
and especially Jesse

Contents

Tables

Figures

Acknowledgments

This book project has taken me to Argentina and back six times over the course of the past several years. I spent hundreds of hours traveling across Argentina to work in government archives, to meet with provincial politicians, and to learn about the country. Over the course of about twenty months in Argentina, I made a number of good friends, saw some of the most beautiful parts of the country, and learned a ton about Argentina and Argentine politics. Despite a number of hiccups along the way – many of which make for great stories now – overall my fieldwork was a major success. And for that, I count myself lucky. Although it took a great deal of tenacity to travel across Argentina alone for months on end, one of the biggest challenges fieldwork introduces is that scholars must often rely on the help of complete strangers to accomplish their goals. Fortunately for me, Argentina is full of kindhearted and generous people. Indeed, this project would not have been possible without the assistance of countless Argentine bureaucrats who helped me obtain data, Argentine politicians who participated in interviews, and other nice people who helped me along the way. To each of them, I owe a great deal of gratitude.

Additionally, this book has benefited from a number of people who provided guidance and support before, during, and after my fieldwork in Argentina. Although there are far too many people to name them all here, and I'm sure I have omitted someone, I would like to take this opportunity to thank some of the people whose influence has been crucial along the way. To begin with, I would like to thank my advisor, Mark Jones. Mark's guidance has been instrumental since the genesis of this project. He helped me acquire the resources and skills needed to carry out extensive fieldwork and to write this book, and he supported me during every stage of the process. He is a wonderful mentor and friend, and I certainly would not be the scholar I am today without him. Thank you, Mark, for all you do.

I would like to thank Maria Escobar-Lemmon, Leslie Schwindt-Bayer, and Michelle Taylor-Robinson for participation in a book workshop at Rice University in the spring of 2014. I was fortunate to have each of them read and comment on my manuscript. The participants in the workshop and the conversations we had (both during and after the workshop) proved invaluable for the development of my book. I am so privileged to call each of these brilliant and talented scholars my mentors and friends.

I'm grateful to Emily Beaulieu, who has become a dear friend, colleague, and mentor. She has been a huge champion of this book and a constant source of both moral support and intellectual inspiration over the past three years. This book benefited from countless conversations with Royce Carroll, and my work is all the better for it. Mirya Holman deserves special thanks for reading most of this book (parts of it multiple times over) and for her unyielding support. Thanks to Mike Alvarez for all the guidance and advice he provided during the later stages of my book project – it proved invaluable!

Further, I am indebted to Stephanie Burchard, Erin Cassese, Miki Kittilson, Heather Silber Mohamed, Diana O'Brien, Randy Stevenson, and Justin Wedeking for reading large portions of my book and giving me excellent comments. This book has also benefited from generous feedback at various stages from Adam Auerbach, Michael Coppedge, Ange-Marie Hancock, Magda Hinojosa, Alice Kang, Mona Lena Krook, Philippe LeMay-Boucher, Richard Matland, Juan Pablo Micozzi, Gabriela Ippolito-O'Donnell, Tracy Osborn, Mark Peffley, Jennifer Piscopo, Charlotte Rommerskirchen, Amelia Scholtz, Meg Shannon, Clayton Thyne, Melody Ellis Valdini, Denise Walsh, Alice Wiemers, Joseph Wiltberger, Christina Wolbrecht, and members of the Gender & Political Psychology Writing Group.

I am lucky to have smart and kind colleagues at the University of Kentucky – especially Horace Bartilow, Emily Beaulieu, Becky Bromley-Trujillo, Stacy Closson, Abby Córdova, Jesse Johnson, Dan Morey, Mark Peffley, Ellen Riggle, Clayton Thyne, Steve Voss, Rick Waterman, Justin Wedeking, and Ernie Yanarella – you are amazing. Jill Haglund and Mike Zilis – I am so happy you are here! Thank you to my wonderful colleagues and professors at Rice, who encouraged and challenged me, shaping me both professionally and intellectually: Santiago Alles, Gina Branton, Stephanie Burchard, Royce Carroll, Songying Fang, Keith Hamm, Jinhyeok Jang, Jesse Johnson, Basia Kataneksza, Jaci Kettler, Seonghui Lee, Ashley Leeds, Lanny Martin, Juan Pablo Micozzi, Marvin McNeese, Cliff Morgan, Monika Nalepa, Ngoc Phan, Andrew Spiegelman, Bob Stein, Randy Stevenson, Carolina Tchintian, and Rick Wilson.

The University of Kentucky supported this project in various, essential ways, including a special fellowship assignment that allowed me to relinquish my teaching duties to spend fall 2013 at the Kellogg Institute for International Studies at the University of Notre Dame to write the initial draft of this manuscript, and several grants that funded fieldwork in Argentina and research assistance. Funding from the National Science Foundation (SES-0921374), the Ora N. Arnold Fellowship, and Rice University's Social Science Research Institute also supported various fieldwork trips to Argentina.

I would like to thank CIPPEC, particularly Fernando Straface and María Marta Page, for their assistance during my fieldwork in Argentina. I also thank Ernesto Risso at Very Important People for his help in obtaining information about Argentine legislators. I would like to thank Adrian Lucardi, Carlos Gervasoni, Leonardo Giacomelli, David Yañuk, and Cristina Tchintian for facilitating numerous contacts for me during my fieldwork in Argentina. Thanks to Pablo Ava for giving me the opportunity to work at Fundación de Investigaciones Económicas y Sociales during the early stages of graduate school so that I could get my footing in Argentina. I would not have thrived during so many months of fieldwork without several dear friends in Argentina. Astrid Lopez Alesanco, you're a gem. Sol Saenz, Rachel Kitch, Alethea Cederberg Dixon, Whitney Fleming, Ignacio Arlotti, and Santiago Alles, I cherish our time together. Thanks to Paula Bertino, Gabriela Rangel, Katie Clark Angie Bautista-Chavez, and Charles Dainoff for excellent research assistance at various stages in the book process.

Robert Dreesen deserves my gratitude. He has been wonderful to work with and I truly appreciate his support. Also, Brianda Reyes merits a special thanks for shepherding me through the publication process. She too is a pleasure to work with. I am grateful to three anonymous reviewers at Cambridge University Press, who supported this project and gave me valuable comments for improving the work.

Finally, I would not have made it this far without the support of my family and friends. To you, I owe my success. Mom (Lori), Dad (Rocky), Addie, Elliot, Cole, Landon, and Luke, thank you for your continued love and support. Nikki and Fanny, your friendships have taken me through so much. But most of all, I thank my partner, Jesse, who gave up a wonderful job at Kansas State and left behind dear friends and colleagues to join me here at the University of Kentucky. I am so thankful that we are here together. Thank you for always being there to celebrate my accomplishments, for enduring endless conversations about my book, and for providing unwavering support throughout both the exciting and the stressful parts of this process. You are a constant source of joy and encouragement in my life.

1

Introduction

"And that's where women in the Senate make a real difference. Women tend to be more collaborative, less concerned about scoring partisan political points and more focused on getting a solution."
                                        – *Republican Senator Susan Collins, Maine, 2013*

Five days into the U.S. government shutdown in 2013, Republican Senator Susan Collins took the Senate floor and challenged her colleagues to work together to put an end to the impasse. In the midst of a fierce partisan standoff, she pieced together a bipartisan coalition – disproportionately comprised of women – that would lay the foundation for the federal fiscal plan later signed into law. Although the large role female senators played in forging a compromise attracted considerable media attention, the senators themselves suggested this was par for the course. Senator Collins explained: "I don't think it's a coincidence that women were so heavily involved in trying to end this stalemate. Although we span the ideological spectrum, we are used to working together in a collaborative way."[1]

Female senators in the United States are certainly not in lockstep politically, but their custom of monthly meetings and their history of collaborating across party lines on other projects set the tone for constructive bargaining to end partisan gridlock. Indeed, women in the U.S. Senate have a track record of crossing party lines to develop legislation that promotes their shared interests. The Airline Passenger Bill of Rights Act (Barbara Boxer, D-CA and Olympia Snowe, R-ME), legislation to provide health care to the first responders to the attacks of September 11, 2001 (Lisa Murkowski, R-AK and Kristen Gillibrand, D-NY), and legislation amending the tax code to meet the needs of stay-at-home moms (Barbara Mikulski, D-MD and Kay Bailey Hutchison, R-TX) are just a few of many examples. Senator Mikulski describes these bipartisan feats

---

[1] Quoted in Weisman and Steinhauer (2013).

and others as "the power of two women building a coalition to accomplish a mutual goal."[2]

This kind of collaborative behavior is not unique to the United States. As women gain access to parliaments worldwide in record numbers, legislative collaboration appears to be on the rise. Stories of women working together to accomplish bipartisan goals appear in popular media and academic discourse across the globe. In Rwanda, two years after the genocide, a bipartisan coalition of women formed the Forum of Rwandan Women Parliamentarians – the first ever caucus in Rwanda where members of the parliament work across party lines to promote legislation. In El Salvador, in 2011, women in the parliament set aside party differences to pass the First Comprehensive Law for a Life Free of Violence against Women. And in Uruguay, female legislators united into a women's caucus, reaching a consensus on legislation to prohibit sexual harassment in the workplace and give female employees access to retirement pensions. Deputy Margarita Percovich of Uruguay described it this way: "Traditional politics, with its endless fighting, had us all tired out. The men emphasized differences, but we did exactly the opposite."[3]

As these examples make clear, collaboration is a vital part of the policy-making process and democratic representation. Yet most scholarship focuses on the competitive aspects of democracy. From Schumpeter's (1942) "competitive struggle" to Dahl's (1971) "contestation and participation," democracy has been defined as a competitive process that determines the power to make decisions. This adversarial understanding of democracy is reflected in the tendency of many scholars to focus on polarization and gridlock (Binder 1999, 2015; Linz and Valenzuela 1993; Mainwaring and Shugart 1997). Legislators are often assumed to have a single-minded focus on defeating their competitors. Still, collaboration occurs, perhaps even often. This is puzzling: *Why, if politicians can secure power to make political decisions via competition, would we ever expect to observe collaboration in the policy-making process?*

This book reexamines traditional notions of competitive democracy by investigating patterns of policy collaboration among Argentine legislators, especially among women. In doing so, it tackles three important questions. The first question is this: *Can democracy be collaborative?* I argue that collaborative democracy is not antithetical to competitive democracy. Although only the majority can secure the power to decide via competition, I explain that all legislators – particularly those who are not in the winning majority – can influence the policy-making process through collaboration. Using bill cosponsorship data, which represents the culmination of the collaborative process, I demonstrate that democracy can be collaborative, that out-of-power legislators collaborate more frequently than those in power, and that women collaborate more than men across the entire range of policy areas.

---

[2] Barbara Mikulski in *Nine and Counting: The Women of the Senate* (Boxer, Collins, and Feinstein 2001).
[3] Quoted in Silveira (2010).

This raises a second question: *Why do women collaborate?* That is, what motivates women's collaboration? Although popular explanations for women's collaboration assume that women are simply socialized to be more collaborative than men, I argue that female legislators – like all legislators – are strategic politicians and they collaborate in an effort to be more effective representatives. Specifically, women collaborate more than men because they face structural barriers that restrict their ability to exert influence on the policy-making process. By collaborating with other women they can overcome structural barriers and attain political power. I show empirically that despite having high levels of descriptive representation as a group and seniority as individuals, women's marginalization exists across a vast array of legislative powers including chamber-wide leadership posts, committee leadership posts, and powerful committee appointments. This marginalization limits women's political power and motivates collaboration among women.

Finally, this leads to a third question: *When do women collaborate?* If women are more motivated to collaborate, why do some female legislators collaborate successfully among themselves, while other women fail to do so? Specifically, I investigate the institutional contexts that condition women's collaboration. I argue that despite the benefits of collaboration, patterns of collaboration vary among female legislators because not all women have the same opportunities to work collaboratively. Different legislative contexts either facilitate or constrain women's collaboration. I show empirically that six key contextual variables, which vary both between and within legislative chambers, shape policy collaboration. First, I examine women's numeric representation and partisan constraints; both factors vary substantially between legislative chambers. Then I focus on affiliation with the executive party, seniority, legislation targeting women's issues, and membership in a women's caucus or committee; each of these factors varies within legislative chambers. Taken together, the answers to these three important questions offer a solution to the puzzle by explaining why and when we can expect to observe collaboration in a democracy where power is obtained via competition.

CENTRAL THEORETICAL ARGUMENT

Can democracy be collaborative? Why do women collaborate? And when do women collaborate? These three central questions motivate this book. In this section, I provide an overview of the theoretical argument that helps me answer these three questions. These ideas are developed in full in Chapter 2.

Can Democracy Be Collaborative?

I argue that democracy can be collaborative and that many of the political behaviors we observe are clearly more collaborative than competitive. The tension between cooperation more generally and competition has figured prominently in the literature on electoral rules and is central in the selection of party authorities to act as delegates for party members (Cox 1997; Duverger 1954; Lijphart 2012). Yet, with few exceptions, modern scholars have paid little attention to the collaborative aspects of the policy-making process.[4] As a result, extant research on legislative behavior gives us an incomplete picture of representative democracy. Shifting from an almost exclusive focus on competition to a focus that incorporates collaboration can improve our understanding of representative democracy and inform our knowledge of how institutions structure the political process.

Whereas classical theories of democracy advocated the idea that power should be vested in the will of the people with the primary purpose of promoting the common good, procedural definitions of democracy focus primarily on competition (Schumpeter 1942). In this view, power is vested in the *majority* and is maintained through exclusion and competition (Lijphart 1984, 2012). Clearly, competition is essential to democracy; but the near-exclusive emphasis on competition runs counter to other core democratic principles and leaves no room for collaboration. If groups of people are continually denied access to power, democracy is likely to be undermined over time (Lijphart 1984; Mainwaring, Brinks, and Pérez-Liñán 2001, 2007). For democracy to be legitimate it needs to incorporate preferences and information from all legislators (not limited to those in the winning majority) beyond the process of simply aggregating preferences through voting procedures or strategic voting that merely maximizes individuals' preferences over a set of predetermined outcomes. The collaborative aspects of democracy are therefore necessary to incorporate the preferences of a wider range of legislators.

Collaboration is not simply coordination. Democratic coordination is characterized as a sequence of choices that include procedures to determine the sets of alternatives at different stages in the decision-making process (Cox 1997). Although coordination may be explicit, it is typically implicit, only requiring actors to anticipate the actions of others and to respond in a strategic way that maximizes the probability of achieving their preferred outcome. Collaboration, by contrast, is a generative process in which legislators work together to produce a wholly new outcome. Collaboration is distinct from coordination because it requires explicit interaction, carried out with the goal of creating something novel rather than simply facilitating preference maximization.

Collaboration enhances democracy by encouraging inclusion and participation of all groups, enabling them to voice their concerns and influence the policy-making process. By collaborating with other representatives – both

---

[4] Notable exceptions of work focused on legislative collaboration include research by Alemán and Calvo (2010), Calvo and Leiras (2012), and Kirkland (2011), which are discussed in more detail in Chapters 2 and 3. For a broader discussion of how institutions promote consensus building in the democratic process, see Clucas and Valdini (2015) and Lijphart (1984).

within their own parties and across party lines – legislators can increase their influence over group decisions, shape the outcome of legislation, and develop more efficient and effective policy. Through collaboration, legislators can raise awareness around an issue, increasing the probability that it gets on the legislative agenda (Krutz 2005; Wilson and Young 1997) and is ultimately passed into law (Alemán and Calvo 2010). All legislators want to exert their influence in the policy-making process, regardless of their majority or minority status. Although only the majority can secure the power to decide via competition, anyone – including those legislators in positions of institutional weakness – can obtain influence through collaboration. An unfortunate reality of democracy is that some group is always likely to be marginalized. But through collaboration, excluded groups can enhance their strength and influence, thus bringing the polity one step closer to the democratic ideal.

Given the strong normative and practical benefits of collaboration, I argue that all legislators have an incentive to collaborate. Nonetheless, collaboration is costly. Consequently, not all legislators will choose to collaborate all of the time. Instead, legislators must determine if the benefits of collaboration outweigh the costs. Legislators in positions of power often do not need to incur the costs of collaboration in order to exert influence in the policy-making process, as they have access to a number of resources they can use to wield influence. By contrast, out-of-power legislators have far fewer resources at their disposal and therefore have a stronger incentive to collaborate to exert influence in the policy-making process. Thus, although I expect to observe widespread collaboration in democracies, legislators in positions of institutional weakness will collaborate more than their powerful colleagues.

Why Do Women Collaborate?

I contend that women are marginalized in the legislatures where they serve and consequently find themselves in a position of institutional weakness. Given this, there is little doubt that they can benefit from collaboration. When women enter into a male-dominated institution, they face formal and informal structural barriers that prevent them from wielding influence in the legislative process. Women are marginalized despite having high levels of descriptive representation as a group and seniority as individuals (Barnes 2014; Krook and O'Brien 2012; Schwindt-Bayer 2010). Women's marginalization is not merely a product of their numeric status in the chamber, but it is also because they lack access to formal and informal positions of power. Women encounter a series of formal structural barriers because they simply do not have the same opportunities as men to hold leadership posts and powerful committee positions in the chamber (Heath, Schwindt-Bayer, and Taylor-Robinson 2005; Kittilson 2006; O'Brien 2015). Legislators holding these positions have disproportionate influence in shaping the legislative agenda, writing the content of bills, and deciding how legislative resources are distributed. Because women are systematically excluded from these powerful positions, they are much less able to shape legislation and allocate resources to their constituents.

Women also face informal barriers that limit their influence in the parliament. They are often excluded from important leadership discussions and professional networks (Barnes 2014; Franceschet and Piscopo 2008; Rosenthal 1998; Schwindt-Bayer 2006). Women are subject to negative stereotypes about their ability to lead, to legislate, and to influence stereotypically masculine policy domains such as economic policy (Duerst-Lahti 2005; Holman, Merolla, and Zechmeister 2011; Kathlene 1994). Together, these formal and informal barriers limit women's legislative power.

Despite these barriers, female legislators, like all legislators, have an obligation to represent their constituents' interests by voicing their concerns and shaping policy. They also have an incentive to behave in a way that allows them to advance their political careers. In order to do their jobs effectively, female legislators must work around these barriers. Because of their marginalization, I contend, women, like other groups not in positions of power, can greatly benefit from collaboration. By collaborating – both within their parties and across party lines – women can attain more power and exert more influence on the policy-making process.

Women stand to benefit from collaboration above and beyond the benefits realized by their male colleagues who are also excluded from power. In a society where women are socialized to be more cooperative and consensual (Forret and Dougherty 2004; Timberlake 2005), not only might women prefer collaboration to competition, but also, women are rewarded for conforming to these gender stereotypes (Eagly and Carli 2007; Heilman and Okimoto 2007). Unlike men, women who are self-assertive or aggressive in pursuing their goals are likely to elicit negative reactions, thus limiting their influence in groups (Burgess and Borgida 1999; Yoder 2001). By contrast, when women take a collaborative and cooperative approach to task performance – such as lawmaking – they can increase their influence over group decisions (Ridgeway 1982; Shackelford, Wood, and Worchel 1996). Consequently, women can wield more power in the legislature by adopting collaborative strategies. Beyond this, women may also derive personal benefits from collaboration, as there is evidence that women in political office enjoy the collaborative elements of politics more than do their male colleagues (Kathlene 1989; Lang-Takac and Osterweil 1992; Tilly and Gurin 1992).

The additional benefits that women incur from collaboration may be sufficient to explain why women are more likely to collaborate than men and, by extension, to choose female collaborators. Still, there are additional reasons why women may choose to work more with women than men. This is because women are also marginalized *within* other out-of-power groups. Beyond the social expectations generated by gender stereotypes, other social dynamics make it particularly rational for women to collaborate with women. In institutions that are traditionally male domains or even mixed-gender settings, men tend to dominate leadership, agenda setting, and deliberation (Karpowitz and Mendelberg 2014; Propp 1995; Thomas-Hunt and Phillips 2004). In collaborating with other women, female legislators find they have more opportunities for influence. Thus, women's unique experiences in the legislature – due to marginalization and socialization – explain why women are more likely than men to collaborate overall, and why they are more likely to collaborate with women.

When Do Women Collaborate?

Despite the benefits of collaboration, patterns of collaboration vary among female legislators because not all women have the same opportunities to work collaboratively. One reason for this variation in women's legislative behavior is that a number of institutional contexts – which vary both between and within legislative chambers – structure women's legislative behavior (Osborn 2012; Schwindt-Bayer 2010). With respect to institutions that vary largely between chambers, both partisan constraints and women's numeric representation should shape women's legislative behavior. I argue that electoral institutions that concentrate power in the hands of party leaders and foster strong party loyalty constrain women's propensity to collaborate. But electoral institutions that allow legislators to act independently of the political parties and tolerate the pursuit of a legislative agenda beyond the parties' platforms impose fewer constraints on women's collaboration. Moreover, this relationship will be stronger or weaker depending on women's numeric representation. As women's marginalization persists regardless of women's numeric status in the chamber, rather than alleviating marginalization, increases in numeric representation *expose* women's marginalization, making it more visible. Because legislators are motivated to collaborate to overcome institutional weakness, this implies that where women hold a larger share of seats in the legislature, women will be further incentivized to collaborate. Thus, I expect that increases in women's numeric representation will spur collaboration among women when they face weak party pressure. At the same time, when there are more women in office, it is more likely that collaboration among women will result in influence over outcomes. Consequently, in contexts where party constraints are strong, increases in women's numeric representation heighten party leaders' incentives to limit women's collaboration.

Women's legislative behavior also varies within legislatures. Specifically, female legislators who are members of the governor's party face fewer partisan pressures than women who are members of the opposition parties; as a result, they have more opportunities to collaborate with female colleagues.[5] With respect to seniority status, I argue that women who have served previous terms

---

[5] In this book, I focus specifically on the Argentine provinces, in which case the executive is the governor. As such, I use the language "governor's party" to refer to the executive. Nonetheless, the theory is general and applies to the executive's party in presidential systems.

in office will have larger political networks within the chamber and are more willing to defy party norms than are their junior colleagues; for this reason they will be more likely to cross party lines to collaborate with women. Next, I argue that because women are more likely than men to prioritize women's issues, women are more likely to seek out female collaborators when working on issues in this area. Finally, women will be more likely to collaborate with other women when they hold membership in a women's caucus or on a women's issues committee. Such organizations serve to solve the coordination problem among women and facilitate collaboration among like-minded legislators. In sum, I expect that women's legislative collaboration will vary both between and within legislative contexts.

EVIDENCE OF WOMEN'S LEGISLATIVE COLLABORATION

To address these three important questions, this book uses a rich combination of qualitative and quantitative data. The primary setting for my analysis is Argentina, where I compare men's and women's legislative behavior at the provincial level in order to capture variation in women's numeric representation and legislative contexts within a single country case. I draw on qualitative evidence from more than 200 interviews with male and female legislators and elite political observers from eighteen Argentine provinces and the autonomous Federal District (herein nineteen provinces). The fieldwork was conducted between 2007 and 2013 during six different trips to Argentina. The map of Argentina in Figure 1.1 depicts the provinces I visited during this time (shaded in gray). My quantitative evidence comes from a novel data set that I developed using archival data from twenty-three Argentine chambers over an eighteen-year period. The data include all cosponsored legislation, committee appointments, and leadership posts for more than 7,000 male and female legislators.

Observing Legislative Collaboration

Collaboration is the process of people working together to produce a desired outcome. Within the legislative context, most collaboration is intended to develop and advance legislation. Legislators can collaborate in a number of ways in an effort to influence the policy-making process. Legislators can collaborate with their colleagues by cosponsoring legislation; by engaging in activities such as networking and organizing informal meetings to collect information on problems in their districts; or by exchanging ideas during party meetings, floor debates, and committee hearings. Collaboration can mean legislators working together within or across party lines. Further, legislative collaboration is not strictly limited to collaboration among legislators themselves. Legislators can collaborate through informal means such as building networks with bureaucrats, experts, and organizations outside the legislature (Alcañiz forthcoming)

FIGURE 1.1. Map of the Argentine provinces.
Note: This map indicates the eighteen provinces and the Federal District (shaded in gray) where I conducted interviews and carried out archival work between 2007 and 2013.

and holding meetings to obtain information, or through formal avenues such as inviting specialists to testify during committee hearings.

Although collaboration can take a number of different forms, some forms of legislative collaboration can be difficult for scholars to observe and even more difficult to systematically measure. For example, it is difficult to observe every time that legislators hold informal meetings or mentor their colleagues. To address this challenge, I take two different approaches to evaluating legislative collaboration. First, in the case of Argentina, I measure collaboration using bill cosponsorship data.[6] Then, I supplement my cosponsorship analysis with a series of case studies to examine more informal types of collaboration.

Cosponsorship data is an ideal measure of collaboration because it represents the culmination of a collaborative process in which legislators work together to consider different perspectives, build consensus, and develop legislation (Alemán and Calvo 2010; Calvo and Leiras 2012; Kirkland 2011). For example, in 2005, eleven female deputies in Córdoba worked together to develop, promote, cosponsor, and pass a law establishing preventative measures for and sanctions against workplace violence. Whereas it is impossible to systematically account for the informal and "behind the scenes" development and promotion of legislation across a large number of cases, we can systematically observe cosponsorship. Most legislatures methodically record bill cosponsorship information. Moreover, I can collect this information and measure it with practically no error. I corroborate evidence from cosponsorship data with numerous qualitative examples of Argentine women's successful and foiled efforts to collaborate. In Chapter 3, I introduce my bill cosponsorship data and detail the reasons why bill cosponsorship is the best measure of collaboration in the Argentine context.

Parties are integral in thinking about the scope of collaboration. As political parties are the organizational units of legislatures, it is not uncommon for legislators to collaborate within their own political parties. Although parties work as agents of coordination to advance the parties' agendas, party leaders can often advance policies without input or even buy-in from rank-and-file members. In such circumstances, if legislators do not collaborate to influence the development of legislation, they may have no involvement in the policy-making process. Thus, my theory indicates that collaboration will vary substantially both within and across parties depending on individual legislators' incentives to collaborate. I evaluate legislators' propensity to collaborate with colleagues *across the entire chamber*, and I also focus specifically on their propensity to *cross party lines* to collaborate.

In Chapter 7, I augment my careful analysis of cosponsorship data with a series of qualitative case studies that examine women's legislative collaboration. This approach, which draws on examples from across the world, allows

---

[6] See Appendix 3.1 for a complete list of the provincial chambers used in the cosponsorship analyses.

me to account for more informal types of collaboration – such as meetings with policy experts outside the legislature, consultations with constituents, and development and promotion of legislation – that occur in the policy-making process. The depth the Argentine analyses provide, coupled with the breadth these additional case studies offer, makes this book the most comprehensive study of legislative collaboration to date.

Why Argentina?

A subnational analysis of women's legislative collaboration allows me to overcome a number of challenges that limited prior research on women's legislative behavior. To evaluate my theory, I need to compare men's and women's legislative collaboration across a large number of chambers that have a sizable share of women over a long duration. To examine how institutions shape women's legislative behavior, I need significant variation in institutions both between and within chambers. Identifying an appropriate sample of legislative chambers to evaluate my theory and collecting data on these chambers was no easy task.

One of the major limitations imposed on cross-national analyses of women's legislative behavior is the fact that there are only a few chambers in the world where women have held substantial proportions of legislative seats for a significant duration of time. Second, studying women's legislative behavior is challenging because many cultural and contextual factors beyond the legislature may influence women's behavior, making it difficult to isolate the effects of institutions. Third, studying women's collaboration in a cross-national setting poses a challenge in terms of identifying a measure of collaboration that can be applied generally across a number of countries with varying party systems and political institutions.

Fortunately, studying Argentina allows me to overcome all three of these challenges by exploiting subnational variation within a single country. A subnational analysis of Argentina allows for interesting comparative analysis across a large number of cases over a long period of time, while effectively eliminating potentially confounding country-level factors (Calvo and Murillo 2004; Lijphart 1971; Linz and de Miguel 1966; Snyder 2001).

As the first country to adopt legislative gender quotas, Argentina is one of the only contexts in the world where women have held a sizable share of seats in a large number of legislatures over a long timeline in a large number of chambers. Gender quotas were first adopted in Argentina at the national level in 1991 as a result of a massive mobilization of over five-thousand women (Carrió 2005; Chama 2001) and skillful lobbying with an appeal to the lasting legacy of Eva María Duarte de Perón, or Evita (Alles 2007, 2008; Jones 1996; Krook 2006, 2009; Lubertino 1992). The following year, quota adoption began to spread rapidly across the provincial legislatures, placing Argentina firmly in the vanguard of the quota adoption movement

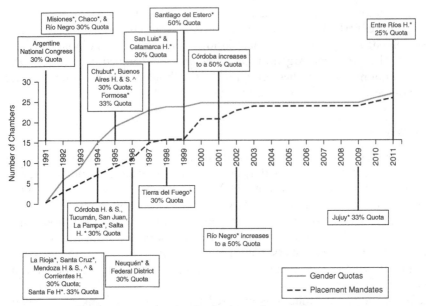

FIGURE 1.2. Gender quota adoption in the Argentine provinces.
* Indicates that the quota legislation included a strong placement mandate. ^ indicates a weak/ineffective placement mandate.
Figure 1.2 graphs the number of provincial chambers adopting gender quotas (out of thirty-two total) on the y-axis and the year of adoption on the x-axis. For detailed information on gender quota laws in the Argentine provinces, see Appendix 1.1.

(Barnes and Jones 2015). Figure 1.2 charts the adoption of gender quotas across the Argentine provinces. Quota adoption was staggered across the 1990s, with six legislative chambers adopting quotas for the first time in 1992, followed by three additional chambers in 1993. By the end of the 1990s, the vast majority of the legislative chambers in Argentina had adopted a gender quota of at least 30 percent (Archenti and Tula 2008; Barnes 2012a; Caminotti 2009). In general, the diffusion of quotas across Argentina resulted in substantial increases in women's numeric representation in subnational legislatures. Thus, a major advantage of the subnational analysis is the sheer number of chambers in Argentina where women hold a sizable proportion of seats (and have for some time now). As such, a subnational analysis of Argentina offers a unique opportunity to examine women's legislative behavior in a large number of cases over a substantial number of years.

Nonetheless, the success of gender quotas varies significantly across chambers because of the large variation in electoral laws used across the provinces (Alles 2009; Jones 1998). This variation is illustrated in Figure 1.3, which graphs women's numeric representation (y-axis) for each subnational chamber in Argentina over time (x-axis). For example, after quota adoption women's

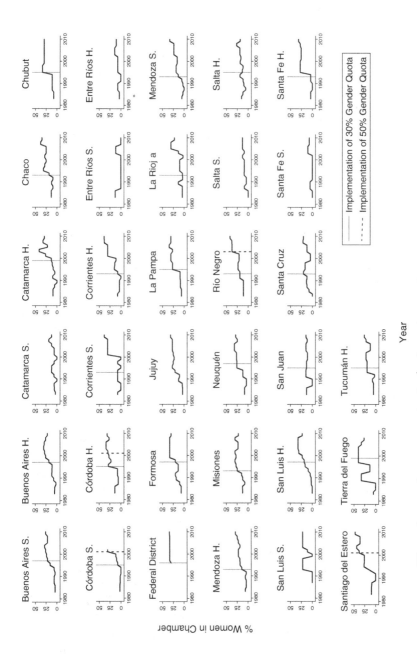

FIGURE 1.3. Women's numeric representation in the Argentine provinces.

Note: Figure 1.3 graphs the number of women in the legislative chamber on the y-axis and the year on the x-axis. The reference lines indicate the adoption of gender quotas in individual provinces.

representation in Chubut increased from 11 percent in 1994 to 26 percent in 1996. In Chubut, legislators are elected from a closed list in one province-wide district and the gender quota legislation requires that women be placed in electable positions on the party list (i.e., a placement mandate). Gender quotas work best when they include a placement mandate and are combined with closed-list electoral systems and large district magnitudes (Alles 2014; Jones 2009; Jones et al. 2012; Schwindt-Bayer 2009). In Salta, Santa Cruz, and San Juan, by contrast, women's representation did not spike after quota adoption. On one hand, the effectiveness of gender quotas in Salta and Santa Cruz has been limited because of the electoral system. Santa Cruz uses a mixed-member electoral system in which one half of the chamber is elected using single-member districts. Salta uses a multimember system in which two-thirds of the legislators are elected from districts with small district magnitudes. Single-member districts and small district magnitudes are more likely to result in low levels of women's numeric representation (Matland 2002; Paxton, Hughes, and Painter 2010) – even when combined with gender quotas (Matland 2006; Tripp and Kang 2008). On the other hand, San Juan adopted a quota without placement mandate language – quotas without placement mandates are not conducive to the election of a large share of women (Jones 1998). This variation in women's numeric representation – which is due primarily to the compatibility between gender quotas and existing electoral rules – is essential for examining how increases in women's numeric representation shape women's legislative collaboration.

Another reason the Argentine legislatures are an ideal setting for studying women's legislative behavior is the significant variation in political institutions used in each of these legislatures (Calvo and Escolar 2005). This variation is important because different political institutions create different legislative incentives, which, I argue, will influence when women collaborate. Of particular interest is the fact that Argentina hosts considerable variation across chambers in terms of the systems used to elect members, which determines the level of party constraints legislators face. Similarly, there is variation within chambers in terms of the number of legislators with seniority status and the number of members affiliated with the governor's party. This variation both across and within chambers in Argentina is essential to test my theory about *when women will collaborate.*

Equally important is the relative ease with which I can draw comparisons between legislators in different chambers. Because of differences in constitutional powers and chamber norms, collaboration might take on different forms in different countries. For example, whereas legislators frequently collaborate to produce cosponsored legislation in Argentina (Alemán et al. 2009; Barnes 2012b; Calvo and Leiras 2012), this same form of collaboration is practically nonexistent in countries where most legislation is handed down from the executive branch and where it is rare for legislators to introduce legislation. These differences make it difficult to systematically compare collaboration across a large number of national chambers. At the subnational level in Argentina, however, each province patterns its own constitution and legislature after the national constitution and national legislature. Deputies in every province have similar legislative authority and uphold similar legislative norms. Hence, legislative collaboration looks similar across Argentina, and there is widespread use of collaboration to develop cosponsored legislation in every province. As a result, I can draw valid comparisons between legislators across a large number of chambers, and I can be more confident that variation in collaboration is not a product of variation in constitutional powers or legislative norms.

Beyond these major advantages to studying Argentina, subnational research is important because a substantial amount of policy making happens at the subnational level in federal systems. Subnational governments typically have jurisdiction over health, education, and social policies, giving them considerable influence over a number of issues that shape the quality of women's lives such as violence against women, reproductive rights, access to contraceptives, and sexual education (Brown 2013, 2014a; Franceschet 2011; Franceschet and Piscopo 2013; Holman 2014; O'Brien 2013; Vickers 2011). But, with few exceptions, scholars have paid little attention to subnational institutions. Taken together, the large number of chambers with a sizable proportion of female legislators and the key sources of variation – both in the proportion of women represented in the legislative chambers and in electoral institutions – make the Argentine legislatures an excellent place to examine women's legislative collaboration. This is one of the best settings to examine the effects of institutions and women's numeric representation on women's legislative collaboration across a large number of chambers while holding many contextual, historical, political, and cultural variables constant.

Beyond Argentina

Although the primary focus of this book is on Argentina, I also extend my analysis in three important ways to demonstrate the generalizability of my theory. First, I move beyond Argentina to examine legislative collaboration in chambers from four additional countries: the Rwandan Parliament, the U.S. Senate, the Uruguayan Congress, and the South African Parliament. Second, I examine countries that have different institutions than the ones used in Argentina, thus allowing the institutional context to vary even more. In particular, the case studies serve as an exploration of how varying levels of party constraints structure women's legislative collaboration across the full range of partisan constraints. Third, I expand my definition of collaboration beyond bill cosponsorship to focus on the policy-making process more generally.

I begin with Rwanda, which represents an example of successful female collaboration. I maintain that despite Rwanda's history of a politically divisive climate, the use of reserved seats for women combined with women-only elections reduces partisan constraints, providing women more autonomy to collaborate with female colleagues. In the case of the U.S. Senate, cross-partisan collaboration among women is well documented. I argue that collaboration among women thrives because legislators face weak party constraints (a product of small electoral districts and competitive primary elections), which my theory implies is conducive to collaboration. In Uruguay, a well-organized women's caucus facilitates coordination among women, and because women comprise only a small portion of the chamber, their efforts to collaborate fly under the radar, attracting little attention from party leaders. Finally, South Africa presents an example of a legislative context where women fail to collaborate among themselves. In this case study, I demonstrate that the use of closed-list ballots with extremely large district magnitude and party leaders' ability to banish defiant members from the parliament foster strong party discipline that constrains women's collaboration. Taken together, these four case studies demonstrate the generalizability of my theory outside of Argentina, using more general measures of collaboration across a larger number of legislative contexts.

THE IMPORTANCE OF STUDYING WOMEN'S LEGISLATIVE COLLABORATION

The study of women's legislative collaboration makes several important contributions to our understanding of representative democracy, women's political power, and political institutions more generally. First, it advances our understanding of democracy and political institutions. Given that most of what we know about legislatures and legislative behavior comes from the study of male legislators and male-dominated institutions, we cannot be sure how much of the behavior we observe is a product of the institution and how much is a product of gendered actors (Driscoll and Krook 2009; Mackay, Kenny, and Chappell 2010; Mackay and Krook 2011). If it is the case that women legislate differently than men, then it is possible that these shortcomings in our understanding of representative democracy – as primarily competitive and not collaborative – are largely gendered. Considering men's and women's legislative behavior side by side in the same institution can help us distinguish between legislative behaviors that are a product of institutional constraints and those that are a product of gender. In doing so, this book contributes to an exciting new research area that investigates the different consequences of institutions for men and women. Whereas recent work focuses on how institutions shape men's and women's mass political attitudes and behavior (Barnes and Córdova forthcoming; Kittilson and Schwindt-Bayer 2012; Morgan and Buice 2013), I evaluate the differential impact of institutions on male and female elites. Moreover, by examining collaboration within the legislative process and not simply legislative outcomes, we get a clearer understanding of how women navigate the legislative system differently than their male colleagues.

Second, the findings from this book imply that women are using their gender-based socialization to make democracy better. This is somewhat counterintuitive because abundant evidence shows women are socialized in a way that limits their ability to wield influence in organizations (Propp 1995; Thomas-Hunt and Phillips 2004). Women do not typically exhibit strong leadership traits that are believed to be important for effective lawmaking. Instead women are socialized to be more collaborative, cooperative, and compromising (Eagly and Karau 2002; Eagly, Wood, and Diekman 2000). Although individual women may wield less power than their male colleagues, I find that women are using their non-agentic skills to make democracy more representative. The fact that women are more skilled at working together to accomplish common goals makes them far better prepared to craft effective legislation (Volden, Wiseman, and Wittmer 2013). The consensus-based leadership styles that women bring to the table are more effective for producing long-term policy solutions (Alcañiz forthcoming; Kathlene 1995). Further, collaboration improves democracy by giving voice to out-of-power groups. I show that women are more collaborative than men, which implies that women's incorporation into politics is making democracy better – above and beyond the added benefit of incorporating a historically marginalized group into government.

Third, this book contributes to our understanding of how and when women will have a voice in the policy-making process. Given that women face a unique set of barriers that limit their political power, it is important to understand how they can work within the system to exert their influence. Women's influence in the chamber is important both for providing different perspectives on the existing legislative agenda and for identifying and introducing new issues that are not a part of the established agenda (Mansbridge 1999; Phillips 1995; Young 1990).

Finally, the study of when women will collaborate is important because it challenges scholars to reconsider conventional wisdom about the political institutions that are best for promoting women's representation. Whereas scholars are typically concerned with engineering institutions that increase the numeric representation of marginalized groups, this book explains why it is important for scholars to also consider how institutions shape legislative behavior once members of these groups are in office. As I explain in the conclusion, the findings in this book imply that institutional mechanisms that are best for increasing women's descriptive representation are not necessarily the best institutions for maximizing women's substantive representation.

ORGANIZATION OF THIS BOOK

Chapter 2 develops my theory of legislative collaboration. The chapter is organized into three main sections. Each section answers one of the three central questions posed in this book: 1) Can democracy be collaborative? 2) Why do women collaborate? 3) When do women collaborate? In doing so, I develop a set of expectations that I test in the subsequent chapters.

Chapter 3 empirically addresses the question: *Can democracy be collabora-tive?* I show, using bill cosponsorship data, that collaboration is widespread in the Argentine provinces. To do this, I first examine legislators' motivations for cosponsoring legislation and explain why bill cosponsorship is the best mea-sure of collaboration in Argentina. Then, I examine patterns of collaboration across different groups of legislators. I show that those legislators who have the least amount of power in the chamber are most likely to collaborate, and that women are more likely to collaborate than men.

Chapter 4 turns to my second question: *Why do women collaborate?* I argue that women collaborate more than men because they are marginalized in leg-islatures. I present empirical evidence that women face structural barriers that limit their influence in the policy-making process. In legislatures, power is dis-tributed via leadership posts and powerful committee appointments. I compare women's and men's leadership posts and committee appointments to show that women are underrepresented in positions of power and consequently do not have the same opportunities as male legislators to influence the policy-making process.

Chapter 5 is the first of two chapters that investigate the question: *When do women collaborate?* I argue that all women have an incentive to collaborate to overcome their marginalized status in legislatures and to attain political power, but that women's collaboration varies between and within chambers because not all women have the same electoral incentive or institutional opportunities to collaborate. Chapter 5 examines how women's collaboration varies *between chambers* as a function of partisan constraints and women's numeric represen-tation. I show that women's collaboration is most likely to unfold where party leaders exercise little control over legislative behavior and women's propensity to collaborate increases when they comprise larger proportions of the cham-ber. By comparison, in districts where party leaders exercise more constraint over legislators' behavior, women are only marginally more likely than men to collaborate with other women and their propensity to do so decreases when women comprise a larger share of the chamber.

Chapter 6 examines how women's legislative collaboration varies *within chambers* as a function of affiliation with the governor's party, seniority status, and the policy domain. I show that female members of the executive's party – who are subject to fewer partisan constraints – are systematically more likely than women from opposition parties to collaborate with women. With respect to seniority, I show that women who have served previous terms in the legisla-ture are systematically more likely than their junior colleagues to cross party lines to collaborate with female colleagues – indicating that senior legislators are more willing to defy party norms. As for women's issues, women are even more inclined to collaborate when working on issues that disproportionately influence the lives of women.

Chapter 7 presents a set of case studies to facilitate the exploration of how institutional arrangements structure women's collaboration outside of the

Argentine provinces. I draw on the Rwandan Parliament, the U.S. Senate, the Uruguayan Congress, and the South African Parliament to demonstrate the generalizability of my argument beyond Argentina. In doing so, I examine countries with different legislative contexts than the ones found in Argentina, thus providing broader tests of how other legislative contexts constrain or facilitate women's collaboration. I argue that, consistent with my theory, women's marginalization motivates collaboration in each of these cases. But, whether or not collaboration unfolds depends on a combination of party constraints and women's numeric representation in each country. In addition to examining chambers with different legislative rules, these case studies adopt different measures of collaboration that focus on multiple aspects of the policy-making process. In the case studies, I account for more informal types of collaboration that emerge in the legislature and during different phases of the policy-making process.

Chapter 8 summarizes my theory and central findings, and synthesizes findings from the country case studies and cross-chamber analyses. I conclude by discussing the broader implications of my theory for thinking about collaboration beyond women's marginalization, the advancement of women's rights agendas, electoral system design, and collaboration among other historically marginalized groups in legislatures. First, my theory argues that marginalization motivates women's collaboration. As women make gains in the legislature, they may begin to achieve equal access to power, and their incentives to collaborate may shift. Yet I explain that collaboration – like other legislative norms – will likely become institutionalized and transcend women's marginalization. Second, I discuss the implications of my research for a better understanding of how champions of women's rights legislation can effectively work within different types of legislatures to get women's rights legislation on the political agenda and shepherd this legislation through the policy-making process. Third, I explain that although, at face value, these findings appear to imply a direct tradeoff between institutions that facilitate the election of women to office, and those that stimulate collaboration among women, this tradeoff is not clear-cut. Instead, the findings from this book suggest that there may be a sweet spot – some combination of electoral systems that are conducive to both women's numeric representation and women's collaboration. Finally, I consider how my theory may be generalized to better understand legislative collaboration of other historically marginalized groups. In doing so I explain how different institutions designed to increase the numeric representation of historically marginalized groups shape both the incentives and the opportunities for these groups to collaborate in office.

APPENDIX 1.1: GENDER QUOTA LAWS IN THE ARGENTINE PROVINCES

District	Uni-/Bicameral	Gender Quota Law	Sanction Date	Election Year Implemented	Placement Mandate	Percent Women
Federal District	Unicameral	Constitution, Article 36	10/1/96	1996	Yes	30%
Buenos Aires[a]	Bicameral	Law 11.733	11/16/95	1997	Yes	30%
		Decree 439 (Enforcing placement mandate)	3/8/97	1997	Yes	30%
Catamarca[b]	Bicameral	Law 4.916	7/10/97	1999	Yes	30%
Chaco	Unicameral	Law 3.858	5/5/93	1993	Yes	30%
Chubut	Unicameral	Law National 24.012 & Decree 137/95 (Decree mandates compliance with national gender quota law)	2/17/95	1995	Yes	30%
Córdoba	Unicameral	Law 8.365	3/3/94	1995	No	30%
		Law 8.901 (Placement mandate)	12/12/00	2001	Yes	50%
Corrientes	Bicameral	Law 4.673	11/25/92	1993	No	30%
		Decree 1.332 (Placement mandate)	6/11/03	2003	Yes	30%
Entre Ríos	Bicameral	Law 10.012	3/15/11	2011	Yes	25%
Formosa[c]	Unicameral	Law 1.155	7/26/95	1997	Yes	33%
Jujuy	Unicameral	Law 5.668	11/25/10	2011	Yes	33%
La Pampa	Unicameral	Law 1.593, Article 18	12/1/94	1995	Yes	30%
La Rioja	Unicameral	Law 5.705	5/7/92	1993	Yes	30%
Mendoza[a]	Bicameral	Law 5.888	8/6/92	1993	Yes	30%

Province	Chamber	Law	Date	Year	Mandate	Quota
		Law 6.831 (Stronger language for placement mandate)	10/10/00	2001	Yes	30%
	Unicameral	Decree 1.641 (New language for placement mandate)	8/23/01	2001	Yes	30%
Misiones	Unicameral	Law 3.011	4/28/93	1993	Yes	30%
	Unicameral	Law 4.080 (Voided Law 3.011; Same language)	7/30/04	2005	Yes	30%
Neuquén	Unicameral	Law 2.161	3/8/96	1997	Yes	30%
Río Negro	Unicameral	Law 2.642	6/17/93	1993	No	33%
		Law 3.717 (Placement mandate)	12/17/02	2003	Yes	50%
Salta[b]	Bicameral	Law 6.782	12/29/94	1995	Yes	30%
		Law 7.008 (Voided Law 6.782; Same language)	11/24/98	1999	Yes	30%
San Juan[b]	Unicameral	Law 6.515	10/13/94	1995	No	30%
San Luis	Bicameral	Law 5.105	3/31/97	1997	Yes	30%
		Law XI-0346-2004 (5542*R) (Voided Law 5.105)	7/16/03	2003	Yes	30%
Santa Cruz	Unicameral	Law 2.302	10/29/92	1993	Yes	30%
Santa Fe[b]	Bicameral	Law 10.802	5/7/92	1993	Yes	33%
Santiago del Estero	Unicameral	Law 6.509	9/5/00	2001	Yes	50%
Tierra del Fuego	Unicameral	Law 408	7/2/98	1999	Yes	30%
Tucumán	Unicameral	Law 6.592	9/8/94	1995	No	30%
		Decree 269/14 (Placement mandate)	2/18/02	2003	Yes	30%

[a] Each of these provinces initially adopted gender quotas with vague placement mandate language (similar to many of the provinces) and later adopted more specific placement mandate language.

[b] The quota law is not applicable to the upper chamber because representatives are elected in single-member districts.

[c] The quota law was adopted before the 1995 election, but the law stipulated that parties must comply beginning in the 1997 election.

2

A Theory of Legislative Collaboration

"Until now, everything we have accomplished was because women got together with women from other parties, reached agreements, gave presentations, and fought for it."

– Female Deputy, Salta Lower Chamber, 2013

Salta, a northwest province of Argentina, is known for its conservative and *machista* society. These characteristics, compounded by the fact that women hold a minority of legislative seats and are excluded from legislative leadership, mean that women's influence is limited in the Salta Chamber of Deputies. As one deputy put it: "There are 11 of us women, out of 60 legislators; that's very few. Salteños are very *machista*. The men are the ones in control; they leave you out for being a woman."[1] Thus, in order for women to have an influence in the chamber, they report that they have to work together – particularly when it comes to women's issues. "In the issues of gender, us women unite, if not we do not accomplish anything."[2]

Despite the need for collaboration, not all women are willing to work together. Multiple women who consider themselves champions of women's rights observe a lack of participation from their colleagues. One notes, "I was the deputy who worked the most in gender issues in this chamber, presenting legislative projects and reporting discrimination problems against women. There have been women who did not join me on this defense. And that is concerning."[3] She speculates about why women are not always willing to join her in defending women's rights and suggests that perhaps it is because "they are obeying a partisan mandate." Another female deputy echoes her concerns about partisan constraints: "Not all women are willing to advance – maybe

---

[1] Interview with female deputy from Salta, Partido Renovador de Salta, July 10, 2013.
[2] Interview with female deputy from Salta, Partido Justicialista, July 10, 2013.
[3] Interview with female deputy from Salta, Acción Cívica y Social, July 10, 2013.

out of fear of losing their positions, their job. Maybe they say 'I can't go against this government, or against my party's president.' It is not easy, these battles are tough."[4]

These women's experiences illustrate the relationship between women's marginalized status in the legislature and their compromised ability to exert influence in the policy-making process. Given their lack of power, women view collaboration as a tool for overcoming marginalization and shaping policy. Still, deputies from Salta report that multiple factors limit collaboration among women.

In this chapter, I address these important topics. I present a theoretical framework that links these issues – incentives to collaborate, women's status in the legislature, and institutional constraints on legislative behavior – to explain why and when women collaborate. This chapter is organized into three parts. First, I tackle the question: *Can democracy be collaborative?* Then, I turn to the question: *Why do women collaborate?* In the third part, I examine the final major question addressed in this book: *When do women collaborate?*

CAN DEMOCRACY BE COLLABORATIVE?

I argue that the answer to this question is yes – democracy can be collaborative, and many of the political behaviors we observe are clearly more collaborative than competitive. Whereas only the majority has the power to influence outcomes when decisions are made through a competitive process (e.g., voting to elect representatives and to pass policy), all legislators – particularly those who do not have power – can influence the policy-making process through collaboration. Collaboration enhances the quality of democracy by ensuring that diverse voices are heard in the policy-making process. As a result, I argue that all legislators have an incentive to collaborate, but the incentive should be strongest among legislators who are not in positions of power.

Democracy and Competition

Classical theories of democracy frequently defined democracy in terms of the source of power and the purpose of the institution, advocating the idea that democracy should be vested in the will of the people with the primary purpose of promoting the common good. These views were in sharp contrast to procedural definitions of democracy, which focused primarily on procedures and institutions used to select leaders. Proceduralists championed the idea that democracy was about the "competitive struggle" for power (Schumpeter 1942, 269). These philosophical debates largely characterized political science in the first half of the twentieth century. But by the 1970s, "the debate was over, and Schumpeter had won" (Huntington 1991, 6). The hallmark of democracy is competition.

---

[4] Interview with female deputy from Salta, Partido Justicialista, July 10, 2013.

In contemporary politics, the primary emphasis on democracy as a competitive exercise endures. Every modern indicator of democracy includes a measure of competition.[5] The quality of representative democracy is most often defined by the procedures used to select leaders, not by the outcomes the leaders and the institutions produce. It is widely accepted that without contested elections, democracy ceases. The emphasis on competition characterizes the study of virtually all aspects of democracy, including the study of competition in the electorate and competition in office.

This is not to say that scholarship has not considered strategic coordination in the pursuit of elective office. Indeed, a wealth of research on elections (Cox 1997; Lijphart 1984) and cabinet formation (Carroll and Cox 2007, 2012; Laver 1998; Laver and Schofield 1990; Martin and Stevenson 2001; Martin and Vanberg 2005) emphasizes the importance of coordination to gain power. Nonetheless, research on electoral coordination typically privileges the idea of competition (Downs 1957; Laver and Shepsle 1996; Riker 1962), often assuming that politicians engage in strategic coordination only to achieve their electoral goals or to compete more effectively (Cox 1997).

Research on behavior of legislators in office also emphasizes competition over collaboration. As Carroll, Cox, and Pachón explain, "parties neither cease to exist nor cease to compete for office when the general election is over. Instead, a new round of competition begins" (2006, 154). Indeed, most theories of legislative behavior in office assume that policy outcomes are a zero-sum game in which legislators have an incentive to protect their own interests (March and Olsen 2010; Shepsle 1978). Legislators compete among themselves to secure scarce resources within the chamber (Cox and McCubbins 1993; Shepsle and Weingast 1994), to take home pork to their constituents (Cain, Ferejohn, and Fiorina 1987; Crisp et al. 2004a; Mayhew 1974), and to allocate government contracts to their supporters in the private sector (Mainwaring 1999; Samules 2002b).

Further, legislative behavior is primarily driven by legislators' desire to better compete in future elections (Mayhew 1974). Legislators' policy initiatives are motivated by efforts to curry favor with constituents by funneling private goods or targeted public goods to specific constituencies, designing policies to target special interest groups or a subset of voters (Carey and Shugart 1995; Carroll and Kim 2010; Crisp, Kanthak, and Leijonhufvud 2004; Samules 1999), and delivering goods in accordance with their electoral schedules (Shepsle et al. 2009). This view assumes that competition drives legislators to alter their policy positions to gain an edge over their opponents (Cox 1987, 1990; Downs 1957; Eaton and Lipsey 1975) and incentivizes them to avoid

---

[5] For example, see work by Alexander, Inglehart, and Welzel (2012); Alexander and Welzel (2011a); Altman and Pérez-Liñán (2002); Cheibub, Gandhi, and Vreeland (2010); Collier and Levitsky (1997); Dahl (1971); Mainwaring and Pérez-Liñán (2013, 2014); Marshall and Gurr (2013).

taking controversial positions prior to close elections (Theriault 2005). Even legislators who are ineligible to compete for reelection or who aspire to hold a different position in the future structure their behavior with an eye toward competition (Micozzi 2013, 2014a, 2014b; Samules 2002a, 2003).

Theories that characterize democracy as a competitive enterprise are useful for understanding legislative behavior, but this paradigm overlooks a huge portion of what legislators actually do in office. Although the tension between coordination and competition has figured prominently in the literature on electoral rules and is central in the selection of party authorities to act as delegates for party members, until recently, research has not considered the incentives for individuals to collaborate while in office to promote common policies. As a result, research on legislative behavior gives us an incomplete picture of representative democracy. Shifting from an almost exclusive focus on competition to a focus that incorporates collaboration can improve our understanding of representative democracy and inform our knowledge of how institutions structure the political process.

Clearly, competition is paramount to democracy. Nonetheless, many of the political behaviors we observe are more collaborative than competitive. This is puzzling: *Why, if politicians can secure power to make political decisions via competition, would we ever expect to observe collaboration in the policy-making process?*

In this book, I argue that only those in the winning majority can secure the power to decide via competition, but *all* legislators can influence the policy-making process through collaboration. By collaborating with other legislators – both within their own parties and across party lines – legislators can ensure their voices are heard, increase their influence over group decisions, shape the outcome of legislation, and develop more efficient and effective policy. For this reason, I expect to observe widespread collaboration among legislators. Nevertheless, collaboration can be quite costly, thus not all legislators have an incentive to incur the cost of collaboration all the time. Instead, I expect that collaboration is more common among legislators who are in positions of institutional weakness because they have fewer opportunities to exert influence in the policy-making process. In the remainder of this section, I first explain in more detail the incentives legislators have to collaborate. Then I describe the costs associated with collaboration and explain why legislators who are out of power have stronger incentives to collaborate than their powerful colleagues.

Incentives to Collaborate

There is substantial evidence that collaboration increases the influence of individual legislators and groups of legislators in the policy-making process. Specifically, scholars examining legislative policy collaboration using cosponsorship data find that collaboration allows legislators to exert more influence over the legislative process than they otherwise could through voting alone (Calvo and Leiras 2012; Kirkland and Williams 2014). When multiple legislators come together in support of an issue, it is more likely to receive attention in the chamber because it signals to legislators and party leaders that the legislation is of particular interest to multiple representatives (Alemán 2008; Campbell 1982; Koger 2003; Mayhew 1974; Swers 2013). Thus, policy collaboration can increase the probability that an issue gets on the legislative agenda (Browne 1985; Krutz 2005; Wilson and Young 1997) and is ultimately passed into law (Tam Cho and Fowler 2010) – particularly when collaboration occurs across party lines (Alemán and Calvo 2010). This is likely because cosponsorship functions as a commitment mechanism – legislators who renege on their cosponsorship agreements later have difficulty garnering support for their own bills (Bernhard and Sulkin 2013). Thus, cosponsorship represents a credible commitment to support legislation if it advances to a vote on the floor.

Collaboration also allows legislators to develop effective legislation (Kessler and Krehbiel 1996; Kirkland 2014) and increases the likelihood that legislators produce landmark legislation (Tam Cho and Fowler 2010). By collaborating, legislators from multiple different parties can wield more power in the chamber than they can if they oppose one another (Kirkland 2012). Even when collaboration does not lead to the passage of legislation, it can still have policy consequences by increasing the probability that the proposed initiative is incorporated into subsequent legislative proposals (Koger 2003). Overall, both the development and the passage of legislation is typically a product of legislators working together to advance their legislative goals.

The benefits of collaboration extend well beyond the passage of legislation. Collaboration gives legislators the opportunity to articulate different group interests, which is an extremely important aspect of representation regardless of the ultimate success of the legislation (Escobar-Lemmon and Taylor-Robinson 2014a; Osborn and Mendez 2010; Piscopo 2011). Indeed, although legislators' goal is to pass legislation, the passage of legislation is not necessary for representation. Instead it is important that different perspectives, priorities, and concerns are articulated in the policy-making process (Swers 2013). As collaborators often assist in shaping legislation from an early stage, they have influence over the substance of legislation that permits far more input than their colleagues who merely provide an up or down vote on the floor. By shaping the content of legislation, these legislators can move legislation closer to their preferred outcomes and ensure that different perspectives are considered in the policy-making process.

Collaboration is also an important tool for networking with like-minded colleagues and developing coalitions of support to advance shared interests (Kirkland 2012; Koger 2003; Swers 1998, 2002; Wawro 2001). Networks within the chamber are extremely valuable. Legislators who are better connected are more influential in the chamber overall and have more influence over the content of policy. For example, in the context of the U.S. Congress, legislators who collaborate more frequently have more success amending legislation during floor debates, allowing them to move legislation closer to their ideal policy positions (Fowler 2006). In sum, legislators can obtain more influence in the legislative process, increase their influence over group decisions, shape the outcome of legislation, articulate their constituents' interests, and develop more efficient and effective policy by collaborating with their colleagues.

Costs of Collaboration

Given all of the benefits of collaboration, we might expect that all legislators should collaborate all of the time. Indeed, if collaboration were costless, legislators would have an incentive to contribute to the development and advancement of any legislation they support (Harward and Moffett 2010). In practice, however, legislators only contribute collaboratively to a small portion of the legislation they favor. This is because collaboration is costly. Collaboration imposes costs in terms of information acquisition and coordination; it tampers legislators' ability to claim exclusive credit for legislation; it increases legislators' responsibility for any controversial aspects of legislation; and it requires legislators to compromise on the content of legislation.

Legislators looking to collaborate must invest time and resources in coordinating with other leaders, and in acquiring information they may lose resources through transaction costs (Calvo and Leiras 2012). In particular, seeking out potential collaborators is costly (Kirkland 2014). As there are a large number of legislators with competing interests, priorities, and preferences, it may be difficult to identify potential collaborators. Moreover, given the high number of bills introduced in a given legislative session, and each legislator's limited amount of time and resources, selecting which bills will receive attention is itself a time-intensive act (Fowler 2006).

Legislators are seen as responsible for legislation on which they collaborate – particularly those legislators who are subject to high levels of public scrutiny (Koger 2003). If legislators collaborate to develop policies that disproportionately benefit one group over another or that advance a controversial issue, they risk sanctions by party leaders or supporters (Balla et al. 2002; Weaver 1986). Legislators who receive a disproportionate amount of media attention thus tend to cosponsor fewer bills in an effort to eschew public scrutiny and avoid alienating a subset of their supporters (Koger 2003). This accountability underscores the importance of properly vetting both colleagues and policy initiatives prior to deciding to partake in collaboration.

Collaboration may also compromise legislators' credit-claiming ability. One of the primary motivations for introducing legislation is to claim credit to constituents, donors, and party leaders (Fenno 1978; Jacobson 2004; Mayhew 1974). Although legislators can still claim credit for legislation that is developed collaboratively, they must share credit (Calvo and Leiras 2012;

Kirkland 2012), which is not always in legislators' best interests. Legislators elected in candidate-centered electoral districts, who benefit primarily from developing their own personal reputations, for example, have little incentive to share credit for their legislative initiatives. Similarly, legislators elected in party-centered legislative districts may have little incentive to share credit for policy proposals with representatives from different political parties.

Finally, collaboration may require legislators to compromise over the content of legislation. When legislators author legislation on their own, they can include all of their preferred content – and only their preferred content – in the legislation. Legislators who rely on collaboration to exert their influence in the policy-making process, however, must be willing to negotiate the bill's content (Evans 1994, 2004). This process can be complicated because legislation that benefits other legislators' districts or constituents does not always advance the interests of one's own constituents (Kirkland 2012). Further, the negotiation process is costly, as it is time-consuming and may result in policy concessions.

Although substantial incentives to collaborate imply that all legislators can benefit from collaboration, collaboration is costly. Thus, not all legislators will choose to collaborate. Instead, legislators must assess whether the benefits of collaboration outweigh the costs. Legislators who have other means by which to advance their legislative agendas are thus unlikely to be willing to sustain the cost of collaboration.

Out-of-Power Legislators and Incentives to Collaborate

Given the costs associated with collaboration, some legislators have a stronger incentive to collaborate than do others. In particular, legislators in positions of power have access to a number of resources they can use to advance their preferred policies rather than incurring the costs of collaboration. They have more influence over the legislative agenda and they are more likely to succeed when they propose amendments to legislation. Thus, legislators in positions of power have fewer incentives to collaborate.

The governor's party, for example, has a disproportionate amount of power (Calvo 2007; Jones 2002, 2008).[6] In presidential systems, executives have the authority to issue decrees, introduce legislation, set the legislative agenda, and veto legislation (Carey and Shugart 1998; Cheibub, Elkins, and Ginsburg 2011; Schibber 2012). Together these powers give the governor substantial sway over the policy-making process. The executive, moreover, has the authority to establish budget spending and revenue levels, and to determine budget priorities (Payne, Zovatto, and Díaz 2007). Even if the executive lacks a

---

[6] Recall that in this book, I focus specifically on the Argentine provinces, where the executive is the governor. I use the language "governor's party" to refer to the executive. Nonetheless, the theory is general and applies to the executive's party in presidential systems and to parties in the governing coalition in parliamentary systems.

majority in the chamber, holding particularistic resources and political capital are all that is necessary to advance the party's legislative agenda. For example, executives can build legislative coalitions to support policies by allocating pork-barrel projects and political appointments to key legislatures (Pereira and Melo 2012). Strong party discipline – like that found in Argentina – facilitates this process by enabling executives to negotiate agreements with a small number of party leaders rather than cultivating support from each individual legislator needed to advance legislation (Cheibub, Figueiredo, and Limongi 2009; Figueiredo and Limongi 2000).

Similarly, majority-led governments have more power than do plurality-led governments or smaller opposition parties (Calvo 2014; Calvo and Sagarzazu 2011; Llanos and Schibber 2008). The majority party can secure the power to decide without collaboration, as it has enough votes to ensure the success of its initiatives. In legislatures, power is distributed through political parties (Crisp and Schibber 2014; Jones, Sanguinetti, and Tommasi 2000; Morgenstern 2002; Müller 2000). Members of the majority, therefore, access a disproportionate number of leadership posts (Bowler, Farrell, and Katz 1999; Carroll et al. 2006; O'Brien 2015), valuable committee appointments (Barnes 2014; Cox and McCubbins 2005; Heath et al. 2005; Krehbiel, Shepsle, and Weingast 1987), and other important agenda-setting and gatekeeping positions (Anzia and Jackman 2013; McAllister 2007; Poguntke and Webb 2005). Consequently, the majority party can manage the structure and process of the legislature, exercising negative agenda control to keep bills that divide the majority party from coming to a floor vote (Alemán 2006; Jones and Hwang 2005a; Kiewiet and McCubbins 1991). For these reasons, the legislative process is "stacked in favor of the majority party interests" (Cox and McCubbins 1993, 2).

Given these institutional advantages, legislators in positions of power do not need to incur the costs of collaboration to exert influence in the policy-making process. This does not imply that legislators in positions of power never have an incentive to collaborate. Even the executive cannot always negotiate an agreement with the legislature – particularly in cases of divided government (Binder 1999, 2003; Mayhew 2011). Similarly, chambers governed by a majority sometimes fail to advance policy (Brady and Volden 1998; Krehbiel 1998). Still, on average, legislators in positions of power have numerous resources to advance their interests and do not need to rely on collaboration as a primary means of exerting influence on the policy-making process.

By contrast, out-of-power legislators have far fewer resources at their disposal (Davidson and Oleszek 2005; Harward and Moffett 2010). They cannot secure the power to decide via competition, they have minimal access to important leadership and committee posts, and they have limited influence during later stages of the policy-making process. Collaboration is one of the only tools they have to advance their legislative agendas. Given their limited influence over the policy-making process, for legislators in positions of institutional weakness, the benefits of collaboration more often outweigh the costs. Although all legislators can influence the policy-making process through collaboration, it is more valuable to legislators who are not in positions of power. Thus, I expect that collaboration will be more common among legislators in positions of institutional weakness as compared to their colleagues with relatively more legislative power. Further, given the limitations of working within their own parties, I anticipate that these legislators will prioritize cross-partisan collaborations to develop larger coalitions of support in the legislature.

A number of different features determine the amount of power and influence that legislators have in office. Similar to legislators from opposition parties and members of the minority, legislators from historically excluded racial, ethnic, or religious groups are often in positions of institutional weakness. Thus as I discuss in Chapter 8, legislators from historically marginalized groups can also benefit from collaboration. Argentina, however, ranks among the least culturally diverse countries in the world (Morin 2013). Therefore, in my analysis of Argentina, I focus specifically on three types of legislators in positions of institutional weakness: legislators in opposition parties, legislators in the legislative minority, and women legislators. In particular, *I expect that legislators who are not in the governor's party will collaborate more frequently than legislators who are members of the governor's party*; and, on average, these legislators *will be more likely to cross party lines to collaborate with colleagues in different political parties*. I expect to find a similar pattern between legislators who are and who are not in the majority party. *Minority legislators will collaborate more frequently than legislators in the majority and they will be more likely to cross party lines to do so*. This is a notable distinction because the governor's party does not always have a majority in the chamber. Finally, I argue that relative to men, women also have access to fewer legislative resources that afford legislators disproportional influence in the policy-making process. As such, *I expect that women will be more likely to collaborate than men*.

To evaluate these expectations, I examine patterns of collaboration in Chapter 3. I demonstrate that democracy can be collaborative, that opposition members (or those not in the governor's party) collaborate more than legislators from the governor's party, legislators from minority parties collaborate more than legislators from majority parties, and women collaborate more than men. Given the institutional circumstances described earlier, it may seem obvious that, on average, legislators in opposition parties and those in minority parties have less power than legislators in the governor's party and those in the majority. At this point, it may be less clear, however, why women are more likely to collaborate than men. As such, this raises a second question: *Why do women collaborate?*

WHY DO WOMEN COLLABORATE?

I argue that women's unique experiences in the legislature – due to marginalization and socialization – motivate their collaboration. Yet, unlike other numeric minorities, women's minority status is not the only important factor that explains their marginalization in the legislature. Women entering a male-dominated institution face structural barriers that extend beyond numeric underrepresentation and prevent them from influencing the decision-making process. Thus, women are one such group that can benefit more from collaboration. By collaborating, women can overcome structural barriers in the legislature and exert their influence on the policy-making process. In this section, I first discuss the ways that women are marginalized in the legislature. To be clear, women's marginalization is not simply a product of their minority status. Indeed, given the cultural and institutional barriers they face, previous research examining the potential for underrepresented groups to influence policy outcomes finds that increases in *simple numeric representation are not sufficient to influence policy* (Dodson 2006; Grey 2002; Htun and Power 2006; Piscopo 2014a; Reingold 2000; Tremblay and Pelletier 2000; Vincent 2004). Then I explain how collaboration can help women to wield their influence in the policy-making process despite their marginalized status.

Women Are Marginalized in the Legislature

In recent years, women have gained access to parliaments around the globe in record numbers. Yet we should not assume that women always have an opportunity to influence the policy-making process just because they gain access to legislative positions. Rather, these groups need to hold *formal* positions, such as committee chairs and leadership posts, within the legislatures that provide additional influence over policy decisions. Additionally, influence requires *informal* incorporation into professional and social networks that are important for developing social capital (Propp 1995). As of yet, women entering historically male-dominated institutions are not being fully incorporated into the legislature. Instead, women are marginalized in the legislature, and this prevents them from influencing the legislative process.

Despite increases in numeric representation and a growing number of women in legislative seniority, women are routinely excluded from formal positions of power within government, political parties, and legislatures (Barnes and O'Brien 2015; Escobar-Lemon and Taylor-Robinson 2005, 2009; Kittilson 2006; Krook and O'Brien 2012; O'Brien 2015). In Latin America, for example, women are less likely to hold leadership positions or to preside over committees; when women do preside over committees, they are likely to be committees with little influence (Barnes and Schibber 2015; Rodriguez 2003; Schwindt-Bayer 2010). Not only are they absent from the leadership, but women are also unlikely to be appointed to serve on powerful committees (Arnold and King 2002; Barnes 2014; Heath et al. 2005; Kerevel and Atkeson 2013; Pansardi and Vercesi forthcoming; Towns 2003). Women's exclusion from leadership posts and powerful committees is evident regardless of whether women are in the majority or the minority party. Instead, they are more likely to serve on social issue committees or women and family committees. Although this overrepresentation on certain committees may reflect women's preferences to serve on such committees (Bækgaard and Kjaer 2012; Carroll 2008; Thomas 1994), underrepresentation on powerful committees is not a reflection of women's committee preferences and is more appropriately attributed to discrimination (Frisch and Kelly 2003; Schwindt-Bayer 2010).

Women are also typically sidelined from the benefits of informal incorporation. Social and professional networks in historically male-dominated institutions tend to be structured by sex, and as a result women are excluded from important formal and informal networks. For example, women in U.S. state legislatures – even the (few) women in leadership positions – report being excluded from "circles of power" and "good ol' boy networks" (Rosenthal 1998, 49–50). Similarly, in Argentina and Chile women are excluded from important policy-making networks that govern political advancement (Franceschet and Piscopo 2008, 2014; Hinojosa 2012). As a result women are regularly cut off from important leadership discussions, have limited access to timely strategic information, and are not consulted for advice.

Although some social norms and gender stereotypes benefit women (Barnes and Beaulieu 2014, 2015; Streb and Frederick 2009), more often they work to disadvantage women and limit their influence. Female legislators are subject to negative stereotypes about their ability to lead and to legislate (Alexander and Andersen 1993; Burrell 1994; Huddy and Terkildsen 1993; King and Matland 2003; Matland 1994). Gender stereotypes typically assume that women are less competent, especially when working in historically male domains such as politics (Fiske, Cuddy, and Glick 2007; Holman et al. 2011). As a result, information provided by women is less likely to influence legislative decisions (Propp 1995; Thomas-Hunt and Phillips 2004).

Despite expectations that circumstances for women will improve as more enter the legislature, research demonstrates that these problems may actually worsen as increasing numbers of women are elected (Barnes 2014; Heath et al. 2005). Higher numeric representation may pose a threat to the dominant group's favored status and provoke backlash from male legislators (Krook 2015). This may result in a hostile work environment in which men become more dominant, assertive, and verbally aggressive (Kathlene 1994), or become more impervious to women's influence (Thomas-Hunt and Phillips 2004). Women are likely to perceive these attitudes from their male colleagues and feel discouraged from contributing to the development of ideas and legislative solutions to problems within their communities.

Formal and informal exclusion of women in the legislature may be an intentional effort for male leaders to preserve their power. Men can maintain their dominance in the legislative arena by creating a conflictual environment where women feel isolated and are excluded from informal meetings and political activity (Kathlene 1994; Schwindt-Bayer 2006). Even without intentional efforts to exclude women, deep-rooted cultural norms that determine how people organize and interact within institutions can provide challenges for women's political incorporation (Beckwith 2005; Chappell 2006, 2010; Duerst-Lahti 2005; Krook and Mackay 2011; North 1990).

Taken together, I argue that female legislators face a number of formal and informal structural barriers to influence in the legislature. The formal and informal exclusion of women are mutually reinforcing. As decisions about access to formal positions of power are political decisions, it is difficult for women to access these posts if they have not established informal networks and social capital within the institution. Exclusion from formal positions of power makes it difficult to forge informal networks and to cultivate social capital. Collectively, these obstacles imply that we should observe fewer women in formal positions of power. This does not imply that no women will ever have the opportunity to serve in leadership positions or on powerful committees, but that on average women will be systematically disadvantaged. Specifically, *I expect that female legislators will be disproportionately underrepresented across a vast array of legislative power including chamber-wide leadership posts, committee leadership posts, and powerful committee appointments.* I test these expectations in Chapter 4.

Women Collaborate to Overcome Marginalization

Women's marginalization motivates women to collaborate to overcome structural barriers. Female legislators, like all legislators, have an obligation to represent their constituents' interests, and a desire to influence policy and advance their political careers (Fenno 2003; Mayhew 1974). Thus, if female legislators want to do their jobs as representatives, they must find a way to work around structural and cultural barriers. I argue that, because women face both formal and informal barriers to power, female legislators are an out-of-power group that can benefit greatly from collaboration. By collaborating – both within their parties and across party lines – women can acquire more power and exert more influence on the policy-making process.

Women stand to benefit from collaboration beyond the benefits realized by their male colleagues who are not in positions of power. Women are socialized to be more collaborative than men (Diekman and Schnider 2010; Eagly and Karau 2002). Gendered patterns of socialization are prevalent across countries (including those in North and South America and Europe), and have persisted over time (Alexander and Welzel 2011b; Diekman et al. 2005; Retamero-Garcia and López-Zafra 2009; Wilde and Diekman 2005). In organizations and society more generally, women are rewarded for behaving in the socially expected manner. Unlike men, women are socially penalized for adopting traditional leadership qualities (Heilman and Okimoto 2007; Ridgeway 2001).[7] Female

---

[7] See Bauer, Harbirdge, and Krupnikov (2015) for a discussion of when citizens (rather than group members – i.e., fellow legislators) punish female politicians for not compromising.

legislators who use the same strategies as their male colleagues for promoting their legislative agendas are unlikely to be effective. Instead, women who are self-assertive, dominant, or aggressive are met with negative reactions and limited success (Burgess and Borgida 1999; Eagly and Karau 2002; Yoder 2001). By contrast, women can wield more influence in the legislature by conforming to traditional gender roles. Specifically, male and female legislators are more likely to be receptive to and supportive of women who take a cooperative and collaborative approach to lawmaking. Indeed, numerous studies show that women can actually attain more power in groups by establishing their intentions to be collaborative (Eagly and Carli 2007; Meeker and Weitzel-O'Neill 1977; Ridgeway 1982; Shackelford, Wood, and Worchel 1996). As women are limited in their ability to exert their influence via competition, and they are rewarded for collaborative behavior, collaboration is a rational strategy.

In addition to their ability to wield influence, women may derive personal benefits from collaboration. Women are socialized to be more collaborative and to avoid conflict (Miller, Danaher, and Forbes 1986). Thus, they may feel more comfortable with collaboration and prefer it to competition (Forret and Dougherty 2004; Timberlake 2005). For example, women tend to choose careers that are intended to achieve communal goals rather than careers that bring them individual recognition and power (Diekman et al. 2010). Similarly, women in political office enjoy the collaborative elements of politics more than do their male colleagues (Duerst-Lahti and Johnson 1990; Kathlene 1989; Lang-Takac and Osterweil 1992; Tilly and Gurin 1992; Rosenthal 1998). As such, women are discouraged from partaking in politics when participation is determined by power and competition (Alexander 2011), but inspired to participate when political involvement is motivated by helping others and working with people (Schneider et al. forthcoming).

Given the expectations for women to collaborate and the professional and personal payoffs they gain from doing so, it should not be surprising that women choose to collaborate more than men and by extension that they choose female collaborators. Still, there are additional reasons why women may choose to work specifically with other women. For instance, unlike other out-of-power groups such as members of the minority party or members of the opposition, women are also marginalized *within* other out-of-power groups. As a result, women face both formal and informal barriers to power regardless of their political parties' access to power.

Beyond the social expectations generated by gender stereotypes, other social dynamics also make it especially rational for women to collaborate with other women. In institutions that are traditionally male domains or even mixed-gender settings, men tend to dominate agenda setting and deliberation (Karpowitz and Mendelberg 2014; Propp 1995; Thomas-Hunt and Phillips 2004). Men are likely to view women as less competent and to discount the contributions of women who take initiative (Fiske, Cuddy, and Glick 2007). By contrast, women are more likely than men to perceive female legislators as possessing the qualities they need to be effective leaders (Alexander 2012, 2015; Barnes and Beaulieu 2014; Beaman et al. 2009; Deal and Stevenson 1998; Norris and Wylie 1995)[8] and are more receptive to women's ideas and contributions (Ridgeway 1982). This implies that when women collaborate *with women* they have more opportunities to influence the policy-making process. Indeed, even when addressing similar issues as their male colleagues, female politicians are more inclusive and work to include more voices in the policy process (Barnes 2012b; Gilligan 1982; Holman 2015; Kathlene 1994; but see Funk 2015). For example, in the United States, women are more likely to take others' opinions and perspectives into account during committee debates (Rosenthal 1998). Female legislators are more likely than their male colleagues to encourage others to contribute and seek to build consensus (Forret and Dougherty 2004; Rosenthal 1998; Timberlake 2005). Thus, it seems rational that female legislators who are looking to collaborate may seek out female colleagues, particularly because they are more likely than men to value contributions by women.

Additionally, as women are largely excluded from the established professional networks that exist in the legislatures, they can compensate for their exclusion by developing professional networks with female colleagues. These networks can provide women with a number of professional benefits, including information about navigating the institutional culture and about overcoming discrimination (Forret and Dougherty 2004; Timberlake 2005).[9] Female legislators can sidestep the issue of not being able to exert proportional influence during floor debates and committee hearings by working together to craft legislation, solicit each other's opinions, or take into account others' experiences, expertise, and perspectives during the formative stages of policy development. As a result, collaborating with female colleagues allows women to take an active role in the policy-making process, which may not otherwise be afforded to them because of their gender. This does not imply that female legislators will agree about every issue, or that they will never debate policy differences. Rather, their preferred method of governing may involve a more cooperative and integrative approach that acknowledges differences and seeks to resolve

---

[8] Research from social psychology and organizational science has documented a gendered shift in the use of gender stereotypes to evaluate women in leadership positions. In the 1970s and 1980s, research consistently found that when male and female respondents were tasked with identifying the characteristics associated with leaders, men, and women, all respondents (both male and female) associated leaders and men with the same characteristics, and women with a distinct set of characteristics (Powell and Butterfield 1989; Schein 1973, 1975). Since the 1990s, replication of these studies shows that male respondents continue to employ gender stereotypes when evaluating women in historically masculine domains, indicating that women's use of stereotyping in evaluating leadership has changed while men's has not (Schein and Mueller 1992; Schein et al. 1996). Women, on the other hand, have begun to associate leadership with both feminine and masculine characteristics (Deal and Stevenson 1998; Norris and Wylie 1995).

[9] See Barnes, Beaulieu, and Krupnikov (2015) for a discussion of how female networks benefit women in other male-dominated institutions.

them through compromise. Thus, collaboration with female colleagues facilitates the opportunity to influence the policy-making process. In sum, women's unique experiences in the legislature – due to marginalization and socialization – explain why women choose to collaborate more than men, and disproportionately choose to collaborate with women.

WHEN DO WOMEN COLLABORATE?

Until this point, I have explained that democracy can be collaborative and described why women collaborate more than men. Nonetheless, patterns of collaboration vary among female legislators. This leads to my final question: *When do women collaborate?* I argue that patterns of collaboration vary among female legislators because not all women have the same opportunities to work collaboratively. Instead, a number of institutional contexts – that vary both between and within legislative chambers – structure women's legislative behavior (Osborn 2012; Schwindt-Bayer 2010). In this section, I develop the theoretical expectations to explain when women collaborate while in office. First, I consider factors that vary largely between legislative chambers – specifically, I explain how partisan constraints and women's numeric representation structure women's collaboration during the policy-making process. Then I turn to factors that vary within legislative chambers. In particular, I posit that affiliation with the governor's party, seniority, legislation targeting women's issues, and membership in a women's issues committee and women's caucuses each influence women's legislative collaboration. In the text that follows, first I discuss factors that vary largely between chambers and explain how they structure women's behavior, then turn to the factors that vary within chambers.

Between-Chamber Variation

In this book I focus specifically on two factors that vary substantially between chambers: party constraints and women's numeric representation. In short, I argue that institutions that foster relatively weak party constraints over legislators' behavior impose few limitations on legislators, allowing women's collaboration to unfold. By contrast, institutions that promote strong party constraints allow party leaders to restrict women's collaboration. Further, the magnitude of this relationship will vary depending on numeric representation. Specifically, I expect that increases in numeric representation will spur collaboration among women when they face weak party constraints. By contrast, when party constraints are strong, increases in numeric representation will stymie collaboration among women. Figure 2.1 depicts this relationship. As I explain later, party constraints and numeric representation work together to structure women's legislative collaboration.

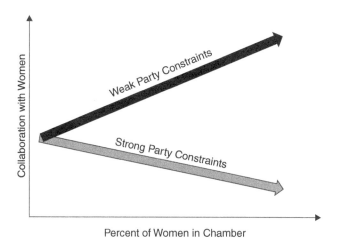

FIGURE 2.1. Between-chamber variation and women's collaboration.

Party Constraints

Institutions structure legislative behaviors by determining the amount of control party leaders have over legislators and by fostering different legislative incentives. Broadly speaking, some institutional contexts afford party leaders more control over rank-and-file legislators' behavior and create greater incentives for members to toe the party line. Meanwhile, other institutional contexts give legislators more autonomy and foster incentives for members to develop their own legislative interests. Provided they are not tarnishing the party name, such context affords legislators more flexibility to behave independently from the party (Carey and Shugart 1995).

Electoral systems serve as the fundamental determinant of the amount of control party leaders have over rank-and-file members (Mainwaring and Shugart 1997). Many different components of electoral systems influence political parties' strength and legislators' incentives. For example, district size, party leaders' control over access to the ballot, the order in which candidates are elected from the party ballot (i.e., open or closed list), and the pooling of votes across candidates to determine the parties' overall seat share influence how much political parties can constrain legislators' behavior (Ames 1995, 2001; Carey 1996; Crisp et al. 2004a; Crisp and Ingall 2002; Samules 1999; Taylor 1992; Taylor-Robinson 2010).

Not all of these features of electoral systems vary within every country. In Argentina, the primary case examined in this book, there is rich variation in district size (i.e., the number of legislators elected to each district in a single election ranges from a low of one to a high of sixty-six). For this reason, I examine how district size in closed-list electoral systems shapes party constraints, and, in turn, how these party constraints influence women's collaboration. Still, it is important to point out that my theory is generalizable beyond the specific institutions I focus on in Argentina. In fact, I draw on a number of case studies to explore the generalizability of my argument to other institutions in Chapter 7.

In closed-list systems, like those found in Argentina, voters cast their ballots for political parties and not individual candidates. A candidate's position on the ballot is extremely important because the seats each party wins are allocated to candidates based on their position on the ballot. In practice, parties do not win enough votes to elect their entire list of candidates. Thus, candidates at the top of the list are far more likely to be elected to office than are those toward the bottom. Party leaders are responsible for selecting candidates to run for office and for determining the order in which those candidates' names appear on the party ballot.[10] Rank-and-file members of the party do not have a strong influence on either of these processes (De Luca, Jones, and Tula 2002). In general, these systems are known for cultivating strong party constraints where party leaders can credibly demand party loyalty and legislators have a strong incentive to toe the party line in an effort to ensure future access to the party ballot (Carey and Shugart 1995; Gallagher and Marsh 1987). Importantly, however, this relationship varies significantly depending on district size: when a district is small or medium, legislators face relatively weak party constraints; when a district is large, legislators face strong party constraints (Carey and Shugart 1995; Shugart, Valdini, and Suominen 2005).

In small and medium districts with closed-list ballots, legislators face relatively weak party constraints because individual legislators have more influence over their own political careers (Carey and Shugart 1995). Voters are more likely to recognize the names of individual candidates in small districts, and this recognition means that candidates are able to lure additional votes to the party ballot by developing an individual reputation. Equally important, the nomination procedure for candidates from small and medium districts is typically less centralized than the nomination procedure used to nominate candidates to one (or a few) large districts (Langston 2008; Samules 2003; Winckler 1999). Whereas local party leaders may wield influence over individual legislators elected from small and medium districts, the centralized party leadership has considerably less control over legislators' behavior. In the case of the Argentine National Congress, for example, legislators are elected mostly from small and medium districts with closed-list ballots and are nominated and placed on the party ballot by local party bosses – not a central party boss (De Luca, Jones, and Tula 2002; Jones and Hwang 2005a). Thus, the central party leadership has relatively limited control over legislators' behavior. In sum, the personal vote-earning nature of smaller districts and the decentralized nomination procedure mean that legislators owe less allegiance to central party

---

[10] See Clucas and Valdini (2015, 60) for a discussion of closed-list proportional representation ballots.

leaders, have more freedom to behave independently of the parties, and face fewer party constraints.

In large districts with closed-list ballots, legislators face stronger party constraints. The more candidates there are on the ballot and the more seats there are in a district (i.e., the larger the district size), the less name recognition and popular support for individuals influence the election process. Party leaders have almost exclusive control over these legislators' career prospects, including controlling access to the ballot and the order of candidates on the ballot. Candidates at the top of the ballot have a higher probability of election. As individuals do not benefit from their own reputations, they have weak incentives to exert their influence in the policy-making process (Jones 2002). Instead, they have an incentive to promote the parties and display strong loyalty. They do so by focusing their time and energy on policies that are consistent with the party platforms and by allowing the political parties to take full credit for successful legislative initiatives. The parties have little to gain from individuals establishing cross-partisan collaboration because this would require the party to share credit for policy proposals. Moreover, given the control party leaders have over individuals' political careers, party leaders can demand party loyalty and exercise strong party discipline to discourage cross-partisan collaboration.

Party Constraints and Women's Collaboration

These same institutional constraints and incentives have specific consequences for women's legislative behavior. Like men, women elected in districts with weaker partisan constraints have more autonomy. Under these circumstances, I argue, they will be more likely to pursue activities that will make their individual voices heard in the policy-making process. As previously argued, female legislators are marginalized in the legislature and have a limited ability to wield influence in the policy-making process. Yet women can attain more influence in the chamber by collaborating with female colleagues. Thus, *I expect female legislators who are elected in districts with weak partisan constraints to be more likely than their male colleagues to collaborate with other women in the chamber.*

When party leaders have more control over legislative behavior, women are unlikely to behave differently than their male colleagues. As exerting personal influence in the legislature is disincentivized, women will not be motivated to work more frequently with women inside their party or across party lines to overcome their marginalized status in the chamber. Instead, women (like men) in these districts have an incentive to toe the party line, display party loyalties, and promote the party brand name. Moreover, women elected under party-centered electoral rules may be even more constrained than men because female legislators operating in male-dominated institutions face discrimination (Schwindt-Bayer 2010). As the male-dominated party leadership controls access to resources in these institutions that are important for career advancement, women are under more pressure to exhibit party loyalty if they want to ensure their future political careers. Because deviating from the party could be very costly in terms of their legislative careers, my theory suggests, women elected in systems where the party has immense control over legislators' careers and behavior do not have a strong motivation to ensure their voice is heard in the policy-making process. As a result, *I expect that strong partisan constraints will limit female legislators' incentives and opportunities to collaborate*. Instead, women in these districts should behave similarly to their male colleagues.

Women's Numeric Representation

A second important feature that varies significantly between chambers and can influence collaboration is women's numeric representation. Previous research has dedicated copious amounts of attention to the issue of how increasing women's numeric representation structures women's legislative behavior and their access to power in the legislative chamber. This research has provided useful insights on how increases in the numeric representation of a marginalized group shape the dynamics of the legislature, and how increases in women's numeric representation may change women's incentives and opportunities to collaborate.

It is an unsettled question, however, as to whether increases in numeric representation result in heightened marginalization. Some scholars posit that increases in numeric representation spur backlash and hostility from male colleagues (Krook 2015), and some find empirical support for this relationship (Barnes 2014; Heath et al. 2005; Kathlene 1994; Schwindt-Bayer 2010). Other research finds that increasing numbers of women may have no effect on women's experiences in the legislature or may even cause discrimination to dissipate (Barnes and Schibber 2015; Bækgaard and Kjaer 2012; Bratton 2002; Brown et al. 2002; Holman 2014; Kerevel and Atkeson 2013; Thomas 1994).

In this book, I assume that increases in the number of women in office raise awareness and visibility of women's marginalization and validate women's experiences with marginalization in the chamber. The extent to which marginalization of women *actually* increases or decreases as women's representation grows is an empirical question, and is likely to vary across places and legislatures depending on a number of factors including culture, women's status in society, and the duration of time that women have been a sizable part of the legislature (Barnes 2014; Beckwith 2007). Regardless, having more women in office serves to make legislators – particularly female legislators – more aware of women's status in office and cognizant of the structural barriers women face.

When a chamber has only a few women, it is very difficult to know if individuals' experiences are idiosyncratic or systematic. For example, if only a few women hold seats in the chamber and they are disproportionately relegated to serve on committees that are viewed as unimportant and have little power, it is hard to know if this circumstance is specific to the few women who are in office or if it is due to systematic marginalization. It could be the case that the chamber leadership does not value women's contributions or thinks women are not competent to legislate on powerful committees. Women may also self-select onto these committees because of their personal interests. Or it may simply be the luck of the draw. After all, not every legislator can serve on the budget committee every time. When women occupy a very small share of seats, it could be fairly easy to explain away gender differences. Moreover, if these same women face *informal* barriers such as a hostile work environment or struggle to exert power in the legislature, it is difficult to make the case that this is due to discrimination because the exclusion happens in subtle or invisible ways. For these reasons, when women comprise a small share of the chamber, it is easy for both male and female legislators to dismiss individual experiences as idiosyncratic.

Female legislators may also feel unjustified in identifying their experiences as discriminatory and may be more likely to blame themselves. The stigma associated with being the victim of discrimination may cause women to feel self-conscious or embarrassed by their experiences. Rather than confronting these obstacles, women may choose to maintain low profiles and avoid conflict, which is accomplished by displaying strong party loyalties, supporting established party programs, and promoting the party brand name rather than challenging the status quo (Beckwith 2007). Although this behavior may mitigate the negative consequences to individual women by keeping them out of the limelight and drawing less attention to their behavior, it does not work to advance women's status in the chamber or increase their influence.

When women comprise a larger proportion of the chamber (even if they are still a minority), the existing structural barriers that women face become more evident. When many female legislators encounter the same obstacles, idiosyncratic justifications for their negative experiences are no longer valid, and allegations of systematic marginalization are substantiated. In this way, increases in numeric representation serve to validate women's experiences and raise consciousness about women's plight in the chamber.

Earlier I explained why marginalization motivates collaboration among women. If increases in numeric representation expose women's marginalization, this implies that increases in numeric representation would motivate collaboration among women. When women are aware that their individual experiences are common among their female colleagues, they are more likely to acknowledge the structural barriers they face as both systematic and problematic. Female legislators are more likely to discuss their status with female colleagues, share information about how to overcome discrimination, and debate how to exert influence in the chamber. As a result, women may be more likely to find ways to work together within the system to be effective. Under these circumstances, female legislators may feel less pressure to display strong party loyalties. Rather, they may feel more freedom to exert their influence in the policy-making process when and how they see fit.

Additionally, collaboration with female colleagues becomes a more viable strategy as women's numeric representation increases. If there are only a few token women in office it may not be very practical for women to work collectively in hopes of advancing their legislative agendas and attaining more political power. But as women's numbers increase, working with women becomes more beneficial, and, as a result, the incentive to collaborate with women becomes stronger. In sum, increases in numeric representation expose women's marginalization and mobilize female legislators to respond to *growing* incentives to collaborate more frequently with female colleagues.

Notably, I argue that increases in numeric representation will motivate collaboration *above and beyond the additive effects* of simply increasing the number of women in office. In Chapters 5 and 6, I account for this explicitly in my analyses of women's collaboration. This is important for disentangling women's motivations to collaborate. If women are only more collaborative because they are socialized to be more cooperative, then we should not expect increases in numeric representation to spur more collaboration among women – at least not beyond the additive benefit of increasing the share of women in office. Instead, if collaboration is motivated only by socialization, we should expect women to behave the same regardless of numeric representation. Yet my empirical analysis shows that numeric representation is important for understanding when women collaborate, thus, indicating that women's marginalization motivates collaboration.

Impact of Women's Numeric Representation Conditional on Party Constraints

Finally, in thinking about how legislative contexts that vary between chambers shape women's collaboration, my theory implies that the relationship between numeric representation and women's collaboration is conditional on party constraints. Recall that not all women have the same incentives and opportunities to collaborate, given the partisan and chamber environment. I argue that collaboration varies as a function of partisan constraints such that women who face strong party constraints have fewer opportunities and incentives to collaborate. For this reason, my theory implies that increases in numeric representation will spur collaboration only when women have institutional opportunities and electoral incentives to collaborate.

Figure 2.1 depicts the expected relationship for female legislators between collaboration with women and increases in numeric representation conditional on party constraints. The x-axis in the figure represents increases in numeric representation and the y-axis represents collaboration with women.[11] As indicated by the top line in the figure labeled "weak party constraints," *I expect that*

---

[11] If women's numeric representation continues to increase, and women begin to gain power within legislatures, their marginalized status may end (albeit this circumstance is highly unlikely) and their incentives to collaborate may shift. In Chapter 8, I consider the implications of this for my theory.

increases in women's numeric representation will be associated with increased collaboration among women in districts with weak party constraints.

By contrast, women in districts with strong party constraints do not have the same opportunities to collaborate. As a result, I do not expect increases in numeric representation to spur more collaboration among women in these districts. If anything, in districts with strong party constraints, women may be more likely to collaborate when they comprise a small share of the chamber than when they comprise a larger share. This is because, when there are only a few women in the chamber, collaboration among them is unlikely to have a sizable impact on legislative outcomes. Thus party leaders have little incentive to expend energy and resources constraining collaboration. In other words, when there are only a few women in office, they can fly under the radar and draw little attention to themselves.

As the proportion of women in the chamber increases, however, collaboration among women, and in particular collaboration across party lines, is more likely to empower women, allowing them to influence outcomes. If women can use collaboration to gain influence in the chamber, their behavior will attract more attention from party leaders. Under these circumstances, party leaders are more likely to exercise party discipline to constrain women's collaboration. In sum, as women's numeric representation increases, they may be subject to more party constraints and forced to toe the party line, behaving like other rank-and-file party members (i.e., other male legislators). The bottom line labeled "strong party constraints" in Figure 2.1 represents my expectations for women who are subject to strong party constraints. Specifically, *I expect that increases in women's numeric representation will be associated with less collaboration among women – particularly among women from different parties.*

Within-Chamber Variation

In addition to cross-chamber variation, there is also important variation within chambers that structures women's legislative collaboration. In particular, I focus on how four factors that vary within the legislature shape women's legislative collaboration: the governor's party, seniority, legislation focused on women's issues, and membership on a women's issues committee or women's caucus. Figure 2.2 summarizes these relationships. Specifically, I theorize that women who are members of the governor's party face less pressure from party leaders than women who are members of the opposition parties. As a result, women who are members of the governor's party have more opportunities to collaborate with female colleagues. With respect to seniority, I argue that women with previous experience in the legislature likely have larger political networks in the chamber and will be more likely to defy party norms than their junior colleagues. For these reasons, they will be more likely to cross party lines to collaborate with women in other political parties. I also expect that women will be more inclined to collaborate with other women when they

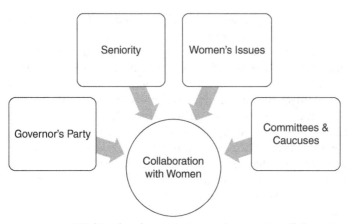

FIGURE 2.2. Within-chamber variation and women's collaboration.

work on issues that disproportionately influence the lives of women. Finally, I posit that women's issues committees and caucuses facilitate coordination among women. In the remainder of this section, I explain in more detail how each of these factors structure women's legislative collaboration.

Governor's Party

One important type of variation among legislators within the same chamber is their affiliation with either the governor's party or opposition parties. In this section, I argue that legislators who are members of the governor's party face weaker constraints and come under less pressure to promote the party. Under these conditions, both male and female members of the governor's party have fewer incentives overall to collaborate to exert influence in the chamber. Yet, I argue that within this context (i.e., among legislators who are members of the governor's party), women representatives have more incentive to collaborate with women than do men, particularly with co-partisans.

To begin with, in presidential systems, the chief executive has the resources and incentives to advance his or her party's agenda and promote the party's reputation. In most Latin American countries, for example, executives have a number of legislative powers, including the ability to introduce legislation, set the legislative agenda, establish budget spending and revenue levels, and determine budget priorities (Mainwaring and Shugart 1997; Payne et al. 2007). Although legislators are expected to vote in favor of the party's agenda (Mainwaring and Pérez-Liñán 1997), they are not responsible for initiating and promoting it. The governor's ability to influence the legislative agenda has two implications for legislators. First, members of the governor's party face weaker constraints than members of the opposition, and as long as they do not damage the party's reputation or oppose the governor's agenda, they have more opportunities to pursue their own legislative priorities (Crisp et al. 2004a;

Nielson and Shugart 1999; Shugart 2001; Shugart and Carey 1992). Second, given the party's access to important resources, party members have relatively weak incentives to collaborate to attain more power for their political party. Thus, as previously explained, *overall levels of collaboration will be lower among members of the governor's party than among opposition members.* But, because they face weaker constraints than do members of the opposition, when members of the governor's party do collaborate, they have more flexibility to choose whom they want to work with.

Yet, despite the fact that members of the governor's party are institutionally stronger than members of the opposition, women continue to experience marginalization *within* the governor's party. Even though the party can advance its agenda and members of the governor's party have disproportionate access to leadership posts and other political resources, women have little influence within the party. Few women hold party leadership positions, and women are less likely than men to attain access to powerful resources and committee appointments. Thus, female legislators in the governor's party are more likely than men to rely on collaboration to attain political power *within* their party. Moreover, as members of the governor's party do not need to advance the party's agenda and face fewer constraints, when women from the governor's party do collaborate, they can devote more of their collaborative efforts to working with women to attain their own political power. Notably, affiliation with the governor's party should primarily influence female legislators' propensities to collaborate with co-partisans. By definition, for members of the governor's party to collaborate across party lines, they must be collaborating with someone who is not from the governor's party. Unlike other political contexts that motivate collaboration, affiliation with the governor's party should not result in more collaboration between women across party lines. Together, I expect overall levels of collaboration to be lower among members of the governor's party, but I posit that *when women from the governor's party do collaborate, they will collaborate with female co-partisans more than male co-partisans.*

By contrast, legislators from the opposition are the only members from their parties with the means to promote their parties' legislative agendas. Under these circumstances, party leaders exert more party discipline over members, pressuring them to devote the bulk of their time to furthering the party's interests and upholding a cohesive party reputation. As such, affiliation with the opposition has two implications for women's collaborative patterns. As previously explained, *out-of-power legislators (those affiliated with the opposition) will rely more on collaboration to accomplish their goals than in-power legislators.* But opposition legislators face pressures from their party to use their time and resources to advance the party's agenda. As such, when women from the opposition collaborate, *they will collaborate with both male and female co-partisans.* Their incentives to collaborate more frequently with women will be offset by pressure to advance the party's agenda and their electoral incentives to attain power for their party.

Seniority

Variation in seniority status within chambers is another important factor that shapes legislative behavior. For multiple reasons, I argue that women with seniority status are more likely than their junior colleagues to cross party lines to collaborate.[12] To begin with, senior women have more experience and are more familiar with navigating the legislature. They may be more willing to help newcomers in their own political party learn to navigate the legislative process to work within the system to accomplish their goals (Barnes 2014). Indeed, extant research on female leadership indicates that women are more likely than men to mentor and support junior colleagues (Eagly, Johannesen-Schmidt, and Van Engen 2003). As such, senior women may be more likely to engage junior women in formal collaboration such as cosponsorship and informal collaboration such as networking.

Additionally, female legislators who served previous periods in office are likely to have developed relationships with other women – including women from other political parties – who also served previous terms. They may have a larger professional network from which to draw on when choosing their collaborators. Senior women may also be less responsive to party discipline and more likely than junior women to defy party norms and directives (Beckwith 2007). Together, these three points imply that *senior women will be more likely than junior women to engage in collaboration with women – particularly collaboration across party lines.*

Women's Issues Legislation

I argue that when working on legislation that disproportionately impacts the lives of women (henceforth women's issues), women are more likely to collaborate with female colleagues than with male colleagues. Although there is not one definition of women's issues (see Escobar-Lemon and Taylor-Robinson 2014a; Schwindt-Bayer and Taylor-Robinson 2011), as I detail in Chapter 6, I classify legislation as a women's issue if it concerns women's rights and quality of life, women's health, or issues focused on children, family, and youth. This subset of women's issues is not limited to any one ideological position nor does it assume all women have the same policy preferences (Barnes 2012b). Instead, these

---

[12] There is reason to believe that, on average, legislators with seniority status in chambers with entrenched seniority norms like the U.S. Congress may be less likely to collaborate because they have more influence over the legislative agenda and do not need to rely on policy collaboration to achieve their legislative goals (Davidson and Oleszek 2005; Harward and Moffett 2010). This is not the case in countries like Argentina, where there is no seniority system like the one found in the United States (Jones et al. 2002). For example, Argentine legislators with seniority status are not systematically rewarded with better committee appointments or leadership posts (Barnes 2014). Moreover, even in systems with entrenched seniority norms, senior women tend to have less influence and power than senior men. Under such circumstances, my theory implies that when senior women collaborate, they will be more likely than their junior colleagues to cross party lines to work with women.

issues are derived from women's interests more generally, but they are limited in scope as they address only those components or aspects of women's interests that become proposed legislation (Beckwith 2011, 2014). Women's issues often cut across party lines and impact women from diverse backgrounds (Smooth 2011) who are motivated by a number of different identities and social perspectives (Weldon 2011). Thus women's issues likely vary considerably over time and across political contexts (Reingold and Swers 2011).

I argue that female legislators are more likely to collaborate with women when they are working on this subset of issues because they are more likely than male legislators to prioritize women's issues in the first place. Historically marginalized groups have a number of "overlooked interests" (Phillips 1995). Because many of these issues have not previously been part of the legislative agenda, they are often not fully articulated (Mansbridge 1999). Legislators can better understand the problems of these groups and represent their interests if they incorporate a variety of perspectives. Thus, legislators should be even more inclined to collaborate when working on women's issues.

Further, members of these groups (in this case, women) may be more likely and better suited to represent these interests. This may be because descriptive representatives are more likely to have shared life experiences that give them different perspectives on a broad set of issues (Dovi 2002; Mansbridge 1999; Phillips 1995). Indeed, Baldez argues that, when women's issues are framed in terms of women's shared experiences of exclusion, they are more likely to cooperate across partisan lines to advance women's rights (2002, 2003). Alternatively, it may simply be because they have increased awareness of the group's interests and are more likely to empathize with the group's concerns and take interest in learning about its welfare (Weldon 2002).

Indeed, female politicians tend to have some priorities that are distinct from their male colleagues (Wängnerud 2015), spend more of their time proposing legislation relevant to women's issues, and are more responsive and receptive to female constituents and women's groups (Brown and Banks 2014; Holman 2013; Htun and Power 2006; Kittilson 2008, 2011; Piscopo 2011). In Latin America, female legislators frequently sponsor legislation on a range of women's issues and are more likely to do so than male legislators (Jones 1997; Schwindt-Bayer 2010; Taylor-Robinson and Heath 2003).[13] In particular, in the case of Argentina, women introduce more legislation specifically pertaining to women's rights and children and family issues (Franceschet and Piscopo 2008; Jones 1997; Schwindt-Bayer 2006). Given that women tend to have a distinct set of priorities from their male colleagues, women working on women's issues may be more likely to choose to collaborate with female colleagues.

---

[13] Women's tendencies to prioritize different issues than men and to introduce legislation that disproportionately affects the lives of women are not unique to Latin America. An abundance of research finds similar trends in the United States (Bratton 2002, 2005; Bratton and Haynie 1999; Gerrity, Osborn, and Mendez 2007; Swers 2002, 2005, 2013; Thomas 1994; Thomas and Welch 1991; Wolbrecht 2002).

There are also sociological reasons to suggest that women may be more likely to seek out female collaborators when working on women's issues. In group settings where women are in the minority, they have less influence than men (Propp 1995; Thomas-Hunt and Phillips 2004) and are often less confident discussing women's issues around men (Karpowitz and Mendelberg 2014). Thus, when working on women's issues, women may be less likely to collaborate with men and may prefer to work with women.

Women's propensity to prioritize women's issues more than men, and women's inclinations to avoid deliberation on women's issues when they are in male-dominated groups, implies that women will be more likely to seek out female collaborators when working on a women's issue. Thus, *I expect that collaboration among women will be even more likely on a subset of legislation that focuses on women's issues.* Further, given that women's issues cut across partisan cleavages, women should be particularly inclined to cross party lines to collaborate on this subset of legislation.

Membership in a Women's Committee or Women's Caucus

A final way that legislative context can influence when women collaborate is by creating an institution in the legislature that is explicitly designated for collaboration on issues pertaining to women or the plight of women in office. Specifically, women's issues committees and/or women's caucuses are instrumental in facilitating collaboration among women, and in particular collaboration across party lines (Kanthak and Krause 2012). Women's issues committees (and some women's caucuses) are designed specifically to address women's issues, to promote the development of a gender-equality agenda, and to foster the discussion and exchange of information pertaining to gender-related initiatives. Women's caucuses, both formal and informal, are often created to promote women's incorporation into the legislature through networking and mentorship (Piscopo 2014b). Typically, the committees and caucuses are disproportionately comprised of women (Barnes 2014; Heath et al. 2005). As a result, women may be more likely to cultivate relationships with female colleagues on the committee or caucus (Ross 2002) and to work with female colleagues in the future.

Beyond simply being associated with more women, the all-female or primarily female setting in women's issues committees and women's caucuses creates an environment where women are more inclined to participate in the policy-making process and form collaborative relationships. When women are in the minority, they are more likely to refrain from participating in conversations and debates necessary to influence policy. By contrast, women are more likely to participate when women are in the majority (Karpowitz and Mendelberg 2014). Given that women are underrepresented in legislatures, they may be less likely to participate in male-dominated settings such as a plenary session or during male-dominated committee meetings, but may be more likely to take an active role on women's issue committees and in women's caucuses. In these female-dominated settings, women have the opportunity to work together and influence the development of legislation.

Further, as committees and women's caucuses are typically comprised of legislators from different political parties, collaboration on issues that influence women may be more likely to occur across party lines. Collaboration across party lines may be aided by the jurisdiction of the legislation addressed in the committee. Many issues that affect women's lives cut across partisan cleavages (Htun 2004). As a result, women may be more willing to cross party lines to work together. *I expect membership on a women's issue committee or in a caucus will increase collaboration among women – particularly collaboration across party lines.*

A growing number of chambers worldwide have established committees with a jurisdiction focused specifically on women's issues more narrowly, or on women, family, and children matters more generally. Nonetheless, in the case of Argentina, there is little variation in membership in women's issues committees and on women's caucuses because so few chambers have women's issues committees or caucuses, and those that do have only had them for a short period of time. This limits my ability to systematically examine the impact of caucuses and committees on collaboration in Argentina. Instead, I empirically examine this expectation in Chapter 7 in a number of different case studies.

CONCLUSION

In this chapter, I provided answers to the three central questions that motivate this book. In doing so, I developed a number of expectations (summarized in Table 2.1) that I will test in the following chapters. First, I explained that democracy can be collaborative. Whereas only the majority can secure the power to decide via competition, all legislators – particularly those who do not have power – can influence the policy-making process through collaboration. I expect collaboration to be widespread, but I posited that out-of-power legislators will collaborate more than those in power. These expectations are summarized in the first section of Table 2.1. To evaluate this expectation, I explore patterns of legislative collaboration in Chapter 3.

Second, I explained that women collaborate more than men because female legislators entering a male-dominated institution face structural barriers that limit their influence in the legislative process. In order to do their jobs effectively, female legislators must work around these barriers. As a result of marginalization, I argued that women are one such out-of-power group that can benefit from collaboration. As summarized in the second section of Table 2.1, we should observe women's marginalization across a vast array of legislative power. I evaluate these expectations in Chapter 4 by examining women's access to chamber-wide leadership positions, committee leadership posts, and powerful committee appointments.

TABLE 2.1. *Summary of Expectations*

---

1. Can democracy be collaborative?
   - Legislators in opposition parties will collaborate more than legislators in the governor's party.
   - Minority party members will collaborate more than majority party members.
   - Women will collaborate more than men.

2. Why do women collaborate?
   - Women will be less likely than men to receive chamber-wide leadership posts.
   - Women will be less likely than men to receive committee leadership posts.
   - Women will be less likely than men to receive powerful committee appointments.

3. When do women collaborate?
   Variation Between-Chambers
   - Women in districts with weak party constraints will be more likely than men to collaborate with female colleagues both within their parties and across party lines.
   - Women in districts with strong party constraints will behave similarly to men.
   - Increases in women's numeric representation will be associated with increased collaboration among women in districts with weak party constraint.
   - Increases in women's numeric representation will be associated with decreased collaboration among women in districts with strong party constraint – particularly collaboration across party lines.

   Variation Within-Chambers
   - Women in the governor's party will be more likely than women from opposition parties to collaborate with female co-partisans.
   - Senior women will be more likely than junior women to cross party lines to collaborate with female colleagues.
   - Women will be more likely to collaborate with female colleagues both within their parties and across party lines when they are working on women's issues than when they are working on other issues.
   - Women will be more likely to collaborate both within their parties and across party lines when they are members of a women's caucus or women's issues committee.

Third, despite incentives to collaborate, I explained, not all female legislators have the same institutional opportunities or electoral incentives to collaborate more frequently with other women. Legislative contexts that vary both between and within institutions structure women's collaboration. The third section of Table 2.1 summarizes my expectations for how six key contextual variables that vary both between and within legislative chambers shape policy collaboration. Chapter 5 examines how factors that vary between chambers in Argentina structure women's propensity to collaborate with female colleagues, and Chapter 6 focuses on factors that vary within legislative chambers. Finally, Chapter 7 uses case studies to examine the generalizability of my theory in a cross-national context.

3

Can Democracy Be Collaborative?

Examining Patterns of Collaboration

> *"We tried to bring everyone together so that each person would give their opinion about the project and to address solutions for the improvement."*
>
> – *Female Deputy, Mendoza, 2013*

In 2012, a group of eight female deputies from across the political spectrum in Mendoza worked together to develop legislation that would create a Special Prosecution Unit for Crimes of Gender. The unit would exist within the Ministry of Public Prosecutions and be staffed with personnel trained to assist female victims of violence against women. Although there is a strong national law addressing violence against women, many provinces are not equipped to enforce the law because they lack the resources and infrastructure to provide victims with assistance. To address this challenge, one deputy explained, legislators needed to learn more about the "kind of problems public officials encountered when they wanted to assist the women."[1] To this end, the deputy spearheading the project in Mendoza brought together a number of experts from different branches of government, including specialists from the provincial courts, the provincial executive branch, the municipalities, and nongovernmental organizations such as the National Institute Against Discrimination and Xenophobia. Female deputies interested in addressing violence against women met with these experts on multiple occasions to identify the challenges the experts faced when implementing the national legislation, to develop solutions, and to fine-tune the proposed legislation.

The project, cosponsored by eight female deputies, was officially proposed in May 2012 and is making its way through the legislative process. The deputy leading the project explained: "This project has been going for one year and I am fighting to sanction it. We have a bicameral system. So it is necessary

---

[1] Interview with female deputy from Mendoza, Frente para la Victoria, June 26, 2013.

for it to be approved by both chambers. I have been fighting for the house's approval."[2] In May 2014, the project finally advanced from the General Legislation and Constitutional Issues Committee but did not go to a vote on the house floor. In the meantime, female deputies collaborated with female senators in the Bicameral Committee for Gender and Diversity in the Mendoza Legislature, and arranged for a female Senator to introduce the same bill in the Mendoza Senate. The legislation was approved in the Senate on May 27, 2015 along with three other bills designed to address violence against women. The passage of the legislation in the Senate coincided with a national protest #NiUnaMas (not one less) denouncing femicide in Argentina. Although the legislation has not yet passed in the Chamber of Deputies, female deputies continue to champion this project and push for approval.

In this example, legislators collaborate with each other and with policy experts outside the legislature to develop legislation that better represents the needs and concerns of constituents. The example represents one of the most common and important types of collaboration that take place inside the legislature and exemplifies why collaboration is an important aspect of the policy-making process and of democratic representation. Although previous research on legislative behavior focuses primarily on the competitive aspects of democracy, a big part of what legislators actually do involves collaboration; yet legislative collaboration has largely gone overlooked.

In this book, I argue that *democracy can be collaborative*. Recall that I explained in Chapter 2 that by collaborating in the development of legislation, legislators can exert more influence during the legislative process. Their involvement in policy development allows them to shape the content of policy and legislative priorities more generally. Given the benefits of collaboration, I expect collaboration to be widespread in legislatures. Because only those legislators who are in positions of power can acquire the right to decide via competition, I argue that legislators who are not in positions of power can attain more influence in the policy-making process via collaboration. Therefore, I expect legislators who are in positions of institutional weakness to collaborate more than legislators who are in power.

In this chapter, I examine patterns of collaboration among legislators. Specifically, I compare collaboration between groups of legislators who are and are not in positions of power. Although legislators can collaborate in a large number of ways, in this book, I look specifically at policy collaboration. As with previous research on Argentina (Alemán and Calvo 2010; Calvo and Leiras 2012), I use bill cosponsorship data to examine policy collaboration. I first discuss the reliability, validity, and comparability of bill cosponsorship as a measure of collaboration. Specifically, I explain that cosponsorship is a reliable measure of collaboration because most legislatures document and archive the introduction of all legislative proposals. As a result, I can systematically

---

[2] Ibid.

quantify bill cosponsorship and measure cosponsorship behavior with practically no error. Drawing on interview evidence to gain a better understanding of legislators' motivations for cosponsoring legislation, I show that bill cosponsorship is an intuitive and valid measure of legislative collaboration. It marks the culmination of a collaborative process in which legislators work together to consider a diversity of perspectives, build consensus, reach compromise, and develop legislation to exert their influence on the policy-making process. Further, because each Argentine legislature included in this study follows similar rules and norms for introducing legislation, I can reliably draw comparisons between chambers.

After discussing the advantages of using bill cosponsorship as a measure of collaboration, I examine patterns in bill cosponsorship data to evaluate how frequently collaboration occurs in the Argentine context. Specifically, I evaluate the first part of my theory, which argues that out-of-power legislators will collaborate more frequently than legislators in power. I show that policy collaboration is quite common in Argentina as is, perhaps surprisingly, collaboration across party lines. The data demonstrate that despite a divisive party system and relatively strong party discipline across Argentina, a large part of what legislators do is collaborative. Although collaboration is common among all legislators, I find legislators who are not in power collaborate more. In particular, I show that legislators from the opposition party collaborate more than legislators from the governor's party, that legislators from minority parties collaborate more than legislators from majority political parties, and that women collaborate more than men.

LEGISLATIVE COLLABORATION: BILL COSPONSORSHIP DATA

Most collaboration among legislators is aimed at developing and advancing legislation, and legislators can collaborate using a variety of methods in an effort to influence the policy-making process. For example, legislators can cosponsor legislation; network; organize informal meetings to exchange ideas and gather information on problems in their districts; or simply encourage colleagues to speak out and share their opinions during party meetings, floor debates, and committee hearings.

Legislative collaboration is not strictly limited to collaboration among legislators themselves; legislators also build networks with experts and organizations outside the legislature through informal activities such as meetings to exchange information, or via formal avenues such as inviting specialists to testify during committee hearings. For example, in 2011, about eighty female lawmakers and experts convened at the city legislature in Buenos Aires to inaugurate the Women's Parliament, an organization aimed at expanding the scope of women's rights and women's quality of life in Argentina. Similarly, in Salta, a deputy explained that female legislators from all political parties get together with women in the community – women from universities, professional organizations, and nonprofit organizations, as well as stay-at-home moms – to address issues of common concern.[3] In a number of cases, women in the Argentine provinces have organized groups or meetings to fuel collaboration between female legislators and other branches of government, women's advocacy groups, and policy experts. Although it is not the focus of this book, an important aspect of legislative collaboration reaches beyond the legislature. Indeed, legislators stand to benefit from formal and informal collaboration both inside and outside of the chamber.

Collaboration can take several different forms, but most legislative collaboration has the same end goal of influencing the development of legislation and policy outcomes. In this book, I focus specifically on bill cosponsorship in the Argentine provinces. As I explain in more detail later, cosponsorship is an ideal measure of collaboration because it is reliable, valid, and comparable across provinces. In the remainder of this section, I elaborate on each of these three advantages associated with using bill cosponsorship data to examine legislative collaboration.

Bill Cosponsorship: A Reliable Measure of Collaboration

When deciding how to measure concepts, it is important to identify a measure that is reliable – that is, a measure that produces the same results when applied at different times or by different researchers (King, Keohane, and Verba 1994, 24–25). As previously mentioned, legislators participate in a large number of collaborative behaviors, ranging from informal meetings and networking to participating in policy debates. Many of these forms of collaboration, however, can be difficult for scholars to observe and impossible to measure reliably. Public records do not account for the number of informal meetings, conversations, or mentoring sessions that colleagues share. Similarly, many legislatures do not keep complete records of legislative debates or of policy experts called to testify during committee hearings. The lack of available data makes it difficult to systematically account for most forms of collaboration and to develop a reliable measure of collaboration.

This is not the case for bill cosponsorship data. Cosponsorship is a reliable measure of collaboration because most legislatures document and archive the introduction of all legislative proposals along with each of the bill's cosponsors. Consequently, I can quantify and measure cosponsorship behavior with practically no error. Indeed, a growing number of studies in political science quantify cosponsorship data to study legislative behavior (Alemán et al. 2009; Alemán and Calvo 2010; Barnes 2012b; Calvo and Leiras 2012; Kirkland 2011).[4]

---

[3] Interview with female deputy from Salta, Frente para la Victoria, July 10, 2013.

[4] Most legislatures in the Argentine provinces, unlike the Argentine National Congress and the U.S. legislatures, do not distinguish between the primary sponsor and cosponsors; nor do they differentiate between cosponsors and coauthors – they use the terms interchangeably.

Nonetheless, obtaining cosponsorship data for subnational legislatures in a developing country is no small feat. For the vast majority of provinces in Argentina, cosponsorship data are not available online or in the nation's capital. In provinces for which data were available online, data were typically only available for the most recent legislative session. To obtain these data, it was necessary to travel to each individual province to collect the data from the archives.

To carry out this research, I traveled to nineteen provinces (twenty-seven chambers – eight bicameral and eleven unicameral) to collect bill cosponsorship data. It was not feasible for me to travel to all provincial legislatures; thus, with the exception of two bicameral legislatures (Entre Ríos and Corrientes) and two provinces in the region of Patagonia (Chubut and Santa Cruz), I did not include any provinces in my sample that do not have at least thirty legislators in the lower chamber.[5] I successfully obtained individual-level bill cosponsorship data for legislators from twenty-three Argentine chambers for an eighteen-year period from 1992 (the year before quota implementation) to 2009.[6] The data include all cosponsored legislation for more than 7,000 male and female legislators. These data serve as the foundation for the empirical analyses in this chapter and in Chapters 5 and 6. During my fieldwork in the Argentine provinces, I also interviewed more than 200 legislators, politicians, and elite political observers. In the next section, I draw on this information along with previous research on bill cosponsorship to explain why bill cosponsorship is a valid measure of collaboration.

Bill Cosponsorship: A Valid Measure of Collaboration

Cosponsorship is a valid measure of collaboration because it represents the culmination of a collaborative process. Recall that validity refers to the degree to which the measure corresponds to the concept (King et al. 1994). To better understand the meaning of cosponsorship data in the Argentine context and to evaluate how well the data capture the concept of collaboration, I asked provincial-level legislators why they cosponsor bills and how they choose their cosponsors. There are two prevailing perspectives on why legislators cosponsor and how cosponsorship comes about. First, cosponsorship is sometimes used to signal support for legislation. Second, cosponsorship is a collaborative

---

[5] I did not travel to Santa Cruz. It is one of the few provinces that archived bill cosponsorship data online, enabling me to include such data in my analyses. Additionally, I was able to obtain committee assignments and leadership appointments (used in Chapter 4) for Santa Cruz via e-mail correspondence with the provincial legislature. I included the two additional provinces in the region of Patagonia because small legislatures (those with fewer than thirty members in the lower chamber) are overrepresented in Patagonia. I did not want to bias my sample by under-sampling this region because the other regions are well represented in the sample.

[6] A list of the chambers and years included in the analysis is available in Appendix 3.1.

process; legislators work together to develop legislation that represents constituents. One deputy from Córdoba summarized this nicely:

"Sometimes projects are developed jointly, and in that case each author signs [the bill]. In other cases, the project is authored by one person and the author accepts or solicits the rest of their bloc to accompany them."[7]

Similarly, a number of interviewees reported that sometimes they cosponsor legislation because the entire political party signs on to the legislation or because someone in their political party is looking for support for their bill. This signaling device is more than just "cheap talk." When legislators pledge their support for legislation via cosponsorship, reneging is quite costly. Legislators who renege on cosponsorship commitments damage their relationships with colleagues and hurt their own ability to develop coalitions of support in the future (Bernhard and Sulkin 2013).

Argentine legislators also indicate that cosponsorship is a result of collaboration wherein multiple legislators discuss problems of mutual concern and work together to develop a solution. This may involve developing the legislation together from the ground up or amending legislation to incorporate the ideas and perspectives of multiple legislators. For example, a deputy from Jujuy explains: "usually projects have more than one author."[8] According to her, the motivation for cosponsoring is that it allows legislators to share their ideas with their colleagues and to incorporate their colleagues' perspectives:

"Once the author of a project gets other people to support it, they ask for the other legislators to modify the project if there is a possibility for any modifications. The [cosponsor] shares their ideas, signs the project, and accompanies the author as a coauthor."[9]

This process, in which one legislator develops legislation and seeks out cosponsors to amend and support the legislation, is consistent with the idea that cosponsorship provides an avenue for legislators to incorporate diverse perspectives and build consensus on legislation. Similarly, other deputies describe a process in which they directly engage with their cosponsors during the development of the legislation. When asked about her cosponsorship activity, a female deputy from Mendoza describes her cosponsors as a *team* of people working together to develop the project:

"We are about to present a project that addresses the issue of policemen with guns who commit violence against their wives. We have a team working on a project to address those cases."[10]

In the same spirit, another legislator explains how legislators choose with whom to work. She depicts an environment in which legislators seek out their colleagues with common interests and work together to find solutions to

---

[7] Interview with male deputy from Córdoba, Unión por Córdoba, November 11, 2009.
[8] Interview with female deputy from Jujuy, Partido Justicialista, October 29, 2009.
[9] Ibid.
[10] Interview with female deputy from Mendoza, Frente para la Victoria, June 27, 2013.

problems. This description is distinct from the idea that legislators sign on to any legislation that comes their way or use partisan shortcuts to decide what legislation to cosponsor. As she described it:

"[Cosponsorship] could happen when two or more legislators are educators, and dedicate their lives to that, or if we are from the same place, and we propose solutions for problems in our community."[11]

Her explanation of cosponsorship activity illustrates that legislators are careful and thoughtful when choosing whom to work with. In particular, she emphasizes that legislators choose to collaborate with colleagues who have shared priorities and interests. Along the same lines, others indicate that they seek to work with colleagues who have expertise in the relevant policy domain. For example, one deputy from Salta explained that when he introduced legislation pertaining to health care, he asked his colleague, who is a doctor by trade, to cosponsor the legislation because it would give him more authority and allow him to draw on his colleague's expertise.[12]

These examples of cosponsorship as collaboration and the perception that cosponsorship is an opportunity for legislators to work together on legislation are common, and interviews with legislators across Argentina reinforce this idea. A deputy from Río Negro notes that cosponsorship allows legislators to "discuss [their] points of view to develop legislation."[13] A deputy from Salta notes that cosponsorship is a way for legislators to "reach a common agreement."[14] Similarly, a deputy from Chaco describes cosponsorship as an avenue for legislators to "attain a better law and reach a consensus."[15] In sum, cosponsorship is often an activity in which multiple legislators collaborate, exchange ideas, and mutually influence legislation.

Cosponsorship is also important for raising awareness around issues and for establishing a network of supporters over time. A deputy from Catamarca explains: "When a project has more than one author it is more likely that it will receive support."[16] Others echo the idea that cosponsorship is a way to expand the base of support for legislation, and many legislators think that it increases the probability of legislation being passed into law. Even when legislation is not successful, cosponsorship can be useful for raising awareness around an issue and generating support for the future. A legislator from the Federal District explained that even if legislation is not passed into law or is never debated on the house floor, there is still an incentive to introduce and cosponsor legislation:

"Sometimes we know that we aren't going to fix the problem, but we still talk about it and discuss it. We make the theme public and put it out there. Sometimes that is what

---

[11] Interview with female deputy from Catamarca, Frente para la Victoria, November 17, 2009.
[12] Interview with male deputy from Salta, Partido Renovador de Salta, October 20, 2009.
[13] Interview with female deputy from Río Negro, Unión Cívica Radical, December 9, 2009.
[14] Interview with female deputy from Salta, Frente para la Victoria, October 21, 2009.
[15] Interview with female deputy from Chaco, Alianza Frente de Todos, March 10, 2010.
[16] Interview with female deputy from Catamarca, Partido Justicialista, November 16, 2009.

the projects are for. Not everything is discussed in the sessions. But it is a way for it to get visibility outside [the legislature] – in the unions or in the neighborhood groups."[17]

By introducing legislation and talking about an issue among interested members, legislators can call attention to the issue and raise awareness about relevant problems in society (Swers 2013). Cosponsorship is an important vehicle through which legislators can voice their opinions, discuss problems with other legislators, and influence the policy-making process – all of which are important aspects of representation.

Finally, interviews with legislators illustrate that cosponsorship is a tool legislators can use to exert influence on the legislative process. Consider, for example, comments from a female senator in Mendoza:

"In general, for all of these projects, men usually make the decisions. But all of the issues that have to do with social or psychological themes have a bigger female involvement [in developing the legislation]. Our group of female senators is interdisciplinary, which is very good; there is a mix that works really well, with [names legislator] and [names legislator]. We make sure to have this involvement because when it comes to the official speech, it is a struggle to introduce this psychological theme, the ones with a feminine aspect [but] having people from different backgrounds helps us see things from that perspective."[18]

The female deputy from Mendoza clearly acknowledges that "men usually make the final decisions" when it comes to the passage of legislation; but she explains that in order for women to have the biggest possible impact on legislation, women collaborate among themselves early in the legislative process (during the development of the idea) to ensure that they have an opportunity for their voices to be heard and their opinions to be reflected in the legislation.

In sum, a few lessons emerge from the discussion of cosponsorship in the Argentine context. First, cosponsorship is sometimes used as a mechanism to build consensus around a topic. This may involve legislators simply signing onto legislation to indicate their support for a project or legislators building coalitions of support and soliciting others' opinions in the development of legislation. Second, cosponsorship is often the product of a collaborative process in which multiple legislators work together to incorporate multiple perspectives, produce better legislation, and exert influence on the policy-making process.

With respect to the first lesson, evidence from interviews indicates that it is not accurate to characterize cosponsorship as *exclusively* an artifact of collaboration. Nonetheless, even if some cosponsorship is not the result of collaboration, this is not problematic for my research. To begin with, if cosponsorship is just a costless signaling device for legislators to indicate their support for legislation, it will be more difficult to observe systematic patterns of collaboration among women or other out-of-power groups. When cosponsorship is used as

---

[17] Interview with female deputy from Federal District, Buenos Aires para Todos, July 19, 2013.
[18] Interview with female senator from Mendoza, Unión Cívica Radical, June 26, 2013.

a signaling device, cosponsorship should be more consistent with party lines and should mask gender differences, potentially biasing my results in favor of a null result.

Additionally, even though it is impossible to know which cosponsors were collaborators and which only signed a project to signal their position, we can make some assumptions about the data. In particular, we may assume that projects for which an entire political party signs the bill are not projects that were developed in a collaborative manner. One way to address this issue is to exclude from my analysis all legislation that is cosponsored by an over-whelming majority of any given political party. Because party-level decisions to cosponsor legislation are not consistent with the concept of collaboration that I am interested in measuring, I eliminate legislation cosponsored by the vast majority of any single political party or cosponsored by the vast major-ity of the legislative chamber. The results presented in this chapter as well as in Chapters 5 and 6 rely on legislation that is not cosponsored by entire (or near-entire) political parties or by the entire chamber.[19] Although the results presented in this book are robust to this decision (i.e., my results hold even when I include all cosponsored legislation), omitting this legislation improves the validity of my measure of collaboration.

With respect to the second lesson, it is clear from the evidence presented here and from numerous interviews I conducted with Argentine legislators that bill cosponsorship is often the product of a collaborative process in which legislators work together to develop legislation. Importantly, the responses I heard from legislators in Argentina were consistent with previous work on policy collaboration that views bill cosponsorship as the result of collabora-tion (Alemán and Calvo 2010; Calvo and Leiras 2012; Kirkland 2011). Similar to extant research on bill cosponsorship, the interviews here show that bill cosponsorship represents the result of a collaborative process in which legis-lators develop networks and coalitions with like-minded colleagues (Alemán and Calvo 2013; Barnes 2012b; Koger 2003; Swers 2013; Wawro 2001) to craft legislation (Kirkland 2011; Tam Cho and Fowler 2010) and exert their influence on the policy-making process (Kessler and Krehbiel 1996; Kirkland 2012, 2014; Swers 2002, 2013). Put succinctly, cosponsorship is the culmina-tion of the collaborative policy-making process, and thus, it is a valid measure of collaboration.

---

[19] Specifically, I eliminate legislation for which 80 percent of the authors of a given party signed the bill if those legislators make up 80 percent of the signatories on the bill, provided that the party in question holds more than two seats in the chamber and provided that more than 25 percent of the chamber signed the legislation in question. These restrictions are put in place to avoid eliminating small parties that hold only a few seats in the chamber. I also eliminate all bills for which 95 percent of a single party signed the bill, provided the party in question holds more than two seats and 35 percent of the chamber signed the bill. Finally, I eliminate bills signed by more than 90 percent of the chamber.

Bill Cosponsorship: A Comparable Measure of Collaboration

Another advantage of using bill cosponsorship data to measure legislative collaboration in the Argentine context is the relative ease with which I can draw comparisons between legislators in different chambers. In cross-national analyses it can be difficult to compare legislative behavior across a large number of chambers because chambers vary substantially in the constitutional powers afforded to legislators and the institutional norms that drive legislative behavior. As a result, collaboration might take different forms in different places. For example, whereas it is meaningful to examine policy collaboration using cosponsorship data in Argentina (Alemán and Calvo 2010; Calvo and Leiras 2012), this same form of collaboration is practically nonexistent in Rwanda, where the introduction of legislation by legislators is extremely rare (Pearson 2008; Wilber 2011). Thus, when comparing legislative collaboration across a large number of chambers, it can be difficult to draw reliable comparisons between groups. By contrast, a major benefit of subnational data is the ability to make meaningful comparisons across units (Boulding 2014).

With respect to legislative collaboration in the Argentine provinces, there is widespread use of collaboration to develop cosponsored legislation. Because each of the provinces in Argentina patterns its own constitution and legislature after the national constitution and national legislature, deputies in every province have similar legislative authority. As a result, bill cosponsorship has a similar meaning in every province, enabling me to draw comparisons in cosponsorship behavior between different chambers with relative ease.

Cosponsorship is both a reliable and valid measure of collaboration that can be compared consistently across the Argentine provinces. I can systematically observe and measure bill cosponsorship. Equally important, the act of cosponsorship nicely captures the concept of collaboration. Finally, this measure of collaboration allows me to generalize across a large number of legislative chambers. For these three reasons, cosponsorship is an ideal measure of collaboration in Argentina.

EVIDENCE OF COLLABORATION: COSPONSORSHIP PATTERNS IN ARGENTINA

In this section, I compare patterns of collaboration for out-of-power legislators with those of legislators who are in power. Using cosponsorship data from twenty-three chambers in Argentina covering an eighteen-year period, I examine the number of bills that an average legislator cosponsors in a two-year period (herein session) and the number of cosponsorship relationships that an average legislator forms in a session. I expect that legislators who are out of power will collaborate on a larger number of bills and form a larger number of collaborative relationships. I also examine legislators' propensity to collaborate with colleagues in their own party and to cross party lines to collaborate.

I expect that all legislators will collaborate frequently but that legislators who are out of power will cross party lines to collaborate at a higher rate than will legislators in positions of power. Cross-party collaboration is particularly important for out-of-power legislators because it allows them to knit together larger coalitions of support for legislation, allowing them to wield more political power. I compare patterns of collaboration for different groups of legislators who typically have more or less power in the chamber. Specifically, I compare patterns of collaboration for legislators who are members of the governor's party with those of members of the opposition; for legislators who are members of the majority legislative party with those of members of other smaller political parties; and for male legislators with those of female legislators.

Patterns of Collaboration for the Governor's Party and Opposition Parties

In presidential systems, like the ones found in Argentina, the executive's party (or, in this case, the governor's party) has a significant amount of power, even when the governor's party lacks a majority in the legislature. In the case of Argentina, governors wield considerable influence over provincial-level public policy, possessing both the ability to introduce legislation and the authority to disburse government funds (Calvo 2007; Jones 2008; Jones et al. 2002). Governors are the most powerful politicians in the province, and they directly introduce a large proportion of the governing party's legislative agenda. As one legislator explains, "in the governor's party, the vast majority of the projects that we treat originate in the executive."[20] Even when the governor's party lacks a majority in the legislature, the governor can advance the party's platform. The governor can take advantage of the authority to disburse government funds in an effort to influence powerful legislators (even those from other political parties) and to secure the votes needed to pass the party's preferred legislation. For this reason, legislators from the governor's party have a larger number of both formal and informal resources at their disposal for accomplishing their goals. Consequently, members of the governor's party do not need to incur the costs associated with collaboration in order to exert influence in the policy-making process. By contrast, legislators from the opposition party are the only politicians in their party with access to the resources necessary to promote their legislative agenda. If they want to successfully advance their legislation, they need to build allies in the legislature and find other avenues for influencing legislation. Specifically, I argue that they can attain more political power by collaborating. Taken together, I expect that members of the governing party will be less likely than members of the opposition party to collaborate.

To evaluate this expectation, I compare patterns of collaboration for these two groups of legislators in Figure 3.1. The two columns on the left represent

---

[20] Interview with male deputy from Córdoba, Unión por Córdoba, November 12, 2009.

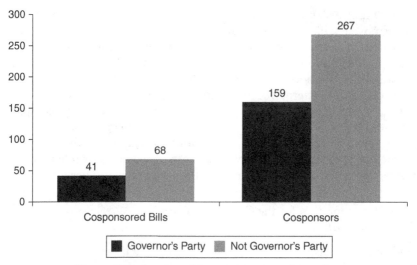

FIGURE 3.1. Comparing the opposition and governor's parties: average number of cosponsored bills and cosponsors.
Note: The two columns on the left represent the *average number* of bills legislators cosponsor for legislators from the governor's party and those not from the governor's party. The two columns on the right represent the *average number of cosponsors* with whom each legislator collaborated for legislators from the governor's party and those not from the governor's party.

the *average number* of bills that legislators from the governor's party and those not from the governor's party cosponsor in a given legislative period.[21] It is clear from this figure that all legislators in Argentina collaborate frequently. The average legislator cosponsors fifty-three bills per two-year period and has an average of 3.8 collaborators per bill. Still, cosponsorship patterns differ between legislators in the governor's party and legislators in the opposition.

Legislators from the opposition party cosponsor more frequently than do legislators from the governor's party. Specifically, Figure 3.1 shows that legislators in the governor's party cosponsor an average of only forty-one bills per session, whereas their colleagues in other political parties cosponsor an average of sixty-eight bills per session. This difference of twenty-seven bills per session is statistically significant at the 95 percent level and indicates that members of the opposition are far more likely than their powerful colleagues to introduce cosponsored legislation.[22]

Opposition members also establish a larger overall number of collaborative relationships than do legislators from the governor's party. The two columns

[21] For consistency across chambers, all data span a two-year period.
[22] Unless noted otherwise, all differences presented in this chapter are statistically significant at the 95 percent level on the basis of the two-tailed t-test.

on the right represent the *average number of cosponsors* with whom each legislator collaborated in a given two-year period for legislators from the governor's party and those not from the governor's party. The total number of cosponsors for each legislator is calculated by summing the number of cosponsors a legislator has on each cosponsored bill he or she introduced in the two-year period. If a legislator introduced multiple bills with the same colleague, the cosponsor is included in the count multiple times (one time for each jointly cosponsored bill). The figure demonstrates that the average legislator from the governor's party had 159 cosponsors in a two-year period. By comparison, the average legislator from the opposition political parties had 267 cosponsors in a session – 108 more cosponsors per session than the average legislator from the governor's party. Figure 3.1 illustrates two interesting trends in the data. First, bill cosponsorship occurs fairly regularly. The routine nature of policy collaboration suggests that collaboration is a very important aspect of democracy. Second, the figure provides evidence that legislators in power – in this case, members of the governor's party – collaborate less than those not in power (members of the opposition).

It may not be surprising to find that legislators collaborate regularly with co-partisans to develop legislation. This could even be consistent with competitive notions of democracy. For example, Downs argues that parties are simply "teams of men" seeking to maximize their electoral support to win control over the government by formulating "policies to win elections, rather than [winning] elections in order to formulate policies" (1957, 28). If legislators are only cosponsoring legislation to formulate policies that will help them win elections, we should not observe collaboration across party lines on a frequent basis. Instead, legislators should collaborate with co-partisans so that their own political party will receive full credit for legislation they propose and so that they can distinguish themselves from other political parties.

In Chapter 2, however, I have argued that collaboration extends beyond strategic coordination and that legislators use collaboration to attain political power in the policy-making process. If this is the case, we should observe collaboration beyond partisan boundaries. In particular, given that members of the opposition have less political power, we should expect them to cross party lines to collaborate more frequently than would members of the government party.

I find that although legislators are more than twice as likely to collaborate with a co-partisan than with a non-co-partisan, they work with colleagues from different political parties (non-co-partisans) on a frequent basis. Figure 3.2 shows how often legislators cosponsor legislation with colleagues in their own party (co-partisans) and colleagues outside of their party (non-co-partisans). The columns on the left represent the rate that legislators from the governor's party and those from opposition parties cosponsor with colleagues in their same party. The columns on the right represent the rate that legislators from the governor's party and those from opposition parties cosponsor

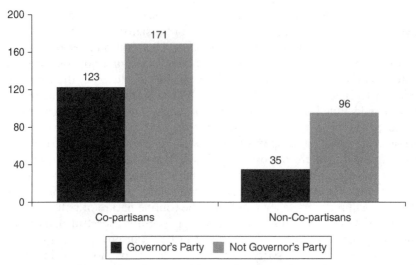

FIGURE 3.2. Comparing the opposition and governor's parties: average number of co-partisan and non-co-partisan cosponsors.

Note: Figure 3.2 shows how often legislators cosponsor legislation with colleagues in their own parties (co-partisans) and colleagues outside of their parties (non-co-partisans). The columns on the left represent the frequency with which legislators cosponsor with colleagues in their same parties. The columns on the right represent the frequency with which legislators cosponsor with colleagues of a different party.

with colleagues of a different party. Unsurprisingly, the largest share of collaboration appears to take place between co-partisans. Still, non-co-partisan cosponsors make up about one-third of the average legislator's cosponsorship relationships in a given session, indicating that collaboration is not limited to strategic coordination.

That said, members of the governor's party do not collaborate as frequently as legislators from opposition parties. Members of the opposition cosponsor on average forty-eight more bills per session with co-partisans than do members of the governor's party. They are also far more likely to work with non-co-partisans. Opposition legislators cosponsor almost three times as many bills with non-co-partisans as do members of the governor's party, and collaboration with non-co-partisans accounts for a larger share of their overall collaborative efforts. Specifically, collaboration with non-co-partisans accounts for only 22 percent of the collaboration performed by members of the governor's party, whereas it accounts for 36 percent of all collaboration performed by members of the opposition party. These data suggest that legislators who are in positions of institutional weakness are more proactive in establishing collaborative relationships with legislators outside of their own political party than is the case for members of the governor's party.

My theory posits that opposition members collaborate to attain more political power. A deputy from the governor's party in Córdoba indicated that opposition members adopt tactics of this nature in an effort to influence the legislative process. He explained that legislators from the opposition party sometimes seek out cosponsors from the governor's party as a way to generate more support for their legislation. He reported being frequently sought after as a cosponsor:

"There are opposition lawmakers who have projects that are very good, and they fear that if they present them alone their projects will face discrimination. Many times, they seek me [as a cosponsor]. If the project is good, I have the habit of accompanying them. And they are guaranteed my support, which is important."[23]

This example illustrates that collaboration is an important part of the legislative process for opposition legislators. By cooperating with other legislators, they can cultivate support for their legislative initiatives and improve their chances of success. According to this logic, we should expect to observe other out-of-power legislators behaving in similar ways.

Patterns of Collaboration for Majority and Minority Political Parties

Majority parties are very powerful and possess a number of institutional advantages in the legislature. It is important to consider patterns of collaboration for the majority party in addition to such patterns for members from the governor's party. Although the governor's party typically wins a large share of seats, it does not always win a majority in the legislature or even the largest share of seats in the chamber. In particular, during concurrent legislative and executive elections, the governor's party may win or lose seats (although it typically loses seats) during midterm elections (Hicken and Stoll 2011; Jones 1995). Given the large number of chambers in Argentina that use midterm elections, it is not uncommon for the governor's party to lack a majority in the chamber after midterm elections. Additionally, it is not uncommon in Argentina for no party to hold a majority in the legislature after an election. Many chambers use proportional representation electoral districts to elect members to office, which often results in a larger number of parties in office and no legislative majority. In my sample, the governor's party has a majority in the legislature only 67 percent of the time. Majority-led governments have distinct advantages over plurality-led governments (Calvo 2014; Calvo and Sagarzazu 2011).

Majority governments can monopolize legislative roll call voting in committees and during the plenary session. In many chambers – including the Argentine provincial legislatures – voting is highly structured by party discipline and legislators are required to vote in lockstep with their parties (Barnes 2012b; Carey 2009; Jones and Hwang 2005a). Thus, if any one party holds a

---

[23] Interview with male deputy from Córdoba, Unión por Córdoba, November 12, 2009.

majority, party leaders have the ability to ensure the party's legislation garners a majority of votes during all stages of the legislative process (Barnes 2012b). As a result, the majority party is advantaged during the committee process and the plenary session.

In the Argentine provinces, the majority party is further advantaged in the committee process because committee appointments are distributed among parties in proportion to each party's seat share in the chamber (Barnes 2014). Thus, in practice, the majority party almost always holds a majority in every legislative committee, providing it the necessary votes to advance its agenda in committees. Even when the committee is presided over by a legislator from an opposition party, the majority party has substantial power to influence the committee agenda and determine the fate of legislation. A member of the majority party in Córdoba explained that committee presidents from minority parties have limited power and are even restricted in their ability to set the committee agenda: "Even when the president is not from the Peronist Party, the majority of the members are from the Peronist Party and they will force the president to treat the projects they [the majority] want."[24] A member of the opposition party in Córdoba offered a similar account of the majority party's power in the committee process: "Even if we chair the committee, the majority of the members still belong to the ruling party. For a bill to be passed out of the committee, we still need a consensus from the legislators from the ruling party."[25]

The majority party is also advantaged during the plenary session, owing to a combination of strong party discipline and adequate votes from within the party to pass legislation. The party's position on each vote is predetermined in the *reunión del bloque* [the bloc's meeting] prior to floor votes, and legislators are expected to represent the party's preference, not their own (Barnes 2012b). Legislators who vote against their parties may incur sanctions and even expulsion from the political parties. Elite political observers such as journalists have often noted that, when voting on the chamber floor, legislators do not think for themselves – they simply raise their hands when they are told to do so. A deputy from Jujuy confirms: "There are very few times that people vote against [their party bloc]."[26] Thus, the majority party is virtually always able to advance its agenda without the support of other parties. The deputy from Jujuy explains: "Due to its numbers [the majority party] does not need support from others to make a quorum or to approve projects, except for the ones that need two-thirds of the vote. If there is a project that needs the two-thirds, then there is a discussion."[27] In Mendoza, a senator also noted: "the ruling party has a majority and this permits them to pass whatever they want."[28] Because the

[24] Interview with male deputy from Córdoba, Peronist Party, November 12, 2009.
[25] Interview with male deputy from Córdoba, Unión Cívica Radical, November 12, 2009.
[26] Interview with female deputy from Jujuy, Partido Justicialista, October 29, 2009.
[27] Ibid.
[28] Interview with female senator from Mendoza, Frente para la Victoria, June 27, 2013.

majority party can advance its legislation without the support of other political parties, the majority party has no incentive to collaborate in order to influence policy outcomes.

By contrast, members of minority parties cannot easily advance their legislative agendas. As one senator from Mendoza put it:

"[Passing legislation] is an arduous task because when you present a project, it goes to a committee, sometimes more than one committee. And then it is debated. At first there might be agreement, but then a lot of other questions are raised…. You have to work a lot, have a lot of dedication; it is a very arduous task…. In general, the ones proposed by the majority party are approved first, the opposition ones take a little more. You have to argue a lot."[29]

A deputy from Salta also sees it this way: "It is not common that the opposition's projects are approved. They don't pass through the committees….When the projects are from the ruling party, they are approved imminently."[30] If opposition members want to influence the legislative process, they have to find allies within the chamber and work hard to advance their agendas. Thus, I expect that members of the minority will be more likely than members of the majority to rely on collaboration as a means to obtain political power.

Minority legislators do collaborate more than majority legislators. The two columns on the left in Figure 3.3 show the average number of bills legislators cosponsor in a given session. Numbers are displayed separately for members of the majority party and members of the minority parties. I refer to political parties that hold more than 50 percent of the seats in the legislature as majority parties and parties that hold 50 percent or fewer of the seats in the chamber as minority parties. As previously mentioned, it is possible that no political party has a majority in a given session. I anticipate that even members of the plurality party will have a strong incentive to collaborate to advance their legislative agenda given the lack of a majority in the chamber. The figure demonstrates that the average legislator from the majority party cosponsors twenty fewer bills per session than does the average legislator from a minority political party.

The average legislator from a minority party, moreover, has a larger number of relationships than does the average legislator from a majority party. The two columns on the right in Figure 3.3 represent the *average number of cosponsors* with whom each legislator collaborated for legislators from the majority party and those from other parties. Legislators from minority parties establish on average sixty-three more relationships per session than do their colleagues from the majority party. These patterns are similar to those observed in Figure 3.1 and provide additional support for my expectations that out-of-power legislators collaborate more frequently than do legislators in positions of power.

---

[29] Interview with female senator from Mendoza, Unión Cívica Radical, June 26, 2013.
[30] Interview with female deputy from Salta, Acción Cívica y Social, July 10, 2013.

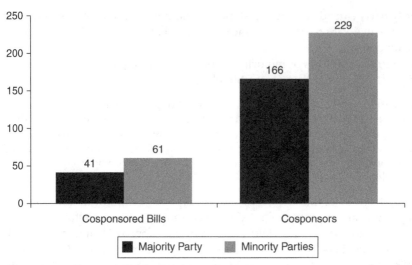

FIGURE 3.3. Comparing the minority and majority parties: average number of cosponsored bills and cosponsors.

Note: The two columns on the left represent the *average number* of bills legislators cosponsor for legislators from the majority party and those from minority parties. The two columns on the right represent the *average number of cosponsors* with whom each legislator collaborated for legislators from the majority party and those from minority parties.

Figure 3.4 graphs collaboration broken down by co-partisans and non-co-partisans. Looking first at collaboration among co-partisans (left two columns) we see that legislators frequently collaborate with colleagues from their own political parties and that collaboration with co-partisans accounts for the majority of collaborative relationships. Moreover, the average legislators from majority and minority parties establish similar numbers of relationships with colleagues in their own political parties. Minority party members cosponsor only six more bills per session than do legislators from the majority, and the difference is not statistically significant. It is interesting that members of the majority are just as likely as members of the minority to collaborate with co-partisans because it indicates that the variation in legislative behavior observed in overall levels of collaboration (as seen in the right two columns in Figure 3.3) cannot be explained by collaboration with co-partisans. Instead, this variation is explained mostly by collaboration with non-co-partisans.

It is evident from Figure 3.4 that legislators in minority political parties are far more likely to collaborate with non-co-partisans than are legislators in the majority party. The right two columns in Figure 3.4 show the rate at which legislators cross party lines to collaborate with colleagues outside their party. The figure indicates that legislators from minority parties establish more than three times as many relationships with non-co-partisans as do legislators

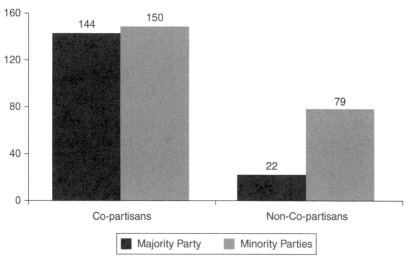

FIGURE 3.4. Comparing the minority and majority parties: average number of co-partisan and non-co-partisan cosponsors.

Note: Figure 3.4 shows how often legislators cosponsor legislation with colleagues in their own parties (co-partisans) and colleagues outside of their parties (non-co-partisans). The columns on the left represent the frequency with which legislators from the majority party and minority parties cosponsor with colleagues in their same parties. The columns on the right represent the frequency with which legislators from the majority party and minority parties cosponsor with colleagues of a different party.

from majority parties – a statistically significant difference of fifty-seven collaborative relationships per session. Cross-partisan collaboration accounts for 34 percent of all collaboration from members of minority parties. By contrast, cross-partisan collaboration accounts for only 13 percent of the majority party's collaboration.

These patterns demonstrate support for my argument that out-of-power legislators have more to gain from collaboration with non-co-partisans. If they want to influence the policy-making process, out-of-power legislators need to either collaborate with members of the majority or develop coalitions of support with other non-co-partisans to advance their legislative agendas. As one deputy from Salta sees it: "As a member of the minority party, it is better to get signatures from other parties; this means they will vote in favor [of my legislation]."[31] A deputy from Jujuy also sees this as a good strategy: "Usually all projects have more than one author. In fact, because there isn't the influence of the minority in the committees, the way to get all parties to agree is to present projects signed by legislators from different blocs."[32] She explains that because

[31] Interview with female deputy from Salta, Frente para la Victoria, October 21, 2009.
[32] Interview with female deputy from Jujuy, Partido Justicialista, October 29, 2009.

members of the minority party do not have much influence over legislation during the committee process, they can develop support for their legislation by courting colleagues from different parties. These examples illustrate that out-of-power legislators seek to collaborate with other legislators in order to attain more political power.

Together, the patterns observed here reinforce the finding from the previous section, strongly supporting my expectation that legislators in positions of institutional weakness are more likely to collaborate than are those in power. Because only legislators in positions of power have the ability to decide via competition, it is not surprising that legislators who are out of power seek to work within the legislature to find different ways to influence policy making. Given the numerous benefits of collaboration outlined in Chapter 2, it is reasonable that legislators who lack power may seek to influence the legislative process by developing collaborative relationships with their colleagues and attempting to advance collaborative projects.

Patterns of Collaboration for Men and Women

Women are marginalized in the legislature and face barriers to influence. During interviews, many women in Argentina indicated that female legislators have less influence in the legislature because they are a minority, are excluded from leadership, and are not in positions to make important decisions. As one deputy put it: "I think the male legislators have more power; they get more done. Women are the minority in the chamber."[33] Her colleague from a different party views women's positions similarly: "The problem with us is that we are a minority. [In our party, women] are three out of twenty-seven deputies. The majority of times we address the issues brought up by men, and then sometimes we address the ones from women, but if you look at it objectively, it is not often."[34] As a result, women perceive that their projects do not receive as much attention and that they have to work harder to advance their legislative agendas than do male legislators. If it is the case that women are marginalized in the legislature, then it follows that women are one such group that can benefit from collaboration. In this section, I demonstrate that not only do women collaborate more than men, but they are also more likely than men to collaborate with women.

Women cosponsor a larger number of bills and establish a larger number of relationships than do men. The left two columns of Figure 3.5 show that in Argentina, the average woman introduces sixty-five cosponsored bills in a two-year session and the average man introduces fifty-one cosponsored bills. The figure illustrates that both women and men cosponsor frequently but that women do so more than men. The average female legislator cosponsors about 28 percent more bills per session than does the average male legislator.

[33] Interview with female deputy from Salta, Partido Renovador de Salta, July 10, 2013.
[34] Interview with female deputy from Salta, Frente para la Victoria, July 10, 2013.

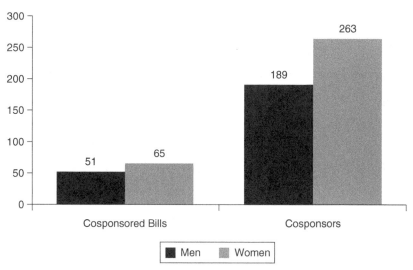

FIGURE 3.5. Comparing women and men: average number of cosponsored bills and cosponsors.
Note: The two columns on the left represent the *average number* of bills legislators cosponsor for men and women. The two columns on the right represent the *average number of cosponsors* with whom each legislator collaborated for men and women.

Furthermore, women have a larger total number of cosponsors than do men. The right two columns show that the average female has 263 cosponsors per session whereas the average male has 189 cosponsors per session, a statistically significant difference of 74 cosponsors. This is a substantial difference; on average, women have about 40 percent more cosponsors than do men.

Women's tendencies to work with more cosponsors overall are not only due to the fact that they cosponsor a larger number of total bills, but also a product of their inclinations to collaborate with a larger number of colleagues on any given bill. Male legislators average approximately 3.7 cosponsors on each of their cosponsored bills and female legislators average 4 cosponsors per cosponsored bill. Once legislators have identified supportive colleagues and fostered collaborative relationships among themselves, it is common (although not inevitable) for the same group of legislators to present several bills together. For example, in the Córdoba Chamber of Deputies in 2000, all ten women from Unión por Córdoba along with two men from the party worked as a group to present nine different projects over a two-year period. Trends like this emerge in other chambers as well. For instance, in Misiones in 2008, the same seven deputies (from two different parties) worked together to cosponsor ten different bills. A subset of this group (again, non-co-partisans) cosponsored six additional bills. It appears that legislators identify a few colleagues who have similar interests and priorities and work with the same group of cosponsors on

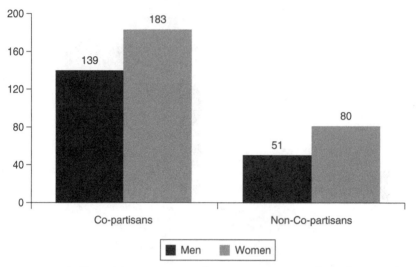

FIGURE 3.6. Comparing women and men: average number of co-partisan and non-co-partisan cosponsors.
Note: Figure 3.6 shows how often women and men cosponsor legislation with colleagues in their own parties (co-partisans) and colleagues outside of their parties (non-co-partisans). The columns on the left represent the frequency with which men and women cosponsor with colleagues in their same party. The columns on the right represent the frequency with which men and women cosponsor with colleagues of a different party.

a number of projects. This helps to explain how some legislators can work on a large number of bills in a two-year session.

Women are more likely than men to collaborate with colleagues in their own political parties and are also more likely to cross party lines to collaborate. Figure 3.6 graphs collaboration for men and women broken down by co-partisans and non-co-partisans. We see that women cosponsor with colleagues both within their own parties and in other parties substantially more than do men. The left two columns in Figure 3.6 show that the average male legislator has 139 co-partisan cosponsors in a session, whereas the average female legislator has 183 co-partisan cosponsors per session. That is, the average woman has 44 more co-partisan cosponsors per session than the average man.

Women's collaboration with non-co-partisans also outpaces men's collaboration. The right two columns in Figure 3.6 show the number of non-co-partisan cosponsors that the average male and female legislator has in a given session. The average male legislator has fifty-one non-co-partisan cosponsors in a given session, whereas the average female legislator has eighty non-co-partisan cosponsors per session. Women collaborate with a larger number of non-co-partisans than do men, and the data show that women cosponsor with non-co-partisans for a larger share of their cosponsorships than do men. Specifically, women collaborate with non-co-partisans 30 percent of the time, whereas men collaborate with non-co-partisans 27 percent of the time that they are collaborating.

All told, women collaborate more frequently than men, both in terms of the overall number of bills they cosponsor and in terms of the collaborative relationships they form. Women's behavior is very similar to that of other out-of-power groups, suggesting that their collaboration is likely motivated by marginalization in the legislature. Consistent with this, a female deputy from Salta observed that women have less influence over legislation. She explains that in Salta, only a limited number of legislative projects can be discussed during the plenary session every week and the projects that get discussed are usually ones proposed by men. She suggests women's struggles to have their legislation heard on the floor are a product of women's marginalized status in the chamber.

"It might not be just women but the ones who are the minority and those who cannot just express their ideas or a project. I think that situation is uncomfortable for anyone [in the minority]. Because women are always the minority, we have to get used to this situation, but it should not be the norm."[35]

She describes women as having limited power, similar to other legislative minorities. Because they wield little influence in the chamber, women are compelled to work together to advance shared concerns. Her explanation for women's legislative collaboration is consistent with the argument laid out in Chapter 2. Specifically, I posited that female legislators entering a male-dominated institution face structural barriers that limit their influence over the policy-making process and that this marginalization motivates women's collaboration. If women are marginalized, then it should be no surprise that women behave like other out-of-power groups, collaborating more frequently in an effort to attain political power. Thus, in demonstrating these gendered patterns of collaboration, this chapter presents preliminary evidence that women's collaboration may be fueled, at least in part, by women's marginalization.

Patterns of Collaboration with Female Colleagues

In contrast to members from minority parties, for women, marginalization in the legislature is not explained solely by their minority status. Rather, in Chapter 4, I present copious evidence that women's marginalization extends beyond their numeric representation. Women face both formal and informal barriers to influence. Moreover, women are marginalized not only in the chamber as a whole, but also *within other out-of-power groups*. Thus, unlike other numeric minorities, women are not proportionally represented in influential

---

[35] Ibid.

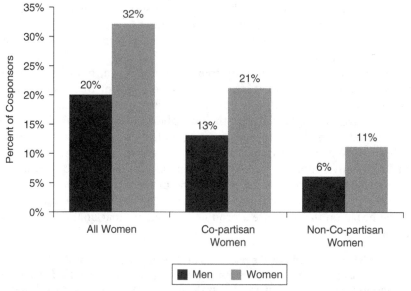

FIGURE 3.7. Women collaborating with women.
Note: Figure 3.7 shows how often women and men cosponsor legislation with women. The first set of columns represents the overall rate at which legislators have a female cosponsor, regardless of party. The center columns represent the rates at which men and women cosponsor with women in their same parties. The columns on the right represent the rates at which men and women cosponsor with women of a different party.

committee appointments and leadership posts. They are excluded from power-ful informal networks within their parties, and their ability to lead and legislate is constantly challenged. For this reason, I posited in Chapter 2 that women have incentives to collaborate not only with their colleagues in general, but also specifically with female colleagues.

Consistent with this expectation, I find that women are more likely than men to work with female colleagues. Figure 3.7 shows how often women and men cosponsor legislation with other women. The first set of columns represents the overall rate of having a female cosponsor, regardless of party. Men cospon-sor with female colleagues 20 percent of the time and women cosponsor with female colleagues 32 percent of the time. On average, women hold 20 percent of the seats in the Argentine chambers; hence, men work with women at a rate proportional to their seat share. Women, on the other hand, work with each other at a much higher rate. The proportion of female cosponsors that women choose to collaborate with is more than 50 percent larger than women's seat share in the chamber, indicating that women choose to cosponsor with women at a disproportionately high rate.

Women cosponsor with female colleagues both within their own parties and in other parties substantially more than men cosponsor with women. In Figure 3.7, the center columns represent the rate that men and women cosponsor with women in their same parties. Men cosponsor with female co-partisans about 13 percent of the time. Women, by comparison, collaborate with female colleagues 21 percent of the time. Not only are women more likely to collaborate with female colleagues than are men, but also, collaboration among female co-partisans is proportionally larger than the rate at which we would expect women to collaborate with female co-partisans given their seat share in the chamber. This indicates that women intentionally collaborate more frequently with other women in their same parties.

Women are almost twice as likely as men to cosponsor with women from a different party. The columns on the right represent the rate at which men and women cosponsor with women of a different party. Women cosponsor about 11 percent of their total cosponsored bills with female non-co-partisans. Men, by contrast, cosponsor with female non-co-partisans only 6 percent of the time. These broad trends indicate that women have an incentive to collaborate not only more frequently than men, but also specifically with women. In short, a disproportionate number of women's cosponsorship efforts are dedicated to working with female colleagues.

These trends represent the *average* woman in my sample, but I expect women's legislative behavior to vary significantly both between and within chambers. Recall, in Chapter 2 I posited that not all women have the same opportunities or incentives to collaborate. Different legislative contexts either facilitate or constrain women's collaboration. I further investigate these patterns of collaboration in Chapters 5 and 6 to develop a clear understanding of *when women collaborate.*

CONCLUSION

In conclusion, I have demonstrated in this chapter that democracy can be collaborative. In doing so, I have identified a useful measure of collaboration and examined patterns of collaboration across Argentina. Specifically, I have demonstrated that cosponsorship data are a reliable, valid, and generalizable measure of collaboration in the Argentine context. The cosponsorship data presented here illustrate one of the many collaborative aspects of democracy and show that Argentine legislators collaborate frequently. We see legislative collaboration unfold in the policy-making process among legislators from the same political party and from different political parties. Indeed, the average legislator cosponsors a large number of bills each session and works with a large number of collaborators. Moreover, the data show that out-of-power groups collaborate more frequently than do legislators in power. Consistent with my expectations, legislators in the opposition party and those in minority parties collaborate more frequently than do their counterparts in the governor's party or the majority party.

Equally important and of particular interest in this book, I have shown that across the board, women collaborate more than do men. Women cosponsor a larger number of bills and have a larger number of overall cosponsors than do men. Women are more likely to cross party lines to collaborate and to collaborate with women. These trends present compelling evidence that women collaborate more than men and raise a second question: *Why do women collaborate?* I tackle this question in the next chapter.

APPENDIX 3.1: PROVINCIAL CHAMBERS INCLUDED IN THE
COSPONSORSHIP ANALYSES

Chamber	Years in Sample	District Type	District Magnitude	# of Seats
Santa Fe Senators	1992–2009	19 Single-Member Districts	1	19
Salta Senators	1992–2009	23 Single-Member Districts	1	23
Córdoba Senators	1992–2000	26 Multimember Districts	1 to 3	67
Salta Deputies	1992–2009	23 Multimember Districts	1 to 9	60
Buenos Aires Senators	1992–2009	8 Multimember Districts	3 to 9	46
Mendoza Senators	1992–2009	4 Multimember Districts	4 to 6	38
Mendoza Deputies	1992–2009	4 Multimember Districts	5 to 8	50
Buenos Aires Deputies	1992–2009	8 Multimember Districts	6 to 18	92
Tucumán Deputies	1992–2009	3 Multimember Districts	11 to 18	49
Chaco Deputies	1992–2009	At-Large District	16	32
Chubut Deputies	1994–2009	At-Large District	27	27
Federal District Deputies	1998–2009	At-Large District	28	60
Córdoba Deputies	1992–2000	At-Large District	66	66
Corrientes Deputies	1992–2009	At-Large District	13	26
Formosa Deputies	1996–2009	At-Large District	15	30
Misiones Deputies	1992–2009	At-Large District	20	40
Jujuy Deputies	1992–2009	At-Large District	24	48

Chamber	Years in Sample	District Type	District Magnitude	# of Seats
Entre Ríos Deputies	1992–2009	At-Large District	30	28
Corrientes Senators	1992–2009	At-Large District	4 or 5	13
Santa Fe Deputies	1992–2009	At-Large District	50	50
Santa Cruz Deputies	1992–2009	Mixed-Member	1 & 10	28
Córdoba Unicameral	2002–2009	Mixed-Member	1 & 44	60
Río Negro Deputies	1996–2009	Mixed-Member	3 & 19	46

Note: Legislatures included in cosponsorship analyses in Chapters 3, 5, and 6.

4

Why Do Women Collaborate?

Evidence of Women's Marginalization

In 2009, Linda Suarez became the first woman to be elected vice president of the legislature. This powerful leadership position is the highest legislative appointment and the third-ranking position in the province – below only the positions of governor and vice-governor. In recent years, a few talented, well-connected women have risen to the top ranks of politics in Argentina. Ask most male politicians in Argentina and they will tell you that, without a doubt, women now have equal opportunities in politics; after all, Argentina has elected a female president. Similarly, many politicians from Vice President Suarez's province boast that a woman holds the top position in the legislature, frequently citing her as proof that women are on even footing politically in the province.

One would expect that Vice President Suarez would be very proud to serve as the first female vice president in her province and that she likely views it as an accomplishment and a testament to her hard work. Yet, when asked if she was the first woman to hold such a prestigious appointment in the legislature, Vice President Suarez had a surprising response:

"Yes, the first one. It is embarrassing, huh? It is the twenty-first century and the truth is it is not pretty to say that I am the first woman: there should have been a lot more."[1]

Where many people use her position to illustrate their opinion that women have equal access to power, Vice President Suarez views her experience as exceptional and not representative of women's status in politics. Instead, she suggests that female legislators face a number of obstacles and disadvantages. In this chapter, I empirically evaluate women's marginalization in the Argentine provincial legislatures. I compare women's and men's access to leadership posts

---

[1] Interview with female legislator. Her name and the date she assumed office were changed to protect her anonymity. I do not provide information about her province or political party because so few women have held the top-ranking legislative positions in their provinces.

and powerful committee appointments in the legislatures to evaluate whether women and men have equitable political power.

It is important to assess women's access to political power in order to answer one of the central questions in this book: *Why do women collaborate?* Recall, my theory contends that women collaborate more than men because women face structural barriers that restrict their ability to exert influence in the policy-making process. In Chapter 1, I showed that women's numeric representation has increased substantially in the Argentine provincial chambers since the early 1990s. In this chapter, I show that women's numeric representation alone is not sufficient for women to gain political power. Specifically, I compare men's and women's appointments to chamber-wide leadership posts, powerful committees, and committee leadership posts to examine their access to political power. I demonstrate that women are *proportionally underrepresented* in positions of power, even when accounting for previous experience in the chamber.

Thus, these results demonstrate that women's marginalization extends beyond their numeric underrepresentation in politics. Women's *disproportionate* representation in positions of power indicates that women are limited in their ability to shape the legislative agenda and influence policy outcomes beyond the limitations imposed by their numeric minority status. As women remain underrepresented in formal positions of power – even when accounting for their minority status – these results indicate that even if women were to attain parity, they would remain institutionally marginalized.

I first turn to an examination of women's access to the most powerful positions in the legislature – chamber-wide leadership posts. I show that women are underrepresented in these coveted leadership posts. After examining trends in women's chamber-wide posts, I assess how legislative power is distributed through powerful committee appointments and committee leadership positions. Additionally, I draw on qualitative interview evidence throughout this chapter to demonstrate how informal barriers reinforce women's marginalization in the chamber and further restrict their access to power.

WOMEN'S POLITICAL POWER: ACCESS TO CHAMBER-WIDE LEADERSHIP POSTS

Chamber-wide leadership posts are some of the most powerful positions in the legislature. Most chambers are organized to include a president, vice presidents, and secretaries. The chamber president – also commonly referred to as the speaker – is the most powerful member of the chamber. Most important, the president has the authority to set the legislative agenda. That is, the president decides what bills will be discussed on the chamber floor, when they will be discussed, and if they will come before the chamber for a vote. This gives the president immense influence over the fate of legislation. The president also presides over the chamber, moderates floor debates, and recognizes members to speak.

In the Argentine provinces, the vice-governor presides over the chamber in unicameral legislatures and over the senate in bicameral legislatures. In bicameral legislatures, the president of the lower house is chosen from within the chamber. In this case, the chamber president is a legislator from the ruling party (or the party with the most seats in the chamber).

The vice president has considerably less power than the president, but this leadership post is still prestigious and desirable. In the absence of the president, the vice president may preside over the chamber. When a legislator presides over the chamber (i.e., lower chambers in Argentina), the vice presidents (if there are multiple vice presidents) typically come from the second and third largest parties in the chamber. But, in chambers where the vice-governor presides over the chamber, the first vice president is almost always a legislator from the largest party and is regarded as the most powerful member of the chamber.

In some countries a legislator holds the secretary position. Under these circumstances, the secretary is regarded as a relatively important leadership post. This is not the case in Argentina. Rather, most secretary positions at the chamber level are strictly administrative positions and are not held by an elected official. For this reason, I do not consider chamber-wide secretaries in my analysis.

Figure 4.1 graphs the average percentage of chamber-wide leadership posts held by women in twenty-three provincial legislatures (nine bicameral and fourteen unicameral) in the Argentine provinces from 1992 to 2008.[2] The top panel displays women's leadership appointments in the lower chamber in provinces with bicameral legislatures. The bottom panel displays women's leadership appointments in upper chambers (senates) and unicameral chambers. I group the chambers in this way to distinguish between those chambers where a legislator presides over the chamber (top panel) and those where the vice-governor presides over the chamber (bottom panel).

In the lower chambers in the Argentine provinces, women have rarely held presidential posts. In the top panel of Figure 4.1, the black solid line graphs the percentage of presidential posts held by women. Between 1992 and 1997, no women held the presidential post in a lower chamber. In 1998, Gladys Bailac de Follari of the Frente Partido Justicialista in San Luis became the only woman to preside over a chamber of deputies. At this time, she was one of four women, and twenty total legislators in her party bloc (20 percent women). She was first elected to office in November 1993, served a four-year term, and was reelected in November 1997. She was selected to preside over the chamber at the beginning of her second term, but her tenure was short-lived. In 1999 she was replaced by the vice president, Ruben Angle Rodriguez, and she went on to hold the vice presidential post herself.

---

[2] Córdoba was bicameral until 2002, when it became unicameral. In this reference, Córdoba is counted as bicameral, although it later reformed.

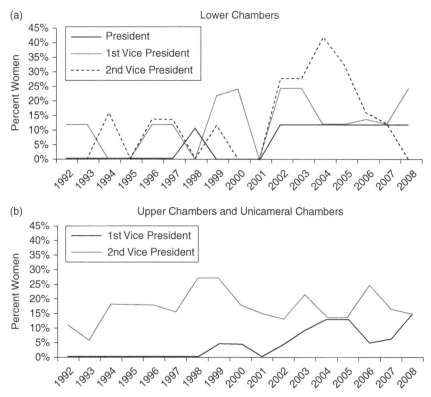

FIGURE 4.1. Percentage of chamber-wide leadership posts held by women.
Note: Figure 4.1 graphs the percentage of women in chamber-wide leadership posts in the Argentine provincial chambers over time. The percentage of women in each category is aggregated across chambers by year.

A woman was not elected to the presidential post again until 2002, when Deputy Josefina Angelica Meabe from the Alianza Frente de Todos was elected to preside over the Chamber of Deputies in Corrientes. The Alianza Frente de Todos had a total of eleven members in the party bloc, three of whom were women (27 percent). She served in this capacity for seven years, until she was elected to the National Senate in 2009. Today she still represents Corrientes in the National Senate and is the president of her new political party, Partido Liberal de Corrientes. Overall, only two women held the presidential post in the lower chamber between 1992 and 2008. Of the nine chambers included in this category, seven of them never elected a female president.[3]

Women also have limited opportunities to serve as vice president in the lower chambers. The gray solid line in the top panel in Figure 4.1 plots the

[3] The Córdoba Chamber of Deputies is included in this figure from 1992 to 2001. After 2001 Córdoba transitioned to a unicameral chamber.

percentage of women in vice presidential posts. Although women began serving in this capacity as early as 1992, they have never held more than two first vice president positions (i.e., 25 percent) in the lower chambers at any given point in time. But, unlike the presidential posts, women's access to vice presidential posts has not been limited to a small number of provinces. Instead, women have held the vice presidential post in five of the eight chambers: Catamarca, Mendoza, Salta, San Luis, and Santa Fe. Similar trends emerge for the position of second vice president. On average one or two women have held a second vice presidential post in a lower chamber at any given point in time. The major exception is the period from 2002 to 2005 during which women occupied between 29 percent and 33 percent of second vice presidential posts.

On the whole, it is clear that women do not have equitable opportunities to hold chamber-wide leadership posts in the Argentine lower chambers – and in particular presidential posts. Female deputies in the lower chambers recognize that there are limited prospects for women to be elected into leadership positions. When asked if women have many opportunities to hold leadership positions in the Salta Chamber of Deputies for example, one female deputy from the Frente para la Victoria party replied: "Leadership-wise, very little. There are very few [women in leadership]. The ones who are better represented are men.... The leadership issue is a struggle."[4] A number of women in the Salta Chamber of Deputies share this concern. A second deputy from Frente para la Victoria noted:

"Usually they [men] are the ones who are in the positions to make decisions. The president is a man, the vice president is a man, all of the authorities in the chamber are men. I think there is only one woman who is presiding over the culture committee. And that is recent.... We women are always noting that when you get to the authorities, they are all men. Where are all the women?"[5]

Her colleague from the Acción Cívica y Social political party similarly notes that women are missing in leadership posts and perceives this as problematic:

"Our representation should not just be in a committee to analyze all of the problems women face, but we need to be represented in the authorities of the chamber. I have complained many times that not even one of the people who preside over the chamber is a woman. They are all men!"[6]

Similar trends in women's leadership exist in senate and unicameral chambers. The bottom panel of Figure 4.1 charts women's share of first vice presidential posts (or the provisional president) and second vice presidential posts for twenty-three senate and unicameral chambers. Recall, the vice-governor presides over these chambers. I am interested in female legislators specifically and not executives; therefore, I do not account for vice-governors. No woman

---

[4] Interview with first female deputy from Salta, Frente para la Victoria, July 10, 2013.
[5] Interview with second female deputy from Salta, Frente para la Victoria, July 10, 2013.
[6] Interview with female deputy from Salta, Acción Cívica y Social, July 10, 2013.

held the post of first vice president in these chambers until 1999, when Deputy Marcela Lilian Oyarzún of the Movimiento Popular Fueguino was elected as the first vice president in Tierra del Fuego. She was one of only three members and the only woman in her party bloc. She occupied this post for only a year. The following year, in Chubut, a woman was elected to serve as the first vice president; Deputy Elsa Ines Zarcos from the Partido Alianza served in this capacity in 2000 and again in 2002. Women held 31 percent of legislative seats in the Partido Alianza bloc when President Zarcos was appointed to office. From 2002 forward, there was typically at least one female first vice president at any given point in time in the Argentine provinces. Although this is an improvement from the 1990s, there was never a period of time when women held more than three of the twenty-three first vice president seats (i.e., 13 percent).

Women's chamber-wide leadership trends are more positive when we consider their presence in second vice presidential posts. Between 1992 and 2008, at least one woman held a second vice presidential post at all points in time. In 1998 and 1999, women held 27 percent of second vice presidential posts. During this two-year period, Chaco, La Rioja, Río Negro, Santa Cruz, Santiago del Estero, the Salta Senate, and the San Luis Senate each had a female second vice president. Nonetheless, on average women's opportunities to hold chamber-wide leadership posts in the provinces do not keep pace with their seat share in the chamber. As one legislator from the Federal District put it: "There is larger women's representation in places where women were not before [referring to legislatures].... But we are still lacking the other half, the positions of power."[7]

This is not to say that all women in the Argentine provinces are always marginalized and that none of them ever have access to powerful positions. Clearly some women have held important leadership posts, but on average it appears that women do not have the same opportunities as men to hold leadership posts. Although their share of chamber-wide leadership posts has improved over the past decade, there is no clear evidence of an upward trajectory. Female legislators are aware of these gender disparities in leadership posts, and they do not think these disparities reflect their abilities to govern. When asked if women have the same opportunities to hold leadership posts as men, a female deputy from Catamarca responded: "No; when the parties make up their list for different positions, it is a struggle for women. Men still get the most representation."[8] She goes on to explain that it is more challenging for women to get into positions of power: "They have to be very strong, very firm, and have a lot of knowledge." The prevailing perception among women is that they have to be twice as good as a man in order to prove they are qualified and to combat the widespread stereotype that women elected through quotas are not qualified

[7] Interview with female deputy from the Federal District, small third party, July 19, 2013.
[8] Interview with female deputy from Catamarca, Partido Justicialista, November 16, 2009.

(Barnes 2014; Franceschet and Piscopo 2008; Murray 2010; O'Brien 2012b). A senior female in the senate leadership in Mendoza explains that women are held to a double standard and it stifles women's ability to exert influence in politics. For women to attain the same level of influence as men, it takes "more education and more time."[9] She elaborates:

"It is like we have to double the amount of time and years. If someone starts their political career at a certain time, whatever it takes men five years to get, it takes women ten years. You see it in the intermediate jobs that women are the ones that work so much, not only in the public sector but also in the private one. It is about time and effort, because sometimes work done by women is valued differently than by a man."

Women's limited access to chamber-wide leadership posts does not bode well for women's overall political power in the Argentine chambers. Nonetheless, political power is not solely concentrated in the hands of the chamber president and vice presidents. A number of powerful posts in the chamber give legislators substantial influence over the policy-making process. To understand women's political power, it is necessary to examine women's representation in these key positions as well. In the remainder of this chapter, I focus on women's appointments to powerful committees and to committee leadership posts. After briefly describing the importance of these positions more generally, I discuss how committee appointments and committee leadership posts are decided in the Argentine provinces, and then investigate women's representation in these powerful positions.

LEGISLATIVE POWER: COMMITTEES AND LEADERSHIP POSTS

In addition to chamber-wide leadership posts, power is distributed via committee appointments and leadership posts within committees. Committees are one of the most important features of legislative organization. They are responsible for examining and amending bills, and providing the chamber with a recommendation that the legislation either be considered during the plenary session or tabled (Calvo 2014; Krehbiel, Shepsle, and Weingast 1987). Committee membership gives legislators considerable influence in the chamber. But not all committees are created equal (Cox and McCubbins 2005; Heath, Schwindt-Bayer, and Taylor-Robinson 2005); some committees have more power and influence than others. For this reason Sinclair argues that "the distribution of valued committee positions provides the single best observable indicator of the distribution of influence in Congress" (1988, 277).

In most legislatures, the budget committee is extremely powerful because this committee hears legislation that determines how money will be allocated. In the Argentine provinces, the general legislation committee also stands out as having a great deal of power. This committee can hear legislation on any issue

---

[9] Interview with female senator from Mendoza, Frente para la Victoria, June 25, 2013.

and often acts as a clearinghouse for legislation. When asked what committees have the most power, a deputy from Córdoba responded: "Basically, economy and general legislation, because the majority of legislation passes through these two committees."[10] Consistent with this observation, the vast majority of the legislators I interviewed agree that the budget committee and the general legislation committee are the two most influential committees. As a result, these posts are coveted among members of parliament.

In addition to holding powerful committee appointments, legislators can wield influence by serving in the committee leadership. Committee leadership typically consists of a president, a vice president, and a secretary. The committee president (also known as the committee chair) is the most powerful committee member (Calvo 2014; Calvo and Sagarzazu 2011; Cox and McCubbins 2005; Krehbiel 1996; Weingast 1989). As one legislator described it: "[Committee presidents] have the authority to convene meetings, address issues, prioritize issues, and try to pursue and achieve consensus."[11] Among these responsibilities, the most valuable is the ability to set the committee agenda and determine what legislation the committee hears. This gives the chair tremendous influence over the fate of legislation. The chair controls the order in which amendments to legislation are considered during committee hearings, giving him substantial influence over the final content of the legislation (Cox and McCubbins 2005). Equally important, in most circumstances, if legislation does not pass through the committee, it cannot be taken up on the chamber floor. This gives the chair the ability to kill off legislation. As one deputy from Entre Ríos put it:

"[The president] decides which themes are going to be discussed or not. So the president of the budget committee can say: for now we won't deal with the budget. Or they can ask to address their districts' issues, or ask for more contracts for assistants.... As the president of the education committee, if I want to change something regarding education, I have more power to do so."[12]

Still, there are limits to the president's power – particularly if they are not supported by a majority of the committee. As legislators from Córdoba explained, if there is a majority party in the chamber, the majority also holds a majority of seats in all committees and makes up a powerful voting bloc. Presidents from the minority party cannot unilaterally advance their legislative agenda because for a bill to be passed out of committee it needs a consensus.[13] Despite the limitations imposed on presidents from minority parties, it is clear that leadership posts give some legislators disproportional power in the chamber.

[10] Interview with male deputy from Córdoba, Peronist Party, November 12, 2009.
[11] Interview with male deputy from Córdoba, Concentración Plural, November 13, 2009.
[12] Interview with female deputy, July 16, 2013.
[13] Interviews with male deputy from Córdoba, Unión Cívica Radical, November 12, 2009, and with male deputy from Córdoba, Peronist Party, November 12, 2009.

The committee vice president and secretary have considerably less power than the president. The vice president presides over the committee in the absence of the president. The secretary is responsible for keeping minutes. Otherwise, the posts are largely ceremonial. Although they are viewed as less prestigious positions than the presidential post, the vice presidential and secretarial posts are desirable positions – particularly those associated with powerful committees. Taken together, memberships on powerful committees and leadership posts are valuable resources that allow legislators to exert a disproportional amount of influence on the policy-making process.

Committees are an extension of parties' power (Carroll, Cox, and Pachón 2006; Cox and McCubbins 2005), and party leaders have substantial influence over who receives powerful committee appointments and leadership posts within committees (Jones, Sanguinetti, and Tommasi 2000; Morgenstern 2002). If legislators want to be appointed to top committee posts, they need to have a good rapport with the party leader. In addition to professional networks, social capital and perceptions about individuals' expertise and ability to govern all work together to determine who will be appointed to these valuable posts. For these reasons, we can learn a lot about the distribution of power within a legislature by examining the allocation of committee appointments and leadership posts.

How Committee Appointments and Leadership Appointments are Made

In the Argentine provinces, committee appointments are typically distributed to political parties in proportion to their seat shares in the legislature (Barnes 2014). With few exceptions, this allocation method is explicitly stipulated in the chamber rules, and numerous interviews across all provinces indicate that the chamber norm is to distribute committee appointments proportionally among political parties.[14] A deputy from the majority party in Córdoba described the distribution of committee seats as follows:

"The committees replicate the same distribution of the seats in the legislature. Always, in all of the committees we have a majority, because we have a majority in the chamber. For example, the economic committee has eleven members: six are from [the] Peronist party, two are from UCR, two from Frente Cívico, and one from a one-person party. The Peronist [party] decides who are those six, UCR decides who are those two, and the small blocs decide who the others are. And we always have a majority. If there are eleven seats, six are ours; if there are nine (because there are committees that have nine members), five are ours and four from the others."[15]

---

[14] The Córdoba Unicameral Chamber and the former Córdoba Lower House are a slight exception. Here the chamber rules reserve five seats for the majority party, two for the largest minority, and one for the remaining minority parties. In Entre Ríos and Salta, there is no specific language regarding the distribution of committee seats in the official rules, but numerous interviews in these two provinces indicate that the norm is to distribute committee appointments proportionally among political parties.

[15] Interview with male deputy from Córdoba, Peronist Party, November 12, 2009.

Early in the legislative session, each political party holds a meeting where members from that party discuss who will be appointed to the committee posts allocated to the party. Given that legislators typically serve only one or two terms in the provincial legislature in the Argentine provinces, seniority – which is typically regarded as very important for appointments to powerful posts in the U.S. context – is not the most important determinant of committee appointments in Argentina (Barnes 2014; Jones et al. 2002). In contrast, the appointment process is very political. A deputy from Corrientes clarifies this point:

"In this way [the committee appointment process] is different than in the United States because in the United States you have seniority, which has to do with how many years you are in the chamber. In this case – no. It has to do with the negotiation or agreement you can make."[16]

In Argentina, committee appointments are the product of a series of negotiations within political parties and sometimes among different blocs. In the party meeting, legislators can indicate their preference for a committee assignment, but this does not necessarily influence their ultimate committee appointments. Members of the party discuss among themselves and decide who will be appointed to each committee. A female deputy from Salta explains: "We pick the [committees] we want to be a member of. Of course not everyone can go to all of them; it depends on the number [of appointments the party gets]. We select amongst ourselves who we want to represent us."[17] Some committee appointments are seen as more valuable than others. To get the committee appointments you want, you have to be willing to "reach out and fight for it,"[18] as one deputy put it. Even though all members have the chance to make their personal preferences known, depending on the political party's norms and other circumstances, not every deputy can serve on his or her most preferred committees. A deputy from Córdoba explained that at the end of the negotiation when committee appointments have been decided: "Some are more upset; others are more happy."[19] The final decision is sometimes put to an informal vote during the party meeting, decided by a small number of powerful party leaders, or even determined by the party boss himself. Regardless, all appointments are subject to the party boss's approval, giving party leaders a large amount of control over committee appointments.

With respect to committee leadership appointments, the technical committee rules in most provinces state that committee members will elect the committee leadership posts during the first committee meeting. Nonetheless, committee leadership positions are typically a product of elite negotiations among party leaders and within political parties. Generally, the party holding the largest share

[16] Interview with male deputy from Corrientes, Partido Popular, March 3, 2010.
[17] Interview with female deputy from Salta, Frente para la Victoria, October 20, 2009.
[18] Interview with female deputy from Entre Ríos, Frente para la Victoria, July 16, 2013.
[19] Interview with male deputy from Córdoba, Peronist Party, November 12, 2009.

of seats in the chamber holds the majority of presidential posts – particularly those on important committees. The second largest political party in the chamber may get some presidential posts and many vice presidential posts. As the second vice president from the Córdoba chamber put it: "Obviously the presidential posts are distributed among the majority party"; but he goes on to explain that members of his party – a minority party – preside over two committees.[20] In the case of Córdoba, for instance, the second largest party typically presides over two committees, the third largest party presides over two committees, and the largest party presides over the remaining twelve committees.[21] Similarly, in other provinces, the party's seat share partially determines the distribution of presidential posts. Nevertheless, the majority/plurality party is likely to preside over the most powerful and important committees.

Clearly, being appointed to a powerful committee and/or leadership post is indicative of an individual's *informal political power* within the party and the chamber, whereas actually serving in such a position is indicative of an individual's *formal political power*. To understand women's access to political power, it is necessary to consider their appointments to powerful committees and committee leadership posts. In the section that follows I examine patterns of women's committee appointments and leadership posts over time. After evaluating these trends, I offer a systematic analysis of women's and men's committee appointments and leadership posts.

PATTERNS OF WOMEN'S COMMITTEE APPOINTMENTS AND LEADERSHIP POSTS

I use data from twenty-three Argentine chambers ranging from 1992 to 2009 to examine whether women are proportionally represented in powerful committees and committee leadership posts.[22] Table 4.1 provides a list of the provinces included in my analysis in the first column and the year that each chamber is included in the sample in the second column. The third column provides information on the average percentage of women in each chamber, as well as the range of numeric representation. As the table demonstrates, there is large variation in women's numeric representation over time within most chambers. I explained in Chapter 1 that, because of the pervasive adoption of gender quotas in Argentina, most chambers range from having few women in the early 1990s to a sizable proportion of women (around 25–30 percent) by the mid- to late-2000s. I compare the average number of committee appointments and leadership posts held by women to women's numeric representation in the chamber to evaluate whether women's access to powerful appointments is proportional to their seat share in the chamber.

---

[20] Interview with male deputy from Córdoba, Unión Cívica Radical, November 12, 2009.
[21] Interview with male deputy from Córdoba, Unión Cívica Radical, November 11, 2009.
[22] Data for committee appointments is taken from Barnes (2014).

TABLE 4.1. *Characteristics of the Argentine Legislative Committees*

District	Years in Sample	Average Percent Women in Chamber (Range)	# of Standing Committees	# of Seats in Chamber	Average # of Appointments per Member (Range)
Federal District	2002–2009[S]	37 (35–38)	22	60	3.0 (1–8)
Buenos Aires Senators	1992–2009	20 (7–30)	23	46	4.2 (1–10)
Buenos Aires Deputies	1992–2009	22 (7–32)	36	92	3.0 (1–8)
Chaco	1994–2009	29 (13–38)	15	32	3.0 (1–6)
Chubut	1994–2009[V]	26 (11–33)	8	27	2.0 (1–4)
Córdoba Senators	1992–2001	5 (0–12)	18	67	2.7 (1–17)
Córdoba Deputies	1992–2001[S]	17 (4–26)	16	66	2.8 (1–9)
Córdoba Unicameral	2002–2009[S]	33 (27–34)	16	60	2.1 (1–5)
Corrientes Senators	1992–2009[V]	20 (0–38)	11	13	4.2 (1–9)
Corrientes Deputies	1994–2009[V]	25 (4–38)	13	26	2.1 (1–4)
Entre Ríos Deputies	1998–2009[VS]	11 (4–17)	21	28	4.9 (1–13)
Formosa	1996–2009	28 (10–39)	9	30	3.2 (1–7)
Jujuy	1992–2007	23 (10–27)	11	48	2.7 (1–6)
Mendoza Senators	1998–2009	18 (13–24)	13	38	2.7 (1–6)
Mendoza Deputies	1992–2009	17 (4–24)	13	50	2.6 (1–6)
Misiones	1994–2009[S]	28 (25–30)	12	40	2.3 (1–4)

(continued)

TABLE 4.1 (*continued*)

District	Years in Sample	Average Percent Women in Chamber (Range)	# of Standing Committees	# of Seats in Chamber	Average # of Appointments per Member (Range)
Río Negro	1996–2009	27 (22–37)	5	46	1.4 (1–5)
Salta Senators	2000–2009[V]	11 (9–13)	11	23	2.3 (1–6)
Salta Deputies	2000–2007[S]	18 (10–27)	18	60	3.6 (1–8)
Santa Cruz	1992–2009	18 (10–27)	10	28	2.3 (1–6)
Santa Fe Senators	1992–2009[VS]	4 (0–11)	16	19	4.1 (1–9)
Santa Fe Deputies	2000–2009[S]	30 (28–36)	13	50	2.7 (1–6)
Tucumán	1992–2009	18 (8–27)	22	49	3.0 (1–7)

Notes: V indicates the province did not appoint vice presidents during the period under study. The Corrientes House did not start appointing vice presidents until 2008.

S indicates the province did not appoint committee secretaries during the period under investigation. In 1992, 2000, 2002, and 2004, the Corrientes House did not report electing secretaries.

Information was unavailable on the following cases: Formosa did not report vice presidents in 1998 and 2000 or secretaries in 2002 and 2004. The Mendoza House did not report vice presidents in 1996, 1998, and 2000, or secretaries in 2002 and 2004. Santa Cruz did not report secretaries in 2002, 2004, or 2006. Santa Cruz reported VPs only in 2002. I do not have leadership appointment for the Córdoba Senate or for the Santa Fe Senate before 1998.

Women's Committees Appointments

First, I consider women's committee appointments. Recall that in Chapter 2 I argued that women do not have the same opportunities as men to hold positions of power. As a result, I expect that women may be underrepresented on powerful committees and overrepresented on less prestigious committees such as social issue committees and women's issues committees. To evaluate this, I categorize legislative committees into four different types: Women and Family Committees (WFC); Social Issues Committees (SIC); Budget and Economic Committees (BEC); and Power Committees (PC) or committees that have the most influence in the chamber (the committee coding is detailed in Appendix 4.1). WFCs include only committees that focus on legislation pertaining to gender, women, families, and youth. SICs, by comparison, include a larger range of committees that focus on issues such as education, health, housing, and human rights. WFCs and SICs are typically considered low-profile committees with limited resources. These committees do not have the authority to allocate funding, so even when they treat important legislation, they are limited in their ability to ensure the legislation is implemented. By contrast, BECs and PCs are considered prestigious committee posts and budget and economic committees in particular have the authority to allocate resources. Interviews with deputies in each of the chambers in my sample confirm that in the case of the Argentine provinces, PCs are the general legislation committee, budget committee, and constitutional issues committee. As such, BECs are typically a subset of PCs.[23]

I use a one-sample t-test to evaluate whether the percentage of women in each type of committee (i.e., WFC, SIC, BEC, and PC) is statistically different than the percentage of women in the Argentine provincial legislatures for each year in my analysis. The percentage of women in each category is aggregated across chambers by year. Figure 4.2 plots these results. The plot graphs the average percentage of women holding leadership positions in the Argentine provincial legislatures on the y-axis and the year on the x-axis. The horizontal reference lines indicate the percentage of provincial-level female legislators in Argentina for a given year. When the confidence intervals cross the reference line, this indicates that the share of women in a given committee type is not significantly different than the share of women in office.

It is clear from the figure that women's numeric representation at both the chamber and the committee levels increased substantially over this period. In 1992, women occupied fewer than 6 percent of all provincial-level legislative seats. By 1996, this number had more than doubled, reaching just over 17 percent. The year 2006 represented a historic high, with women holding 27 percent of seats in the sample. Similarly, women's appointments to each

---

[23] There are instances in which a subset of the committees included in the BEC category are not included in the PC category. See Appendix 4.1 for more details.

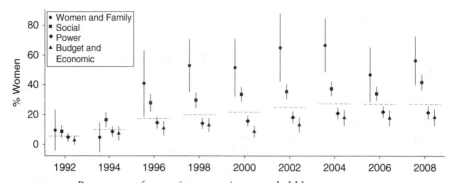

FIGURE 4.2. Percentage of committee appointments held by women.
Note: Figure 4.2 uses a one-sample t-test to compare the percentage of women in committee posts to the percentage of women in the chamber, as indicated by the horizontal reference line. The percentage of women in each category is aggregated across chambers by year.

committee type appear to increase over time. Still, women do not occupy a proportional share of committee seats across the different committees. They are clearly overrepresented in some committees and underrepresented in others.

Women are proportionally *overrepresented* in WFCs during every year in the sample except 1994. These differences are statistically significant for every year in the sample except 1992 and 1994 – years when there were very few women in the legislature. By 1998, when women hold just 19 percent of legislative seats in the sample, they occupy more than 50 percent of the appointments on WFCs. A similar trend, albeit less stark, emerges for committee appointments to SICs. Women are always proportionally *overrepresented* on SICs. By 1996, women hold 28 percent of seats on SICs despite holding only 17 percent of legislative seats. Their share of SICs continues to increase over time with women occupying 42 percent of SICs in 2008.

The opposite is true for women's appointments to PCs and BECs. There is a visible gap between the percentage of women in the chamber and the percentage of women holding PCs and BECs, indicating that women are proportionally *underrepresented* on these committees. On average, men occupy disproportionately more seats on powerful committees from 1992 to 1994, although these differences were not statistically significant for these two years. As women's numeric representation increases, these differences become larger and statistically significant. After 1996, the gap between women's average numeric representation in the chambers and women's average numeric representation on PCs becomes statistically significant, ranging from a low of 14 percent in 1998 to a high of 22 percent in 2006. With only one exception (i.e., BECs in 1996), women's underrepresentation is even more pronounced in BECs. Women held as few as 9 percent of the appointments on BECs in 2000, and never held more than

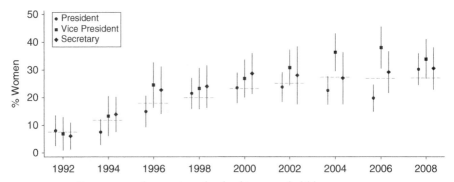

FIGURE 4.3. Percentage of committee leadership posts held by women.
Note: Figure 4.3 uses a one-sample t-test to compare the percentage of women in leadership posts to the percentage of women in the chamber, as indicated by the horizontal reference line. The percentage of women in each category is aggregated across chambers by year.

18 percent of appointments (2008). These differences are statistically significant for every year after 1996. On average, women's appointments to prestigious committees have not kept pace with increases in women's numeric representation in the chambers as a whole. Figure 4.2 clearly shows that women are proportionally overrepresented on low-profile committees and underrepresented on the most powerful committees.

Women's Committee Leadership Posts

To further examine the extent of women's marginalization in the Argentine chambers, I evaluate their representation in committee leadership posts. I use a one-sample t-test to examine if the percentage of women in leadership posts is significantly different than the percentage of women in the Argentine provincial legislatures for each year in my sample. As with the previous analysis, the percentage of women in each leadership post is aggregated across chambers by year. Figure 4.3 plots the results from the committee leadership analysis. The horizontal reference lines indicate the percentage of provincial-level female legislators in Argentina in a given year. When the confidence intervals cross the reference line, this indicates the share of women in a given leadership post is not significantly different than the share of women in office.

For most years in my sample, women are proportionally represented in committee leadership posts. In 1992, women hold 8 percent of presidential posts; this percentage is slightly higher than their total seat share in the sample. Women's share of presidential posts continues to rise over time, more or less keeping pace with increases in women's numeric representation in the chamber. In 2006, the share of presidential posts held by women drops below the share of women in the legislative chamber, to 20 percent, but, in 2008, it rises above the chamber average, to 30 percent. On average, this figure shows that women do not tend to be significantly under- or overrepresented in presidential posts.

Women also tend to be proportionally represented in vice presidential and secretarial posts. In both cases, women's numeric representation slightly outpaces women's average numeric representation in the chambers during most years in the sample. For vice presidential posts, women's appointments are on par with their numeric representation in the chamber, but during two years they are proportionally overrepresented in this post. In 2004 and 2006, for example, women hold about 36 percent and 38 percent of vice presidential posts, respectively, but they comprise an average of only 27 percent of seats in the chamber during both of these years. Similarly, looking at women's appointments to secretarial posts, women are also proportionally represented in these positions. Indeed, according to the sample-wide average, women hold a larger share of secretarial posts than they do seats in the legislature in most years in the sample – but the difference is not statistically significant for any year in the sample. In 1992 and 2004, women were slightly underrepresented in the secretarial posts, but, again, the difference is not significant. Together, the trends presented in Figure 4.3 paint a relatively positive image of women's access to committee leadership posts.

This general analysis of women's committee appointments and leadership posts leaves us with a complex picture of women's status in the legislature. On one hand, a first look at committee appointments shows that women are underrepresented in powerful committees, suggesting that women may not have equal access to power. On the other hand, the descriptive statistics for women's committee leadership posts are more favorable for women. Women are proportionally overrepresented in vice presidential and secretarial posts; in some years, they are even proportionally overrepresented in presidential posts (the most powerful of the three positions). To understand these trends in the data, we need a more detailed analysis.

In particular, it is important to take into account individual-level factors about legislators that may influence their appointments as well as variation across chambers. It is not clear from this analysis, for instance, whether women are underrepresented in powerful committees because they have less legislative experience than their male colleagues. Moreover, it is unclear if and how women's status changes as women's numeric representation increases. With respect to leadership posts, it may also be important to consider the different types of committees over which women preside. Do women have opportunities to preside over powerful committees, or are they presiding over less powerful committees with limited resources? In the two sections that follow, I provide multivariate analyses of women's committee appointments and women's leadership posts to develop a clearer understanding of women's status in the legislature. Then, I offer a disaggregated look at the types of committees over which women frequently preside.

WOMEN'S COMMITTEE APPOINTMENTS:
MULTIVARIATE ANALYSIS

In this section, I offer an empirical analysis to systematically evaluate if women are less likely to be appointed to powerful committees than are their male colleagues and more likely to be appointed to SICs and WFCs. The unit of analysis is an individual legislator. For each of the four categories established earlier, a legislator is coded 1 if he or she sits on a committee in a given category, and 0 otherwise. This coding rule results in four dichotomous dependent variables, one for each of the four committee types.[24] I use a logistic regression to estimate the likelihood of legislators being appointed to Women and Family Committees, Social Issues Committees, Power Committees, and Budget and Economic Committees.[25]

The analysis compares male and female legislators to assess if women are less likely than their male colleagues to receive powerful committee appointments. To account for differences between men and women, I include a dummy variable coded 1 for female legislators and 0 for male legislators. I also account for how women's probability of appointment to powerful posts changes as women's numeric representation increases. Specifically, given that committee assignments are proportionally distributed among political parties and then distributed among members *within* political parties, I control for the proportion of women in the legislative party in a given legislative session. I include an interaction term between the sex of the legislators and the percentage of women in the political party in order to evaluate the relationship between women's numeric representation and the probability that women are marginalized in the legislature.

Control Variables

My statistical analysis also accounts for a number of other factors that may influence committee appointments more generally. First, given that committee seats are distributed proportionally among political parties, and that the biggest party holds the most seats on each committee, I control for whether the legislator is a member of the biggest party in the chamber. Second, to examine whether individuals with seniority or more legislative experience

---

[24] Recall that the categories are not mutually exclusive. BECs are typically a subset of the PCs.

[25] Standard errors are clustered on the legislative session. A complete table of coefficients is available in Appendix 4.2. It is important to reiterate that the four categories for the dependent variable are not mutually exclusive and that representatives serve on multiple committees; thus, being appointed to one committee does not preclude appointment to another committee. Consistent with this logic of committee appointments, the results presented here are robust to different model specifications. Specifically, I obtain substantively and statistically consistent results when I use a seemingly unrelated probit model to estimate the probability of appointment to PCs and SICs.

may be more likely to be appointed to prestigious committees, I control for previous legislative experience in the provincial chamber. Unlike in the United States, it is not common for legislators in the Argentine provincial (or national) chambers to serve multiple terms. On average 22 percent of all legislators in my sample served in a previous term. Given the small share of legislators who actually serve multiple terms in office, I control for previous legislative experience in office using a dichotomous variable that distinguishes between individuals who have and have not previously served in the same provincial chamber.[26] I also include an interaction term between previous experience and the legislators' sex to assess whether female legislators with legislative experience are as likely as their male colleagues to receive valuable appointments.

Additionally, in the Argentine legislative chambers, all legislators are permitted to sit on multiple committees in a given session. Individuals appointed to more posts may be more likely to hold prestigious committee appointments. The number of appointments per member varies among members in the same chamber serving in the same session, across chambers, and over time. Table 4.1 depicts the range of committee appointments per member in each chamber. In every chamber, there are members who hold only one committee appointment, and there are members in the same chamber who hold several appointments. On average, men hold 2.61 appointments per session and women hold 2.78.[27] Similarly, the average number of committee appointments per member varies across chambers. To illustrate, in Río Negro the average number of appointments per member is only 1.4. By comparison, in the Santa Fe, Corrientes, and Buenos Aires Senates, legislators hold closer to four appointments per member. To account for this variation, I control for the number of appointments each individual holds.

It is possible that the adoption of gender quotas may influence women's appointments to prestigious committees. Therefore, I control for the number of legislative sessions since gender quota implementation in each chamber. The number of years since quota adoption ranges from zero to sixteen. To examine whether quota adoption affects women and men's committee appointments in distinct ways, I include an interaction variable between the sex of the legislators and quota years.

I also control for the number of available committee positions in each committee category. In this case, if three committees are coded as Power Committees, and each committee has seven members, then the number of available positions on Power Committees is twenty-one. The more positions there are available in

---

[26] Measuring previous experience as a count variable does not change my results; they are substantive and statistically robust to this decision.

[27] This difference is statistically significant at the 99 percent confidence level using a two-tailed t-test.

a given chamber session, the more opportunities legislators have to serve on a committee in that category.

Finally, I control for the number of committees in a given chamber. There is considerable variation in the number of committees in each chamber. Some chambers have a small number of committees; for example, Chubut and Río Negro have only eight standing committees, and Formosa has nine. Other chambers, such as the Federal District and the Buenos Aires House and Senate, have substantially more, with twenty-two, twenty-three, and thirty-six standing committees, respectively. Chambers with more committees may mean legislators are spread more thinly and less likely to have the opportunity to serve on committees of their choice.

Determinants of Committee Appointment

I begin with a brief discussion of the factors that explain committee appointments more generally, and then I turn to a comparison of women's and men's committee appointments. First, legislators with prior legislative experience are more likely to be appointed to PCs and to BECs. They are no more or less likely to be appointed to WFCs and SICs. Female legislators are just as likely to receive a seniority bonus as are their male colleagues in the chamber. *This does not mean that senior women are just as likely to receive powerful committee appointments as senior men.* On the contrary, as I discuss in detail later, women are less likely to be appointed to powerful committee posts, and legislative experience does not explain or narrow this gap.

All four analyses indicate that legislators appointed to serve on more committees have a higher probability of being appointed to each committee type. With the exception of WFCs, members of the largest party are not systematically more likely to be appointed to any committee type. This result provides support for the notion that committee seats are distributed proportionally among political parties, and the biggest party is not overrepresented on powerful committees or underrepresented on social committees. When quotas have been in place for a longer period of time, women are more likely to be appointed to BECs. This implies that over time, women may be gaining more access to powerful committee appointments. Other than this exception, the number of years since gender quota adoption does not have a significant impact on committee appointments for men or women. Additionally, the results show that, whereas chamber size does not have a significant influence on the probability of being appointed to SICs, it is negatively correlated with the probability of appointment to WFCs, PCs, and BECs. Also, as the number of committees in the chamber increases, the probability of appointment to any one type of committee decreases (with the exception of WFCs). By contrast, as the number of positions in each of these committee categories increases, the probability of appointment to the committee increases.

Women's Access to Power: Gender Differences in
Committee Appointments

Now that we have a general understanding of the factors that determine the committee appointment process, I will compare women's and men's appointments directly. To facilitate the comparison, I use simulated coefficients and calculate sets of predicted probabilities that the average female and male legislator would be appointed to each of the committee types as the percentage of women in their political party increases (King, Tomz, and Wittenberg 2000). Figure 4.4 graphs the predicted probability of appointment on the y-axis and the percentage of women in the political party on the x-axis. The figures allow us to visualize how the probability of appointment to a given committee type changes for male and female legislators as the proportion of women in their party increases. Recall that in Chapter 2, I argued that women entering a male-dominated legislature face structural barriers – such as disadvantages in their committee appointments.

At first glance, it is clear from the top left panel of Figure 4.4 that, on average, female legislators are far more likely to be appointed to WFCs. The average female legislator has a 29 percent chance of being appointed to a WFC compared to the average male legislator, whose chance of being appointed to a WFC is only 7 percent. It is also clear, however, that the probability of being appointed to WFCs changes as the proportion of women in their political party increases. In particular, male legislators are significantly less likely to be appointed to serve on a WFC as the percentage of female legislators in their political party increases. When female legislators comprise only 10 percent of a given party, male legislators have a 9 percent chance of being appointed to a WFC. Yet, as women's percentage of legislative seats increases to 30 percent, male legislators have only a 4 percent chance of being appointed to a WFC. This is a statistically significant difference.

Similar trends do not emerge in other types of committees. In fact, what the data show is that increases in women's numeric representation do not result in a lower probability of male legislators being appointed to SICs or a higher probability of male legislators being appointed to a PC or BEC (although the slope for men is slightly positive in the bottom two figures, it is not statistically significant). On the contrary, male legislators are *always* privileged in their committee appointments – regardless of the gender composition of the political party. Indeed, the top right panel of Figure 4.4 indicates that female legislators are systematically more likely to serve on SICs. When women comprise only about 5 percent of the party, the average woman has a 68 percent chance of being appointed to an SIC, whereas the average man has only a 42 percent chance of being appointed to an SIC. A substantial and statistically significant difference in women's and men's probability of appointments persists across the entire range of the data – regardless of increases in women's numeric representation.

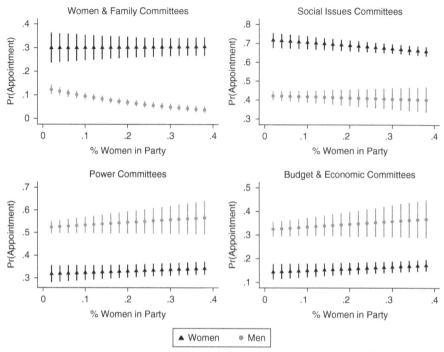

FIGURE 4.4. Probability of appointment to committee, by committee type.

Note: Figure 4.4 graphs the simulated predicted probability of being appointed to each committee type. The predicted probabilities are based on Models 1, 2, 3, and 4, respectively in Appendix 4.2. All values are held at their mean, biggest committee is set to 1, and previous term is set to 0. The confidence intervals indicate whether the differences between the predicted probabilities are statistically significant at the 95 percent confidence level.

In order to evaluate whether the predicted probabilities are statistically different at the 95 percent confidence level, I graphed and evaluated 84 percent confidence intervals for each of the predicted probabilities. An overlap of 84 percent confidence intervals means that we cannot reject the null hypothesis of no difference at the 95 percent confidence level. If the confidence intervals do not overlap, we can reject the null hypothesis and conclude that the difference between two predicted probabilities is statistically significant at the 95 percent confidence level (Julious 2004).

Conversely, the bottom panel of Figure 4.4 indicates that male legislators are always more likely than women to be appointed to serve on PCs and BECs. The differences between men's and women's probability of appointment to PCs are stark, with the average woman having only about a 33 percent chance of being appointed to serve on a PC, compared to male legislators, who have a 54 percent chance of appointment to a PC – a difference of more than

20 percent. Here again, the difference in the probability of appointment for men and women is statistically significant across the entire range of the data.

An even bigger difference exists between men's and women's probability of appointment to BECs. Women's chances of appointment to a BEC (16 percent) pale in comparison to men's chances of appointment (33 percent), with men more than twice as likely to be appointed to a BEC. Regardless of the gender composition of the political party, the difference in men's and women's probability of appointments is always large and significant.

A female deputy from the Federal District explains that it is rare for women to serve on powerful committees – particularly budget committees. Women's underrepresentation on budget committees means they have limited access to political power. As she puts it: "[The budget committee] is where everything is defined. With money, a lot is defined. You decide what others can decide. It is the *mother* of all committees."[28] She says, "*you decide what others can decide*," because any legislation that requires state funding must be approved by the budget committee. Consequently, access to the legislative budget is important for legislators' abilities to represent their constituents more generally and to advance women's rights. She explains that the state needs financial resources to address a number of problems women face in society: "When it comes to violence, *if there are any* women's centers in the city, *there aren't enough workers*. And this happens all over the country. Then there is labor discrimination against women; women are the ones who have the worst jobs – *without social benefits*." Improving the quality of life for women in Argentina requires more resources, and female legislators' limited access to the committees that control these resources makes it difficult for female legislators to successfully promote and advance women's rights.

These results certainly do not reflect positively on the status of women in the Argentine provinces. This analysis reveals that increases in women's numeric representation in the legislature are not sufficient to give women equal access to the policy-making process. Women still face a number of obstacles that prevent them from being appointed to powerful committees. Several female deputies have suggested that "without a doubt"[29] stereotypes about women's role in society shape their paths once they are in office. One deputy from Mendoza explains: "There is also the stereotype: women don't belong in politics; women should be involved in more humanitarian professions. You can even see it inside the legislature, where women go to the culture committee rather than the housing or public services ones."[30] A deputy from the Federal District suggests the same stereotypes play out in the Legislatura Porteña:

"Just like at work, there are also [stereotypes] when it comes to committee politics. Every committee that is related to services, education, women, health, social

[28] Interview with female deputy from Federal District, small third party, July 19, 2013.
[29] Interview with female senator from Mendoza, Frente para la Victoria, June 26, 2013.
[30] Interview with female senator in Mendoza, Partido Justicialista, Frente para la Victoria, June 25, 2013.

advancement, all have women as a majority. Because that's where men think they should be and women too."[31]

Gender stereotypes often preclude women from serving on powerful committees – despite their experience in office – and result in an inequitable distribution of power. In the case of Salta, a deputy points out: "here, you do not get the job by ability. Here the personnel and women are designated in a different way. That makes the discrimination easy to see. You don't really see a number of women in relevant positions."[32] These comments reveal a clear perception that structural barriers prevent women from climbing the political ladder and from influencing the policy-making process. Similarly, the analysis demonstrates that in the Argentine provinces women do not have equal access to powerful committees. There is no doubt that inequitable committee appointments impede women's influence in the legislature.

WOMEN'S LEADERSHIP APPOINTMENTS: MULTIVARIATE ANALYSIS

In this section, I analyze men and women's access to committee leadership posts. First, using the different leadership categories (i.e., president, vice president, and secretary), I construct three dependent variables. Each legislator is coded 1 if he or she was appointed to a leadership post in the respective category and 0 otherwise. To examine if women are systematically less likely than men to be appointed to leadership posts, I analyze their appointment to each of these positions separately. I include all of the same independent variables in my model as I did in the previous analysis of committee appointments. The only change to this model is that I no longer control for the number of committees in a chamber-year, because the number of positions available per chamber-year (e.g., the number of presidential posts) and the number of committees per chamber-year are the same given that there is only one president per committee. As before, I will use a logistic regression to estimate the likelihood of legislators being appointed to each of the leadership posts.[33]

Determinants of Leadership Posts

I briefly discuss the general factors that explain leadership appointments and then I explicitly compare women's probability of appointment to men's. The biggest party in the legislature is significantly more likely to receive presidential posts and less likely to receive vice presidential posts. This result is consistent with the description of how leadership posts are allocated in Argentina's provincial chambers. It is interesting to note that legislators with previous experience are more likely to be appointed to presidential posts, but they are not any

---

[31] Interview with female deputy from the Federal District, small third party, July 19, 2013.

[32] Interview with Salta, Acción Cívica y Social legislator, July 10, 2013.

[33] Standard errors are clustered on the legislative session. A complete table of coefficients is available in Appendix 4.3.

more likely to hold vice presidential posts, and they are actually less likely to hold secretarial appointments. Given that members of the biggest party are not more likely to hold secretarial posts, and that experienced legislators are not more likely to hold secretarial posts, we can infer that, unlike presidential appointments, secretarial posts are not necessarily highly sought after.

My results also show that women have a slightly larger seniority bonus than their male colleagues with respect to presidential appointments. But women with legislative experience are neither more nor less likely than their male counterparts to be appointed to vice presidential or secretarial posts. The number of years since the implementation of a gender quota does not influence women's appointments to legislative leadership. As chamber size increases, the probability of being appointed to presidential and vice presidential posts decreases. This seems logical because in larger chambers there are more people vying for leadership posts. Conversely, as the number of presidential appointments in a chamber increases, the probability of receiving one of these valuable appointments increases. But, as the number of both vice presidential and secretarial appointments in the chamber increases, the probability of being appointed to one of these positions does not increase or decrease significantly. At first glance this seems odd, but it is not uncommon for one person to hold more than one secretarial post. In fact, for chambers that do appoint committee secretaries, enough secretarial positions are available that, on average, 37 percent of the members could hold this position if no legislator held multiple secretarial posts. In practice, only 15 percent of legislators hold a secretarial post, and among those members who hold a secretarial post, on average they each hold 1.26 posts. Interestingly, it is those chambers that have a larger number of secretarial posts that are most likely to have deputies who hold multiple secretarial posts.

Women's Access to Power: Gender Differences in Leadership Posts

Now, I turn to the differences in men's and women's probability of appointments. Figure 4.5 graphs the predicted probabilities of the average female and male legislator being appointed to leadership posts as the percentage of women in the political party increases. As in the previous figure, the y-axis depicts the probability of appointment and the x-axis depicts the percentage of women in the political party.

The top left panel of Figure 4.5 graphs the probability of appointment to a presidential post. The figure shows that when women comprise only a small proportion of a political party (less than 12 percent), women are not significantly less likely to hold presidential posts than are their male counterparts. As the proportion of women in the party increases, however, the difference between the probability of male and female legislators being appointed to leadership posts increases. Once women comprise more than 12 percent of the political party, a statistically significant difference emerges and persists across the range of the data.

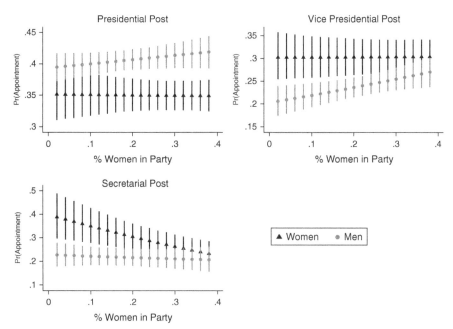

FIGURE 4.5. Probability of appointment to committee leadership.
Notes: Figure 4.5 graphs the simulated predicted probability of being appointed to each committee type. The predicted probabilities are based on Models 1, 2, and 3, respectively, in Appendix 4.3. All values are held at their mean, biggest committee is set to 1, and previous term is set to 0. The confidence intervals indicate whether the differences between the predicted probabilities are statistically significant at the 95 percent confidence level.

The perception among women that female legislators are absent from presidential posts is common across Argentina. A deputy from Catamarca explains that it is a struggle for women to hold leadership posts because, "Society is very *machista.*" The idea of women holding leadership posts does not square with people's ideas about what role women should fulfill in society. As a result, she observes: "[In the legislature,] the majority of committees are led by men." And this is not because women do not want to be in leadership positions. Rather, she explains, "it is a struggle for us due to this *machismo.*"[34] Her colleague had a similar observation; when asked if there were only a small number of women holding committee chair positions, she responded, "Yes, three. Because there is a lot of inequality." She elaborated:

"My goal is for more women to preside over committees, that they will participate more in political issues and in political decisions.... [My goal] is to have more participation in

[34] Interview with female deputy from Catamarca, Partido Justicialista, November 17, 2009.

political parties and the decision-making positions. [Men] always just let us know when it's all decided. We want to be a part of these political decisions."[35]

Whereas women have fewer opportunities than men to hold presidential posts, they are actually more likely than men to be appointed to vice presidential and secretarial posts when they occupy only a small portion of the party. Yet this difference does not hold across the range of the data: as the proportion of women in the party increases, the difference in men's and women's probability of appointment to these two positions narrows and women are no longer advantaged in these appointments. To summarize, when women occupy a small proportion of membership in political parties, they are not underrepresented in presidential leadership posts and they are slightly overrepresented in other committee leadership posts. However, when the proportion of women in the party is larger, women are systematically less likely to be appointed to presidential posts and are equally likely to be appointed to vice presidential and secretarial posts.

These results are consistent with the notion that increases in women's numeric representation may cause male legislators (the traditionally dominant group) to feel that their status in the legislature is being threatened by female legislators who will likely demand to occupy scarce resources such as leadership posts (Heath et al. 2005). This point is illustrated by a female deputy's observation that men occupy the majority of powerful positions in the Salta Chamber of Deputies. She notes that among men "there may be a fear that they will lose their positions because, for women to gain these positions, men have to lose them."[36] Male legislators may therefore respond by bypassing women for powerful political appointments in an effort to preserve power for themselves (Bauer and Britton 2006; Beckwith 2007; Zetterberg 2008). As a result, despite major gains in women's numeric representation in legislative bodies across Argentina, women are not making gains within the legislature at the same rate.

Leadership Appointments by Committee Type

These trends in leadership appointments may not tell the whole story because the analysis treats all committee leadership posts as equal – regardless of the committee type. Given that some committees are more powerful than others, it logically follows that some committee leadership posts are also more powerful (Patty et al. 2015). Thus, to understand women's status in the legislature, it is important to consider the types of committees where they are likely to hold leadership posts. To investigate this relationship, I categorize leadership posts by committee types (i.e., WFCs, SICs, PCs, and BECs) and conduct a series of

[35] Interview with female deputy from Catamarca, Partido Justicialista, November 16, 2009.
[36] Interview with female deputy from Salta, Frente para la Victoria, July 10, 2013.

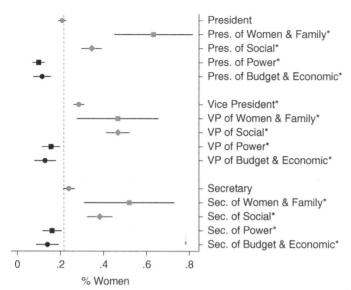

FIGURE 4.6. Percentage of leadership posts held by women, by committee type.
Note: Figure 4.6 plots the percentage of leadership posts occupied by women and 95 percent confidence intervals on the x-axis and the y-axis indicates the different type of leadership posts. The vertical reference line indicates the percentage of women in the entire sample. An asterisk indicates that there is a statistically significant difference (using a two-tailed t-test) between the percentage of female legislators holding a given type of leadership post and the percentage of female legislators in the chamber.

t-tests to determine if female legislators are proportionally over- or underrepresented in leadership posts on different types of committees. Figure 4.6 graphs the percentage of women in leadership posts by committee type, as compared to women's overall seats share in the chamber. The averages are constructed by pooling the data across all the chamber-years in the sample, with the asterisk indicating that the percentage of women in the chamber and the percentage of women in leadership posts are statistically different at the 95 percent level using a two-tailed test. The vertical line serves as a reference for the average percentage of female legislators in the sample.

Figure 4.6 reveals, that on average, women are not proportionally underrepresented in either presidential or secretarial posts, and they are overrepresented in vice presidential posts. Still, a closer look reveals that this trend does not hold across the different committee types: women are proportionally overrepresented in the leadership in some committee types and underrepresented in the leadership in others.

For all three types of leadership posts (i.e., presidential, vice presidential, and secretarial), female legislators are overrepresented on WFCs and SICs – the less powerful committee posts. The figure reveals that women are president for 63 percent of WFCs, vice president for 47 percent of WFCs, and secretary for 52 percent of WFCs. A similar, albeit weaker, trend appears for SICs: a larger share of women holds presidential, vice presidential, and secretarial posts as compared to their overall presence in the provincial legislatures. It is not surprising that women would be overrepresented in the leadership in these committees, as previous research has indicated that it is not uncommon for women to prioritize these issues (Schwindt-Bayer 2010).

By contrast, women are proportionally underrepresented in leadership posts on powerful committees. Figure 4.6 reveals that women rarely preside over PCs or BECs in the Argentine provinces. Thus, not only are women under-represented in the chamber more generally (comprising less than 50 percent of each chamber in my sample), but also leadership posts on powerful committees are not proportionally distributed among the women in office. A female deputy from the Federal District described the distribution of committee leadership appointments between men and women in the following way: "[Leadership positions] are divided, but some committees are more important than others ... and those are led by men."[37] She went on to explain how women are passed over for powerful posts:

"I think there are two [women on the budget committee]. A woman from the PRO was going to preside over the committee. She wasn't an economist, but studied [the topic]. And then at the last minute they put someone else in charge. He was new, and usually people who are new do not preside over committees, but the change was because she was a woman, so they did not let her do it."[38]

Her comments suggest that female deputies are aware that they do not have the same opportunities to hold leadership posts on powerful commit-tees. Moreover, women's underrepresentation in leadership posts on powerful committees is not perceived as a product of women's qualifications. As she explains, women are often overlooked for these positions and instead assigned to committees related to service, health, women, and social advancements.

Taken together, the data in Figures 4.5 and 4.6 illustrate that the problem is not that women have not held leadership posts, but that they are unlikely to hold leadership posts in powerful committees. Moreover, many women believe that the absence of female legislators in powerful positions is a product of discrimination in the legislature that reflects chauvinistic views in society more generally. A deputy from Salta summarizes this point nicely:

"The positions of power are still lacking. But that is about how women are seen in the sessions – in politics in general. There is still a lack of equality. If we are going to elect someone, it has to be because of qualifications. We are still lacking that step. We have to keep working and empowering women for that."[39]

---

[37] Interview with female deputy from the Federal District, small third party, July 19, 2013.
[38] Ibid.
[39] Interview with legislator in Salta, Acción Cívica y Social, July 10, 2013.

CONCLUSION

Even after years of successful gender quotas, which have helped to increase women's numeric representation in the Argentine legislatures, women remain woefully underrepresented in the most powerful leadership posts. The data in this chapter paint a bleak picture of the status of women in Argentina. In fact, some may even call it "embarrassing."[40]

Putting aside whether women's inferior status in the legislature is viewed as socially unacceptable, their subordinate status has serious implications for their ability to influence the policy-making process. On average, women hold fewer chamber-wide or powerful committee leadership posts than men. Moreover, they are much less likely to receive powerful committee appointments than are their male colleagues. The data demonstrate that this trend is consistent for appointments to Power Committees and Budget and Economic Committees regardless of women's numeric representation in parties. This finding is particularly troubling given that the budget committee controls the distribution of the state budget and decides the funding priorities of the legislatures. The exclusion of women from these committees directly translates into women being cut off from decisions to fund legislation that influences their constituents more generally and legislation that disproportionately influences the lives of women.

Even more troubling, the data show that women's access to committee presidential posts decreases as women's numeric representation increases. This finding suggests that increases in women's numeric representation may result in backlash from male colleagues. The data clearly demonstrate that when women comprise only a small proportion of the chamber, they are about as likely as their male colleagues to be appointed to presidential posts. But as women's numeric representation increases, this gender equity disappears, with women being systematically less likely to preside over committees. A fine-grained analysis of leadership appointments by committee type indicates that even when women do preside over committees, they are not likely to preside over Power Committees and Budget and Economic Committees.

Further, the gender gap in powerful appointments cannot be explained by seniority. Even when controlling for legislative experience, women are systematically less likely to be appointed to powerful committees and powerful leadership posts. Indeed, women with seniority status are less likely than men with seniority status to receive committee leadership posts and powerful committee appointments.

The findings from this chapter clearly demonstrate that women's marginalization extends beyond their numeric minority status in the chamber. Rather than alleviating women's marginalization in the legislature, increases in women's numeric representation further expose women's marginalization. As more

[40] Interview with female senator in Mendoza, Partido Justicialista, Frente para la Victoria, June 25, 2013.

women enter office and women continue to be proportionally underrepresented in formal positions of influence and denied informal access to power, it becomes clear that women's marginalization is systematic. Indeed, marginalization is institutionalized in the Argentine provinces. This marginalization cannot be addressed by simply increasing women's numeric representation. For women to be on equal footing with men, they need equal access to formal and informal political power.

In addition to providing a clearer understanding of women's status in the Argentine provinces, this chapter establishes the generalizability of the Argentine case. Although not universal,[41] research that has examined women's status in the legislature often finds that women are less likely to receive powerful committee posts (Barnes and Schibber 2015; Dolan and Ford 1997; Heath et al. 2005; Kerevel and Atkeson 2013; Swers 2013; Thomas 1994; Towns 2003). Women are less likely to chair influential committees (Rodriguez 2003; Schwindt-Bayer 2010), to hold top party-wide leadership posts (O'Brien 2015; Schwindt-Bayer 2010), or to occupy chamber-wide leadership posts (O'Brien and Rickne forthcoming). In parliamentary systems, where cabinet ministers are drawn directly from the parliament, women are also unlikely to hold prestigious appointments (Barnes and O'Brien 2015; Claveria 2014; Krook and O'Brien 2012; O'Brien et al. 2015).

Instead, women are more likely to serve on social issue committees, that is, committees with small or nonexistent budgets, essentially rendering them powerless. As in the Argentine chambers, women are also more likely to serve on women's issues committees (Dolan and Ford 1997; Funk and Taylor-Robinson 2014; Heath et al. 2005; Pansardi and Vercesi forthcoming; Schwindt-Bayer 2010; Towns 2003; Zetterberg 2008). Thus, women's status in the Argentine chambers is not unlike that of women across Latin America, the United States, or Western Europe.

Finally, these findings provide strong evidence for my explanation of *why women collaborate*. Women's marginalization across a vast array of legislative power – including chamber-wide leadership posts, committee leadership posts, and powerful committee appointments – implies that women do not have the same opportunities to influence the policy-making process as men. As a result, women who want to exert influence on the legislative process must legislate differently than men. I argue that, by collaborating with female colleagues, women can successfully navigate these barriers to power. In the next chapter, I turn my attention to women's collaboration.

[41] In the case of the Mexican Chamber of Deputies, Kerevel and Atkeson (2013) show that despite their underrepresentation on economic committees (arguably the most important committees), women are not less likely to be appointed to other powerful committees or to hold committee chair positions more generally. In a study of three state legislatures in the United States, Bratton (2005) finds little evidence that women are less likely to be appointed to leadership posts. Also, in the case of the British House of Commons, O'Brien (2012a) finds that women and men have the same likelihood of obtaining select committee appointments (special oversight committees).

Chamber	Women and Family	Social Issues	Budget and Economic	Power Committees
Buenos Aires Deputies	Childhood, Adolescence, Family, & Women[a]	Public Health; Edu. & Culture; Cultural Issues; Human Rights & Guarantees; Prevention & Control of Human Rights Abuses; Drug Dependency & Trafficking; Addiction Prevention; Development & Human Rights	Budget & Taxes; Treasury; Foreign Commerce; Mercosur; Regional & Interior Issues	General Leg. I; General Leg. II; Budget & Taxes; Treasury; Constitutional & Justice Issues
Buenos Aires Senators	Children & Family Issues[b]	Public Health; Edu. & Culture; Interior Advancement & Development; Social Legislation; Human Rights & Guarantees; Addiction Prevention	Budget & Taxes; Treasury; Foreign Commerce; Mercosur Politics & Regional Integration	General Leg. I; General Leg. II; Budget & Taxes; Treasury; Constitutional Issues & Agreements
Chaco	None	Social Assistance, Public Health, Drug Addiction Prevention, Family & Population Development; Edu. & Culture; Land, Human & Rural Habitat Regularization & Development; Human Rights; Human Development & Health	Treasury & Budget	General Leg. & Justice; Treasury & Budget; Constitutional Issues
Chubut	None	Social & Health Legislation; Social, Labor, & Human Rights Legislation; Human Development & Environment	Treasury & Public Works	General Leg., Health, Culture, & Education; Treasury & Public Works; Constitutional & Justice Issues

(continued)

Appendix 4.1 (cont.)

Chamber	Women and Family	Social Issues	Budget and Economic	Power Committees
Córdoba Deputies	None	Public Health; Culture, Edu., Science, & Tech	Economy	General Leg.; Economy; Constitutional & Municipal Issues, Petitions, & Power
Córdoba Senators	Family & Minors	Public Health; Edu. & Culture; Youth Rights, Sports, Recreation, & Politics of Drug Addiction Prevention; Human Rights & Consumer Rights[c]	Budget & Treasury	General Leg.; Budget & Treasury; Constitutional, Institutional, & Municipal
Córdoba Unicameral	Family & Minors	Public Health; Edu. & Culture; Youth Rights, Sports, Recreation, & Politics of Drug Addiction Prevention; Justice, Agreements & Human Rights	Budget & Treasury	General Leg.; Budget & Treasury; Constitutional, Institutional, & Municipal
Corrientes Deputies	None	Labor, Public Health, & Social Assistance; Public Edu. & Culture; Human Rights, Security, Constitutional Guarantees, & User & Consumer Rights	Budget & Taxes; Treasury	Constitutional Issues & General Leg.; Budget & Taxes; Treasury; Constitutional & Legislative Affairs
Corrientes Senators	None	Education & Culture	Taxes & Budget; Treasury & Public Works	Leg. & Constitutional Issues; Taxes & Budget; Treasury & Public Works
Entre Ríos Deputies	None	Public Health; Edu.; Culture; Human Rights; Addictions & Drug Dependency	Treasury, Budget, & Accounts; Commerce, Cooperativism, & Mercosur	Legislation; Treasury, Budget, & Accounts; Constitutional Issues

Federal District	Family, Women, & Minority[d]	Health; Edu, Science, & Tech; Social Advancement & Economic Activities; Culture & Communication;[e] Human Rights, Guarantees, & Antidiscrimination; Equal Opportunities; Mental Health	Treasury & Budget;[f] Economic Development, Mercosur, & Employment Politics	General Leg. & Labor; Treasury & Budget;[g] Constitutional Issues
Formosa	None	Public Health & Drug Addiction Issues; Social Well-being, Culture, & Edu.; Development & Advancement of Tourist Affairs	Economic Issues & Public Works; Regional Issues, Tariff Free Zone, Mercosur, & Intl Agreements	Legislation & Constitutional Issues; Economic Issues & Public Works
Jujuy	None	Public Health; Culture & Edu.; Social Issues	Economy; Finance	General Leg.; Economy; Finance; Institutional Issues
Mendoza Deputies	None[h]	Public Health; Culture & Edu.; Social & Labor Legislation; Youth	Economy, Commerce, & Consumption; Treasury & Budget	Economy, Commerce, & Consumption; Treasury & Budget; Legislation & Constitutional Issues
Mendoza Senators	None	Health; Culture, Edu., Science & Technology; Social Issues & Labor	Economy & Foreign Commerce; Treasury & Budget	Legislative & Constitutional Issues; Economy & Foreign Commerce; Treasury & Budget; Rights & Guarantees
Misiones	Gender, Family, and Adolescence	Social Issues, Public Health, & Edu.	Budget, Taxes, & Treasury	General Leg. & Justice; Budget, Taxes, & Treasury; Constitutional & Municipal Issues, & Political Justice

(continued)

Appendix 4.1 (*cont.*)

Chamber	Women and Family	Social Issues	Budget and Economic	Power Committees
Río Negro	None[i]	Culture, Edu., & Social Communication; Social Issues	Planning, Economic Issues, & Tourism; Budget & Treasury	Constitutional Issues & General Leg.; Planning, Economic Issues, & Tourism; Budget & Treasury
Salta Deputies	None	Health; Edu.; Culture & Sports; Human Rights	Bicameral for Investment Accounts; Treasury & Budget; Mercosur & Regional Integration	General Leg.; Bicameral for Investment Accounts; Treasury & Budget
Salta Senators	None	Public Health, Social Security, & Sports; Human Rights & Indigenous Issues; Drug Addiction, Trafficking, & Consumption	Economy, Public Finance, & Budget; Border & Limits	General Leg. for Labor & Provisional Regime; Economy, Public Finance, & Budget
Santa Cruz	None	Social Action, Public Health, & Housing; Edu., Culture, Science, & Tech	Budget & Treasury	General Leg.; Budget & Treasury; Constitutional Issues, Justice, Power, Petitions, & Regulations
Santa Fe Deputies	None	Public Health & Social Assistance; Edu.; Culture & Social Communication; Human Rights & Guarantees	Budget & Treasury	Constitutional Issues & General Leg.; Budget & Treasury

Santa Fe Senators	None	Public Health & Environment Protection; Edu.; Culture & Social Communication	Economy, Agriculture, Livestock, Industry, & Commerce; Budget & Treasury; Foreign Commerce	Constitutional Issues & General Leg.; Economy, Agriculture, Livestock, Industry, & Commerce; Budget & Treasury
Tucumán	Family, Minors, & Disabled	Public Health; Edu. & Culture; Social Legislation & Public Health; Family, Minors, & Disabled; Human Rights; Narco-Trafficking & Drug Dependency; Prevention & Assistance for Addictions	Economy & Production; Treasury & Budget	General Leg.; Economy & Production; Treasury & Budget; Constitutional & Institutional Issues

Source: Adapted from Barnes (2014).

[a] Previously Childhood, Adolescence, and Family. In 1998, the Women's Issue Committee was created. In 2002, these two committees were consolidated to make Childhood, Adolescence, Family, and Women.

[b] Previously Childhood, Adolescence, and Family.

[c] Previously Justice, Human Rights, and Agreements.

[d] Previously Women, Childhood, Adolescence, and Youth.

[e] Previously Culture.

[f] Previously Budget, Administration, Financial Administration, and Tributary Politics.

[g] Ibid.

[h] The Mendoza Chamber of Deputies created a special committee focused on gender in 2009. Every female in the Chamber of Deputies was a member of the committee in 2009.

[i] In 2000, Río Negro created a special committee called the Special Committee on the Study of Gender. It is not a standing committee and does not meet on a regular basis.

APPENDIX 4.2: PROBABILITY OF APPOINTMENT TO COMMITTEE

	(1) Women & Family	(2) Social Issues	(3) Power	(4) Budget & Economic
Female	1.435***	1.234***	−0.931***	−1.271***
	(0.344)	(0.164)	(0.182)	(0.241)
Biggest Party	0.283**	0.029	−0.057	−0.067
	(0.100)	(0.039)	(0.043)	(0.038)
Previous Term	−0.286	−0.100	0.534***	0.175*
	(0.325)	(0.080)	(0.078)	(0.087)
Previous Term X Female	0.112	−0.065	0.094	0.093
	(0.492)	(0.168)	(0.194)	(0.233)
# of Appointments	0.407***	0.441***	0.339***	0.298***
	(0.044)	(0.028)	(0.030)	(0.031)
Percent Women in Party	−0.036***	−0.006*	−0.002	0.001
	(0.008)	(0.003)	(0.003)	(0.003)
Percent Women in Party X Female	0.037***	−0.002	0.005	0.005
	(0.010)	(0.004)	(0.005)	(0.005)
Quota Years	0.050	−0.014	−0.006	−0.027
	(0.039)	(0.013)	(0.014)	(0.017)
Quota Years X Female	−0.133	0.009	0.023	0.065*
	(0.074)	(0.031)	(0.032)	(0.033)
Chamber Size	−0.008**	−0.002	−0.013***	−0.014***
	(0.003)	(0.003)	(0.003)	(0.003)
# of Committees	−0.023	−0.048***	−0.052***	−0.035***
	(0.012)	(0.006)	(0.008)	(0.008)
Available Positions	0.051***	0.022***	0.041***	0.046***
	(0.013)	(0.003)	(0.005)	(0.011)
Constant	−2.941***	−1.294***	−0.457**	−0.742***
	(0.380)	(0.104)	(0.149)	(0.181)
Number of Legislators	2030	6084	6106	4946
Log Pseudo-likelihood	−639.5789	−3773.5387	−3880.8606	−2857.4652

Robust standard errors clustered around the legislative session in parentheses.
*p < 0.05, ** p < 0.01, *** p < 0.001.

APPENDIX 4.3: PROBABILITY OF APPOINTMENT TO COMMITTEE
LEADERSHIP POSTS

	(1) President	(2) Vice President	(3) Secretary
Female	−0.256	0.445	0.778*
	(0.174)	(0.269)	(0.352)
Biggest Party	0.718***	−0.408**	−0.106
	(0.088)	(0.133)	(0.178)
Previous Term	0.173*	−0.132	−0.429*
	(0.088)	(0.123)	(0.207)
Previous Term X Female	0.338*	−0.043	−0.323
	(0.166)	(0.222)	(0.352)
# of Appointments	0.053**	0.367***	0.946***
	(0.018)	(0.035)	(0.065)
Percent Women in Party	0.277	0.988	−0.358
	(0.293)	(0.537)	(0.865)
Percent Women in Party X Female	−0.298	−0.967	−1.694
	(0.451)	(0.666)	(1.204)
Quota Years	−0.009	−0.000	−0.038
	(0.011)	(0.022)	(0.047)
Quota Years X Female	0.023	0.027	0.004
	(0.032)	(0.039)	(0.048)
Chamber Size	−0.031***	−0.006	−0.008
	(0.002)	(0.004)	(0.010)
# of Presidential Posts	0.081***	−	−
	(0.006)		
# of VP Posts	−	0.017	−
		(0.010)	
# of Secretary Posts	−	−	−0.020
			(0.028)
Constant	−1.132***	−2.692***	−5.016***
	(0.135)	(0.206)	(0.425)
Number of Legislators	5328	4096	3310
Log Pseudo-likelihood	−3170.5963	−2123.75	−1033.1182

Robust standard errors clustered around the legislative session in parentheses.
*p < 0.05, ** p < 0.01, *** p < 0.001.

5

When Do Women Collaborate?

Explaining Between-Chamber Variation

> *"There is an impressive party discipline that dominates individual members who are part of that political party."*
>
> *– Female Deputy, Jujuy, 2009*

Party discipline is key to understanding legislative dynamics. In Chapter 2, I argued that women have incentives to collaborate more frequently than men with female colleagues to exert their influence on the legislative process. Nonetheless, not all women have the same opportunities to collaborate. In particular, some institutional contexts – such as the extreme party discipline described in the quote above – permit party leaders to constrain legislative behavior and disincentivize legislators from behaving independently of their political parties.

In the case of Jujuy, a deputy describes one such environment in which political parties exercise absolute control over legislative behavior. "In the majority party, there are four or five who lead and direct the issues. The rest have to support them. They can present projects, but [party leaders] don't encourage it."[1] Given that women are typically absent from leadership, they likely wield very little influence in the chamber. Women may even be discouraged from introducing new issues to the legislative agenda or collaborating with female legislators in their own political parties. Instead, they are expected to toe the party line and provide unwavering support for party leaders. As the deputy from Jujuy sees it, "[Party leaders] end up eliminating the possibility for debates that enrich and cultivate different views – even debates within [their own parties]."[2] Moreover, when political institutions give party leaders substantial control over legislators' behavior, party leaders have very little tolerance for behavior that may be viewed as disloyal. In such environments,

[1] Interview with female deputy from Jujuy, October 28, 2009.
[2] Ibid.

116

party leaders do not allow any disagreement from rank-and-file members. "Legislators can be very angry or even opposed to their part[ies], but the party discipline is very strong. There are legislators who are part of the majority party who have not opened their mouth[s]; they don't speak."[3] She indicates that legislators do not openly challenge party leaders. When legislators disagree with party leaders, their only option is to abstain from the discussion. In Chapter 2, I explained that strong party constraints of this nature limit women's legislative collaboration.[4] Nonetheless, such uncompromising party discipline is not constant across all Argentine settings; rather, there is considerable variation both between and within legislative chambers. For this reason, I argue that examining legislative contexts will lead to a clearer understanding of *when women collaborate*.

This is the first of two chapters that empirically test the third part of my theory, which argues that legislative contexts shape legislative collaboration. In Chapter 2, I outlined six key contextual factors that influence when women will collaborate. In this chapter, I examine two of these factors that vary widely *between chambers*: party constraints and women's numeric representation. In the next chapter, I examine factors that vary *within chambers*.

Recall in Chapter 2, I argued that increases in women's numeric representation and party constraints influence when women will collaborate. In this chapter, I demonstrate that when party leaders have *weak* control over legislative behavior, as women's numeric representation increases, women are *more* likely than men to collaborate with female colleagues. By comparison, in districts in which party leaders exercise *strong* control over legislators' behavior, women are only marginally more likely than men to collaborate with other women, and their propensity to do so actually decreases when women comprise a larger share of the chamber. When women make up only a small part of the chamber, they have little influence over legislative outcomes. As a result, party leaders are unlikely to police their behavior or limit their collaboration. But as their seat share increases, women pose a bigger threat – if they work collectively, they can wield more influence in the chamber. This threat incentivizes party leaders to impose even more restrictions on women's legislative behavior. Put succinctly, in an environment in which party leaders have *strong* control over legislative behavior, increases in women's numeric representation suppress women's collaboration, to the point where women will be no more likely to collaborate than men.

---

[3] Ibid.

[4] Even in chambers with strong party discipline, in which individual legislators have little influence over the policy-making process, there are still a number of benefits to serving in the provincial legislature. Legislators may gain access to additional pork in order to cultivate specific political constituencies (Calvo and Murillo 2004). Further, legislators who demonstrate strong party loyalty may be more likely to obtain other, more influential political posts such as mayoral posts or political appointments that are controlled by the party in the future.

EVALUATING LEGISLATIVE COLLABORATION

The analysis in this chapter seeks to understand when women are more likely than men to collaborate with other women, and how women's collaboration changes when their share of the legislature increases. The most intuitive way to think about legislators' collaboration with women is simply to consider the proportion of time that women and men cosponsor with female colleagues as a proportion of their total cosponsorship efforts. But given that I want to examine how collaboration with female colleagues increases as women's numeric representation increases, this approach may be problematic. Recall, I argued that increases in women's numeric representation will motivate collaboration *above and beyond* the additive effects from simply increasing the share of women in office. It may seem obvious that as women's numeric representation increases, women (and men) will naturally cosponsor more legislation with women. This is because even if legislators were randomly choosing cosponsors – for example, drawing their cosponsors' names from a hat – increasing the percentage of women in the legislature increases the probability that all legislators will cosponsor more with women. To continue with the selection from a hat analogy, this is because as more women's names are added to the hat, legislators will be more likely to draw a female name from the hat. In fact, if the cosponsorship process were random, we would expect cosponsorship with female legislators to be equal to women's seat share in the legislature. Therefore, in order to evaluate how increases in women's numeric representation shape women's and men's decisions to collaborate with female colleagues, I need to account for increases in women's presence in the chamber. For this reason, I measure collaboration with female legislators – my dependent variable – as a proportion of the times that each legislator actually cosponsors with female colleagues minus the proportion of times that each legislator would cosponsor with female colleagues if cosponsorship were random (or if legislators were randomly drawing their cosponsors' names from a hat). I call this measure the Gender Cosponsorship Score (GCS).

To get a clear understanding of how I calculate the GCS, consider the following example from two Argentine legislators. Deputy Lilian Juncos (a woman) and Deputy Alfonso Mosquera (a man) served in the Córdoba Chamber in 2006. Seventy legislators worked in this chamber – twenty-four women and forty-six men. This means that both Deputy Juncos and Deputy Mosquera had sixty-nine colleagues; twenty-three of Deputy Juncos' colleagues were women and twenty-four of Deputy Mosquera's colleagues were women. Given this, if Deputy Juncos and Deputy Mosquera were randomly choosing their cosponsors' names from a hat, we would expect for Deputy Juncos to cosponsor with women 33 percent (or 23/69) of the time and for Deputy Mosquera to cosponsor with women 35 percent (or 24/69) of the time.

In practice, 89 of Deputy Juncos' 103 cosponsors (86 percent) were women. Accordingly, her GCS is 53 (or 86–33). Nineteen of Deputy Mosquera's 59 cosponsors (32 percent) were women. His GCS is –3 (or 35–32).

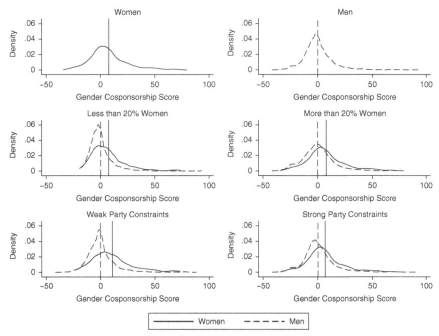

FIGURE 5.1. Distribution of the chamber-wide gender cosponsorship score.
Notes: Figure 5.1 graphs the distribution of the GCS for different groups of interest to my analysis. The vertical references indicate the mean GCS for each group (solid lines for women and dashed lines for men).

The Gender Cosponsorship Score provides an intuitive way of thinking about gendered patterns of collaboration. Negative values of the GCS indicate that the individual legislator works with women less than one would expect if representatives were choosing their cosponsors randomly. Deputy Mosquera's GCS takes on a negative value because in practice he cosponsored less with women than we would expect if he were randomly choosing his cosponsors. Conversely, positive values of the GCS indicate that the individual legislator works with women more than one would expect if representatives were choosing their cosponsors randomly. This was the case with Deputy Juncos, who worked with women 86 percent of the time. By the same logic, a value of zero indicates that the legislator works with women at the same rate as would be expected if the cosponsorship process were completely random.

Figure 5.1 graphs the distribution of the GCS for different groups of interests. The top panel compares the GCS for women and men. The subsequent panels graph women and men on the same plot to facilitate the comparison of their collaborative patterns in different legislative contexts. The vertical reference lines in each figure (solid lines for women and dashed lines for men) mark the mean GCS for each sample. The mean GCS in the full sample is 1.7,

indicating that, on average, legislators are only slightly more likely to cosponsor with women than they would be if they were selecting their cosponsors randomly. It is clear from the figure that the average GCS for most groups is close
to zero, but there is some variation across the different subsamples. For example, the average GCS for women in my sample is 7.2 and 0.2 for men. This is
a statistically significant difference of 7.0.[5] This is consistent with the general
trends presented in Chapter 3 (Figure 3.7) showing that women are more likely
than men to collaborate with female colleagues. The distributions for women
(and the vertical lines indicating the mean GCS for women) are shifted slightly
to the right of the distributions for men in each of the figures, indicating that,
on average, women are more likely to cosponsor with women than are men.
Statistically significant gender differences in the GCS exist across each subsam-
ple of my data. The center panel graphs the distribution of the GCS for women
and men by the proportion of women in the chamber. The gender difference in
the GCS is 6.8 in chambers with less than 20 percent women and 6.9 in chambers with more than 20 percent women. The bottom panel graphs the distribution by the strength of party constraints. As explained later, in the section "Key
Factors: Sex, Women's Numeric Representation, and Party Constraints," the
strength of party constraints is determined using district size, with legislators
from small districts confronting relatively weak party constraints and legislators from large districts confronting relatively strong party constraints. The
bottom left panel shows that the difference in GCS is biggest between women
and men from districts with weak party constraints (i.e., small districts). Here,
the average GCS is 10.4 for women and 0 for men – a statistically significant
difference. The gender difference in districts with strong party constraints (i.e.,
large districts) is 5.8 – slightly smaller but still significant (bottom right panel).

In addition to examining how likely legislators are to cosponsor with female
colleagues in general, I theorized that under some circumstances, women
would be more likely to cross party lines to collaborate with female colleagues.
To evaluate this, I examine an alternative measure of the GCS. Specifically,
I calculate the rate at which representatives *cross party lines* to cosponsor with
women outside their parties. This alternative measure is calculated in exactly
the same way as the first measure, except that I calculate the rate at which
legislators *cross party lines to cosponsor with women* minus the rate at which
they would cross party lines to cosponsor with women if they were choosing
their cosponsors randomly.

Figure 5.2 graphs the distribution of the GCS across party lines for different
subsamples of legislators. The vertical references indicate the mean value for
each group (solid lines for women and dashed lines for men). The average GCS
across party lines in my sample is –5.9 percent. The negative value indicates
that most legislators cross party lines to cosponsor with female colleagues at a

[5] All differences in this section are statistically significant at the 99 percent level using a two-tailed
t-test.

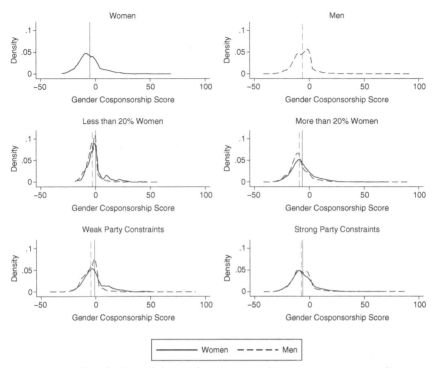

FIGURE 5.2. Distribution of the gender cosponsorship score, across party lines.
Notes: Figure 5.2 graphs the distribution of the GCS across party lines for different groups of interest to my analysis. The vertical references indicate the mean GCS across party lines for each group (solid lines for women and dashed lines for men).

lower rate than they would if they were randomly choosing their cosponsors. This is not surprising given that most cosponsorship in any legislature occurs between co-partisans. Figure 5.2 also shows that there are some interesting differences between women's and men's average GCS across party lines. Men's average scores (−6.1) are slightly lower than women's scores (−4.9); this difference of 1.2 is statistically significant.[6] There is a significant difference between women's and men's scores in each of the subsamples examined in my data. Of particular interest here, in districts with less than 20 percent women, women's average score is positive (0.2) but still close to zero. Women from districts with weak party constraints also have an average score close to zero (−0.9). This indicates that women cross party lines to cosponsor with female colleagues at about the same rate as would be the case if they were choosing their cosponsors randomly. This may seem surprisingly high given that most cosponsorship

---

[6] The differences between women's and men's GCS across party lines reported in this section are all statically significant at the 99 percent level using a two-tailed t-test.

takes place between legislators from the same political party, but my theory explains that women have an incentive to cross party lines to collaborate with female colleagues. By collaborating on legislation, women can ensure that their voices are heard in the policy-making process and can exert more influence in the chamber.

Taken together, Figures 5.1 and 5.2 illustrate some interesting differences between men and women legislators. It is impossible, however, to understand women's and men's cosponsorship behavior without taking into account a number of different factors that shape legislative behavior. Next, I discuss the key factors that I expect to explain differences in cosponsorship behavior.

Key Factors: Sex, Women's Numeric Representation, and Party Constraints

The part of the theory I test in this chapter suggests that three factors interact to influence the GCS: 1) the sex of the legislator; 2) women's numeric representation in the chamber; and 3) party constraints. To estimate the relationship between these three factors and the GCS, I measure each of these factors as follows. First, in order to evaluate whether women behave differently from men, I include a variable to account for the legislators' sex. This variable is coded 1 for female legislators and 0 for male legislators. The second key variable in my analysis is women's numeric representation, which I measure as the percentage of women in the chamber. As I explained in Chapter 1, women's numeric representation varies significantly between the chambers in my sample and within the chambers over time. But given that women's numeric representation is largely driven by the adoption of gender quotas in the Argentine provinces, the percentage of women is relatively consistent across political parties within the same chamber in the same legislative session. I expect that increases in women's numeric representation will have a substantial impact on women's collaborative behavior but not on men's. To determine how these two factors interact to influence legislative collaboration, I include an interaction between the percentage of women in the chamber and the sex of the legislators.

The third key factor in my analysis is the level of party constraints in a chamber. In Chapter 2, I argued that the level of constraints that institutions afford political party leaders influences women's collaborative behavior. As previously explained, Argentine provincial legislatures use closed-list systems to elect representatives. In closed-list systems, the strength of party discipline depends on the district size, with large districts enabling party leaders to exercise more control over legislators' behavior and small districts affording party leaders less control over legislative behavior. As Figure 5.3 illustrates, the Argentine legislatures employ a wide range of district magnitudes to elect members. The y-axis in Figure 5.3 shows the total number of seats in a chamber. The districts in each province are represented on a single bar. Each segment of the bar represents a different district, with black segments depicting single-member districts,

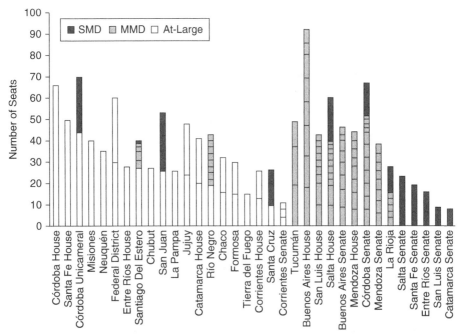

FIGURE 5.3. Variation in district size in the Argentine provincial legislatures.
Notes: Figure 5.3 shows the distribution in district size and type between the Argentine provincial legislatures.

gray segments depicting multimember districts, and white segments depicting at-large (or province-wide) districts.

At one extreme, district size ranges from a low of one in several chambers in which only one deputy is elected in each electoral district. In the Salta Senate, for example, twenty-three senators are elected from single-member districts. On the other extreme, several chambers have electoral districts where more than twenty deputies are elected from the same district. In the Córdoba House, sixty-six members are elected from one at-large district; in Jujuy, twenty-four members (half the chamber) are elected every two years from an at-large district. Between these two extremes, several provinces use multimember districts. For example, the Mendoza Senate uses districts ranging from four to six members to elect thirty-eight senators to office. Other provinces have mixed-member districts, which use a combination of single-member districts, multimember districts, and at-large districts.

The substantial variation in district size between the Argentine legislative chambers results in sizable variation in partisan constraints.[7] This variation,

[7] In my sample, district size (and thus party constraints) varies somewhat within chambers. Most variation, however, occurs between chambers. Indeed, thirteen of the chambers in my analysis

moreover, is necessary for me to examine how partisan constraints structure patterns of collaboration with female legislatures. For the purposes of my empirical analysis, I define electoral systems with *strong* party constraints as closed-list systems with *large* district magnitudes (i.e., electoral district size of 9 or larger).[8] I define electoral institutions with relatively *weak* party constraints (hereafter "weak party constraints") as closed-list systems with *small and medium* district magnitudes (i.e., electoral district size ranging from 1 to 8).[9] To evaluate whether women behave differently depending on the institutional context, I analyze and compare the results from two subsamples of data: 1) legislators elected in small and medium districts; and 2) legislators elected in large districts. Analyzing subsamples of my data allows me to easily examine whether increases in women's numeric representation are associated with increased collaboration among women in districts with weak party constraints and decreased collaboration among women in districts with strong party constraints. In addition to these key independent variables, I account for a number of variables that may influence legislators' GCS. There is a complete discussion of these variables in Appendix 5.1 in this chapter.

Empirical Model

Given the nature of my data (i.e., legislators are nested within sessions, which are nested within legislative chambers), I use a hierarchical linear model (HLM), to evaluate legislative cosponsorship. The HLM model allows me to account for unmeasured variation that exists within my data (Gelman and Hill 2007; Rabe-Hesketh and Skrondal 2005).[10] I include a random intercept for each legislative session in order to relax the assumption of independence of errors between the legislators in a given legislative session. I also include a random intercept for each legislative chamber to relax the assumption of independence of errors between legislative sessions in a given chamber.

As previously noted, I analyze two separate models for each specification of the dependent variable. The first model examines legislators elected in small

---

feature no within-chamber variation either because they elect legislators from one at-large district or because all legislators are elected from single-member districts.

[8] This is not to say that party leaders have no influence over legislative behavior in small and medium districts with closed-list systems; rather, relative to districts with large magnitudes, they have less control. If the comparison included open- and unblocked-list electoral systems, I would expect that legislators elected in this type of system with large district magnitudes would have extremely weak party constraints by comparison with those in closed-list systems.

[9] This coding decision is based on logic presented in previous research (Carey and Hix 2011; Carey and Shugart 1995; Shugart, Valdini, and Suominen 2005). Results are not sensitive to this decision; coding medium districts as slightly smaller or larger does not alter my substantive conclusions.

[10] Specifically, I include a random intercept for each legislative session, in order to relax the assumption of independence of errors between the legislators in a given legislative session. Results are robust to estimations using province and year fixed effects and clustered standard errors.

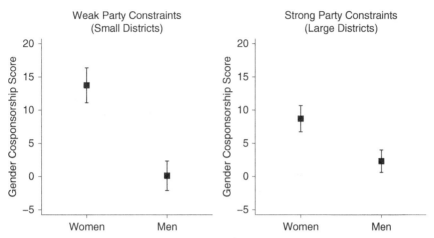

FIGURE 5.4. Chamber-wide collaboration: expected Gender Cosponsorship Score.
Notes: Figure 5.4 graphs the expected GCS on the y-axis for women and on the x-axis for men. All other values are held at their mean. Dummy variables are set to the mode. The point estimates are surrounded by 95 percent confidence intervals. The estimates in the left and right panels are based on Models 1 and 2, respectively, in Appendix 5.3.

and medium districts, and the second examines legislators elected in large districts. I will turn my attention first to chamber-wide cosponsorship behavior and second to cosponsorship that takes place across party lines specifically.

DETERMINANTS OF WOMEN'S CHAMBER-WIDE COLLABORATION

To evaluate support for my argument, I graphed the results from my analysis in Figure 5.4. I calculated the expected value of the GCS for different values of interest while all other values are held at their mean and dummy variables are set to the mode. The point estimates are surrounded by 95 percent confidence intervals. Figure 5.4 graphs the results for small districts on the left panel and for large districts on the right panel.[11]

I argue that under certain circumstances, female legislators have a greater incentive to collaborate with female colleagues than do men. The first step in evaluating this argument is to determine if women behave differently from men. Therefore, Figure 5.4 charts cosponsorship patterns for men (x-axis) and women (y-axis). Recall that the GCS is the difference between the actual rate of cosponsorship and the random probability that a legislator will cosponsor

---

[11] Appendix 5.3 in this chapter provides estimates for the coefficients and standard errors for the HLMs for the GCS for legislators from both small and large electoral districts.

with a female legislator. Negative (positive) values indicate that legislators cosponsor with females at a lower (higher) rate than they would if the cosponsorship process were random. A value of zero indicates that legislators cosponsor with females at the same rate at which they would if cosponsorship were completely random.

We can see from this graph that, on average, the expected GCSs take on positive values for female legislators from districts with both weak party constraints and strong party constraints. By contrast, the expected GCSs for male legislators from districts with weak party constraints are not statistically different from zero, and the GCSs for male legislators from districts with strong party constraints are only slightly above zero. The difference between the expected GCSs for female and that for male legislators is statistically significant in both types of districts, but the magnitude of the difference varies by district type. The difference between women's behavior and men's in districts with weak party constraints is larger than the difference between women's and men's in districts with strong party constraints. Figure 5.4 indicates that the expected GCS in districts with weak party constraints is 13.64 for female legislators and −0.03 for male legislators – a statistically significant difference of 13.67. Similarly, the GCS for representatives in districts with strong party constraints is 9.03 for female legislators and 2.06 for male legislators. This difference of 7.07 is about half the size of the gap between female and male legislators' GCS from districts with weak party constraints.

These broad trends demonstrate a few important points. Female legislators are more likely to cosponsor with their female colleagues than are male legislators. Further, women are more likely to cosponsor with female colleagues than we would expect if they were randomly choosing their cosponsors. This indicates that women are making intentional efforts to cosponsor more frequently with female colleagues. Still, this finding does not mean that male legislators are not likely to cosponsor with female colleagues; rather the figure shows that men are about as likely to cosponsor with female colleagues as they would be if they were randomly choosing their cosponsors. The expected values for male legislators in districts with both weak and strong party constraints are very close to zero, indicating that male legislators do not cosponsor with their female colleagues any less than we would expect if they were choosing their cosponsors randomly. Interestingly, men from small and large districts behave quite similarly to one another. This provides preliminary evidence to suggest that men's chamber-wide collaboration with female colleagues is not structured by party constraints.

It is also clear from this figure that female legislators from districts with weak party constraints and those from districts with strong party constraints behave differently from each other. Figure 5.4 indicates that women behave differently depending on institutional constraints. Specifically, female legislators from districts with strong party constraints behave more similarly to their male colleagues. Recall that the gap between female and male legislators from districts with strong party constraints, as plotted in Figure 5.4, is less than half the size of the gap between male legislators and female legislators from districts with weak party constraints.

My theory posits that all women have an incentive to collaborate more frequently with women than do men but that not all women have the same opportunities to do so. Specifically, women from districts with strong party constraints face more pressure to toe the party line and to behave more similarly to rank-and-file party members. By contrast, women from districts with weak party constraints have more opportunities to work cooperatively with female colleagues. Figure 5.4 shows evidence in support of this argument.

Chamber-wide Collaboration: The Effects of Women's Numeric Representation Conditional on Party Constraints

In addition to institutional incentives, I argue, women's legislative behavior is influenced by the demographic composition of the legislature, conditional on party constraints. I examine this part of my argument in this section. To evaluate how legislative collaboration changes as women's numeric representation increases, I have graphed the results from my analysis in Figure 5.5. I calculated the expected value of the GCS and 95 percent confidence intervals for different values of interest while all other values are held at their mean or mode. I plot the expected values across the range of women's numeric representation. Figure 5.5 shows the results for small districts on the top panel and for large districts on the bottom panel.[12] Specifically, Figure 5.5 charts how men's and women's cosponsorship patterns (y-axis) change as the percentage of women in the chamber increases (x-axis).

It is clear from the figure that women almost always cosponsor more frequently with female colleagues than do men. Moreover, it is apparent that women's propensity to collaborate varies significantly depending on the gender composition of the legislature, but men's propensity to collaborate is relatively constant regardless of women's numeric representation. When women comprise only a small portion of the legislature, all female legislators, regardless of their district type, are more likely to work with female colleagues than we would expect if they were choosing their cosponsors randomly. Figure 5.5 indicates that when women comprise 5 percent of the chamber, the expected GCS is above zero for all women, but as the percentage of women in the legislature increases, women's collaborative behavior changes. To understand how women's behavior changes, it is important to take into account party constraints. As the proportion of women in the chamber increases, women facing strong party constraints behave differently from women facing weak party constraints.

First, consider how women from districts with weak party constraints behave. As the percentage of women in the legislature increases, women facing

---

[12] The estimates in the top and bottom panels are based on Models 1 and 2, respectively, in Appendix 5.3.

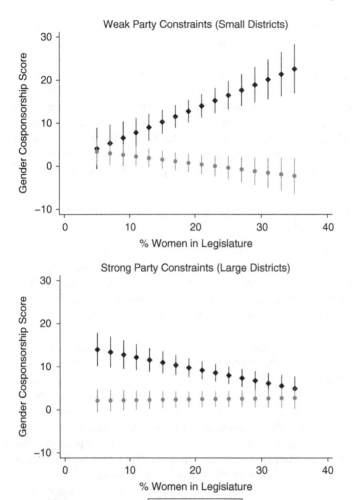

FIGURE 5.5. Chamber-wide collaboration, conditional on women's numeric representation: expected Gender Cosponsorship Score.
Notes: Figure 5.5 graphs the expected GCS on the y-axis and the percentage of women in the legislature on the x-axis. All other values are held at their mean. Dummy variables are set to mode. The point estimates are surrounded by 95 percent confidence intervals. The estimates in the top and bottom panels are based on Models 1 and 2, respectively, in Appendix 5.3.

weak party constraints become more likely to cosponsor legislation with their female colleagues. The left panel in Figure 5.5 shows a strong positive relationship between women's numeric representation and women's GCS. Specifically, it demonstrates that when women comprise 30 percent of the chamber, female legislators from districts with weak party constraints are more than *four times* more likely to cosponsor with female colleagues than are female legislators from the same districts in which women comprise only 5 percent of the chamber. This provides strong evidence in support of my argument that given women's marginalized status in the Argentine legislatures, women collaborate among themselves in an effort to attain political power and exert their influence on the policy-making process. I posit that growths in women's numeric representation raise consciousness among women about their status in the chamber and increase the likelihood that women rally and collaborate among themselves. The analysis in this chapter shows that women who come under weak party pressure are more likely to collaborate as women's numeric representation increases. Indeed, several female legislators have suggested that women collaborate among themselves in an effort to navigate the sometimes chauvinistic legislative environment. As one female legislator put it:

"I would say there is this moral support among women to get through complicated situations that are presented in our *machista* society, where people believe women don't have the ability to lead."[13]

Despite the incentive female legislators have to work together, not all women have the same opportunities to collaborate. Indeed, Figure 5.5 reveals that women from districts with strong party constraints behave very differently than women from districts with weak party constraints. The left panel in Figure 5.5 shows that when women comprise only a small portion of the chamber, they are more likely than their male colleagues to collaborate with other women. Although men are just as likely to collaborate with women as they would be if they were choosing their cosponsors randomly, women are systematically more likely to choose a female cosponsor. Even though these women are subject to strong party pressures, this finding is not surprising. As I explained in Chapter 2, when women comprise only a small portion of the chamber, women's efforts to collaborate are likely to fly under the radar, attracting very little attention from male party leaders. Given women's marginalized status in the legislature, the presence of only a few women does not pose a strong threat to male leaders because they are unlikely to mobilize enough support to bring about change or influence the legislative agenda. Given the relatively benign consequences, party leaders have little incentive to constrain women's behavior; as a result, their legislative behavior goes effectively unchecked. This is consistent with the trend we see in Figure 5.5.

As the percentage of women in the chamber increases, however, women pose a bigger threat to the status quo. Therefore, when institutions allow party leaders to constrain legislative behavior – similar to the situation described in Jujuy at the beginning of this chapter – increases in women's numeric representation are likely to trigger more pressure from party leaders to toe the

---

[13] Interview with female senator from Mendoza, Unión Cívica Radical, June 26, 2013.

party line. Under this pressure, female legislators from large districts have little incentive to collaborate in an effort to ensure their voices are heard in the policy-making process. Because the male-dominated party leadership controls access to resources that are important for career advancement, women have an incentive to cave to party pressures and toe the party line if they want to ensure their future political careers. Consistent with these expectations, Figure 5.5 shows that as the percentage of female legislators in a chamber increases, the rate at which female legislators from districts with strong party constraints work with other female colleagues decreases. In fact, female legislators begin to behave more like their male colleagues. Once women comprise approximately 30 percent of the chamber, they are no more likely to work with other women than are their male colleagues, and the expected value of their GCS nears zero.

These results tell a very compelling story about how institutions structure legislative behavior. Specifically, the results show that when women have more autonomy from party leaders and their behavior is unchecked, their legislative behavior is gendered – they work more frequently with women than do their male colleagues, and their propensity to do so increases as their share in the chamber increases. But when women are subject to extreme party discipline, they behave more like their male colleagues. Taken together, these results provide strong support for my argument that 1) given women's marginalized status in the chamber, they have an incentive to collaborate more frequently with women to attain political power; 2) institutions that foster weak party constraints permit women's collaboration to unfold, whereas institutions that concentrate power in the hands of party leaders constrain women's legislative behavior and curb their opportunities to collaborate; and 3) in districts with weak party constraints, women's incentive to collaborate with women increases as the proportion of women in the chamber increases and their marginalized status becomes more visible.

DETERMINANTS OF WOMEN'S COLLABORATION
ACROSS PARTY LINES

At this point, I have demonstrated that female legislators from districts with weak party constraints are more likely than men to collaborate with female colleagues, and that their propensity to do so increases as the percentage of women in the chamber increases. My theory also indicates that under some circumstances, women will be more likely than men to cross party lines to collaborate with female colleagues. In this section, I evaluate this part of my argument. It is particularly important to consider collaboration across party lines because most collaboration that occurs in the Argentine provinces is among co-partisans. Unlike collaboration between co-partisans, collaboration between female colleagues in other political parties is more costly because it is clearly distinct from typical partisan behavior. Indeed, female legislators

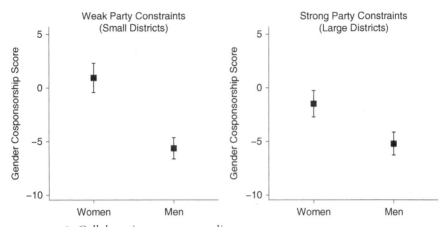

FIGURE 5.6. Collaboration across party lines.
Notes: Figure 5.6 graphs the expected GCS on the y-axis for women and on the x-axis for men. All other values are held at their mean. Dummy variables are set to mode. The point estimates are surrounded by 95 percent confidence intervals. The estimates in the left and right panels are based on Model 3 and 4, respectively, in Appendix 5.3.

collaborating with women from the opposition party may even be viewed as disloyal, particularly in legislatures known for their strong party constraints.

In order to examine the extent to which female legislators cooperate with female colleagues from opposition political parties, I turn to my second dependent variable: the GCS across party lines. Using the same statistical model as before, I examine the extent to which electoral incentives and the gender composition of the chamber influence women's patterns of collaboration.[14] Figure 5.6 graphs the expected value for the GCS across party lines on the y-axis for women and men on the x-axis when all other values are held at their mean or mode.

Recall, the dependent variable for this analysis examines the rate at which legislators collaborate with women from different political parties minus the rate at which they would cross party lines to collaborate if they were choosing their cosponsors randomly. As a result, a value of zero indicates that legislators cross party lines at the same rate as if they selected their cosponsors randomly.

It is evident from Figure 5.6 that men and women do not collaborate with women in other parties at the same rate. The left panel indicates that women from districts with weak party constraints collaborate with women in other parties at a surprisingly high rate. Their expected GCS is 0.98, whereas men's expected GCS is –5.66. That is, women from small districts cross party lines to

[14] Appendix 5.3 in this chapter provides estimates for the coefficients and standard errors for the HLMs for the GCS across party lines for legislators from both small and large electoral districts.

collaborate at the same rate we would expect if they were randomly choosing their cosponsors. This is very high considering that most collaboration takes place among co-partisans. Men, however, are far less likely to cross party lines. The results in the left panel provide support for my argument that women are more willing than men to cross party lines when they face weak party pressure.

A different trend emerges when we consider legislators from districts with strong party constraints (right panel). Here, we see that women's expected GCS is −1.42, whereas men's is −5.31. In these districts, women are less likely to cross party lines to collaborate than we would expect if they were choosing their collaborators randomly, but they are still more willing to do so than are their male colleagues. Further, this figure indicates that men's behavior is similar regardless of the level of party constraints they face. That is, all men are unlikely to cross party lines to collaborate with women, whereas women's behavior varies considerably under different levels of party pressure. Nonetheless, these patterns are highly conditional on women's numeric representation.

Collaboration across Party Lines: The Effects of Women's Numeric Representation Conditional on Party Constraints

To consider how women's numeric representation structures legislators' collaboration, Figure 5.7 plots legislators' expected GCS across party lines on the y-axis and women's numeric representation across the x-axis. I graph these values for male and female legislators from districts with weak party constraints on the left panel and for those from districts with strong party constraints in the right panel.[15] The first thing to note is that, as shown in Figure 5.7, I have found that women are (almost always) more likely than men to cross party lines to collaborate with female colleagues. This supports the argument that women have an incentive to collaborate more frequently with female colleagues than do men. Moreover, this finding indicates that women's collaboration goes beyond partisan boundaries – that women do not just collaborate with female co-partisans, but are also more willing than men to cross party lines to collaborate.

Second, my results indicate when a chamber has a relatively small number of women – regardless of party constraints – female legislators are much more willing to cross party lines to cosponsor than we would expect if they chose their cosponsors randomly. Figure 5.7 shows that women's expected GCS (as depicted by the black diamonds) is at or above zero when women comprise less than 15 percent of the chamber. Given that most collaboration in legislatures happens among members from the same political party, this is unexpectedly high. It is surprising to think that in Argentina, a country known for strong party discipline, any legislator would cross party lines to collaborate at such

[15] The estimates in the right and left panels are based on Models 3 and 4, respectively, in Appendix 5.3.

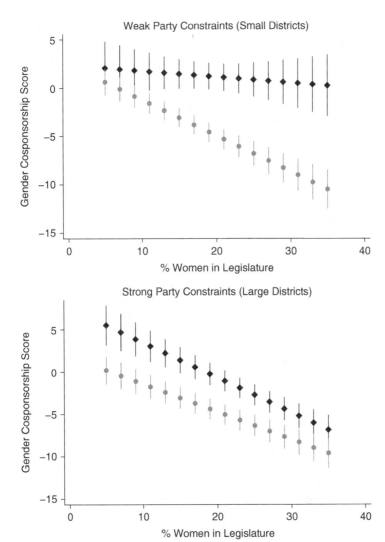

FIGURE 5.7. Collaboration across party lines, conditional on women's numeric representation: expected Gender Cosponsorship Score.
Notes: Figure 5.7 graphs the expected GCS on the y-axis and the percentage of women in the legislature on the x-axis. All other values are held at their mean. Dummy variables are set to mode. The point estimates are surrounded by 95 percent confidence intervals. The estimates in the top and bottom panels are based on Models 3 and 4, respectively, in Appendix 5.3.

a high rate; yet, when they hold a very small share of seats, women from both types of districts cross party lines quite frequently.

Despite these general trends in women's legislative collaboration, the results indicate that women's propensity to collaborate is influenced by both women's numeric representation and the strength of political party constraints. First, I will take a closer look at the collaborative patterns of women from small districts – those with relatively weak party constraints.

Women from districts with weak party constraints behave the same regardless of the proportion of women in the chamber. Figure 5.7 shows women's behavior remains constant as their numeric representation increases. The line for women may appear to have a slight negative slope, but there is no statistical difference in women's behavior between when they occupy 5 percent of seats in the chamber and when they occupy 35 percent of seats. Moreover, women from small districts are just as likely to cross party lines to cosponsor with female colleagues as they would be if they were choosing cosponsors randomly. It is worth repeating that this is an unexpectedly high rate of non-co-partisan collaboration given that under normal circumstances, we would expect representatives to intentionally cosponsor *less* with their colleagues from other parties than if they were choosing cosponsors randomly. Dozens of interviews I conducted in the Argentine provinces with male and female legislators indicated that it is rare to cosponsor with legislators from other parties. One male deputy from Córdoba explains:

"Generally, coauthors are from the same bloc, from the same party. There may be other lawmakers who sign who are from other parties … but it is not common. It is common that people from the same bloc sign the same project."[16]

Nonetheless, data from Argentina indicate that female legislators who are subject to relatively weak partisan pressures cross party lines relatively frequently. Furthermore, when I asked women specifically about working with other women, they told me that it was quite common to cross party lines to collaborate. For instance, a female legislator from the Mendoza Chamber of Deputies, a chamber that uses small electoral districts to elect legislators, states:

"Here, we have a lot of harmony among women. We are capable of going past the partisan barriers to get involved in gender issues."[17]

Her colleague from a different political party also emphasizes women's cooperation and explains that it extends beyond traditional gender issues.

"There is a lot of solidarity among women not only in gender issues but also other issues as well. There is a bigger sense of togetherness."[18]

[16] Interview with male deputy from Córdoba, Unión Cívica Radical, November 11, 2009.
[17] Interview with female deputy from Mendoza, Frente para la Victoria, June 26, 2013.
[18] Interview with female senator from Mendoza, Bloque Nuevo Encontro, June 27, 2013.

Collaboration among female legislators in Mendoza is evident in the legis-lation they sponsor. Women from different political parties work together on a range of issues beyond women's rights, including education, development, tourism, security, and health care, just to name a few. For example, in 2008, a group of four women and one man from three different parties cosponsored legislation to improve citizens' access to clean water in rural areas of Mendoza. The proposed bill created tax exemptions for cooperatives and community associations that manage community water centers. In the same period, a group of four women (from two different parties) introduced legislation aimed at promoting tourism in the province, and a group of three women (also from two different parties) introduced legislation to establish safety regulations in public areas intended for children. Consistent with these examples, the data in this analysis show that women from districts with relatively weak party con-straints are more likely than men to cross party lines to collaborate with other women, and they do so at an unexpectedly high rate.

The same pattern does not hold for men. Men from small districts are fairly likely to work with women from outside their parties when women comprise only about 5 percent of the legislature, crossing party lines at the same rate we would expect if they were randomly choosing their coauthors. As women's share of the chamber increases, however, men become far less likely to work with women outside their political parties. The differences between men's and women's behavior become even more pronounced as the gender composition of the legislature changes.

Turning now to districts with strong party constraints, it is clear that wom-en's tendencies to cross party lines to collaborate are conditional on the gender composition of the legislature. When women comprise only a small share of the chamber, female legislators are fairly likely to collaborate with women out-side of their chamber, but cross-party collaboration among women decreases sharply as the proportion of female legislators increases. When female legisla-tors comprise 15 percent of the chamber, the expected GCS for female legisla-tors in large districts drops well below zero. This result illustrates that women become less likely to deviate from the party line – and instead behave more similarly to male colleagues – as the share of women in the chamber increases. That is, both male and female legislators from districts with strong party con-straints become less likely to cross party lines to collaborate with female col-leagues, with female legislators only slightly more likely to do so than their male colleagues. Once women occupy more than 30 percent of the seats in the chamber, women are no more likely to cross party lines to collaborate than are their male colleagues. These findings are consistent with my theory that legislators from large districts face more pressure to toe the party line and to devote their energy to partisan activity. Moreover, this pressure to behave like rank-and-file party members increases as the proportion of women in the chamber increases.

Interviews with Argentine legislators reveal that legislators do face pressures to demonstrate their loyalty to the party leaders. People notice when legislators work with colleagues outside of their parties, and there is pressure not to cross party lines to collaborate. Comments from a female deputy from Catamarca illustrate how partisan pressures constrain legislative behavior:

"I have presented projects with people from the opposition. It is not common. That is why I am criticized sometimes, because they don't understand how I can work with the opposition."[19]

In Catamarca, legislators are elected to the Chamber of Deputies from one at-large district. This large district size concentrates power in the hands of party leaders and fosters strong party loyalty. Women from other provinces have spoken of similar challenges to women's cross-partisan collaboration. A female deputy from the Jujuy, another chamber in Argentina using an at-large electoral district, commented: "We work together in many different things. It is hard, but yes there is a commitment from the women who are in different political parties."[20] She explained that even though there is a commitment among women to collaborate across party lines, this commitment is difficult to fulfill. In legislatures with strong party discipline, like Jujuy, women are more likely to face pressures to devote their time and energy to party-oriented activities. Also of interest, she noted that women's commitment to collaborate is a commitment to not simply promote women's rights, but also to collaborate on a range of issues. Here, comments are consistent with the results from my analysis, which show that under some circumstances, women are more likely than men to collaborate with female colleagues regardless of the issue area. But women's collaboration is clearly constrained as women's numeric representation increases. Indeed, although interviews with women from both large and small districts indicate that female legislators collaborate on a broad spectrum of issues, it is still evident from the results presented here that female legislators from small districts collaborate with female colleagues on a larger share of legislation than do female legislators from large districts.

Finally, it is worth noting that a similar trend emerges for men from districts with both weak and strong party constraints. Figure 5.7 shows that when there are few women in the chamber, men are about as likely to cross party lines to cosponsor with women as we would expect if they were choosing their cosponsor randomly. But, similar to women from districts with strong party constraints, as the proportion of women in the chambers increases, men's propensity to cross party lines sharply declines (as illustrated by the steep negative slope on the lines depicting men's behavior). This trend may be a result of the supply of female coauthors. If, for some reason, a legislator wants to coauthor with a woman and all or most of the women are from different political

[19] Interview with female deputy from Catamarca, Partido Justicialista, November 17, 2009.
[20] Interview with female deputy from Jujuy, Unión Cívica Radical, October 27, 2009.

parties, he/she may have no choice but to cross party lines to collaborate. But as the proportion of women in the chamber increases, legislators have more potential female cosponsors to choose from and, as a result, cross party lines less frequently.

CONCLUSION

This chapter presents several findings that are key to understanding *when women collaborate*. First, on average, women are more likely than men to collaborate with both women in the same political party and women outside their political party. This supports my theory that women have strong incentives to collaborate in an effort to overcome structural barriers in the legislature. Evidence from interviews with female legislators in the Argentine provinces corroborates my empirical analysis and provides face validity to the findings that women have an incentive to collaborate more frequently with other women and that they use cosponsorship as an avenue for doing so.

The second finding to emerge from this chapter shows that despite these incentives, not all female legislators collaborate more than men. Indeed, my analysis demonstrates that although women from small and medium districts devote a considerably higher share of their cooperative efforts to collaborating with female colleagues than do men, women from large districts with strong party constraints behave more similarly to their male colleagues. My theory posits that when institutions permit party leaders more control over legislative behavior, party leaders will limit women's collaboration with female colleagues in the same political party and restrict their efforts to cross party lines. Meanwhile, female legislators who face comparatively weak party constraints come under less party pressure to toe the party line and have more opportunities to work with women both inside and outside of their own political parties. In the case of Argentina, I focus specifically on how district sizes in closed-list systems determine party constraints, which, in turn, structure women's collaboration. Outside of Argentina, variation in a number of different institutions determines party constraints. My theory is generalizable, and as I demonstrate in Chapter 7, the same logic helps us understand why women's collaboration varies between chambers beyond Argentina. This finding is of particular importance because it contributes to both our broader understanding of how institutions structure legislative behavior and a small but growing body of literature that seeks to understand how institutions may impose additional structure on women's legislative behavior (Osborn 2012; Schwindt-Bayer 2010).

Finally, these results show that the gender composition of the chamber does influence the behavior of female legislators but that this relationship is conditioned by institutional incentives. Increases in the proportion of female legislators strengthen women's incentives to toe the party line in districts with strong party constraints and to collaborate with female colleagues in districts with weak party constraints. This analysis provides strong support for the idea that legislative context shapes women's legislative behavior in distinct ways.

The analysis in this chapter is limited to two key legislative contexts that structure women's legislative behavior: party constraints as a product of district size in closed-list electoral systems and women's numeric representation. Although these two factors – which vary largely between legislative chambers – are key to understanding women's legislative behavior in the Argentine context, I posit that other factors that vary *within* legislative chambers should also influence the extent to which women have both opportunities and incentives to collaborate. In the chapter that follows, I examine how legislators' affiliation with the governor, legislators' seniority, and the content of legislation help us further understand *when women collaborate*.

APPENDIX 5.1: CONTROL VARIABLES FOR EMPIRICAL MODELS

In addition to my main variables of interests, I control for a number of factors that may influence legislators' Gender Cosponsorship Scores. In this section, I describe the control variables used in the analysis. First, given that changes in women's numeric representation are typically brought about by the adoption of legislative quotas, I control for the number of years since quotas were implemented. This variable is a count and ranges from 0 to 16. Given that women's numeric representation is believed to shape women's behavior differently than men's, I include an interaction between quota years and sex.[21] Second, I control for affiliation with the governor; recall from Chapter 2 that members of the governor's party may be subject to fewer party constraints. I will test this expectation explicitly in the following chapter; here I simply control for affiliation with the governor in my analysis. Legislators affiliated with the governor are coded 1 and those members not in the governor's party are coded 0.[22] I also

---

[21] District magnitude is another factor known to influence the percentage of women in the legislature. In the Argentine provinces, however, few districts without gender quotas, regardless of the district size, elect a sizable proportion of women. Increases in women's numeric representation in the Argentine provinces are largely due to the adoption of gender quotas. In my sample, the correlation between the percentage of women in the chamber and district magnitude is 0.28. The correlation between the percentage of women in the chamber and the adoption of gender quotas is 0.62. On average, provinces using small districts combined with gender quotas elect women at almost the same rate as provinces using large districts combined with quotas. Related to this point, in Argentina increases in women's numeric representation are best explained by the adoption of gender quotas (Jones 1998). Gender quota laws require that *every party* in *every district* comply with the gender quota to be eligible to compete in elections, thus women are not more likely to be elected in more liberal districts or by more woman-friendly parties (Barnes 2012b).

[22] Additionally, one may think that representatives would be more likely to cosponsor with people they interact with in committees. In the Argentine provinces, legislators serve on several committees, facilitating interaction with a wide range of colleagues on a regular basis. Given that my research design examines individual level legislative behavior, and not the relationship between two legislators, committee assignment is unlikely to influence my results.

control for the use of a sub-party list to elect members to office. This is a variant in the electoral system that is used in some Argentine provinces. Legislators elected with a sub-party list are coded 1 and those elected without a sub-party list are coded 0.

Third, I control for seniority: legislators who served in the previous term are coded 1 and those with no previous experience in the same legislative chamber are coded 0. The vast majority of legislators in Argentine provincial chambers do not serve multiple legislative sessions. Only 22 percent of all legislators served more than one term in my sample. Given the small number of legislators who actually serve multiple terms in office, I control for previous legislative experience in office using a dichotomous variable that distinguishes between individuals who have and have not previously been elected to serve in the provincial chamber. In the following chapter, I examine more carefully how seniority shapes women's legislative collaboration.

Fourth, it is reasonable to assume that women who represent urban and/ or economically developed districts may behave differently from women who represent rural and/or economically depressed districts, so I added a control variable for economic development for each province-year. I measure this using the province-level infant mortality rate (Development), which has been found to correlate strongly with economic development. Fifth, I control for social inequalities between men and women in a given province. It is reasonable to suspect that female legislators may behave differently in provinces with higher levels of gender equality. I measure this variation using the Gender-Related Development Index (GDI), which accounts for gender disparities in life expectancy rates, adult literacy rates, and standards of living such that as disparity increases, GDI decreases. I include an interaction between Development and sex and between GDI and sex to account for the fact that these variables may be more likely to influence women's GCS than men's. Finally, representatives who cosponsor more legislation may be as a matter of course more likely to cosponsor with females, so I include a control variable for the total number of cosponsored bills proposed by each member in each session. The full models for my analysis are presented in Appendix 5.3.

APPENDIX 5.2: ALTERNATIVE SPECIFICATIONS

I find that my results are robust to a number of alternative model specifications. First, my results are robust to the inclusion of control variables that account for individual legislators' political party affiliation. I do not include this control variable in the main model presented in this chapter, however, because I do not have theoretical expectations for how political party would be correlated with women's legislative behavior in Argentina. Some research finds that leftist parties are more hospitable to women in Western Europe (Kittilson 2006, 2011), Latin America (Escobar-Lemmon and Taylor-Robinson 2005), and the United States (Barnes, Branton, and Cassese forthcoming;

Osborn 2012; Palmer and Simon 2006). In the case of the United States, this is largely because parties in the state and national legislatures are organized along a left–right, liberal–conservative ideological continuum (Clark et al. 2009; Poole and Rosenthal 2001; Wright and Birkhead 2014). Despite this, research outside of the United States often finds that leftist parties do not stand out as being more women friendly (Barnes and O'Brien 2015; O'Brien 2015; Wylie 2015a), indicating that these findings are not generalizable to other political party systems. In particular, there is no evidence to suggest that some political parties are more hospitable to women than others in Argentina (Barnes 2012b; Franceschet and Piscopo 2008; Jones 1997, 1998; Lopreite 2012, 2014). To begin with, political parties in Argentina are not organized along a left–right continuum nor do they consistently occupy the same ideological position from year to year, from province to province, or even from legislator to legislator within the same chamber (Jones and Hwang 2005a, 2005b). Over the past two decades, for example, presidents from the Partido Justicialista have occupied multiple ideological positions (Barnes and Jones 2011): President Menem (1989–1999) was conservative, President De la Rúa (2000–2001) a centrist, and President Kirchner (2004–2007) and President Fernández (2008–2015) both progressive. Evidence from elite survey data further underscores this point, as Congress members from the main Argentine parties (i.e., the PJ and the UCR) are "indistinguishable in terms of their ideological self-placement" (Jones and Hwang 2005b, 133). In contrast to the U.S. Congress, political party affiliation in Argentina is not indicative of women's substantive (Franceschet and Piscopo 2008; Lopreite 2012, 2014) or descriptive representation (Barnes and Jones 2011; Jones 1998). For these reasons, I do not have theoretical expectations about how legislators' political party affiliations will influence their patterns of collaboration. Future research, however, should consider the ways ideology shapes women's propensity to collaborate with other women.

Second, Models 3 and 4 are robust to the inclusion of a control variable that accounts for the number of political parties in a given chamber. At first glance it may seem reasonable to think as the number of political parties in the chamber increases, the share of cross-party collaborations will also increase, all else equal. However, the dependent variable in Models 3 and 4 is measured at the individual level and it only takes into account the rate at which legislators are crossing party lines to collaborate with *any female legislators* outside of their party – regardless of their colleagues' party affiliations – minus the rate they would cross party lines to collaborate with women if they were randomly choosing their collaborators. This is important because increases in the share of female legislators outside of an individual's political party are unrelated to the overall number of parties in the legislature. Moreover, I do not have reason to believe that legislators are more or less likely to cross party lines to collaborate with women if women are from a large number of parties or all from the same opposition party – particularly given that party affiliation is not indicative of legislators' ideology in Argentina (Jones and Hwang 2005b). Given this discussion, it is not surprising that my results are robust to alternative model specifications controlling for the number of political parties in a given chamber.

Finally, although it is often the case that more developed and urban regions have higher district magnitudes compared to less developed and rural regions, in the Argentine provinces, district magnitude is not highly correlated with development or urbanity. Some of the most and least developed provinces elect legislators from at-large districts. Moreover, some legislators in urban centers of Argentina, such as Buenos Aires, are elected using multimember districts, whereas many legislators from rural provinces, such as Chaco, are elected from at-large districts. My results are robust to the exclusion of large chambers – both those with large district magnitudes and those with small district magnitudes – that could potentially drive my results.

APPENDIX 5.3: DETERMINANTS OF GENDER COSPONSORSHIP SCORE

	(1)	(2)	(3)	(4)
	Chamber-wide GCS		GCS Across Party Lines	
	Small	Large	Small	Large
Female	−282.211***	−34.326	−90.042**	−8.057
	(43.280)	(24.176)	(28.002)	(14.258)
Percent Women	−0.184	0.032	−0.378***	−0.339***
	(0.096)	(0.059)	(0.045)	(0.040)
Percent Women X Female	0.813***	−0.328***	0.305***	−0.093*
	(0.137)	(0.076)	(0.088)	(0.045)
Quota Years	0.301	0.138	0.170*	0.114
	(0.182)	(0.134)	(0.084)	(0.091)
Quota Years X Female	−1.187***	0.276	−0.540***	−0.174*
	(0.213)	(0.143)	(0.138)	(0.085)
Development	0.026	0.147	−0.049	0.022
	(0.164)	(0.129)	(0.073)	(0.089)
Development X Female	0.073	−0.095	0.033	−0.104
	(0.216)	(0.147)	(0.139)	(0.087)
GDI	−72.171	−4.405	−40.120	16.190
	(55.250)	(33.163)	(23.221)	(21.433)
GDI X Female	354.234***	59.962*	115.404**	20.621
	(54.265)	(27.449)	(35.102)	(16.189)

(continued)

Appendix 5.3 *(cont.)*

	(1)	(2)	(3)	(4)
	Chamber-wide GCS		GCS Across Party Lines	
	Small	Large	Small	Large
Seniority	0.011	0.123	−0.019	0.539
	(0.643)	(0.521)	(0.414)	(0.307)
Governor's Party	1.911***	2.079***	1.763***	2.250***
	(0.558)	(0.439)	(0.355)	(0.260)
Sub-party List	−1.268	−1.910	0.048	−1.295
	(1.555)	(1.065)	(0.698)	(0.721)
# Bills Authored	0.016**	−0.006*	−0.005	−0.014***
	(0.005)	(0.003)	(0.003)	(0.002)
GDP	0.000	−0.000	0.000**	0.000
	(0.000)	(0.000)	(0.000)	(0.000)
Constant	56.913	1.922	30.598	−13.888
	(44.573)	(28.137)	(18.763)	(18.309)
Random-effects Parameters				
Province	0.868*	0.853**	−0.172	0.328
	(0.365)	(0.277)	(0.509)	(0.306)
Year	1.390***	1.172***	0.439*	0.931***
	(0.115)	(0.110)	(0.175)	(0.091)
Residual	2.525***	2.660***	2.093***	2.130***
	(0.014)	(0.010)	(0.014)	(0.010)
N-Legislators	2497	4738	2497	4738
N-Chambers	12	18	12	18

Standard errors in parentheses. * $p < 0.05$, ** $p < 0.01$, *** $p < 0.001$.

6

When Do Women Collaborate?

Explaining Within-Chamber Variation

> *"Women work together on legislation that affects women. Since everyone has different ideologies and perspectives, we discuss our points of view to develop legislation that better represents women."*
>
> *– Female Deputy, Río Negro, 2009*

In the previous chapter, I showed that factors that vary widely *between* legislative chambers are important for explaining *when women collaborate*. Patterns of collaboration also vary *within* chambers. For instance, many women explain that they are more likely to collaborate with female colleagues when working on women's issues legislation. When asked if women work together, a female deputy from Entre Ríos responded: "Yes, above all partisan differences. We all represent the different parties. We tend to think the same way and agree on the same things, because we believe in this process of generating and carrying out women's rights."[1] Similarly, in Río Negro, women look beyond partisan divisions in order to achieve common goals. As one deputy reflected, "we work together, we work with our colleagues in our party, and with other parties."[2]

Collaboration among women on women's issues legislation ranges from crafting legislation to participating in debates, organizing meetings, and contributing to discussions about policies. To illustrate, a female deputy explained that in Salta, legislators from all different parties get together to address women's issues. They establish relationships with women outside of the legislature to get input on the development of legislation designed to promote women's rights. When asked how women have made progress over time, she responded: "With a lot of fight and with the unification of women presenting projects in the chamber. There were women in the chamber who took charge

---

[1] Interview with female deputy from Entre Ríos, Frente para la Victoria, July 16, 2013.
[2] Interview with female deputy Río Negro, Unión Cívica Radical, December 9, 2009.

and fought for their projects to be approved."[3] Women from across Argentina maintain that collaboration has important implications for women's abilities to influence the policy-making process.

In addition to women's issues legislation, I posit that other legislative contexts that vary within chambers also influence when women collaborate. Specifically, three factors that vary significantly within the Argentine legislatures should influence women's collaboration: 1) affiliation with the governor; 2) seniority status; and 3) women's issues legislation.[4] In this chapter, I empirically investigate how these three factors structure legislative collaboration.

GOVERNOR'S PARTY AND WOMEN'S LEGISLATIVE COLLABORATION

I begin with my investigation of how affiliation with the governor shapes women's propensity to collaborate with female colleagues. In Chapter 2, I explained that the governor has both the incentive and resources necessary to promote the governing party's reputation and policy agenda. As a result, members of the governor's party have less incentive to collaborate to promote their party. Thus, *overall levels* of collaboration are lower among legislators affiliated with the governor's party than among those in opposition. Indeed, in Chapter 3, I showed evidence that opposition party members collaborate more frequently than do members of the government. This same trend holds when we look specifically at women's legislative collaboration. The average female legislator from the governor's party cosponsored forty-seven bills in a session. In contrast, the average female legislator from the opposition party cosponsored eighty-five bills – almost twice as many as women from the governor's party. Women from the governor's party also work with far fewer colleagues when coauthoring legislation: They have an average of 193 cosponsors per session, whereas women from the opposition party have an average of 364 cosponsors per session. On the whole, it is clear that women from the governor's party are less likely to collaborate than are women from the opposition. This is consistent with my expectation that legislators who are out of power will collaborate more frequently.

Although legislators from the governor's party have less incentive to collaborate – and as a result collaborate less frequently than do members of the opposition – they also face weaker pressures from party leaders and have fewer obligations to promote their party than do members of the opposition. Therefore, when legislators from the governor's party do collaborate, they have

---

[3] Interview with female deputy from Salta, Frente para la Victoria, July 10, 2013.

[4] Recall that in Chapter 2, I argued that membership in women's issues committees or women's caucuses should also increase women's collaboration. Variation across the Argentine provinces is not sufficient to allow for systematic examination of this expectation here. I therefore return to the issue of women's caucuses and women's issues committees in Chapter 7.

more flexibility to choose those with whom they will work. This implies that women from the governor's party have more opportunities to collaborate with women in their own party. Thus, in Chapter 2, I explained that when women do collaborate, I expect women from the governor's party will be more likely than women from the opposition party to work with women. In contrast, total levels of collaboration are higher among opposition legislators, but women from the opposition come under more party pressures and are more compelled to use their collaborative efforts to promote the *party's* agenda than are women from the ruling party. Thus, I expect that *when women from the governor's party collaborate, they are more likely than women from the opposition party to collaborate with female co-partisans.*

The logic for this argument is based on research on presidents that shows that the chief executive has all the necessary resources and incentives to advance the party's political agenda and promote the party's reputation (Crisp et al. 2004a; Payne, Zovatto, and Díaz 2007; Mainwaring and Shugart 1997). This frees legislators from the executive's party to devote their energy and resources elsewhere (Nielson and Shugart 1999; Shugart 2001; Shugart and Carey 1992). The same logic applies for governors in the case of Argentina. Each of the provinces in Argentina patterns its own constitution after the national constitution, and executives in every province have similar authority and access to the resources that allow them to promote their parties' agendas. Governors are the most powerful politicians in each province. They wield considerable influence over provincial-level public policy, having the ability to introduce legislation and the authority to disburse government funds (Jones 2008; Jones et al. 2002). Numerous interviews with provincial legislators in Argentina confirm the prevailing view that at the provincial level, governors possess unparalleled power and directly initiate a large proportion of the governing party's legislative agenda. As one deputy described it, "The executive has the power [to present legislation] and sends the laws that he thinks are necessary.... But more than anything the executive controls the budgetary contribution to the legislature."[5] Given the strong executive power of governors in Argentina, I can easily examine my expectations for how affiliation with the executive influences legislative collaboration more generally using the case of the Argentine provinces.

Empirical Investigation: Governor's Party

In this section, I empirically test my expectations about affiliation with the governor and women's legislative collaboration. To evaluate these expectations, I need variation in the proportion of legislators affiliated with the governor's party. Indeed, this proportion varies significantly within chambers over time and between chambers. Figure 6.1 graphs the average size of the governor's party for each province for the years included in my sample. It is clear from the

---

[5] Interview with female deputy from Mendoza, Frente para la Victoria, June 27, 2013.

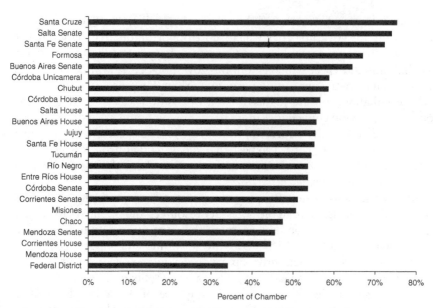

FIGURE 6.1. Percentage of legislators in the governor's party.
Notes: Figure 6.1 graphs the average percentage of seats held by the governor's party
for each chamber in my analysis.

figure that, on average, the governor's party tends to win very large seat shares
in some chambers, whereas in other chambers, the governor's party averages
less than 50 percent of the seats in a given year. In Santa Cruz, for example,
the governor's party holds a majority of seats in every year included in my
analysis. In contrast, in other chambers, the proportion of seats the governor's
party holds tends to be much smaller. In the cases of the Corrientes Chamber
of Deputies, the Mendoza Chamber of Deputies, and the Mendoza Senate, the
governor's party frequently holds less than 50 percent of the seats. The size of
the governor's party within chambers also varies notably over time. In the Salta
Chamber of Deputies, for instance, the governor's party held more than 70 percent of seats from 1996 to 2003. But in 1992 and 2008, the governor's party
held less than 30 percent of seats. This rich variation within the Argentine legislatures is useful for evaluating my argument that women's legislative behavior
varies as a function of affiliation with the governor.

To evaluate my expectation that *when women do collaborate, women from
the governor's party will be more likely than women from the opposition party
to work with women,* I use the same two dependent variables that I utilized in
Chapter 5. I first examine the relationship between affiliation with the governor
and legislators' Gender Cosponsorship Score (GCS). Then I turn to legislators'
Gender Cosponsorship Score-Across Party Lines (GCS across party lines). My
empirical analysis builds on the baseline models from Chapter 5. This model

is appropriate because I need to examine the relationship between women's collaboration and affiliation with the governor's party within the broader legislative context. In Chapter 5, I showed that party constraints and women's numeric representation structure women's legislative collaboration. Thus, by using the model I developed in Chapter 5, I can explicitly account for these two important legislative contexts when evaluating my expectations about how affiliation with the governor's party influences collaboration. Specifically, by examining subsets of my sample, as I did in Chapter 5, I can examine whether the factors that vary within legislative chambers have similar influences on women's legislative collaboration in districts with strong party constraints (i.e., districts with large district magnitudes) and in districts with weak party constraints (i.e., districts with small district magnitudes). Moreover, by examining the interplay between affiliation with the governor's party and women's numeric representation, I can account for the effect of women's numeric representation on legislative collaboration.

The baseline model from Chapter 5 already includes a variable that accounts for affiliation with the governor's party. Here, I use a series of interaction terms to evaluate the effects of affiliation with the governor's party on women's legislative collaboration. First, I use an interaction term between affiliation with the governor and the sex of the legislators to examine how affiliation with the governor influences women's collaboration differently from the way it influences men's. Then, to evaluate the interplay between affiliation with the governor and women's numeric representation, I use an interaction term between affiliation with the governor and the percentage of women in the chamber and a three-way interaction between these three variables.[6] I examine the Gender Cosponsorship Score (GCS) for the entire chamber and GCS across party lines using the same estimation technique as before. The results for this analysis are reported in Figures 6.2 and 6.3. The complete table of coefficients is available in Appendix 6.1 in this chapter.

Results: Governor's Party and Chamber-wide Collaboration

To gain a clear understanding of how affiliation with the governor influences women's legislative collaboration, I calculate the expected value of legislators'

---

[6] Another important contextual factor that would be interesting to evaluate is whether the gender of the governor influences collaboration with female legislators. Unfortunately, I cannot test this question empirically in the present analysis as there are no female governors in my sample. To date, there have only been three female governors in Argentina – Fabiana Rios in Tierra del Fuego (2007–present), Lucia Corpacci in Catamarca (2011–present), and Claudia Ledesma Abdala de Zamora in Santiago del Estero (2013–present). Two of these women came to power after my sample ended, and Tierra del Fuego (a chamber of only twelve members) was excluded from my sample selection owing to the chamber size. As women increasingly take on executive power, however, studying the relationship between an executive's gender and other contextual variables would be an interesting extension of this research.

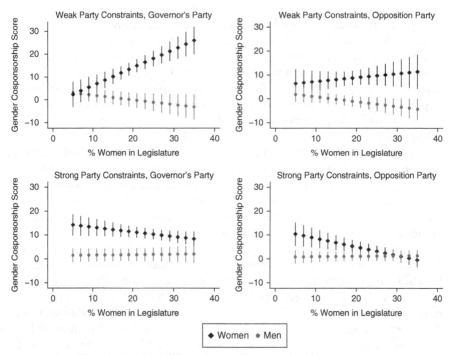

FIGURE 6.2. Chamber-wide collaboration: affiliation with the governor.
Notes: Figure 6.2 graphs the expected GCS on the y-axis and the percentage of women in the legislature on the x-axis. All other values are held at their mean. Dummy variables are set to 0. The point estimates are surrounded by 95 percent confidence intervals. The estimates in the top and bottom panels are based on Models 1 and 2, respectively in Appendix 6.1.

GCS for different values of interest in my sample. Figure 6.2 graphs the expected value of women's and men's GCS on the y-axis and the percentage of women in the chamber on the x-axis for four different groups of legislators: 1) governor's party legislators facing weak party constraints; 2) opposition legislators facing weak party constraints; 3) governor's party legislators facing strong party constraints; and 4) opposition legislators facing strong party constraints. Recall that the GCS measures the difference between the actual rate of cosponsorship and the random probability that a legislator will cosponsor with a woman. Negative (positive) values indicate that legislators cosponsor with women at a lower (higher) rate than they would if the cosponsorship process were random. A value of zero indicates that legislators cosponsor with women at the same rate at which they would if cosponsorship were completely random.

The general trend in my results is consistent with the broad patterns seen in Chapter 5. Figure 6.2 shows that women facing strong party constraints (bottom panel) behave more similarly to their male colleagues than do women from districts with weak party constraints (top panel). As in Chapter 5, the magnitude of this relationship changes as women's numeric representation increases such that women from districts with weak (strong) party constraints are more (less) likely to collaborate with women as women's numeric representation increases. Nonetheless, it is also evident from the figure that affiliation with the governor's party has a substantial impact on women's legislative collaboration.

In districts with weak party constraints (top panel), women are far more likely than men to collaborate with women – particularly those women who are affiliated with the governor's party. The left panel shows that when women comprise a small share of the legislature, men and women from the governor's party behave similarly. As the proportion of women in the chamber increases, women become increasingly likely to collaborate with female colleagues and men become slightly less likely to do so. As a result, the difference between men's and women's expected GCS increases, such that when women hold 35 percent of seats in the chamber, female legislators' expected GCS is twenty-nine points higher than men's.

The same general trend is present among legislators from the opposition. Nevertheless, the magnitude of the relationship between women's numeric representation and legislators' GCS is much weaker for opposition women. In this case, when women comprise 35 percent of the chamber, the difference in men's and women's expected GCS is only fifteen points. The gap is half the size of the gap observed between men and women from the governor's party. These differences are due almost entirely to differences in women's behavior. In contrast, men from the opposition behave very similarly to men from the governor's party: Their GCS is largely unaffected by their affiliation with the opposition. Men do not face strong incentives to collaborate with women; therefore, their tendency to do so does not vary as a function of affiliation with the governor.

A comparison of the two graphs indicates that women from the governor's party behave differently from women from the opposition party. Specifically, at high levels of women's numeric representation, women from the governor's party are *more than twice* as likely to collaborate with female colleagues than are women from the opposition. When women hold 30 percent of the seats in the chamber, the expected GCS is about twenty-five for women from the governor's party but only ten for women from the opposition parties. According to my theory, these differences emerge because women from the governor's party come under less party pressure to toe the party line and have more freedom to pursue their own legislative agendas. Women from the governor's party therefore collaborate among themselves to attain more political power and increase their influence in the policy-making process. In contrast, women from the opposition party behave more similarly to their male colleagues because they face more pressure to represent the party's interest and advance the party's agenda by participating in party-oriented behaviors.

It is evident from the figure that affiliation with the governor's party also exerts an influence on women's collaboration in districts with strong party constraints (bottom panel). Women from the governor's party are more likely than men to collaborate with female colleagues. The bottom left panel indicates that women's propensity to collaborate with women decreases slightly as women's numeric representation increases, but women's behavior remains distinct from their male colleagues regardless of women's numeric representation. Even when women hold 35 percent of the seats in the chamber, women's GCS is about eight points higher than men's GCS. The behavior observed here is consistent with my theory that women from the governor's party come under less partisan pressure than do women in opposition and instead are afforded more legislative autonomy, which they use to collaborate with female colleagues.

Women from the opposition parties, in contrast, behave more similarly to their male colleagues. The bottom right panel shows that when women comprise only a small share of the chamber, women from the opposition party are more likely than men to collaborate with female colleagues. But as women's numeric representation increases women become less and less likely to collaborate with female colleagues, to the point that their behavior becomes indistinguishable from that of their male colleagues. This pattern supports my argument that members of the opposition are more likely to exert their legislative efforts to engage in party-oriented behavior and to behave similarly to other rank-and-file members.

Together, the top and bottom panels in Figure 6.2 show women from the governor's party are more likely than women from the opposition party (and men) to collaborate with women in their own party. These results provide strong support for my expectations and illustrate how affiliation with the executive party – an important contextual factor that varies within virtually every legislature – influences women's behavior. In the next section, I continue my investigation of how affiliation with the governor shapes collaboration by examining patterns of collaboration across party lines.

Results: Governor's Party and Collaboration across Party Lines

Although affiliation with the governor's party is important for understanding when women will collaborate, my theory indicates that women who share affiliation with the governor should not cross party lines to collaborate with women more frequently than women from the opposition. Figure 6.3 graphs the expected GCS across party lines (y-axis) as women's numeric representation increases (x-axis) for legislators from districts with weak party constraints in the top panel and legislators with strong party constraints in the bottom panel. Women in the governor's party are depicted in the left panel and women from the opposition are depicted in the right panel.

The figures demonstrate that affiliation with the governor's party is not important for understanding when women will cross party lines. Women from the governor's party cross party lines at the same rate as women from the opposition. Party constraints are more important than affiliation with the

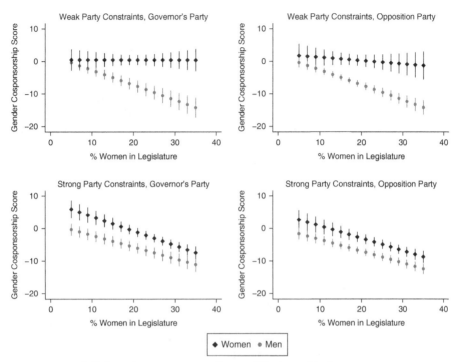

FIGURE 6.3. Collaboration across party lines: affiliation with the governor.
Notes: Figure 6.3 graphs the expected GCS on the y-axis and the percentage of women in the legislature on the x-axis. All other values are held at their mean. Dummy variables are set to 0. The point estimates are surrounded by 95 percent confidence intervals. The estimates in the top and bottom panels are based on Models 1 and 2, respectively, in Appendix 6.1.

governor's party for explaining cross-party collaboration. The top panel illustrates that among those women facing weak party constraints, women from the governor's party are no more likely to cross party lines to collaborate with female colleagues than are women from the opposition party. Affiliation with the governor is also not important for understanding when women will cross party lines to collaborate in districts with strong party constraints (bottom panel). Women behave similarly to one another, and similarly to their male colleagues, regardless of their affiliation with the governor's party. Consistent with my theory, Figure 6.3 illustrates that party constraints are more important than affiliation with the governor's party for understanding legislators' collaboration with women outside their party.

In sum, affiliation with the governor's party is key to understanding collaboration among women. The results presented in this section demonstrate support for my expectation that female legislators from the governor's party are more likely than women from the opposition party to collaborate with women. Women from the governor's party spend a large share of their collaborative efforts working with women; by comparison, women from the opposition party behave more similarly to their male colleagues. This finding is important because most work on legislative behavior has considered how electoral systems and legislative rules structure such behavior but has not considered the important role of affiliation with the executive;[7] yet the results here clearly indicate that affiliation with the governor is important for understanding legislative behavior and should be taken into account in future studies of both women in politics and legislative behavior more generally.

SENIORITY AND WOMEN'S LEGISLATIVE COLLABORATION

Seniority is another important factor for understanding when women will collaborate. In Chapter 2, I identified multiple reasons for senior women legislators' greater propensity for collaboration with female colleagues relative to junior women legislators. Senior women may be more willing to help newcomers learn to navigate the legislative process. In doing so, they are likely to engage in more formal collaboration such as cosponsorship and informal collaboration such as mentoring. Moreover, women with previous experience in the same chamber have likely developed professional networks with other women during previous terms, making them more likely than junior women to cross party lines to collaborate. Finally, senior women may be more willing than junior women to defy party norms by cosponsoring with women outside their own political parties. For these reasons, I expect that *female legislators with seniority are more likely than junior women to collaborate with female colleagues both in their own parties and in other political parties.*

Empirical Investigation: Seniority

In this section, I empirically investigate the relationship between seniority status and collaboration. To evaluate my argument, I need variation in deputies' legislative experience. In Argentina there are no term limits. As a result, legislators can run for reelection as many times as they like. Nonetheless, similar to the National Congress in Argentina, there is not a strong norm that deputies stand for reelection. Even after a gender quota has been in place for a long period of time, a large share of the female legislators serving in a given legislative session are new members. In contrast to other chambers such as the U.S. House and Senate and the Chilean House and Senate, where the norm is for legislators to seek and win reelection, a relatively small proportion of legislators in Argentina have served a previous term in office. As a result of the high legislative turnover in Argentina, the number of legislators who have served

---

[7] For a notable example, see Crisp et al. 2004a.

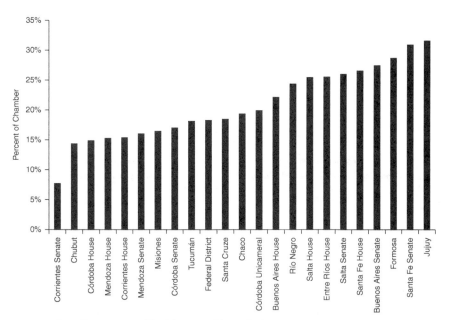

FIGURE 6.4. Percentage of legislators with seniority.
Notes: Figure 6.4 graphs the average number of legislators with seniority status (i.e., legislators serving their second term or more) for each chamber in my analysis.

previous terms in office varies considerably. Nonetheless, few legislators in Argentina go on to serve more than two terms. For this reason, to test my arguments about the role of seniority, I differentiate between legislators who have and have not previously held office.[8] Figure 6.4 shows the average number of members who served a previous term in office (y-axis) for each chamber in my sample (x-axis). The share of senior legislators varies from a low of 7 percent in the Corrientes Senate to a high of 32 percent in Jujuy. Overall, 22 percent of legislators served a previous term in the average chamber in my sample. I leverage this variation within the Argentine chambers to evaluate my expectations.

As with the previous analysis in this chapter, I build on the baseline model from Chapter 5 to evaluate my expectations. Recall that this allows me to explicitly take into account contextual factors that vary between provinces (i.e., party constraints and women's numeric representation) when evaluating the relationship between seniority and collaboration. In this analysis, legislators who served in the previous legislative term are coded 1 for the seniority variable, and first-term legislators are coded 0. Similar to the previous analysis, I use a three-way interaction term to investigate the effects of seniority.

---

[8] Measuring legislative seniority as a count variable does not change my results. The results are substantively and statistically robust to this decision.

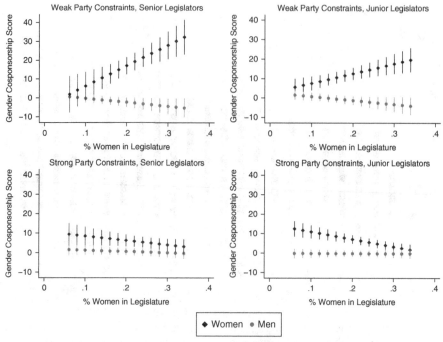

FIGURE 6.5. Chamber-wide collaboration: seniority.
Notes: Figure 6.5 graphs the expected GCS on the y-axis and the percentage of women in the legislature on the x-axis. All other values are held at their mean. Dummy variables are set to 0. The point estimates are surrounded by 95 percent confidence intervals. The estimates in the top and bottom panels are based on Models 1 and 2, respectively, in Appendix 6.2.

To examine how senior women behave compared with senior men, I inter-act seniority with the sex of the legislators. Then, to evaluate the interplay between seniority and women's numeric representation, I use an interaction term between seniority and percentage of women in the chamber, as well as a three-way interaction between seniority, sex, and percentage of women in the chamber. These results for the seniority model are presented in Figures 6.5 and 6.6. The table of coefficients can be found in Appendix 6.2.

Results: Seniority and Chamber-wide Collaboration

I first discuss the results for chamber-wide collaboration. To facilitate the inter-pretation of my analysis, I graph the expected value of the GCS (y-axis) and women's numeric representation (x-axis) in Figure 6.5. The figure represents four groups of legislators: 1) senior legislators from districts with weak party constraints; 2) junior legislators from districts with weak party constraints;

3) senior legislators from districts with strong party constraints; and 4) junior legislators from districts with strong party constraints. The general trends from this figure show that the legislative features that vary between chambers – specifically party pressure and women's numeric representation – shape patterns of legislative collaboration in predictable ways. The relationships shown here are consistent with the overall results presented in the previous chapter and in the previous analysis in this chapter. Still, Figure 6.5 offers a more nuanced view of how factors that vary within chambers – in this case, legislative seniority – structure collaboration.

First, I consider variation in legislative collaboration between senior and junior women from districts with weak party constraints. The top panel graphs the expected GCS for women and men from districts with weak party constraints. Both figures exhibit similar trends. When women comprise only a small share of the chamber, both senior and junior women cosponsor with female colleagues at the same rate as their male counterparts, with their expected GCSs just above zero (1.69 for senior women and 3.91 for junior women). As women's numeric representation in the chamber increases, women's expected GCSs increase and become significantly different from those of men's. Nonetheless, it is evident from the figure that the magnitude of this relationship is stronger for women with seniority status than for their junior female colleagues. When women comprise a large share of the chamber (around 35 percent), women with seniority status have an expected GCS of 29.27 – more than thirty-four points higher than their male counterparts. By comparison, junior women have an expected GCS of 18.75 – twenty-two points higher than their male colleagues. These results show that senior women are more likely to collaborate with women than both men and their junior female colleagues.

Turning next to legislators in districts with strong party constraints (bottom panel), senior and junior women behave similarly to one another when women make up a small share of the chamber, but slight differences emerge when women make up a large share of the chamber. Specifically, women from districts with strong party constraints are slightly more likely than their male colleagues to collaborate with women when women comprise a small share of the chamber seats. Women's propensity to collaborate with women decreases as their numeric representation increases and their behavior becomes more similar to their male colleagues. This general trend characterizes the behavior of both senior and junior women, but interesting differences emerge where women comprise a larger share of the chamber. Specifically, when women make up 30 to 35 percent of the chamber, junior women are no more likely to collaborate with female colleagues than are their male counterparts. To illustrate, when women hold 35 percent of the seats in the chamber, the expected GCSs for junior legislators (both men and women) are not significantly different from zero, indicating that they are no more likely to cosponsor with female colleagues than if they were randomly choosing their cosponsors. The same holds for senior men. Senior women, however, behave differently. When women comprise 35 percent of the chamber, senior women have an expected GCS of 6.5 and the confidence intervals do not cross zero, indicating that senior women are systematically more likely to collaborate with female colleagues than if they were randomly choosing their cosponsors. Moreover, this trend for senior women holds regardless of the gender composition in the chamber. Finally, the bottom panel in Figure 6.5 shows that men's legislative behavior is unaltered by increases in women's numeric representation or their own seniority status. Men are always about as likely to collaborate with women as they would be if they were randomly choosing their cosponsors.

Overall, the results from Figure 6.5 indicate that senior women are more likely than junior women to collaborate with women. But the effect of seniority is much stronger in districts with weak party constraints (top panel) than in districts with strong party constraints (bottom panel). This suggests that in districts with strong party constraints, substantial party pressures constrain even senior women's propensity to collaborate. These results are important because they suggest that women with seniority status take the lead in encouraging collaboration among women. My theory states that senior women may be more likely to establish relationships with and mentor newcomers and to help them learn how to navigate the legislative process. Similarly, a female senator from Mendoza explains: "I believe that you need to understand the dynamics and get to know the practical rules of a place. When I started, it was the other women who taught me and guided me."[9] Thus, it appears that senior women may be more likely to promote both formal (e.g., bill cosponsorship) and informal (e.g., mentoring) types of collaboration among women in the chamber. Although the role of senior women is consistent between political contexts, the magnitude of collaboration with other women is contingent upon partisan constraints and the percentage of women in the chamber.

Results: Seniority and Collaboration across Party Lines

My theory also explains that senior women will be more likely than junior women to cross party lines to collaborate with other women. Figure 6.6 graphs legislators' propensity to cross party lines to collaborate. This figure is organized in the same manner as the previous figure. The top panel graphs the expected GCS across party lines for women and men from districts with weak party constraints and the bottom panel graphs the results for women and men from districts with strong party constraints. A few general trends are apparent from this figure. To begin with, the top panel shows that, regardless of their seniority status, when women comprise a small share of the chamber (around 5 percent of all legislators), they are about as likely to cross party lines to collaborate with female colleagues as they would be if they were randomly choosing their cosponsors. Recall that this is a high rate given that most

[9] Interview with female senator from Mendoza, Unión Cívica Radical, June 27, 2013.

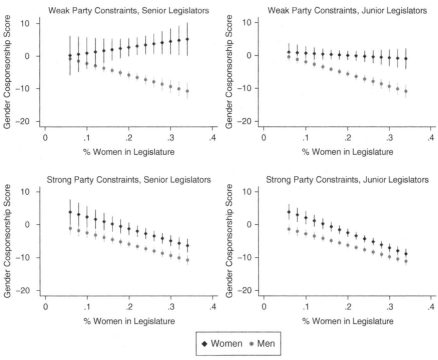

FIGURE 6.6. Collaboration across party lines: seniority.
Notes: Figure 6.6 graphs the expected GCS on the y-axis and the percentage of women in the legislature on the x-axis. All other values are held at their mean. Dummy variables are set to 0. The point estimates are surrounded by 95 percent confidence intervals. The estimates in the top and bottom panels are based on Models 1 and 2, respectively, in Appendix 6.2.

cosponsorship takes place within party lines. Further, the figure shows that as women's numeric representation increases, both senior and junior men become less likely to cross party lines. But women behave differently from their male counterparts. Specifically, as women's numeric representation increases, senior women become slightly *more* likely to cross party lines to collaborate. When women hold more than 20 percent of seats in the chamber, my model predicts that senior women will become more likely to cross party lines to collaborate than they would be if they were randomly choosing their cosponsors. By contrast, junior women's behavior is relatively constant regardless of women's numeric representation. My theory explains that previous legislative experience will likely result in a larger professional network, providing senior women with more opportunities to develop relationships across party lines. It is also probable that legislators with seniority status are more willing to challenge party bosses by crossing party lines more frequently.

Finally, the bottom panel in Figure 6.6 suggests that seniority does not motivate collaboration across party lines among women in districts with strong party constraints. The figure shows that senior women from districts with strong party constraints are no more likely to cross party lines than are their junior colleagues. On average, we see that both senior and junior women are slightly more likely to cross party lines to collaborate than are their male colleagues; but all women, regardless of their seniority status, behave fairly similarly to their male colleagues. The results from my analysis show that strong party constraints in large districts trump the effect of seniority. Consistent with these results, a female deputy in Entre Ríos – a chamber in which members are elected from one at-large district and thus face strong party constraints – explains that the only female legislator in her chamber with previous legislative experience is from another political party. As a result, she is not likely to collaborate with the women from other parties regardless of her seniority status. As she put it: "Since she is from another bloc, politics come into play."[10]

In sum, it appears that seniority status is important for understanding women's collaboration, but it is necessary to consider the relationship between seniority and the broader legislative context to understand when collaboration is most likely to occur. Party constraints and women's numeric representation are key for understanding collaboration, and these factors moderate the effects of seniority. Specifically, senior women from districts with weak party constraints become more likely than men to collaborate with female colleagues as women's numeric representation increases, and they are more willing to cross party lines than their male counterparts. By contrast, women from large districts – those with the strongest party constraints – behave more similarly to their male colleagues as the proportion of women in the chamber increases, regardless of their seniority status. Moreover, party constraints and women's numeric representation moderate women's propensity to cross party lines to collaborate. Senior women facing weak party constraints are slightly more likely to collaborate than their junior colleagues. But senior women facing strong party constraints are no more likely to collaborate than junior women. Instead, all women from districts with strong party constraints behave similarly to their male colleagues, indicating that political and institutional contexts structure women's legislative behavior.

WOMEN'S ISSUES AND WOMEN'S LEGISLATIVE COLLABORATION

The third section of this chapter is dedicated to examining legislative collaboration on women's issues legislation. In Chapter 2, I explained that women are more likely than their male colleagues to prioritize women's issues. Collaboration is particularly beneficial when working on women's issues

---

[10] Interview with female deputy from Entre Ríos, Frente para la Victoria, July 16, 2013.

because these issues have historically been excluded from most legislative agendas and therefore are not fully articulated. Through collaboration, legislators can develop a better understanding of the issues relevant to women and develop legislation that represents a diversity of perspectives. Thus, legislators should be even more inclined to collaborate when working on women's issues. Further, given that women's issues cut across partisan cleavages, women should be particularly inclined to cross party lines to collaborate on this subset of legislation. Beyond this, research shows that although women are interested in discussing issues that disproportionately affect women's lives and do so freely when they are deliberating issues with other women, they are more hesitant to discuss such issues in group settings in which they comprise a minority of the group (Karpowitz and Mendelberg 2014). For these reasons, I expect that women will be even more likely to collaborate with female colleagues when working on women's issues, particularly when women constitute a large percentage of the chamber.

Empirical Investigation: Collaboration on Women's Issues

To assess if women behave differently when they are working on issues that disproportionately influence women's lives, I examine a subset of relevant legislation. I classify legislation as a women's issue if it concerns women's rights and quality of life; women's health; or issues focused on children, family, and youth. Although there is an ongoing debate regarding the definition of women's issues (Escobar-Lemmon and Taylor-Robinson 2014a; Schwindt-Bayer and Taylor-Robinson 2011), I choose this narrow set of issues because there is substantial evidence that in Latin America, and in Argentina in particular, women are more likely to prioritize this subset of issues (Franceschet and Piscopo 2008; Htun, Lacalle, and Micozzi 2013; Htun and Power 2006; Jones 1997; Piscopo 2014a; Schwindt-Bayer 2006, 2010). I do not use the phrase "women's issues" to refer to women's preferences over policies (Beckwith 2011) or assume that women all have the same preferences (Beckwith 2014; Smooth 2011) and priorities (Baldez 2011; Hancock 2014). Nor do I assume that men do not care about this subset of issues. Rather, my primary interest is to gain an understanding of how characteristics that vary within the legislature – in this case different issues on the legislative agenda – motivate women to collaborate across party lines.

On average, approximately 61 percent of Argentine legislators cosponsor women's issues legislation at least once during a two-year legislative period. Specifically, 57 percent of men and 78 percent of women cosponsor a bill in this area. That said, the average number of bills each legislator cosponsors declines significantly when I consider only this subset of legislation. Although the average male legislator cosponsors fifty-one bills per session, only four of these bills address women's issues. Similarly, although women cosponsor an average of sixty-six bills per session, only seven of these bills address women's issues.[11]

As these descriptive statistics make clear, not all women (or men) choose to work on legislation in this area in a given legislative session. Further, as mentioned, the issue coding takes into account only the issue area and not preferences over outcomes. Any legislation pertaining to women's issues, regardless of the intent of the legislation, is included in this analysis. These two points are important to note because women vary in their preferences and advocacy for women's rights (Lopreite 2014; Piscopo 2011). Women may refrain from collaborating on specific issues if the political party opposes efforts to advance the issue (Lopreite 2014). It is important to note, in the Argentine case, this is not driven by *party ideology*, with parties being ideologically weak. They do not tend to take explicit ideological positions on women's rights issues. Instead, any position they take depends on current political party leaders and may vary over time. For example, the Partido Justicialista opposed the expansion of reproductive rights under President Carlos Menem (1989–1999) but strongly supported laws to create a reproductive health program in 2000 (Lopreite 2012, 2014). In Argentina, women's decisions to collaborate on women's issues also vary in terms of women legislators' personal ideas and belief systems, preferences over policy outcomes, and priorities (Barnes 2012b; Piscopo 2011; Schwindt-Bayer 2010). Some women may choose not to work on women's issues because they prefer the status quo, whereas others may prefer the expansion of women's rights but have competing priorities regarding where they choose to devote their time.

This analysis is concerned with understanding collaborative behavior among those legislators who do work on women's issues. I use this subset of women's issues legislation to calculate the *Women's Issues Gender Cosponsorship Score* (GCS). As before, I calculate two dependent variables: one that measures collaboration with women *chamber wide* and one that measures collaboration with women *across party lines*. I use the exact same formula described in Chapter 5 to calculate the Women's Issues GCS in this section. The only difference between the Women's Issues GCS in this section and the GCS in previous sections is that the Women's Issues GCS is calculated for only the subset of legislation that pertains to women's issues.

Figure 6.7 shows the Women's Issues GCS for chamber-wide collaboration across different groups of interest. Similar to the figures showing the distribution of GCS for all issues in Chapter 5, the vertical reference lines in each figure (solid lines for women and dashed lines for men) mark the mean score for each sub-sample. The mean score in the full sample is 10.37. Recall from Chapter 5 that this is much higher than the mean score of 1.7, for all issues. The higher

---

[11] It is worth noting that women do cosponsor more women's issues bills on average than do men. But the difference (an average of three bills per session) is not sufficient to account for the overall gender gap in collaboration (an average of fifteen bills per session). This offers additional support for my argument that women do collaborate on a range of issues, not just on women's issues.

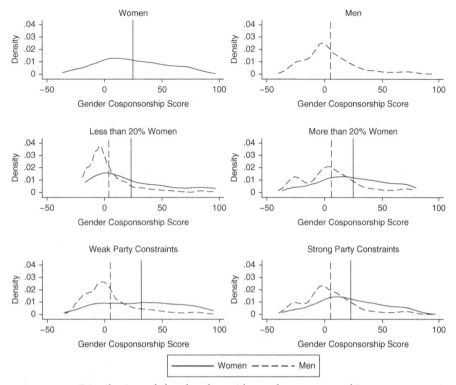

FIGURE 6.7. Distribution of the chamber-wide gender cosponsorship score, women's issues.
Notes: Figure 6.7 graphs the distribution of the women's issues GCS for different groups of interest to my analysis. The vertical references indicate the mean women's issues GCS for each group (solid lines for women and dashed lines for men).

mean for the Women's Issues GCS indicates that all legislators are more likely to collaborate with women when they are working on women's issues than when they are working on other types of legislation.

The mean value for each group in the sample is positive, denoting that when working on women's issues, all legislators are more likely to collaborate with women than they would be if they were randomly choosing their collaborators. This is not surprising given that women in general are more likely to prioritize and author legislation in this issue area. There are, however, interesting differences between different groups in the sample. For example, the average score in my sample is 24.8 for women and 5.1 for men. This difference is large and statistically significant, indicating that, on average, women have higher Women's Issues GCSs than do men.[12] This is consistent with the general trends presented

[12] All differences in this section are statistically significant at the 99 percent level using a two-tailed t-test.

in Figure 6.7. The distributions for women (and the vertical lines denoting the means) are shifted to the right of the distributions for men in every group depicted in the figure, indicating that, on average, women are more likely than men to cosponsor with female colleagues when working on women's issues. The center panel depicts the distribution by the proportion of women in the chamber. The difference between women's and men's scores is 19.5 in chambers with less than 20 percent women and 18.9 in chambers with more than 20 percent women – the average differences do not change much as women's numeric representation increases. The bottom panel shows the distribution by the strength of party constraints. Similar to the trends observed in Chapter 5, the bottom panel demonstrates that the difference in scores is largest between women and men from districts with weak party constraints. The average score is 31.9 for women and 4.9 for men – an extremely large and statistically significant difference. The gender difference is smaller, but still significant, in districts with strong party constraints. Here, the average score is 22.7 for women and 5.11 for men. As with previous analyses in this book, men's behavior does not vary much across district types, whereas women's behavior does.

Figure 6.8 shows the distribution for the Women's Issues GCS across party lines for women's issues legislation. Recall that this alternative measure of the Women's Issues GCS is calculated in exactly the same way as the first measure, but this time I measure the rate at which legislators *cross party lines to cosponsor with women* minus the rate at which they would cross party lines to cosponsor with women if they were choosing their cosponsors randomly. Again, for this analysis, the legislation in the sample is limited to women's issues.

The average Women's Issues GCS across party lines in my sample is –3.1, indicating that most legislators cross party lines to cosponsor with female colleagues at a lower rate than they would if they were choosing their cosponsors randomly. This is expected, given the partisan nature of cosponsorship. Still, the average is slightly higher than the average value of the GCS across party lines for the *full sample of legislation* as shown in Chapter 5. Figure 6.8 also shows interesting differences between women's and men's average scores. Overall, men's average score (–5.3) is lower than women's score (2.9) – a statistically significant difference of 8.3.[13] In each of the subsamples examined in my data, the men's average score is lower than that of women. When women hold less than 20 percent of the seats in a legislature, both men (–1.4) and women (7.5) have higher average scores than the sample mean. But their scores decline to –7.9 for men and 1.8 for women when women hold more than 20 percent of the seats in the chamber.

Finally, the bottom panel of Figure 6.8 shows important differences in Women's Issues GCS across party lines for legislators from districts with weak

---

[13] The differences between women's and men's GCS across party lines reported in this section are all statically significant at the 99 percent level using a two-tailed t-test.

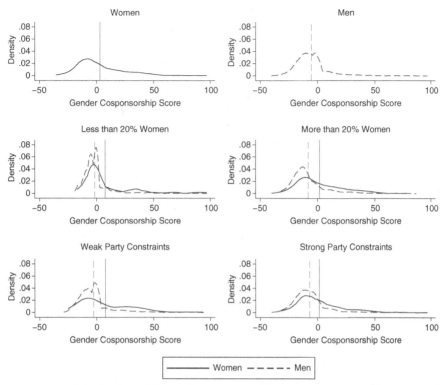

FIGURE 6.8. Distribution of the gender cosponsorship score, across party lines, women's issues.

Notes: Figure 6.8 graphs the distribution of the Women's Issues GCS across party lines for different groups of interest to my analysis. The vertical references indicate the mean Women's Issues GCS across party lines for each group (solid lines for women and dashed lines for men).

and strong party constraints. Both women and men from districts with weak party constraints are more likely to cross party lines to collaborate with women on women's issues than are legislators from districts with strong party constraints. Despite these differences, the gap between men's and women's behavior persists across the different subsamples presented in Figure 6.8.

Together, Figures 6.7 and 6.8 illustrate a few important points. First, all legislators are more likely to collaborate with female colleagues when they are working on women's issues legislation. The average Women's Issues GCS for men and women is higher than the GCS for all legislation shown in the previous chapter. This may be due to the fact that, on average, women are more likely to introduce legislation related to women's issues. Second, significant differences exist between men's and women's collaborative patterns. As expected, women are more likely than men to collaborate with women. Third, women's and men's behavior varies substantially across different subsamples of my data. In the next section, I use these dependent variables (i.e., Women's Issues GCS and Women's Issues GCS across party lines) to test my expectations that women will be more likely to collaborate with female colleagues when working on women's issues legislation and to evaluate how this relationship varies as a function of important legislative contexts.

To examine legislators' propensity to collaborate with female colleagues on women's issues, I again use the baseline model developed in Chapter 5. As with my analyses of other legislative factors that vary *within* chambers, I expect contexts that vary between chambers – specifically partisan pressures and women's numeric representation – will also structure women's legislative behavior. For this reason, the model I used in the previous chapter is appropriate to examine my expectations about collaboration on women's issues. The only difference in the model presented here and that presented in Chapter 5 is that the latter takes into account legislative collaboration on *all issues*. In the following analyses, I focus exclusively on *women's issues*. As I explained previously, fewer legislators cosponsor legislation in this area; thus, there are fewer observations in the analysis. The results for the analysis on women's issues are reported in Figure 6.5. The complete table of coefficients can be found in Appendix 6.3.

Results: Women's Issues and Chamber-wide Collaboration

The top panel of Figure 6.5 graphs legislators' expected Women's Issues GCS for chamber-wide collaboration. It is clear from the top panel in Figure 6.5 that all legislators, regardless of their sex or district size, are more likely to coauthor with a female colleague when working on women's issues than they would be if they were choosing their coauthors randomly. The expected Women's Issues GCSs for both men and women are above zero across the entire range of the data. This is interesting because it suggests that both men and women seek out female cosponsors when they are working on women's issues. This seems reasonable when we think about the reasons legislators choose cosponsors. In Chapter 3, I explained that Argentine provincial deputies often choose cosponsors who have similar interests and priorities or who have expertise in the issue at hand. It is therefore not surprising that men and women are both more likely to cosponsor with women when they work on women's issues.

Despite the fact that all legislators are more likely to collaborate with women on women's issues, there are still important differences between men and women, between legislators facing different partisan constrains, and between legislators from chambers with different gender compositions. First, I discuss the behavior of legislators from small districts – those facing relatively weak party constraints. Then, I turn to legislators from large districts.

The top left panel in Figure 6.9 graphs men's and women's expected Women's Issues GCSs for legislators facing weak party constraints. This panel

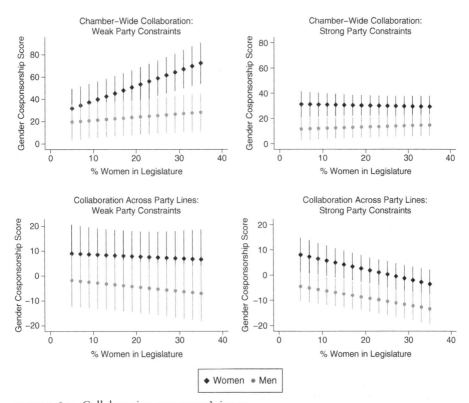

FIGURE 6.9. Collaboration on women's issues.
Notes: Figure 6.9 graphs the expected Women's Issues GCS on the y-axis and the percentage of women in the legislature on the x-axis. All other values are held at their mean. Dummy variables are set to 0. The confidence intervals indicate whether the differences between the expected values are statistically significant at the 95 percent confidence level. The left and right figure in the top panel and the left and right figure in the bottom panel are based on Models 1, 2, 3, and 4 in Appendix 6.3, respectively.

illustrates that men are just as likely as women to collaborate with female colleagues when women comprise a small share of the chamber. As women's numeric representation increases, important gender differences emerge. Consistent with the results from Chapter 5, there is a strong positive relationship between women's numeric representation and female legislators' scores. This indicates that women who face weak party constraints become more likely to collaborate with female colleagues as the proportion of women in the chamber increases. Moreover, the relationship here is much stronger than that observed in Chapter 5, where I examined collaboration on all issues – further supporting my expectation that women are more likely to work with female colleagues when legislating on women's issues. Men's propensity to collaborate with female colleagues, in contrast, remains constant across the entire range of the data, indicating that their score is not structured by women's numeric representation.

The top right panel compares men and women from large districts – those districts with strong party constraints. Similar to the results from Chapter 5, when women comprise a small share of the chamber, women from large districts are more likely to collaborate with female colleagues than are men. But in contrast to the results in Chapter 5, Figure 6.9 shows the relationship between the proportion of women in the legislative chamber and the expected Women's Issues GCS is flat and consistently above zero across the entire range of the data. (Recall from Chapter 5 that women's GCSs decrease as their numeric representation increases.) This indicates that women in districts with strong party constraints are also more likely to collaborate with female colleagues on women's issues than when working on a wider range of legislative issues.

Accounts from numerous interviews with Argentine deputies corroborate this finding. Collaboration on women's issues is particularly important because these issues are often not part of the traditional legislative agenda and cut across multiple class and party cleavages, affecting different groups of women in a variety of ways (Beckwith 2014; Hancock 2014). Collaboration enables legislators to identify the concerns of a broader range of constituents, consider diverse perspectives, and develop legislation that better meets constituents' needs. One deputy from Río Negro explains that this is one reason women find it important to collaborate on women's issues legislation:

"Women work together on legislation that affects women. Since everyone has different ideologies and perspectives, we discuss our points of view to develop legislation that better represents women."[14]

Río Negro employs a mixed-member electoral system that combines small districts with a magnitude of 3 with one at-large district with a magnitude of 19. In Río Negro, most female legislators are elected from the at-large district, where legislators face relatively strong party constraints and have less incentive to exert influence in the legislature. Despite strong party constraints, female legislators see the value in collaborating on this subset of issues.

Examples of collaboration among women on women's issues emerge in chambers across Argentina. In 1994, the National Congress passed the Protection against Family Violence Law, which drew widespread attention to issues of family violence and violence against women. Following the adoption of this law, groups of women in provinces such as Chaco, Córdoba, Río Negro, Misiones, Mendoza, Salta, and Santa Fe formed coalitions within political parties – and in some cases across party lines (e.g., in Río Negro and Santa Fe) – to develop and cosponsor legislation that raised awareness about family violence and to pressure the provincial governments to adopt measures to comply with the national law. Similarly, in Buenos Aires in 2009, four female deputies from Frente para la

---

[14] Interview with female deputy from Río Negro, Unión Cívica Radical, December 9, 2009.

Victoria allied to introduce legislation to create a provincial program focused on reproductive health. In the course of the legislative session, this group of female legislators introduced eight other bills together on a number of women's rights issues, including the maternal mortality rate, teen pregnancy, sexually transmitted diseases, and human trafficking. Although women collaborate among themselves on a range of issues (as seen in Chapter 5), they are even more likely to collaborate with female colleagues when working on women's issues.

Notably, men are also more likely to collaborate with female colleagues on women's issues than we would expect if they were choosing their cosponsors randomly. Men's expected GCS for women's issues legislation is above zero for the entire range of the data. As with men in districts with weak party constraints, we see that male legislators are more likely to choose to cosponsor with female colleagues on women's issues legislation than when working on other types of legislation.

The top panel in Figure 6.9 supports my expectation that all women – both those facing strong party constraints and those facing relatively weak constraints – are more likely to collaborate with female colleagues when working on women's issues legislation than when working on other issues. Moreover, these findings offer additional support for the ways women's numeric representation and party constraints structure collaboration with other women.

Results: Women's Issues and Collaboration across Party Lines

The bottom panel in Figure 6.9 shows men's and women's propensity to cross party lines when working on women's issues. The bottom panel plots the relationship between women's numeric representation and legislators' expected Women's Issues GCS across party lines for legislators from small districts (on the left) and large districts (on the right). In this analysis, the differences between male and female legislators and between those from small and large districts are not clear-cut. Recall, there are far fewer legislators working on women's issues (only about 61 percent of legislators cosponsor at least one bill in this area during the two-year period), and the average number of bills cosponsored per legislator is significantly smaller for this subset of data. As a result, the estimates in this analysis are less efficient and some of the differences observed in this analysis do not attain conventional levels of statistical significance. Nonetheless, the trends from this analysis are interesting and merit careful consideration.

First, consider the collaborative patterns among legislators from districts with weak party constraints. This analysis finds that women from small districts are more likely to collaborate with female colleagues in other parties when working on women's issues than if they were choosing their coauthors randomly. This is a remarkably high rate of collaboration across party lines considering the cosponsorship norm of collaborating with co-partisans. The observed relationship provides evidence that women see an added benefit to crossing party lines to collaborate on women's issues. This is consistent with women's characterizations of their behavior. A deputy from Mendoza explains:

For questions of gender in general, we work among all blocs and all initiatives come from women. There is solidarity among us women to defend questions of gender, even though we may be from different parties.[15]

Similarly, a female legislator from Salta described women from different political parties forming alliances to introduce and promote legislation that advances women's rights. By collaborating with women from other political parties who serve different constituents, legislators can better identify problems facing female constituents and develop more effective solutions. She suggests women commonly form gender-based alliances around "issues that have emerged through gender."[16] In this regard, she cites the example of legislation introduced to establish a registrar for sex offenders and notes that because the issue affects the lives of all women, female legislators worked together to find "a common agreement."

The data also demonstrate that men who choose to work on women's issues are more likely to engage with their female colleagues when working on such legislation than when they are working on other types of legislation. Figure 6.9 indicates that men's expected Women's Issues GCS across party lines is zero – signifying that men work with women in other political parties at the same rate as would be expected if they were choosing their cosponsors randomly. Notably, however, this is higher than the rate at which male legislators cross party lines to work with women on the universe of issues. Recall from Chapter 5 that the results depicting men's behavior when they work on all legislative issues is negative and significant. Given that women's rights affect the lives of women from all political parties, it is not surprising that male legislators working on such issues would cross party lines to do so. A female deputy from Mendoza explains:

"There are male legislators who stand out for their gender consciousness. For example, [names male legislator] is one who stays and listens, respects, thinks about [gender issues].... [Some male legislators] stand out, but there are some who don't and I won't name them."[17]

Unsurprisingly, the male deputy she identified (along with a few other male deputies) cosponsored legislation with multiparty coalitions of women to advance the status of women in the chamber and in Mendoza more generally. In 2012, along with eight female deputies (from multiple parties), he cosponsored legislation intended to make the gender committee a permanent committee rather than a special one. Male legislators may choose to join a group of

[15] Interview with female senator from Mendoza, Frente para la Victoria, June 27, 2013.
[16] Interview with female deputy from Jujuy, Partido Justicialista, October 29, 2009.
[17] Interview with female senator from Mendoza, Frente para la Victoria, June 26, 2013.

women collaborators when they prioritize similar issues (as in this example), but they may also be the ones to initiate collaboration with female colleagues on new legislation. Men who want to advance women's issues legislation may seek out feedback and insights from female colleagues, or they may believe that working with female collaborators will add credibility to their legislative initiatives.

Different trends emerge among legislators from districts with strong party constraints. The bottom right panel in Figure 6.9 demonstrates that women are more likely than their male counterparts to cross party lines to collaborate with female colleagues. When women comprise only a small portion of the legislature, they cross party lines frequently to collaborate with female colleagues on women's issues. As the proportion of women in the district increases, women are less likely to cross party lines. When there are more women to choose from, female legislators are more likely to find a female collaborator within their own parties, rather than having to look to women from different parties. Collaboration with female co-partisans may be preferred, as women from large districts face strong partisan pressures to work with other legislators within their own parties. Yet, even when women's numeric representation is high, women are still about as likely to cross party lines to collaborate with women as they would be if they were choosing their coauthors randomly. This is much higher than the level of cross-partisan collaboration observed among women from large districts when they are working on the full array of legislative issues (shown in Chapter 5). Thus, it is clearly not uncommon for women to cross party lines to collaborate to promote women's issues – even when faced with strong party constraints.

Numerous examples underscore the importance of cross-party collaboration for developing and promoting women's issues. In 2000, a group of ten female deputies from the Union por Córdoba political party in the Córdoba Chamber of Deputies worked together to introduce legislation to establish the Provincial Women's Council. The council was intended to coordinate government officials, nongovernmental agencies, and advocates to promote women's rights. Although ten women from the same political party initially introduced the legislation to create the council, by 2002, the coalition of actors who influenced and advocated for the development of the council had expanded to include the vast majority of female legislators. In 2002, twenty-three women, representing every political party in the chamber, worked together to identify problems with the existing structure of the chamber and cosponsored legislation amending the structure of the council's executive bureau. This bill represents one of twenty-five bills cosponsored in the Córdoba Chamber in 2002 by a coalition of five or more female deputies.

Interview evidence also reveals that even in the face of strong party constraints, women engage in cross-partisan collaboration. A female legislator from the Catamarca lower chamber – a legislature that elects members from one at-large district, an electoral system known to foster strong party constraints – reported that she is working on legislation related to women's health, annual exams, and early detection of ovarian and breast cancer. Not only does she work more frequently with women on issues of this nature, but also, despite partisan pressures, she crosses party lines to do so. She reports: "I have a good relationship with women from other blocs, and I work with women in the executive branch ... we work as a group."[18] Similarly, a female deputy from Jujuy, a province that also uses an at-large district to elect members, explains that female legislators are dedicated to working together on women's issues: "We get together to discuss the issues that have to do with gender."[19] For example, she explains that women from different political parties work together on issues such as the Law of Reproductive Health and the Law against Family Violence. Given that gender is a cross-cutting cleavage that influences people from different ideologies and backgrounds in similar ways, it should not be surprising to find that women can collaborate on issues that affect women and can seek common ground.

CONCLUSION

This chapter has examined how legislative contexts that vary within chambers influence women's legislative collaboration. First, I took a closer look at how affiliation with the governor shapes women's legislative behavior. This is particularly interesting because affiliation with the governor varies within electoral districts. That is, members of the governor's party are represented in both districts that foster extremely strong party discipline and those that have relatively weaker party discipline. Yet there is considerable variation in women's legislative behavior depending on their affiliation with the governor. Although members of the opposition party are more likely to collaborate overall, female legislators who are members of the governor's party are far more likely to collaborate *with female colleagues* than are members of the opposition. I argue that this is because the governor has the necessary resources and motivation to advance the political party's agenda. This provides legislators from the governor's party with more autonomy to pursue their own legislative agendas. Conversely, legislators from the opposition must devote more of their time and energy to advancing their party agendas.

Although previous research has discussed the implications of affiliation with the governor for legislative behavior, very few empirical tests of these implications exist. I contribute to this research by demonstrating that affiliation with the governor shapes legislative behavior in various contexts and does so in a way that scholars have not previously considered. Specifically, female legislators from the governor's party are free to collaborate with female colleagues to promote shared interests and exert their influence in the chamber. Men, in

[18] Interview with female deputy from Catamarca, Partido Justicialista, November 16, 2009.
[19] Interview with female deputy from Jujuy, Unión Cívica Radical, October 27, 2009.

contrast, do not have a strong incentive to collaborate with female colleagues, and thus their gender patterns of collaboration are largely unaltered by their affiliation with the governor.

A second major contribution of this chapter is a set of empirical tests that evaluate how seniority influences women's legislative collaboration. I argue that female legislators with seniority status are more likely to collaborate with colleagues within their parties in an effort to mentor and assist junior colleagues in accomplishing their legislative goals. Further, given their previous experience in the legislature, they are likely to have larger networks that facilitate collaboration with both other senior women in their party and women in other political parties. Finally, they may be more willing to deviate from party norms and defy party pressures by collaborating with women outside of their own political parties. Indeed, I show that women with seniority status are more likely than their junior female colleagues to collaborate with female colleagues both within their party and across party lines.

The difference in senior and junior women's behavior is striking given that seniority indicates only one additional term in office. Provincial legislators in Argentina have short legislative careers. It is likely, however, that the effects of seniority may be even stronger in other legislative contexts, where legislators serve much longer terms. One may anticipate, for instance, that women who have served for a longer time may be even more proactive as mentors and may have even larger legislative networks. The U.S. Senate case, discussed in the next chapter, offers a compelling example of long-standing senior women's willingness to establish relationships with female newcomers and to mentor them and help them navigate the legislative process.

The third major finding in this chapter is that all legislators are far more likely to choose to collaborate with female colleagues on women's issues, and this pattern is especially strong among female legislators. Nonetheless, women's collaborative patterns are still structured by the larger legislative context such that women from districts with strong party discipline behave more similarly to their male colleagues than do women from districts with weak party discipline.

In its entirety, this book demonstrates that women have strong incentives to collaborate but that opportunities to do so vary significantly by legislative contexts. The Argentine provincial legislatures provide an excellent setting for empirically investigating how different legislative contexts shape women's behavior. Indeed, Chapter 5 shows how factors that vary mostly between legislative chambers (women's numeric representation and partisan pressures) structure women's legislative collaboration. Chapter 6 demonstrates the ways factors that vary *within* chambers (affiliation with the governor, seniority, and the legislative agenda) shape when women will collaborate. Moreover, although affiliation with the governor, seniority, and working on women's issues legislation all increase collaboration with women, the impact of each of these factors varies depending on women's numeric representation and partisan pressures. Thus, the findings in Chapter 6 underscore the importance of considering how electoral incentives and institutional opportunities that vary both between and within chambers work together to structure legislative collaboration.

One of the major advantages of my subnational Argentine study is the sizeable variation in these important contextual variables across a large number of chambers. A single-country study, however, may raise questions regarding the external validity and generalizability of my theory. Namely, can my theory of women's legislative collaboration help us understand women's collaboration outside of the Argentina context? In order to address this concern, I consider women's collaboration in a cross-national context in the next chapter.

APPENDIX 6.1: THE EFFECTS OF AFFILIATION WITH
THE GOVERNOR'S PARTY ON THE GENDER
COSPONSORSHIP SCORE

	(1)	(2)	(3)	(4)
	Chamber-wide GCS		GCS Across Party Lines	
	Small	Large	Small	Large
Female	−264.206***	−51.583*	−88.229**	−4.555
	(43.678)	(24.205)	(28.257)	(14.332)
Percent Women	−0.204	0.021	−0.472***	−0.370***
	(0.104)	(0.063)	(0.052)	(0.043)
Percent Women X Female	0.390*	−0.375***	0.356**	−0.028
	(0.188)	(0.101)	(0.122)	(0.060)
Quota Years	0.299	0.134	0.176*	0.113
	(0.182)	(0.134)	(0.084)	(0.091)
Quota Years X Female	−1.045***	0.265	−0.571***	−0.180*
	(0.215)	(0.143)	(0.139)	(0.085)
Development	0.017	0.129	−0.057	0.025
	(0.165)	(0.129)	(0.072)	(0.089)
Development X Female	0.187	−0.053	0.045	−0.112
	(0.217)	(0.147)	(0.140)	(0.087)
GDI	−71.639	−8.575	−44.285*	18.153
	(55.237)	(33.466)	(22.471)	(21.460)

	(1)	(2)	(3)	(4)
	Chamber-wide GCS		GCS Across Party Lines	
	Small	Large	Small	Large
GDI X Female	335.633***	78.142**	113.573**	14.974
	(54.430)	(27.581)	(35.207)	(16.331)
Seniority	0.005	0.042	−0.063	0.561
	(0.640)	(0.519)	(0.413)	(0.307)
Governor's Party	0.956	0.327	−0.138	1.092
	(1.140)	(1.134)	(0.734)	(0.671)
Governor's Party X Female	−8.143	2.342	−1.693	2.417
	(4.255)	(3.432)	(2.752)	(2.031)
Governor's Party X % Women	0.026	0.010	0.142***	0.062*
	(0.063)	(0.047)	(0.041)	(0.028)
Governor's Party X Female X % Women	0.584**	0.148	−0.041	−0.131
	(0.199)	(0.122)	(0.129)	(0.072)
Sub-Party List	−1.170	−1.917	0.064	−1.320
	(1.559)	(1.067)	(0.690)	(0.722)
# Bills Authored	0.016**	−0.005	−0.004	−0.014***
	(0.005)	(0.003)	(0.003)	(0.002)
GDP	0.000	−0.000	0.000**	0.000
	(0.000)	(0.000)	(0.000)	(0.000)
Constant	57.104	6.684	35.169	−14.958
	(44.584)	(28.354)	(18.192)	(18.328)
Random-effects Parameters				
Province	0.865*	0.874**	−0.272	0.328
	(0.364)	(0.272)	(0.569)	(0.307)
Year	1.395***	1.166***	0.457**	0.934***
	(0.114)	(0.110)	(0.172)	(0.091)
Residual	2.522***	2.656***	2.090***	2.129***
	(0.014)	(0.010)	(0.014)	(0.010)
N-Legislators	2497	4738	2497	4738
N-Chambers	12	18	12	18

Standard errors in parentheses. * $p < 0.05$, ** $p < 0.01$, *** $p < 0.001$.

APPENDIX 6.2: THE EFFECTS OF SENIORITY ON THE GENDER COSPONSORSHIP SCORE

	(1)	(2)	(3)	(4)
	Chamber-wide GCS		GCS Across Party Lines	
	Small	Large	Small	Large
Female	−287.291***	−41.523	−94.222***	−9.347
	(43.436)	(24.307)	(28.106)	(14.351)
Percent Women	−0.164	0.039	−0.379***	−0.343***
	(0.097)	(0.060)	(0.046)	(0.041)
Percent Women X Female	0.732***	−0.350***	0.276**	−0.108*
	(0.142)	(0.082)	(0.092)	(0.049)
Quota Years	0.295	0.131	0.164	0.112
	(0.182)	(0.133)	(0.085)	(0.091)
Quota Years X Female	−1.185***	0.298*	−0.534***	−0.168*
	(0.213)	(0.143)	(0.138)	(0.085)
Development	0.018	0.134	−0.057	0.018
	(0.163)	(0.129)	(0.073)	(0.089)
Development X Female	0.127	−0.027	0.078	−0.088
	(0.218)	(0.149)	(0.141)	(0.088)
GDI	−73.955	−7.769	−40.886	15.429
	(54.093)	(33.132)	(23.280)	(21.478)
GDI X Female	360.465***	66.869*	119.700***	22.021
	(54.331)	(27.506)	(35.149)	(16.239)
Seniority	0.457	−0.211	−0.549	−0.107
	(1.309)	(1.441)	(0.843)	(0.851)
Seniority X Female	−7.510	0.963	−1.843	−1.004
	(6.449)	(4.373)	(4.171)	(2.580)
Seniority X % Women	−0.057	−0.030	0.012	0.014
	(0.071)	(0.058)	(0.045)	(0.034)
Seniority X Female X % Women	0.555*	0.143	0.228	0.089
	(0.274)	(0.153)	(0.178)	(0.090)
Governor's Party	1.904***	2.048***	1.756***	2.247***
	(0.557)	(0.439)	(0.354)	(0.260)
Sub-Party List	−1.299	−1.874	0.012	−1.279
	(1.546)	(1.063)	(0.700)	(0.721)
# Bills Authored	0.016**	−0.006	−0.005	−0.014***
	(0.005)	(0.003)	(0.003)	(0.002)
GDP	−0.000	−0.000	0.000**	0.000
	(0.000)	(0.000)	(0.000)	(0.000)

	(1)	(2)	(3)	(4)
	Chamber-wide GCS		GCS Across Party Lines	
	Small	Large	Small	Large
Constant	58.398	4.881	31.525	−13.039
	(43.652)	(28.104)	(18.805)	(18.339)
Random-effects Parameters				
Province	0.823*	0.852**	−0.168	0.334
	(0.378)	(0.276)	(0.517)	(0.304)
Year	1.397***	1.168***	0.442*	0.928***
	(0.114)	(0.110)	(0.174)	(0.091)
Residual	2.523***	2.659***	2.091***	2.130***
	(0.014)	(0.010)	(0.014)	(0.010)
N-Legislators	2497	4738	2497	4738
N-Chambers	12	18	12	18

Standard errors in parentheses. * p < 0.05, ** p < 0.01, *** p < 0.001.

APPENDIX 6.3: DETERMINANTS OF THE GENDER COSPONSORSHIP SCORE, WOMEN'S ISSUES LEGISLATION

	(1)	(2)	(3)	(4)
	Chamber-wide GCS		GCS Across Party Lines	
	Small	Large	Small	Large
Female	−371.205***	55.960	−137.388*	−47.480
	(98.874)	(46.462)	(66.294)	(29.735)
Percent Women	0.290	0.109	−0.173	−0.297***
	(0.187)	(0.121)	(0.119)	(0.090)
Percent Women X Female	1.069***	−0.170	0.096	−0.088
	(0.312)	(0.153)	(0.209)	(0.098)
Quota Years	0.051	0.262	0.004	0.207
	(0.346)	(0.268)	(0.219)	(0.198)
Quota Years X Female	−1.820***	−0.826**	−0.435	−0.617***
	(0.485)	(0.282)	(0.325)	(0.181)
Development	0.176	0.521*	0.169	0.255
	(0.284)	(0.259)	(0.180)	(0.193)
Development X Female	1.237*	−1.007***	0.493	−0.421*
	(0.485)	(0.289)	(0.325)	(0.185)

(*continued*)

Appendix 6.3 (*cont.*)

	(1)	(2)	(3)	(4)
	Chamber-wide GCS		GCS Across Party Lines	
	Small	Large	Small	Large
GDI	−42.870	20.392	2.272	30.967
	(79.183)	(61.178)	(50.236)	(42.963)
GDI X Female	455.798***	−16.412	176.077*	88.439**
	(124.365)	(52.839)	(83.371)	(33.815)
Seniority	1.107	−0.719	0.071	0.417
	(1.670)	(1.093)	(1.120)	(0.700)
Governor's	2.955*	5.179***	0.250	0.777
Party	(1.401)	(0.930)	(0.937)	(0.597)
Sub-Party List	−1.722	−3.576	0.381	−1.533
	(2.661)	(2.055)	(1.685)	(1.513)
# Bills	0.298*	0.063	−0.024	−0.077
Authored	(0.147)	(0.070)	(0.098)	(0.045)
GDP	0.000	0.000	0.000	0.000
	(0.001)	(0.000)	(0.000)	(0.000)
Constant	28.074	−26.076	−7.862	−32.695
	(64.636)	(52.456)	(40.990)	(37.107)
Random-effects Parameters				
Province	−16.528**	1.349***	−9.871	0.838*
	(6.273)	(0.342)	(7.350)	(0.388)
Year	2.051***	1.804***	1.549***	1.696***
	(0.131)	(0.126)	(0.144)	(0.097)
Residual	3.182***	3.178***	2.785***	2.728***
	(0.020)	(0.013)	(0.020)	(0.013)
N-Legislators	1402	3016	1402	3016
N-Chambers	12	18	12	18

Standard errors in parentheses. * $p < 0.05$, ** $p < 0.01$, *** $p < 0.001$.

7

Collaboration in a Cross-National Context

Evidence from Argentina shows that women entering male-dominated legis-latures face structural barriers and have limited ability to exert influence on the policy-making process. As a result, women have strong incentives to col-laborate in order to overcome such barriers, exert influence in the chamber, and gain a voice in the policy-making process. Despite the many benefits of collaboration, its prevalence varies between legislative contexts because not all women have the same opportunities to collaborate. In Argentina, women facing weak party constraints are more likely to collaborate than their male colleagues, and their propensity to do so increases as women's numeric repre-sentation increases. By contrast, women facing strong party constraints have limited opportunities to collaborate with other women. Instead, these women behave more like their male colleagues and collaborate less frequently. The effects of strong party constraints are mitigated by other factors; notably affili-ation with the executive's party, seniority, and women's issues legislation moti-vate collaboration among women.

In this chapter, I draw on a series of case studies from across the world in order to expand my analysis and to demonstrate the generalizability of my theory beyond Argentina. I evaluate data from four national parliaments: the Rwandan Chamber of Deputies, the U.S. Senate, the Uruguayan Congress, and the South African Parliament. In doing so, I examine countries that have dif-ferent legislative contexts than the ones found in Argentina, thus providing broader tests of how other legislative contexts constrain or facilitate women's collaboration.

I present this set of case studies to facilitate the exploration of how institu-tional arrangements structure women's collaboration outside of the Argentine provinces. As I explain in Chapter 2, electoral institutions that concentrate power in the hands of party leaders and foster strong party loyalty constrain women's collaboration. By contrast, electoral institutions that allow legislators to act independently of political parties impose fewer constraints on women's collaboration. Whereas the Argentine provinces enabled me to test these expectations for both women facing strong party constraints and women facing comparably weaker party constraints (i.e., closed-list PR systems with large district magnitudes and closed-list PR systems with small district magnitudes), these four additional cases allow me to examine collaboration in legislatures across the full range of party constraints.

In all four cases, I argue that women's marginalization motivates collaboration. Whether collaboration transpired or was thwarted, however, was determined by the level of party constraints in combination with women's numeric representation. As an example of extremely low levels of partisan constraints, many women in Rwanda are elected to office through nonpartisan reserved seats for women. Because reserved seats allow women to gain access to the legislature independent of political parties, women in Rwanda are not constrained by party leaders and collaboration unfolds. On the other hand, in South Africa, legislators are elected to office via closed-list PR systems with exceptionally large district magnitudes – which are known to foster tremendous party discipline – and, unlike in Argentina, legislators who break party ranks can be banished from parties and forced to give up their seats in the parliament. In this case study, I show that despite a strong norm of multiparty collaboration among women during the democratic transition, once women gained access to political office, extreme party discipline stifled women's collaboration in South Africa. The U.S. Senate and the Uruguayan Congress fall between these two extremes. In particular, in the U.S. Senate, where party constraints are relatively weak by global standards (Johnson and Wallack 2010), cross-partisan collaboration among women flourishes. In the Uruguayan Congress, legislators face relatively strong party discipline, but because women comprise only a small share of the legislature, they can collaborate because these efforts fly under the radar, attracting little attention from party leaders.

In addition to extending my analysis of how party constraints structure women's collaboration, these case studies adopt different measures of collaboration that focus on different aspects of the policy-making process. These variations are advantageous because I can account for more informal types of collaboration that emerge in the legislature. My analysis of the Argentine provinces measured collaboration using cosponsorship data, which represents the culmination of the collaborative policy-making process. Yet, in Chapter 1, I explained that although most legislative collaboration is intended to develop and advance legislation, legislators can collaborate in a number of ways in an effort to influence the policy-making process. In the case studies that follow, I examine how women's collaboration plays out in more informal settings, such as the "behind the scenes" development and promotion of legislation, peer mentoring among colleagues, networking with experts and organizations outside the legislature, and consulting with constituents. I also consider other more formal types of collaboration such as inviting specialists to testify during committee hearings. In doing so, these case studies explore additional ways that future research may approach the study of collaboration.

In each case, I focus on a different way that legislators collaborate to influence the policy-making process. In the case of Rwanda, for example, I trace the development of legislation criminalizing gender-based violence. I show how women worked together with legislative colleagues, experts, and constituents in their districts to design effective legislation and engender broad-based support for their legislative initiatives. In the case of the U.S. Senate, I examine women's efforts to foster a culture of collaboration among female senators. In particular, I explain how senior women organized regularly occurring informal meetings and established mentoring relationships with junior female colleagues in an effort to develop professional networks among women and to engender legislation with diverse perspectives. Women's collaboration in Uruguay was the result of private meetings in the bicameral women's caucus. Women worked behind the scenes to develop legislation and reach agreements on controversial issues, ultimately allowing them to advance women's rights legislation as a unified bloc. Finally, I explain how women's efforts to collaborate in South Africa were foiled. In this case, we see little evidence of formal or informal collaboration among women.

The case studies outlined in this chapter corroborate my theory that out-of-power legislators – in this case, women – have incentives to collaborate in order to overcome structural barriers and exert an influence on the legislative process. Nonetheless, as I show, not all women have the same opportunities to work collaboratively. These cases further illustrate the importance of partisan constraints for understanding the conditions under which collaboration thrives and under which it breaks down. For each case, I begin by providing a brief overview of my argument. I then use primary and secondary accounts, news articles, and academic sources to bring to bear evidence of women's legislative collaboration. Following this discussion, I describe how women's status in the chamber fosters incentives to collaborate. Next, I discuss the legislative context that structures women's behavior, and explain how different legislative features permit or constrain women's collaboration. Although the focus is primarily on the varying levels of party constraints, as I argue in Chapter 2, other institutional features also influence women's opportunities to collaborate. Thus, after giving careful attention to the ways electoral institutions concentrate or disperse power among party leaders, I highlight other important features of each political context and illustrate how these features further structure women's collaboration.

COLLABORATING TO ADVANCE WOMEN'S RIGHTS IN RWANDA

The Rwandan Chamber of Deputies represents an example of successful female collaboration. Despite partisan and ethnic divisions, female legislators in Rwanda engineered a cross-partisan coalition to pioneer legislation criminalizing gender-based violence (GBV). Collaboration in Rwanda extended beyond the legislature, as female lawmakers worked with nongovernmental organizations (NGOs), women's rights organizations, and even constituents to develop the GBV legislation. In this case study, I argue that women had a strong incentive to collaborate so as to overcome their historically marginalized status in the legislature. Two key features of the Rwandan Chamber of Deputies facilitated women's collaboration. First, and unique to the Rwandan case, most female legislators are elected to seats reserved for women in women-only elections. Women elected through reserved seats are not beholden to political party leaders, and party leaders have limited control over these legislators' political careers. Thus party constraints are weak, allowing collaboration to unfold. Second, the women's caucus in Rwanda is instrumental in coordinating women across party lines and creating an opportunity for collaboration.

Evidence of Collaboration beyond the Legislature in Rwanda

In August 2006, eight members of the Rwanda Chamber of Deputies introduced the "Draft Law on Prevention, Protection and Punishment of Any Gender-Based Violence." Although the Forum of Rwandan Women Parliamentarians (Forum des Femmes Rwandaises Parlementaires, or FFRP) was responsible for initiating and developing the legislation, eight legislators, who were elected from three different political parties and from nonpartisan reserved seats for women, formally introduced the legislation.[1] The FFRP women's caucus, comprised of all female parliamentarians, was the first legislative group in Rwanda to collaborate across multiple parties (Powley 2005; Wilber 2011).[2] This bill not only represented the first bill introduced by a cross-partisan coalition, it was also the first legislature-initiated bill since the ratification of the new constitution in 2003. Prior to this point, all legislation had come directly from the executive branch (Pearson 2008; Wilber 2011). As Rwanda is (by most accounts) not classified as a democratic regime, members of the parliament may have

---

[1] The official bill sponsors were Evariste Kalisa (Liberal Party), Judith Kanakuze (elected from a reserved seat), Claire Kayirangwa (Liberal Party), Donatila Mukabalisa (Liberal Party), Faith Mukakalisa (elected from a reserved seat), Juvenal Nkusi (Social Democratic Party), Aimable Nibishaka (Rwandan Patriotic Front), and Fidele Mitsindo (Rwandan Patriotic Front).

[2] Although the FFRP brings together women from across all legislative parties, the vast majority of legislative seats are concentrated in the hands of the majority party. In September 2003, eight parties competed for seats in the nationwide electoral district. Seven political parties won at least one seat in office; however, five parties ran as an electoral coalition (the Rwandan Patriotic Front – RPF), and the coalition secured 73 percent of the votes and forty seats in the fifty-three-seat nationwide district. Two other parties, the Socialist Democratic Party and the Liberal Party, won seven seats and six seats, respectively. The remaining twenty-seven seats were reserved seats (for women, youth, and handicapped) and were not contested via political parties – still the majority of legislators elected in these seats are sympathetic to the ruling party (Powley 2005). In the 2008 legislative election, the RPF won forty-two seats. The Socialist Democratic Party and the Liberal Party won seven seats and four seats, respectively.

fewer incentives or opportunities to initiate legislation. The FFRP broke with this institutional norm to develop and promote the GBV legislation (Delvin and Elgie 2008). Still, it is important to point out that women in Rwanda have a history of working within the nondemocratic system to advance women's rights – even if the legislation is not introduced from the parliament directly. As Burnet explains, women have "gained enough experience to know how to manipulate the state, even a repressive state, to achieve a common goal" (2008, 377).

The FFRP spent two years cultivating the GBV legislation (Pearson 2008). During this time, the women's forum members met with civil society and international experts, consulted with male and female constituents, and debated among themselves to develop the legislation (Pearson 2008). In an effort to produce effective legislation, the FFRP hired two consultants to engage civil society organizations. The consultants developed a questionnaire to obtain information from civil society groups and compiled a set of best practices from international law addressing issues of sexual violence. This information served as the foundation for a national conference on GBV in Kigali in 2005. After the conference, female MPs spent two days in their districts, explaining the policy-making process, discussing GBV, and soliciting recommendations from their constituents to develop GBV legislation. Upon returning to the legislature, the FFRP members invited two activists from each of Rwanda's twelve districts to assist in information gathering. This collaborative process allowed women from different backgrounds and perspectives to share information and insights that influenced the development of the legislation. Finally, women were strategic in establishing male allies (Powley and Pearson 2007). Men were involved in each stage of the process. One male and one female consultant were hired to participate in drafting the bill. It used gender-inclusive language, each version of the legislation was circulated to male and female members of the parliament, and four male MPs (along with four female MPs) were even tapped to formally introduce the legislation (Carlson and Randell 2013; Delvin and Elgie 2008; Powley and Pearson 2007). According to the president of the FFRP, "Everyone recognized [that] women pushed the process," but it was more important to ensure that men felt "ownership" of the legislation than to demonstrate women's leadership.[3] This inclusive approach was instrumental for establishing a unified women's front in support of the legislation and ultimately pushing it through the legislature. It allowed women to reach agreements among themselves and to cultivate male supporters. Yet it did not win the full support of all male legislators. Indeed, by the time the legislation was finally brought to the parliament floor, all but one of the objections to the proposed legislation were raised by men (Pearson 2008).

Table 7.1 characterizes the different objections raised during the debate in the legislature and shows the gender distribution of the legislators raising the

[3] Interview with Judith Kanakuze, president of the FFRP, cited in Powley and Pearson (2007).

TABLE 7.1. *Objections Raised against GBV Legislation in the Rwandan Parliament*

Objections	Objection Raised by	
	Men	Women
Objections stating that the proposed punishments are too harsh	6	0
Objections stating that there should be allowances for marital rape and/or domestic violence	5	0
Objections to the abolition of polygamy or the requirement for polygamous men to marry their first wife	3	0
Objections stating there were unfair standards of evidence/testimony/accusation	3	0
Objections to the establishment of maternity leave policies	2	1
Objections to provision dealing with adultery	2	0
Objections stating that law will hurt families	2	0
Objections to provision concerning dress code	2	0
Total	25	1

Source: Data were collected and compiled by Pearson (2008).

objections. It is clear from the list of objections that garnering widespread support for legislation intended to reduce GBV was not an easy task in Rwanda. Male legislators were unhappy with a number of aspects in the bill. For example, six male MPs objected to the harshness of punishments proposed for GBV perpetrators. Instead, one male MP suggested community service was an appropriate punishment for GBV offenders (Pearson 2008). Five male MPs objected to the bill's position on marital rape, some even going so far as to suggest: "marital rape is a contradiction in terms" (Pearson 2008, 26). The nature of these objections demonstrates why passing women's rights legislation in Rwanda was no small feat. Female legislators foresaw that GBV legislation would be controversial and knew their only hope for successfully passing the legislation would be to demonstrate cohesive support among female legislators and to cultivate male allies.

Both chambers approved the final GBV legislation in 2008. As with any law, there are still challenges associated with effectively implementing the legislation (Carlson and Randell 2013). However, there is evidence that the new legislation has been effective at raising awareness (Bangi 2012), and numerous steps have been taken to disseminate information, to provide training for practitioners, and to generate social acceptance for the legislation among the public (Carlson and Randell 2013). Although there is still work to be done, crafting effective legislation and gaining widespread support for legislative approval was a crucial first step in the process of addressing violence against women.

In a country characterized by a divisive political scene and a conservative society in which violence against women is widespread and commonplace (Wilber 2011), how were female legislators able to forge cross-partisan relationships and reach agreements to advance women's rights? To explain women's ability to engage in cross-bench collaboration, I examine evidence from three key components of Rwanda's Chamber of Deputies. First, I consider the status of women in the Rwandan Parliament and in society more generally. Given the marginalized status of women in society and in the legislature, my theory implies that women had an incentive to collaborate. Second, I consider how reserved seats for female candidates in women-only elections fostered allegiance to female constituents as opposed to strong party loyalties. The use of reserved seats significantly reduces partisan constraints, which I argue, fosters an environment that is permissive of women's cross-partisan collaboration. Finally, I discuss the role of the FFRP (the women's caucus) in facilitating collaboration among female legislators. Women's caucuses cultivate collaboration among women from different political parties. As such, I argue that the FFRP played a strong role in nurturing collaboration among women.

Women's Marginalized Status in Rwanda

Historically, women occupied important positions in tribal governments, but colonization brought about a shift in gender roles. As the British imposed their own beliefs about women's roles in society and politics in colonial Rwanda, Rwanda became an extremely patriarchal society. Women's primary role was in the home, while men dominated the political scene. As a result, women's representation in decision-making bodies was scarce. Prior to 1994, women never held more than 18 percent of seats in the parliament, and very few women held important governmental posts. Although it is worth pointing out that 18 percent was a relatively high level of representation compared to most other countries in the world in the early 1990s, women were still underrepresented in elected offices.

The 1994 genocide in Rwanda devastated the country and dramatically changed its gender demographics. More than 800,000 were killed, with men disproportionately affected. After the genocide, women comprised about 70 percent of the population. Because of this imbalance, women were required to take on new roles in society and government; they became heads of households and leaders in local governments. Women played a crucial role in rebuilding society after the devastation (Burnet 2012a, 2012b). In particular, women were interested in safeguarding their rights and ensuring fair representation under the new constitution (Bauer and Burnet 2013; Hughes 2009). Women's movements mobilized around the writing of the constitution to guarantee that gender equality would be a foundation of the new government (Powley 2005).

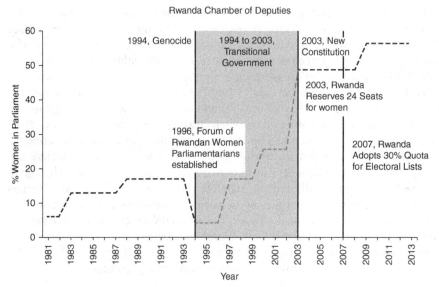

FIGURE 7.1. Women's numeric representation in Rwanda.
Source: IPU (2013) and Paxton, Green, and Hughes (2008).

From 1994 to 2003, record numbers of women were appointed to serve as Members of Parliament during the transitional government, reaching a high of 25 percent in 2000. Figure 7.1 illustrates how women's numeric representation increased during this transitional time. In 2003, Rwanda adopted a new constitution that emphasizes a commitment to gender equality and states that women will be guaranteed at least 30 percent of seats in all government decision-making bodies (Powley 2005). For the first parliamentary election, this mandate was implemented in the form of reserved seats wherein 30 percent of seats in the National Parliament were set aside exclusively for women MPs (see discussion later in this chapter). As Figure 7.1 demonstrates, this resulted in immediate gains for women in the parliament. In the first election after the adoption of the new constitution, women won 30 percent of seats in the Senate and 49 percent of seats in the Chamber of Deputies. In 2007, Rwanda adopted an additional gender quota requiring that political parties reserve 30 percent of their party lists for female candidates. In sharp contrast to their pre-1994 minority status in the legislature, today, women comprise 56 percent of the Rwanda Chamber of Deputies – the highest proportion of seats occupied by women in any national parliament worldwide.

In a society where women's rights have historically been severely compromised, women's numeric representation has been instrumental in giving women a voice in the policy-making process and in the promotion of women's rights. Parliamentarian Mwiza explains: "When men had the majority, we had trouble passing anything that had to do with gender issues. But now, with our numbers, we have a stronger voice than before."[4] Despite major gains in women's numeric representation after the restoration of multiparty politics, women still have a long way to go. The history of women's marginalization both in government and in society established a clear need for women to collaborate among themselves to exert their influence in the legislature. To understand why women were successful in forging cross-party collaboration, it is necessary to consider the legislative context in which Rwandan MPs operate.

Weak Party Constraints: Reserved Seats and Women-Only Elections

Although the majority of legislators in Rwanda are elected through a closed-list proportional representation system, and thus face very strong party constraints, the majority of women in Rwanda are elected through reserved seats – they do not face the same party pressures as legislators elected through closed-list proportional representation. Instead, reserved seats and women-only elections foster weak party constraints for female MPs, which were instrumental for allowing women's collaboration to unfold in Rwanda. The Chamber of Deputies is comprised of eighty members. Rwanda's constitution, adopted in 2003, established the election of members to five-year terms through three separate mechanisms:

1. 53 members are elected from a closed-list proportional representation (PR) system in one nationwide district;
2. 24 seats are reserved exclusively for women;
3. 3 members are elected by the National Youth Council and Federation of the Associations of the Disabled.

Despite the fact that Rwanda exhibits a number of authoritarian characteristics (Burnet 2008, 2011) and is not classified as an electoral democracy (Marshall and Gurr 2013), there is still considerable evidence to suggest that the different mechanisms used to elect members of parliament shape representatives' incentives, priorities, and legislative behavior (Pearson 2008; Schwartz 2004). With respect to the first group of legislators, the closed-list electoral system allows political party leaders to construct their own lists of candidates and decide where candidates will be placed on each list (Burchard 2015). Given the extremely large district size, individual legislators have little influence over their own electoral fortunes. Instead, party leaders have almost exclusive control over legislators' careers. As with the large districts in the Argentine provinces, this electoral system fosters strong party loyalty and enables party leaders to severely constrain legislative behavior. Women facing these conditions have fewer electoral incentives or opportunities to collaborate with

[4] Interview with Espérance Mwiza, a female Member of Parliament, cited in United Nations Development Program (2012).

female colleagues – particularly with women in other political parties. Instead, MPs have an incentive to advance the parties' interests. For example, 83 percent of men and 64 percent of women elected on party ballots rank the promotion of party interests as "very important" (Schwartz 2004, 17). Thus, if all legislators were elected from very large districts in a closed-list PR system, my theory implies that collaboration among female legislators would be extremely unlikely.

The vast majority of women in the Rwanda Chamber of Deputies, however, are not elected to such districts. Thirty percent of the legislature is elected through seats reserved for women.[5] Only women can compete for the twenty-four seats up for grabs in the "women-only elections," and only female constituents can vote in the elections (Powley 2005).[6] Women elected through reserved seats are not selected directly by political parties and their political careers are not directly tied to the success of the political parties. As a result, these women face weaker party constraints than other legislators in the same chamber who are elected from the PR list and should therefore be more likely to collaborate. Moreover, given that they are elected by female constituents, female MPs serving in reserved seats likely feel more loyalty toward female constituents than do members elected from PR lists. As a result, women in reserved seats are more compelled to promote women's rights and represent the interests of the specific constituents who elected them.

Indeed, Pearson argues that "female parliamentarians – particularly the 30 percent that were elected on the 'women's ballot,' as opposed to political party lists – feel an obligation to represent women's interests" (2008, 28). She reports that female parliamentarians viewed promotion of the GBV law as a way to fulfill this obligation. As one MP explained: "Generally the MPs represent a political party which guides their standpoint on different issues. But women elected on quota do not represent a political party; they are elected by mainly women and therefore represent the female population.... I was present during the campaigns, and women in the countryside asked the candidates for the women's seats in what way they could help them."[7] Survey data also indicate that women elected to reserved seats face weaker party constraints and exhibit more loyalty to female constituents. In 2003, of those elected on the PR lists, 64 percent of female MPs report that the promotion of their parties' interests is "very important." By contrast, only 42 percent of female MPs elected

---

[5] Prior to 2006, two women were elected from each of the twelve provinces including the city of Kigali.

[6] In 2007, the Law on Political Organizations and Politicians was amended to include an electoral gender quota for the party lists. The quota law requires that all candidate lists presented for any elective office include at least 30 percent female candidates. The gender quota does not, however, include placement mandate language requiring women to be placed in specific positions on the list. As a result, political parties can place women in non-electable positions.

[7] Interview with anonymous male Member of Parliament, cited in Schwartz (2004).

from reserved seats felt the promotion of party interests was "very important" (Schwartz 2004).

Moreover, most female MPs felt committed to promoting women's issues. One hundred percent of the female legislators elected in reserved seats reported that the promotion of women's interests was "very important," and 93 percent of women elected from the closed-list electoral system felt these issues were "very important" (Schwartz 2004). Evidence from survey data and elite interviews shows that many women, regardless of their paths to office, prioritize women's issues. But the survey demonstrates that women MPs who are elected from party lists face competing pressures because they also have a strong obligation to represent their political parties. Conversely, women in reserved seats do not face competing partisan incentives – they have no obligation to promote a political party agenda. Instead, they have more autonomy to promote women's rights and collaborate with female colleagues in an effort to exert their influence in the chamber. Taken together, the evidence presented here indicates that the use of reserved seats in women-only elections is the key to facilitating women's collaboration in Rwanda.

Forum of Rwandan Women Parliamentarians

Another crucial factor in understanding women's collaboration in Rwanda is the existence of a multiparty women's caucus. In 1996, female MPs joined to form the FFRP. All female parliamentarians in both chambers – regardless of their ethnicity or party affiliation – were members of the FFRP (Pearson 2008). The primary objective of the FFRP was to strengthen the capacity of female MPs, and to establish policy priorities that included reforming legislation that discriminated against women, promoting gender equality, and mainstreaming gender issues in the legislature (Gomez and Koppell 2008). The caucus provided the opportunity for female legislators to discuss shared interests and the issues concerning women in the nation. The caucus is comprised of all female MPs regardless of partisanship or ethnicity. When the caucus was first formed in 1996, women comprised about 17 percent of the chamber; today they comprise more than half of the chamber (about 56 percent). Prior to winning a majority in the parliament, the FFRP spearheaded several policy initiatives to advance women's rights (Burnet 2011). With the transition to a female-majority parliament, the FFRP initially struggled to develop a women's agenda, but in 2006 the caucus unified behind the GBV legislation. Although the strength and unification of the FFRP fluctuated over time, the caucus has been instrumental in facilitating collaboration on women's rights.

Women's caucuses are important for coordinating women within and across party lines (Kanthak and Krause 2012). In Rwanda, political observers see the women's caucus as playing a central role in the development of the GBV legislation (Delvin and Elgie 2008; Gomez and Koppell 2008; Pearson 2008; Wilber 2011). The women's caucus put GBV on the legislative agenda and worked to obtain the information necessary to develop and promote the legislation. The caucus incorporated diverse perspectives from female MPs (Pearson 2008), civil societies, policy experts, and constituents (Gomez and Koppell 2008). Evidence from Rwanda shows that one of the major benefits to collaboration is that it improves policy outcomes by increasing the information brought to bear on an issue, allowing legislators to efficiently create better legislation. Specifically, by collaborating with female constituents and civil societies, female legislators were able to identify constituents' needs and to design legislation that addressed their concerns.

In addition to creating a forum for women to exchange ideas and address women's rights, the caucus helped to forge consensus among female MPs on difficult issues *prior* to the introduction of legislation on the chamber floor. If women present a unified front when legislation comes to the chamber floor, they will have a much higher probability of success. While not every woman is likely to agree on every aspect of the GBV legislation, the caucus ensures that women have the common goal of passing the GBV legislation and provides a forum for female legislators to consider different perspectives and come to agreements on the content of the legislation.

The FFRP has been instrumental in connecting women from across the chamber and, as a result, has strengthened the role of women in the legislature more generally. As one MP notes: "When it comes to the Forum, we [unite] as women, irrespective of political parties. So we don't think of our parties, [we think of] the challenges that surround us as women."[8] The FFRP was central to women's collaboration on GBV legislation in 2006. The caucus has a track record of forging collaborations with civil society to promote women's rights and continues to do so today. Although not formally introduced by the parliament, the FFRP united with women in civil society to develop and promote the adoption of the "Inheritance Law" in Rwanda in 1999 under the transition government (Burnet 2008). Although formally known as the Inheritance Law, the law as passed extended a number of legal rights to women, including the rights to enter into legal contractual agreements, to hold property and bank accounts in their own names, and to seek paid employment. As Burnet explains, women from the FFRP and civil society "worked together closely in formulating policy, crafting the text of the bill, and lobbying decision makers in other ministries and within the inner circle of the RPF, referred to as the akazu, to pass the controversial bill" (2008, 376). Similarly, in 2012, the parliament amended legislation to legalize abortion in cases of rape or incest, or to protect the mother's health (Gogineni 2013). Interviews with female MPs indicate that they will continue to prioritize equality issues, including gender violence and gender inequality.[9]

---

[8] Interview with Member of Parliament Connie Bwiza Sekamana, cited in Powley (2005).
[9] Interview with Member of Parliament Connie Bwiza Sekemana, cited in Gogineni (2013).

Conclusions for the Rwandan Parliament

In Rwanda, the use of reserved seats for women and women-only elections, combined with a strong women's caucus, create a legislative setting favorable to women's collaboration. Reserved seats for women and women-only elections substantially reduce female MPs' allegiances to and reliance on political parties, granting them the freedom they need to form cross-partisan collaborations. Moreover, the women's caucus organizes and encourages efforts to collaborate. Rwanda provides an excellent example of how effective women's caucuses can be at organizing women when their efforts are not thwarted by strong party discipline. Weak political loyalties and a formal women's caucus are an effective combination for promoting women's collaboration.

Overall, the case of Rwanda provides strong support for my argument that women are more likely to collaborate when they face weak party constraints. The findings from this case study corroborate the results from Argentina presented in Chapters 5 and 6. Together these cases show that women facing relatively weak party constraints are far more likely than men to cross party lines to collaborate with women. Further, this case study advances our understanding of women's collaboration by allowing me to evaluate the expectation that women's caucuses facilitate collaboration. Recall there is not sufficient variation across the Argentine provinces to test this part of my theory. The results from Rwanda move our understanding of collaboration forward by illustrating the importance of women's issues committees and caucuses for engendering collaboration among women.

THE U.S. SENATE: A CULTURE OF COLLABORATION

Collaboration among women in the U.S. Senate is particularly well documented. Elite political observers and female senators themselves paint the picture of a collaborative culture among women in the Senate. Women collaborate to develop professional networks, build consensus, engender legislation with diverse perspectives, and promote women's rights. In this case study, I argue that women have historically occupied a marginalized status in the U.S. Senate and this marginalization motivates collaboration. Two fundamental features of the U.S. Senate help explain why women's collaboration unfolds in the U.S. Senate. First, weak party constraints as fostered by small electoral districts with competitive primary elections provide women opportunities to collaborate. Second, entrenched seniority in the U.S. Senate promotes collaboration because women with seniority status are more likely to forge cross-party connections.

Evidence of Women's Collaboration in the U.S. Senate

In the opening pages of this book, I gave the example of female senators forming cross-party alliances to overcome partisan gridlock and end the

U.S. government shutdown in 2013. While women's collaboration during this time attracted considerable attention from the media, female senators suggest that this behavior is not uncommon (Boxer et al. 2001). There are numerous examples of women's bipartisan efforts to exert their influence in the Senate. For instance, after September 11, 2001, Senators Lisa Murkowski (R-AK) and Kirsten Gillibrand (D-NY) joined forces to develop legislation that provided health care to first responders. Senator Barbara Boxer (D-CA) and Senator Olympia Snowe (R-ME) developed the Airline Passenger Bill of Rights Act to limit the amount of time jets could keep passengers sitting on the tarmac.

With respect to collaborating to promote women's rights, or provide substantive representation for women, all seven of the women serving on the Senate Armed Services Committee in 2013 joined forces to champion the prevention and adjudication of sexual assault in the military and to open combat jobs to women (Steinhauer 2013). Similarly, Senators Mikulski and Snowe worked together on a bipartisan resolution urging the National Cancer Institute to reinstate guidelines encouraging mammograms for women in their forties. Senator Mikulski partnered with Senator Kay Bailey Hutchison (R-TX) to pass the Homemaker IRA bill, raising the IRA contribution deductible limit for single-income married couples to match that of two-income married couples. The list of examples of women's collaboration is extensive. As Senator Mikulski put it, these accomplishments and others resulted from "the power of two women building a coalition to accomplish a mutual goal."[10]

Despite this, it is important to recognize that female senators are not collaborating because they all think alike or have the same political ideology. Senator Snowe makes this clear:

"We certainly don't want to communicate that all of the women in the Senate are homogenous, with the women sitting on one side and the men sitting on the other.... Every one of us is different – in our political positions, our styles, our life experiences. However, women just come from a different place than men in terms of being more relationship-oriented and more collaborative."[11]

Senator Susan Collins echoes these sentiments: "There are many different views among the women of the Senate."[12] Indeed, women in the Senate span the ideological spectrum. Nonetheless, Collins explains, "the women in the Senate seem to do the thing that most of the other members cannot – which is work outside of the chamber relationships that cut across party lines." As the number of women in the U.S. Senate grows, the number of perspectives increases too. Indeed, the purpose of collaboration is not to reinforce the same idea or perspective; rather, it is to consider other positions and to incorporate different viewpoints into the policy-making process (Swers 2013). When

---

[10] Barbara Mikulski in *Nine and Counting: The Women of the U.S. Senate* (Boxer et al. 2001).
[11] Olympia Snowe in *Nine and Counting: The Women of the U.S. Senate* (Boxer et al. 2001).
[12] Interview with Senator Susan Collins, cited in Kim (2013).

women's numeric representation in the U.S. Senate finally reached 20 percent in 2013, Senator Debby Fischer explained, "It's nice to have 20 women here ... that offers another point of diversity, which is always good."[13]

Women's collaboration is also recognized among their male colleagues. "I don't want to generalize, because this isn't true of all of them, but they tend to be interested in finding common ground," said Senator Rob Portman (R-OH). "So I think it's going to have, and is having, a positive impact on the Senate."[14] These examples help to illustrate the collaborative culture among women in the U.S. Senate. Accounts from female senators suggest that collaboration is pervasive among them and has been a fundamental tool they use to exert influence in the male-dominated Senate.

What explains the culture of collaboration among women in the U.S. Senate? As in the case of Argentina, I expect that women's marginalized status in the U.S. Senate will motivate collaboration among women. Further, I posit that collaboration comes to fruition in the U.S. Senate because women face weak party constraints that do not restrict their efforts to collaborate. Specifically, legislators in the U.S. Senate are elected using primaries and a first-past-the-post voting system in dual-seat constituencies, which, as I explain later, render party leaders little control over legislative behavior. Finally, I expect that women's seniority status in the U.S. Senate will facilitate cross party collaboration. In the remainder of this case study, I use evidence from three explanatory factors (i.e., women's marginalization, weak party constraints, and legislative seniority) to explain collaboration in the U.S. Senate.

Women's Marginalized Status in the U.S. Senate

Similar to the Argentine case, women in the U.S. Senate have a history of marginalization in the legislature. This is most evident in their lack of numeric representation. Historically, women were virtually absent in the U.S. Senate. It was not until 1992 – commonly touted as "The Year of the Woman" in the United States – that women started to gain ground, winning 5 percent of the Senate seats.[15] Senator Kay Bailey Hutchison (R-TX) picked up a sixth seat in a special election later that year, resulting in women holding 6 percent of seats in the U.S. Senate at the outset of the 1993–1994 congressional term. As depicted in Figure 7.2, the proportion of women in the Senate began to slowly increase over the next two decades. In 2013, the U.S. Senate reached a major milestone with women winning 20 percent of the Senate seats.

In addition to their minority status, women have not held many powerful committee or leadership positions in the Senate. In 1992, women's committee

---

[13] Interview with Senator Debby Fischer, cited in Morton (2013).
[14] Interview with Senator Rob Portman, cited in Steinhauer (2013).
[15] Women won five seats in the general election: Barbara Mikulski (R-MD), Patty Murray (D-WA), Carol Moseley Braun (D-IL), Dianne Feinstein (D-CA), and Barbara Boxer (D-CA).

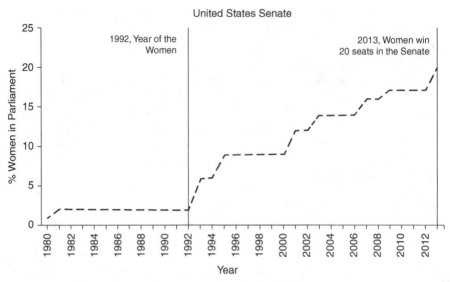

FIGURE 7.2. Women's numeric representation in the U.S. Senate.
Source: IPU (2013) and Paxton et al. (2008).

appointments were considered slightly better than those of the average fresh-man senator. These favorable appointments were likely the product of the Senate leadership's desire to demonstrate the growing diversification of the Senate in an effort to restore positive public perceptions (Arnold and King 2002). Appointments of this nature, however, are not characteristic of women's formal incorporation in the Senate over time. An analysis of women's commit-tee appointments reveals that women are represented on most Senate commit-tees, but they are proportionally underrepresented on the four most powerful committees in the chamber (Arnold and King 2002). Women's status in the chamber has improved some over the past ten years. Today, women do chair a variety of Standing Committees (e.g., Agriculture, Nutrition, and Forestry; Environment and Public Works; Small Business and Entrepreneurship). Albeit, women have not chaired the most powerful committees, and the majority leader, minority leaders, and party whips are all still men (Swers 2013).

Still today, the U.S. Senate is very much a male-dominated institution (Swers 2013). In addition to formal barriers to power, women face a num-ber of challenges with informal integration in the U.S. Senate. Female sena-tors report that they are keenly aware that they operate in a male-dominated organization and are often reminded by subtle forms of sexism. Senator Amy Klobuchar (D-MN) recounts a story that illustrates this point. After Klobuchar had already served six months in the Senate, an unnamed male senator walked into a "Senators Only" elevator, looked at Senator Klobuchar, and asked what she was doing there – clearly not realizing that she was one of his colleagues

(Steinhauer 2013). Despite that she was one of only a handful of women in the Senate, her male colleague was so accustomed to being surrounded by men that he did not recognize her as a senator. In addition to being treated like outsiders, women in the Senate – like women in the Argentine provinces – report having to work twice as hard to prove that they deserve to be in the Senate and are effective politicians. Senator Barbara Boxer (D-CA) recalls: "When I started out it was an absolute disadvantage to be a woman. You had to prove you understood numbers, that you understood history."[16] Senator Dianne Feinstein perceived a similar environment: "The Senate has traditionally and historically been an all-male club.... We are still, in a sense, interlopers. It still is, in a sense, an uphill battle to show that you're just as effective as a male."[17]

Women's marginalization creates incentives for women to collaborate. The formation of the women's monthly dinner club provides some evidence of this incentive. This feeling of being an outsider inspired Senator Barbara Mikulski (D-MD), the longest-serving woman in the Senate, to start a bipartisan women's dinner group shortly after she assumed office in 1987. This informal gathering created the opportunity for women to get to know one another outside of the office and discuss their shared experiences. These regular meetings are often identified as fundamental in fostering bipartisanship, civility, and cooperation among female senators.

In addition to marginalization, it is worth noting, in the U.S. Senate, all legislators may have an additional incentive to collaborate. In Chapter 2 I explained that minority legislators have a stronger incentive to collaborate than do majority legislators because they do not have the power to decide via competition. In the U.S. Senate, however, a majority is not sufficient to guarantee legislators the power to decide. Instead, legislators typically need to rally support from a supermajority in order to avoid a filibuster. This is because the U.S. Senate rules allow senators to filibuster a bill for as long as they want until three-fifths of the senators invoke the cloture rule to bring the filibuster to an end. Thus, this powerful parliamentary device may further incentivize collaboration among U.S. senators as they need to establish filibuster-proof majorities to advance their legislative interests. Nonetheless, this incentive is not unique to women. Indeed, both men and women need to establish filibuster-proof majorities to secure legislative success. Given that female senators collaborate more than their male counterparts, this is clearly not the only incentive women have to collaborate in the U.S. Senate.

I argue here that women in the U.S. Senate also have an incentive to collaborate in an effort to overcome their marginalized status in the Senate. Yet, as in Argentina, institutions influence the extent to which women are successful at forging collaboration. In the next two sections, I examine how the institutions in place in the Senate structure women's legislative behavior.

[16] Interview with Senator Barbara Boxer, cited in Steinhauer (2013).
[17] Interview with Senator Dianne Feinstein, quoted in Morton (2013).

Weak Party Constraints: Primary Elections and Dual-seat Constituencies

Weak party constraints mark the first notable feature of the U.S. Senate that is conducive to collaboration. As shown in the case of Argentina, when party discipline is weak, women are more likely than men to collaborate with their female colleagues and they are more willing to cross party lines to do so. Conversely, strong party discipline constrains women's incentive to collaborate with female colleagues. In the U.S. Senate, members are subject to relatively weak party discipline – even weaker than women from small electoral districts in the Argentine provinces.

In the U.S. Senate, members are elected using primary elections in dual-seat constituencies in which only one senator is elected during a given election. The decision to run for reelection lies almost exclusively in the hands of the legislator (and not the party). Voters cast votes for individual candidates – not political parties – rewarding or punishing them for past performance (Fiorina 1978). As such, election to office depends largely on a candidate's personal reputation with the electorate. This method of election provides legislators a strong incentive to develop their individual reputations and it limits the control that party leaders exercise over individual legislators (Mayhew 1974). As a result, legislators have more freedom to behave independently of the party.

Female legislators facing limited party constraints are more likely to pursue activities that will make their voices heard in the policy-making process. Indeed, multiple examples from the U.S. Senate illustrate how women have come together across partisan lines to make a difference. As Senator Kristen Gillibrand explains, "In the Senate you have to start with a bipartisan core to get things done, and that core is often formed with the women."[18] I argue that the weak party constraints fostered by the electoral system in the United States are key to understanding women's ability to develop a collaborative culture in the Senate. Female senators' efforts to collaborate were largely unhampered by partisan constraints. The evidence presented here corroborates my findings from the Argentine provinces that women's legislative collaboration thrives when party constraints are weak.

Entrenched Seniority in the U.S. Senate

Seniority is a second factor that promotes women's legislative collaboration. The U.S. Senate is known for its extremely high reelection rates and entrenched seniority. Previous research shows that senior legislators are typically less likely to collaborate because they have other avenues through which to influence policy (Davidson and Oleszek 2005; Harward and Moffett 2010). But, because of both formal and informal barriers, even women with seniority status have limited power relative to their senior male colleagues. Thus

[18] Interview with Senator Kristen Gillibrand, cited in Steinhauer (2013).

senior women behave differently than senior men. Senior women are more willing to reach out to newcomers, mentor them, and teach them to navigate the legislative process. For example, Senator Mikulski, elected in 1987 and now ranking among the longest-serving legislators in the Senate, stands out as a senior woman who has invested significant resources into mentoring junior colleagues. In addition to creating a community among women (e.g., starting the women-only dinner group), she takes in newcomers and shows them the ropes. "The other ladies call me Coach Barb. When a new woman is elected to the Senate – Republican or Democrat – I bring her in for my Senate Power Workshop and guide her on how to get started, how to get on the good committees for her state, and how to be an effective senator." [19] Similarly, Senator Feinstein and Senator Boxer, who each served just over ten years, are involved in mentoring female newcomers. Senior women in the U.S. Senate have clearly taken the lead on establishing strong mentorship networks among female senators. Consistent with the evidence from Argentina, senior women are more likely to forge cross-partisan connections and facilitate collaboration among women from different parties.

Conclusions for the U.S. Senate

As in Argentina, the history of women's marginalized status in the United States creates a strong incentive for women to collaborate, and the legislative contexts in the U.S. Senate are particularly conducive to collaboration. Electoral systems that combine open primaries and small districts, like those found in the U.S. Senate, foster weak party constraints. Thus, similar to women in districts with weak party constraints (small districts) in Argentina, women in the U.S. Senate collaborate on a regular basis and frequently cross party lines to work with female colleagues. Moreover, in line with the findings for Argentina, senior women in the Senate facilitate collaborative opportunities for women from all political parties and transmit norms of collaboration to new cohorts of women.

Taken together, the study of the U.S. Senate establishes the generalizability of my findings beyond Argentina by demonstrating that weak party constraints and seniority are important factors that permit women to work within the legislature to exert their influence on policy. The U.S. case shows that women's collaboration is not limited to cosponsorship but extends to other formal and informal types of collaboration – such as networking and mentorship – that shape the policy-making process. Finally, the study advances our understanding of how institutions structure women's collaboration by extending my analysis to institutions that are not found in Argentina (i.e., primary elections with small districts).

---

[19] Interview with Senator Barbara Mikulski, cited in Carlson (2012).

THE COST OF COLLABORATION IN URUGUAY

In recent years, women in Uruguay have forged coalitions among themselves and collaborated to promote women's rights. But for many women, this collaboration has come at a cost. Women who choose to defy party norms have been sanctioned by their parties and excluded from the party ballots in subsequent elections – effectively ending their political careers. Women are marginalized in the Uruguayan Congress and thus have a strong incentive to collaborate to exert their influence. Still, it may seem surprising that women's collaboration would unfold in Uruguay because legislators face strong party constraints. Three different factors explain the patterns of women's collaboration and subsequent partisan costs in the case of Uruguay. First, women's collaboration is largely limited to women's issues legislation. Indeed, in Chapter 2, I posit that women – even those facing strong party constraints – are more likely to collaborate when working on women's issues. Second, women hold a very small proportion of seats. As I explain in Chapter 2, when women comprise only a small share of the chamber, party leaders are less likely to constrain their efforts to collaborate, as women's collaboration is unlikely to have a sizable impact on legislative outcomes. Thus party leaders have little incentive to expend energy and resources constraining women's collaboration. Third, there is a well-organized women's caucus. Similar to the Forum of Rwandan Women Parliamentarians, the caucus unites women from different parties and facilitates cooperation among women. Despite these factors that facilitate women's collaboration, it is not surprising that collaboration is costly for some female legislators. The political factions in Uruguay impose strong party discipline and faction leaders have significant control over legislators' political careers. Thus, when women's collaboration results in the advancement of controversial policies, it attracts the attention of party bosses and results in party sanctions. As such, some women end up paying a premium to collaborate with female colleagues and to support women's rights.

Evidence of Women's Collaboration on Women's Issues in Uruguay

In recent years, women in Uruguay have made headline news for collaborating with women across the political spectrum to advance a women's rights agenda (Silveira 2010). As journalist Silvana Silveira (2010) observed: "Women lawmakers in Uruguay have joined forces across party lines, in spite of criticism from colleagues in their own parties, and have built majorities to approve laws in favor of gender equality and other rights that have been denied for years." As a result of this multiparty collaboration, female legislators in Uruguay have seen several major legislative successes in the past decade. For example, in 2003, legislation was passed granting women the right to restraining orders in cases of domestic violence. In 2000, the Uruguayan Parliament passed a law to promote preventative health care by permitting women the right to take a day off work each year for annual gynecological exams. In 2009, Uruguay adopted gender quota legislation to increase women's numeric representation in the National Parliament.

These major policy accomplishments and others are largely a product of female legislators, from different political parties, coming together to establish a clear women's rights agenda and working among themselves to produce more representative legislation. Senator Margarita Percovich (Broad Front) explains: "We have a common agenda, which includes both draft laws and public policies, whose central aim is gender equity."[20] Women's rights expert Diana González agreed that multiparty collaboration was a cornerstone of these policy successes: "Examining the approval processes of each of these laws shows that including equity and gender elements was due to women lawmakers who united beyond their political positions to contribute shared criteria."[21]

From the outset women's collaboration appears quite profitable; but for some, collaboration was extremely costly. In Uruguay, legislators face strong party/faction constraints (Morgenstern 2001), and not all political parties are supportive of the women's rights agenda (Fernández Anderson 2011). Women from these parties are sometimes forced to choose between party allegiances and promoting legislation they genuinely support. The decision to promote women's rights can come at the expense of their political careers. For example, Deputy Glenda Rondán (Colorado Party) suffered severe partisan consequences for backing legislation to decriminalize abortion (Silveira 2010). Although the Colorado Party does not formally oppose the decriminalization of abortion, historically the vast majority of legislators from the Colorado Party voted against abortion law reforms (Fernández Anderson 2011). But, in 2001, Deputy Rondán publicly supported reforming the abortion law in favor of decriminalization, and the next year, she joined forces with other legislators to coauthor the Defense of Reproductive Health Legislation (Defensa de la Salud Reproductiva) to decriminalize abortion. She explained that supporting women's rights sometimes comes at a price: "When you want to change things, you pay a cost, and if you are a woman you pay three times over."[22] For Deputy Rondán, the price was exclusion from the party's power structure (Silveira 2010).

Another national deputy faced similar consequences for advocating the women's rights agenda against her party's orders. Deputy Beatriz Argimón (National Party) served in the Chamber of Deputies from 2000 to 2010. She defied her party's negative stance on the gender quota law by voting to support the legislation. She explains that she has always defended women's rights but has been met with "strong resistance from some of her colleagues."[23] She

[20] Interview with Senator Margrita Percovich, cited in Castellanos (2006).
[21] Interview with policy expert Diana González, cited in Silveira (2010).
[22] Interview with Deputy Rondán, Cited in Silveira (2010).
[23] Interview with Deputy Beatriz Argimón, cited in "Una Mirada Feminista a la Campaña Electoral 2009" (2009).

reasoned that her party "has serious problems with the fact of women in power."[24] Her decision to support the quota law was met with the ultimate party sanction; when her term in office was up, faction leaders refused to allow her to run for reelection on the faction list (Silveira 2010). Deputy Argimón and her co-partisan Deputy Sandra Etcheverry, both of whom promoted the quota law, "agreed that they were paying the price of having rebelled against the rules of the system that eternally relegated women."[25] These examples illustrate the gravity of party sanctions and the cost of defying party bosses.

Despite this, collaboration on women's issues is widespread in the Uruguayan Congress and has been the driving force behind several landmark advancements in women's rights. Yet, clearly, these women face strong party-faction discipline. At the outset, it may seem puzzling that women's collaboration prevails in the face of strong faction constraints. What allows women to overcome these obstacles in order to advance a women's rights agenda?

To answer this question, it is important to acknowledge that in Uruguay, women's collaboration is largely limited to women's issues. In the case of Argentina, women who face weak party constraints are more likely to collaborate on women's issues regardless of the legislative context. Women are more likely than men to prioritize women's issues, and thus, legislators working on women's issues are more likely to seek out female collaborators. This explains in part why women collaborate in the face of strong faction constraints. A common women's rights agenda provided substantial motivation for women to collaborate. Other legislative contexts also shape women's opportunities and incentives to work together.

I evaluate three additional factors expected to facilitate collaboration among women. First, because Uruguayan women are marginalized in the legislature, I expect them to have incentives to collaborate. Second, as women hold a very small proportion of seats in the chamber, they can fly under the radar, collaborating without attracting much attention from party leaders. Third, an organized caucus – the Bicameral Women's Caucus – coordinates women around central themes and unites them across party lines and across chambers.

Women's Marginalized Status in the Uruguayan Congress

As with the other chambers examined in this book, women's marginalization in the Uruguayan Congress motivates collaboration. In the early 1980s, Uruguay returned to democracy and held its first democratic election in 1984, during which time no women were elected to serve in the national legislature. Figure 7.3 graphs the proportion of women elected to the Uruguayan Senate and House since the restoration of democracy. The first women were

---

[24] Interview with Deputy Beatriz Argimón, cited in Silveira (2010).
[25] Interviewed on the program *Primera Voz*, Radio AM Libre, quoted in *La República* (23/08/2009), cited in Johnson (2013b).

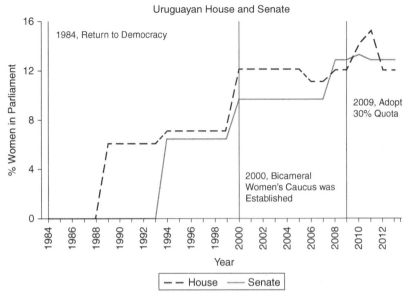

FIGURE 7.3. Women's numeric representation in Uruguay.
Source: IPU (2013) and Johnson and Pérez (2009).

elected to serve in the House in 1989 and won 6.1 percent of legislative seats. In the Senate no women were elected to office until 1994, during which time they won 6.5 percent of seats. Women's numeric representation in Uruguay has slowly inched up over time but continues to lag behind the majority of national parliaments across Latin America (Johnson 2005; Johnson and Pérez 2009). Even today, women hold only a small minority of seats in the Senate and House. As of 2013, women still hold only 13 percent of seats in the Senate and 12 percent in the House. Historically, among the major parties in the parliament, a higher proportion of women have been elected into the Broad Front political party than in any other party. From 1995 to 2010, between 15 percent and 16 percent of the Broad Front party members were women (Johnson and Pérez 2009). By comparison, during this period, only between 6 percent and 11 percent of members from the Colorado Party were women; and the proportion of women in the National Party ranged from zero to 17 percent. In 2009, the Uruguay Parliament adopted a gender quota requiring political parties to reserve at least one in every three seats on their lists for female candidates. The quota was implemented for the first time in the November 2014 legislative elections and 2015 local elections. The law is only a trial to evaluate the law's effectiveness and is not currently intended to extend to future legislative elections. In spite of this reform, women remain woefully underrepresented in the Uruguayan Parliament.

Women's underrepresentation is important for understanding women's collaboration in Uruguay for two reasons. First, women's marginalization motivates women's collaboration. Women are a small minority; they make up a small fraction of the legislative leadership, and typically hold fewer than 20 percent of committee leadership positions (Archenti and Johnson 2006). Women lack the political power needed to advance their legislative priorities. For example, the first domestic violence bill in Uruguay was introduced in 1991, but it was not passed until almost a decade later because women lacked the resources to advance the legislation. Thus, women's marginalization motivates women to collaborate among themselves and to build coalitions of support and attain political power.

Second, as I explain in Chapter 2, when women comprise a very small share of the chamber they collaborate without attracting much attention from party leaders. Because women are unlikely to have much legislative success, it is more costly for party leaders to police their behavior than to ignore them. But, as women grow in numbers, and their power increases, party leaders have a stronger incentive to constrain their behavior. As such, faced with strong partisan constraints, women are more likely to have opportunities to collaborate across party lines when they comprise only a small proportion of the legislature. In the case of the Argentine provinces, I show in Chapter 5 that female legislators who are subject to strong party constraints are more likely to cross party lines to collaborate when women comprise less than 10 percent of the chamber than when women comprise 30 percent of the chamber. During the period under study, women's numeric representation in Uruguay never rose above 15 percent in either chamber. Thus, it is not surprising that women in Uruguay collaborate to promote women's rights even in the face of strong faction discipline.

Strong Faction Constraints: Sub-party Lists in the Uruguayan Congress

The Uruguayan electoral system uses sub-party lists to elect members to the Senate and House. The sub-party lists are closed list and voters choose between lists and not directly between candidates. Thirty senators are elected in a single national district. In the Congress, about half of the chamber is elected from districts of very small magnitudes, while the remainder is elected from large district magnitudes. Specifically, forty-one members are elected from one district in Montevideo, fifteen members are elected from one district in Canelones, and the remaining forty-three members are elected from small districts ranging in size from 2 to 4.

In Uruguay, party-factions are more important than parties. Faction leaders control access to the faction ballot, and for this reason they have the ability to exercise strong constraints over members elected from their faction list (Morgenstern 2001). Party-factions are well organized and institutionalized, and therefore are capable of sanctioning faction members. As a result, legislators are subject to strong party constraints imposed by faction leaders.

Legislators who desire to seek reelection have a strong incentive to toe the *faction* line and appeal to faction leaders. The strong faction constraints help explain why collaboration among women in Uruguay is largely limited to collaboration on women's issues. In Argentina, all women – those facing weak and strong party constraints – are more likely to collaborate when working on women's issues legislation than when working on other types of legislation. In Uruguay, women have been successful in collaborating to promote women's rights, but strong faction pressures stifle cross-party collaboration among women on other issues.

The Bicameral Women's Caucus

Collaboration among women is further enhanced by the presence of a women's caucus. Caucuses create a space for women to interact regardless of political party affiliation. Caucuses – particularly those focused on women's issues – can promote the development of a gender equality agenda and foster the discussion and exchange of information pertaining to gender-related initiatives. In Uruguay, a well-organized women's caucus has been fundamental in coordinating women across party lines.

The Bicameral Women's Caucus (Bancada Bicameral Femenina, or the BBF) in Uruguay was first formed in 2000 when female legislators won 10 percent of Congress for the first time – (a total of fifteen women in the House and Senate combined). The BBF was initiated by a multiparty coalition of legislators (Deputy Margarita Percovich [Broad Front], Deputy Beatriz Argimón [National Party], and Deputy Glenda Rondán [Colorado Party]), and was designed to unite women in the Senate and the House. During the first caucus meeting, all legislators in attendance signed an agreement that they would work together to advance a common agenda to promote gender equality (Johnson 2013a).

This understanding did not mean that women agreed on every policy. There are a number of policies, such as abortion and gender quotas, that are highly contested. Yet, as Deputy Rondán explains, their different stances on issues do not negate the importance of the issues: "In spite of differences, we will always have common concerns."[26] Thus, even though they did not agree on a few controversial issues, women vowed to acknowledge the importance of these issues, to engage in debates on the issues, and to move toward common solutions (Johnson 2009). Senator Susana Dalmás (Broad Front) explains that the caucus represents "the will" of female legislators "to come together to try to agree on certain matters" that should be taken up in the parliament.[27] Deputy Daisy Tourné (Broad Front) echoes this understanding: "It is clear to us that on some matters we are going to disagree and we feel absolutely free

---

[26] Interview with Deputy Glenda Rondán, cited in Silveira (2010).
[27] Interview with Senator Susana Dalmás, cited in Green (2012).

to do so, and that doesn't undermine the unity that we achieve on the underlying issues."[28] Even when members of the BBF disagreed on issues, they had an explicit agreement never to do so publicly, but to limit such disagreement to the caucus meetings (Johnson 2009). This is the same approach that Rwandan women took with the Forum on Rwanda Women Parliamentarians when they agreed to come to a consensus on difficult issues *prior* to introducing the GBV legislation on the chamber floor. This allows them to present a united public image and increases the probability that the chamber would approve the legislation.[29]

Women's collaboration in the caucus soon became a norm. Senator Monica Xavier (Broad Front) explained that the "[caucus emphasizes] the things that unite us ... when citizens see that we can rise above ideological differences ... and work on other issues on which we agree, then we have strength."[30] Moreover, Deputy Argimón explains that the women's caucus was important for confronting women's marginalization in the legislature, establishing a dialogue around gender issues, and promoting legislative initiatives to improve women's lives.[31] The ability to work through issues and develop a common solution has enabled their success in the parliament. The women's caucus is widely seen as a driving force behind numerous women's rights policies. As one expert put it: "There is no doubt that the BBF was behind the success of these bills [advancing women's rights]."[32]

Finally, in addition to several major policy successes, Deputy Argimón also explains the BBF started a public debate and garnered media attention and visibility around many major policy issues.[33] This is an extremely important aspect of representation regardless of the ultimate success of legislation. Indeed, this is one purpose of collaboration that came across in the Argentine case. A deputy from the Federal District explained: "Sometimes we know that we aren't going to fix the problem, but we still talk about it and discuss it. We make the theme public and put it out there."[34] By collaborating on important issues and talking about them with interested colleagues, legislators can call attention to issues (Swers 2013). The BBF was instrumental in allowing women in Uruguay to raise awareness about relevant problems in society and ignite important public discussions.

---

[28] Interview with Deputy Daisy Tourné in the weekly supplement La República de las Mujeres (30/05/2004); also in cited in Johnson (2013a).
[29] See Piscopo (2014b) for a discussion of how compromise in women's caucuses may limit the ability of women in the legislature to use their political power to challenge gender roles.
[30] Interview with Senator Monica Xavier, cited in Green (2012).
[31] Interview with Deputy Beatriz Argimón, cited in Silveira (2010).
[32] Interview with Diana González, a lawyer who specializes in gender issues in Uruguay, cited in Silveira (2010).
[33] Interview with Deputy Beatriz Argimón, cited in Castellanos (2006).
[34] Interview with female deputy from Federal District, Buenos Aires para Todos, July 19, 2013.

Conclusions for the Uruguayan Congress

One of the key factors for promoting women's collaboration in Uruguay is the Bicameral Women's Caucus. The women's caucus united women across party lines, providing a place for women to debate important women's rights issues, develop compromises, and find ways to move legislation forward. Although women's caucuses and women's issues committees are not common in the Argentine provinces, they have increased in popularity in Latin America over the past fifteen years. At the national level in Latin America, women's caucuses have been growing in strength and they are often seen as vital for facilitating dialogue among female legislators (Castellanos 2006). Table 7.2 provides a list of the South American countries where women's caucuses exist. Nine countries have established women's caucuses, and Uruguay's caucus has served as a model for many countries in Latin America and across the globe.

Even though women successfully united across party lines to promote a shared agenda, female legislators in Uruguay still face faction pressures to toe the faction line, and some women are even discouraged from championing women's rights. Deputy Argimón's experience after voting against her party on important women's rights issues demonstrates tangible partisan pressures, and illustrates the gravity of consequences legislators face when they defy party discipline. Finally, faction discipline works to restrict women's collaboration in terms of issue domains. Unlike the example from the United States, where women tend to work across party lines on a number of issues, women's collaboration in Uruguay has been more restricted to women's issues. This is another limitation of the strong discipline imposed by party factions.

THE SOUTH AFRICAN PARLIAMENT: A CASE OF PARTISAN CONSTRAINT

South Africa presents an example of a legislative context where women fail to collaborate among themselves. Similar to the previous case studies, female legislators face structural barriers that limit their influence in the policy-making process, and thus have an incentive to work together to exert their influence in the chamber. However, unlike the cases of the U.S. Senate, the Rwandan Chamber of Deputies, and the Uruguay Congress, women's efforts to mobilize across party lines are continually thwarted in South Africa. In this case study, I argue that two features of the electoral system foster strong party discipline and constrain women's collaboration. First, the use of closed-list electoral systems with extremely large districts gives party leaders immense control over legislators' political careers. Second, the political parties own the rights to all seats won by their lists during elections. Specifically, the constitution requires that the seat share of each party in the parliament remain representative of the election results. Thus unlike other parliaments that allow legislators to freely switch parties (O'Brien and Shomer 2013), legislators in South Africa cannot

TABLE 7.2. *Women's Caucuses across Latin America*

Country	Caucus Name	Year Created	Chamber
Brazil	Bancada Feminina na Câmara (Women's Caucus of National Congress)	1988	Unicameral
Uruguay	Bancada Bicameral Femenina (Bicameral Women's Caucus)	2000	Senate and House
Colombia	Bancada de Mujeres del Congreso (Colombian Congressional Women's Caucus)	2006	Senate and House
Peru	Mesa de Mujeres Parlamentarias Peruanas (Table of Peruvian Women Parliamentarians)	2006	Unicameral
Bolivia	La Unión de Mujeres Parlamentarias de Bolivia (Union of Women Parliamentarians of Bolivia)	2006	Unicameral
Argentina	Banca de la Mujer (Women's Caucus)	2007	Senate
El Salvador	Grupo Parlamentario de Mujeres de la Asamblea Legislativa (Parliamentary Women's Caucus of the Legislative Assembly)	2009	Unicameral
Ecuador	Grupo Parlamentario por los Derechos de las Mujeres (Parliamentary Group for Women's Rights)	2009	Unicameral
Nicaragua	Grupo Institucional de Diputadas y Diputados para la Promoción de la Equidad de Género (Institutional group of Legislators for the Promotion of Gender Equality)	2013	Unicameral

Source: IPU Database on Women's Caucuses (2015).

change parties, become unaffiliated with parties, or be forced out of their parties and remain in the parliament (Mattes 2002). Consequently, legislators who break party ranks can be banished from the parties and forced to give up their seats in the parliament (Mattes 2002). As such, the South African Parliament represents the most extreme case of party control.

Foiled Efforts to Collaborate in South Africa

From 1991 to 1993, a series of negotiations between the white minority government and the opposition led to the end of apartheid in South Africa.[35] During this time, women mobilized across party lines to organize a national women's liberation movement with the goal of influencing the development of the new constitution to ensure women's place in government. The Women's National Coalition (WNC), a multiparty coalition comprised of more than ninety women's organizations (Ginwala 1991), coordinated efforts to spearhead the movement and develop an inclusive platform of action, which is now known as the Women's Charter (Britton 2005; Meintjes 2001).

Despite partisan, ethnic, and class differences, women "united over their exclusion from the constitutional negotiations, their shared patterns of resistance to subordination, and an exclusive focus on gender issues" (Britton 2005). By emphasizing women's shared experiences and focusing on a narrow goal, the WNC was able to minimize women's differences and become the only organization in South Africa to successfully work across party, ethnic, and class lines (Tripp 2000). This unified front positioned women to make demands on both the political parties and the state, eventually winning women a seat at the table during constitutional negotiations.

One may expect that the vital role of multiparty collaboration during the democratic transition would lay the foundation for women to collaborate in the parliament. The conditions described earlier appear ideal for encouraging collaboration. Surprising, once in the parliament, women's collaboration was continually foiled (Britton 2005; Goetz and Hassim 2002; Hassim 2003). For example, after the transition to democracy in 1994 a women's caucus, the Parliamentary Women's Group (PWG), was established to coordinate women from different parties and facilitate the advancement of women's rights. As Britton describes it: "At its inception this multiparty caucus was envisioned as linking women in civil societies and government, mobilizing women from all parties in government, and monitoring the government's efforts to promote gender equality" (2005, 135). But the caucus was not successful in accomplishing these goals. What explains this puzzling outcome?

In the case of South Africa, the electoral system promotes fierce party loyalty and extreme party discipline. As I have argued, women's collaboration is stymied when legislators are subject to strong partisan constraints. To fully appreciate the extent to which political institutions structure women's behavior in South Africa, it is important to consider the following three factors: women's status in South Africa and their role in the democratic transition; the electoral system and the power it grants party leaders; and the crippling effects of party discipline on the women's caucus. I consider each of these factors in turn.

---

[35] See Clucas and Valdini (2015) for a discussion of the negotiations leading to the adoption of a new constitution.

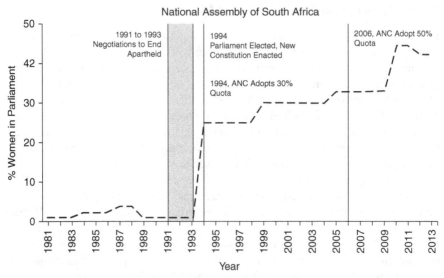

FIGURE 7.4. Women's numeric representation in South Africa.
Source: IPU (2013) and Paxton et al. (2008).

Women's Marginalized Status in South Africa

Historically women have been excluded from the South African Parliament. Prior to the transition to democracy in 1994, women never held more than 5 percent of seats in the parliament. Figure 7.4 charts women's numeric representation in the South African Parliament from 1981 until the present day. From 1981 until 1993, women's numeric representation hovered between 1 percent and 4 percent. The democratic transition marked a new opportunity for women to become more incorporated in politics. Women used this opportunity to pressure the state and individual political parties to guarantee women political representation. They championed the adoption of a multimember electoral system using party lists because this system is known to be the most successful for increasing women's numeric representation (Ballington 1999; Britton 2002). Additionally, women worked within their respective parties to pressure party leaders to reserve space on the party ballot for women.

As a result of these efforts, women won 14 percent of seats in the parliament during the first democratic election in 1994. Later that year, the African National Congress (ANC), the largest political party holding 62 percent of seats, adopted a gender quota of 30 percent. In the following election in 1999, women's numeric representation improved to 25 percent, and has continued to increase. In 2006, the ANC increased the gender quota to 50 percent. In the election immediately following the quota reform, women won 44 percent of the seats in the national parliament, an all-time high. The ANC party quota was very effective at increasing women's numeric representation because the ANC continued to secure the vast majority of seats in office. In 1999 the ANC won 266 seats (67 percent). The second largest party, the Democratic Party, won only 38 seats. This trend continues to dominate party politics in South Africa. In 2004 and 2009 the ANC secured 279 and 264 seats, respectively. The Democratic Alliance trailed behind with only 50 seats in 2004 and 67 seats in 2009.

Women's initial access to the parliament and increases in women's numeric representation were the result of women's multiparty collaboration (Britton 2005). It may seem logical that the presence of the WNC combined with women's history of marginalization would lay the foundation for women's collaboration. Despite women's success in securing access to the parliament and increasing their numeric representation, female MPs have not been successful in establishing cross-partisan collaborations. What explains the lack of collaboration among women in the South African Parliament?

Extreme Party Constraints: Closed-List PR with Large District Magnitude

In South Africa, 400 legislators are elected from a closed-list PR system with an extremely large district size. Two hundred MPs are elected from nine multi-member provincial districts. The number of seats is allocated in proportion to the population and the average district size is 22. The remaining 200 MPs are elected from one nationwide district. In closed-list systems, party leaders are responsible for selecting candidates to run on the party ballot. Rank-and-file members of the party do not have a strong influence in this process, and voters do not have an opportunity to indicate preferences for individual candidates (Burchard 2015; Clucas and Valdini 2015). Legislators' electoral success is directly tied to the parties' success. Because legislators have to depend on a party leader to get their names on the ballot, they do not have a strong incentive to promote legislation that increases their own public visibility or to pursue a legislative agenda beyond the party platform. Popular support does not have a strong bearing on their legislative careers or affect the probability of reelection. Instead, legislators are indebted to party leaders and must display strong party loyalty to ensure the continued possibility of reelection. MPs are strictly accountable to party leaders and have very little incentive to deviate from the party line. As such, South African parties have a culture of strong discipline.

Facing these circumstances, women have both weaker incentives and fewer opportunities to collaborate with female colleagues to influence policy outcomes. Member of Parliament Suzanne Vos acknowledged how party pressures restrict women's ability to promote a clear policy agenda: "There is no doubt that the PR list system ensures that all politicians must remain popular with the (mostly male) party bosses to survive. Male leadership also invariably selects which women are promoted within party structures and within parliament" (1999, 108–109). As such, strong party constraints limit female MPs' ability to articulate policy positions that diverge from those of the party leaders (Goetz and Hassim 2003).

It is evident from this discussion that strong party constraints in South Africa stymie women's collaboration. Party constraints are so strong, in fact, that they stifle women's collaboration in spite of the presence of a women's caucus – an institution put in place to coordinate women across party lines. In the next section, I explain how party discipline foiled the efforts of multiparty women's caucuses.

Women's Caucus Fails to Promote Collaboration

In 1994, the Parliamentary Women's Group (PWG) was created to promote gender equality, to organize women across different political parties, and to institutionalize the work of the WNC (the organization that was instrumental in securing women a place in Parliament). As Britton explains it, "The PWG initially worked to both tackle cultural issues blocking women's participation in Parliament and to provide a clearinghouse for cross-party coalition building on women's issues" (2005, 135). But the organization was not able to accomplish the goal of uniting women across party lines. Britton reports that by 1996 and 1997, most women were not participating in the PWG and had reservations about the viability of a multiparty organization in the South African Parliament where "party loyalty is supreme." By 2003, women's participation in the PWG had dissipated completely. Britton explains that female MPs are compelled to represent their parties and not their constituents. Further, they report not being "allowed" to participate in cross-party collaboration or to promote a shared agenda. As such, Britton concludes that the divisive partisan climate in the South African Parliament "will always limit cross-party collaboration based only on gender" (2005, 137).

This is not to say that women's numeric representation has not had an impact on South African politics. Rather, research finds that women in South Africa have successfully advanced women's rights in a number of areas and women's presence in the legislature has been instrumental in eroding traditional expectations about women's role in politics more generally (Barnes and Burchard 2013). Where multi-partisan efforts were thwarted, some partisan efforts, led by an elite group of women within the ANC, have had success at promoting women's rights (Britton 2005; Goetz and Hassim 2002; Hassim 2003). Most notably, the Joint Standing Committee on the Quality of Life and Status of Women (JMC) passed several pieces of women's rights legislation. Under the direction of Pregs Govender, a high-profile member of the ANC, the JMC established a clear list of priorities and several significant pieces of legislation were passed into law. While the JMC is technically a nonpartisan committee, critics point out that the success of the JMC is a product of strategically placed leaders from the ANC and not a product of cross-party collaboration (Britton 2005).

Despite their thwarted efforts to collaborate, most women report that they support the idea of cross-partisan collaboration and hope it would be fruitful in the future (Britton 2005). While it is not unimaginable that women across the parliament may find a mutual agenda, the dominant ANC has little incentive to share credit for women's rights achievements with other political parties. It benefits more by claiming full credit for its MPs' efforts to advance women's status. As such, it is likely to continue to discourage female MPs from crossing party lines to promote women's rights.

Conclusions for the South African Parliament

Strong partisan constraints in the South African Parliament restrict female legislators' abilities to collaborate to promote women's rights. The divisive political climate in South Africa crippled the efforts of the PWG and paralyzed female MPs. Ironically, multimember electoral systems with large district magnitudes (which women advocated for because they are found to be most effective at increasing women's numeric representation) are known to foster strong party discipline, which I argue stifles women's ability to collaborate.

Obviously this does not preclude women's rights legislation from ever being passed, but it does create the need for more outside pressure. Goetz and Hassim (2002) indicate that in the case of South Africa, most of the progress on women's rights legislation has been an explicit product of pressure from outside of the government. Other scholars have also identified autonomous women's movements as fundamental for advancing women's rights (Htun and Weldon 2012). My research suggests that autonomous women's movements and other external forces are most critical when institutions allow parties to constrain women's collaboration. The limited possibility of collaboration on women's rights legislation is unfortunate because it precludes the consideration of a diversity of perspectives and experiences. Given that women's rights legislation affects the lives of women from a multitude of different backgrounds, the consideration of different perspectives is fundamental to the development of effective policy. This is particularly true in a diverse nation such as South Africa. The lack of collaboration among female MPs implies that influence from outside organizations and autonomous women's movements are imperative to articulate and represent the needs of South African women from different racial and class backgrounds.

COMPARING COLLABORATION ACROSS CASES

An in-depth assessment of collaboration across the four cases shows that legislative contexts are extremely important in understanding *when women will collaborate*. The four cases examined here differ significantly in historic, political, social, and economic terms. Yet the cases tell a cohesive story about how legislative contexts structure women's collaboration and corroborate the findings from the Argentine provinces. Women are more likely to collaborate when they face weak party constraints. Women in both the U.S. Senate and the Rwanda Parliament are subject to weak party constraints and serve as examples of women's successful collaboration. By contrast, women in South Africa are subject to extreme party constraints and their collaborative efforts are consistently foiled. Additionally, these case studies provide strong evidence that women's issues committees and women's caucuses are important – but not sufficient – for facilitating collaboration among women.

Assessing the cases together, South Africa offers the clearest evidence that institutions constrain women's collaboration. Strong party discipline effectively deters women from collaborating across party lines. Although women's collaboration was initially responsible for securing women a place in government and the development of a women's caucus, female MPs in South Africa do not collaborate among themselves. Both primary and secondary sources indicate that women's collaboration in South Africa is thwarted by party constraints. Women's inability to collaborate in South Africa is consistent with the trends we see in the Argentine provinces with the strongest party constraints. Evidence from Chapter 5 shows that women from large districts with closed-list systems – also like the ones found in South Africa – face strong party constraints that discourage women's collaboration.

Uruguay presents evidence of women collaborating across party lines in the face of strong party discipline. Because women comprise only a small share of the chamber, female legislators fly under the radar of party leaders and can work together to promote a shared women's rights agenda. This squares with the findings from Argentina presented in Chapter 6. I show that despite strong party constraints, women are more willing to collaborate with female colleagues when working on *women's issues* than when they are working on other legislative issues. This is particularly the case when women comprise a very small share of the chamber.

The cases of Rwanda and the U.S. Senate offer the clearest examples of where limited party discipline permits female legislators the opportunities to cross party lines, collaborating to accomplish shared goals. In the U.S. Senate, collaboration extends beyond women's issues to a broad set of policy issues. Female senators report that they regularly collaborate on a breadth of issues. In Rwanda, women collaborated among themselves and with women in the broader community to develop effective gender-based violence legislation. The objections raised to the legislation illustrate the challenges associated with advancing women's rights in Rwanda and further exemplify why it was essential for female legislators to collaborate among themselves to ensure legislative success.

Together these four case studies illustrate the generalizability of my theory. Incentives for collaboration among women legislators exist in a number of diverse settings, and women's collaboration is not unique to Argentina. Instead, it is prevalent across a number of countries that vary significantly in their historical, political, cultural, and economic backgrounds. Equally important, the extent to which the incentive to collaborate is realized is highly conditional on institutional opportunities. When institutions permit legislators some autonomy, collaboration flourishes; but when institutions constrain legislative behavior and demand unwavering party loyalty, collaboration is squelched.

8

Conclusion

Collaboration is an essential component of democracy. It is widespread across legislatures, but some legislators have more incentives to collaborate than others. In particular, legislators who are not in positions of power – such as women – can use collaboration to attain political power and influence the policy-making process. Perhaps this is why most scholarship emphasizes the competitive aspects of democracy, paying little attention to collaboration. When we focus primarily on privileged groups – those groups who designed institutions to benefit themselves – we overlook this aspect of democracy. It is only as we focus on groups that face structural barriers in institutions that the need for collaboration becomes apparent.

Although the incorporation of underrepresented groups into political institutions highlights aspects of the democratic process that are typically overlooked, these underrepresented groups still must function within existing institutions. As such, we can see how institutions structure their distinctive motivations. Patterns of collaboration vary among female legislators because not all women have the same opportunities to work collaboratively. Generally, women's collaboration is more likely to unfold where party leaders exercise weak party constraints over legislative behavior. By contrast, when party leaders exercise strong constraints over legislators' behavior, women's legislative collaboration is likely to be foiled.

In this concluding chapter, I address questions about how this book's contributions can advance future studies of legislative collaboration beyond women's marginalization, women's rights legislation, women's representation, and collaboration among other historically excluded groups. With respect to legislative collaboration, my theory argues that women are largely motivated to collaborate in an effort to overcome their marginalized status in the legislature and influence the policy-making process. As women make gains in the legislature and begin to achieve equal access to power, will collaboration cease, or is there room to think about collaboration beyond women's collective marginalization? Where the study of women's rights is concerned, what can the theory advanced here help us understand about the progression and success of women's rights agendas? For example, are some institutions more prohibitive to the advancement of women's rights? If so, what can be done to overcome these challenges? Next, I consider the implications of my findings for institutional design. Specifically, I consider what my findings have to say about how institutions can be designed to maximize women's numeric representation and to simultaneously ensure that women's voices are heard in the policy-making process. Finally, I explain how my theory may be generalized to other historically excluded groups. Before tackling these questions, I provide a brief review of my main argument and findings.

MAIN ARGUMENT AND FINDINGS: SUMMARY

Scholars of political representation are keenly concerned with understanding how members of underrepresented groups can gain a voice in the policy-making process. In the past three decades, international organizations have pressured governments to incorporate women and other marginalized groups into decision-making bodies (Bush 2011; Hughes, Krook, and Paxton 2015). Yet simple numeric representation is not sufficient to attain influences in democracies. Instead, even once women and other marginalized groups gain access to office they often have limited access to power. In its ideal form, democracy vests power within the people and power is used to promote the common good. In practice, democratic power is vested in the *majority* and is maintained through exclusion and competition. Given this, it is unclear under what conditions marginalized groups will attain political power and influence in the policy-making process.

I argue that women and other out-of-power groups can attain influence through collaboration. Thus, despite the traditional emphasis on competition, I maintain that *democracy can be collaborative*. Although only the winning majority can acquire power through competition, all legislators can influence the policy-making process through collaboration. For this reason, I explain that out-of-power legislators collaborate more than those in power.

In particular, *women collaborate more than men because they are marginalized*. Increasing women's numeric representation is not sufficient for women to attain political power. Instead, female legislators encounter structural barriers that limit their influence in decision-making bodies. Thus, women are one such group that can benefit from collaboration. Moreover, because women are marginalized within other out-of-power groups, they particularly stand to benefit from collaborating with female colleagues. Female legislators can overcome barriers imposed by the dominant group and gain a voice in the policy-making process by developing professional networks and working relationships with other female legislators. In doing so, they can exert more influence during the legislative process.

Despite the incentives to collaborate, not all women behave in this way. This book offers an explanation for these puzzling inconsistencies. I argue that *women's collaboration varies depending on legislative contexts that differ between and within chambers.* Six key factors that vary between and within chambers provide different incentives and opportunities for women to collaborate. With respect to factors that vary predominately between chambers, I argue that increases in women's numeric representation will spur collaboration among women when they face weak party constraints. By contrast, when party leaders have strong control over legislative behavior, increases in women's numeric representation will further limit collaboration among women. As for factors that vary within chambers, affiliation with the executive party, seniority, legislation that addresses women's issues, and membership in a women's caucus or committee each make collaboration more likely to unfold.

I pair original data from twenty-three Argentine provinces and interviews with more than 200 Argentine political elites with case studies from four countries across the globe to examine women's legislative collaboration. In doing so, I provide strong empirical support for my theory. First, I show that collaboration is an important feature of democracy. I use cosponsorship data – which represents the culmination of the collaborative policy-making process – to examine patterns of collaboration across Argentina. Collaboration – and, in particular, collaboration across party lines – is pervasive in the Argentine legislatures. Even in a country known for a divisive party system and relatively strong party discipline, an important part of the policy-making process is collaborative. Although collaboration is prevalent among all legislators, legislators who are not in power collaborate more than their colleagues who are in positions of power. Specifically, legislators from the opposition party collaborate more than those from the governor's party, legislators from minority parties collaborate more than those from the majority party, and women collaborate more than men. Interestingly, women not only cosponsor a larger number of bills and have a larger number of overall cosponsors than do men, but also, they are more likely than men to collaborate with women.

Second, I show that women are marginalized in the Argentine legislatures. I demonstrate that, despite substantial increases in women's numeric representation since the early 1990s, women are marginalized across a vast array of legislative power including chamber-wide leadership posts, committee leadership posts, and powerful committee appointments. Women are proportionally underrepresented in these positions of power, even when accounting for previous experience in the legislature. Women's exclusion from formal positions of power indicates that women do not have the same opportunities as men to shape the legislative agenda and influence policy outcomes. This marginalization limits women's political power and motivates collaboration among women.

Finally, I demonstrate that patterns of collaboration among women vary both between and within legislatures because not all women have the same opportunity to collaborate. I examine a number of different legislative contexts and show how electoral incentives and institutional opportunities work together to structure women's legislative behavior. With respect to legislative features that vary widely between chambers, I show that both party constraints and women's numeric representation structure women's collaboration. In Argentina, legislators are elected from closed-list ballots and the strength of political parties is determined, at least in part, by the district size. In particular, large district magnitudes in closed-list systems are known to foster strong party constraints and fierce party loyalty, which limit women's legislative collaboration. Women elected in small and medium districts are subject to relatively weaker party constraints. In institutions where women face weak party constraints, collaboration is more likely to unfold. The magnitude of this relationship varies depending on the gender composition of the legislature, such that increases in the proportion of female legislators strengthen women's incentives to toe the party line in districts with strong party constraints and to collaborate with female colleagues in districts with weak party constraints. These two relationships are evident from a comparison of men's and women's behavior in the Argentine provincial chambers. The case of South Africa further illustrates how strong party constraints have foiled women's efforts to collaborate. By contrast, collaboration thrives in institutions where legislators face weaker party constraints (such as the U.S. Senate and reserved seats in the Rwandan Parliament).

With respect to legislative contexts that vary within chambers, I first show that inter-branch relations are central to understanding legislative behavior. Female legislators affiliated with the executive are more likely to collaborate with one another than are legislators affiliated with other opposition political parties. Additionally, seniority status has an important influence on women's legislative behavior. In Argentina, female legislators with seniority status are more likely than their junior colleagues to collaborate with women outside of their parties. Similarly, senior women in the U.S. Senate facilitate collaboration with junior colleagues – from their own party and from the opposition party – through mentoring, informal meetings, and efforts to jointly develop legislation.

The topic of legislation is also important for understanding when women will collaborate. Across the board, women from Argentina are more likely to collaborate when legislating on women's issues – regardless of other legislative contexts. In the case of Uruguay, women are more willing to defy strong party constraints to advance women's rights legislation, even when they face costly party sanctions. Likewise, in the case of Rwanda, women can find common ground on women's rights legislation despite the strong partisan and racial cleavages that historically dominated Rwandan politics.

Finally, women's issues committees and women's caucuses are instrumental for facilitating collaboration. In the cases of Rwanda and Uruguay, for example, women's caucuses were instrumental in uniting women across party lines and creating a space for women to establish a women's rights agenda, consider diverse perspectives, and develop compromise on legislation. The process of collaboration and compromise among women was essential to the success of women's rights legislation in Rwanda and Uruguay. In a number of circumstances, women's ability to unite behind a single piece of legislation gave them the weight they needed to push for approval from the full chamber. The case of South Africa, on the other hand, clearly demonstrates that women's issues committees and caucuses are not sufficient to facilitate collaboration among women. In the face of extreme party constraints and party loyalty, women's caucuses and committees are not enough to forge cross-partisan alliances. Instead, partisan pressures inhibit potentially beneficial collaboration.

This research has important implications for how we understand democracy more broadly and for understanding how and when marginalized groups will have a voice in the policy-making process. Collaboration improves democracy by better representing the views of out-of-power groups. Despite women's marginalized status in the chamber, women can work within the system to exert their influence in the legislature. Nonetheless, their ability to do so is structured by a number of legislative contexts. In particular, increased collaboration is most likely when women are elected via institutions that give party leaders less control (rather than more) over backbenchers. Thus, the findings from this book advance our understanding of how different legislative contexts structure parliamentary behavior and, by extension, policy outcomes. Beyond contributing to our understanding of why and when women collaborate, this research has important implications for how we think about democracy, the advancement of women's rights agendas, electoral system design, and collaboration among legislators from other historically marginalized groups.

COLLABORATION BEYOND MARGINALIZATION

Our current understanding of institutions is gendered. In this book, I argue that women legislate differently than men and that understanding these differences is paramount to developing a complete model of representative democracy. I demonstrate that women are more likely than men to engage in collaboration. One clear consequence of my findings is this: as women's numeric representation in legislatures across the globe continues to increase, their distinct approach to democratic representation has the potential to change the nature of legislative politics. In particular, the increase of women's representation in office will change democracy more broadly from largely adversarial to more collaborative.

That said, I argue that collaboration is – at least in part – born out of women's efforts to overcome marginalization. If women's numeric representation continues to increase, and women begin to gain more power within legislatures, their marginalized status may end. The end of women's marginalization implies that their high levels of collaboration would then also end.

Nonetheless, I argue that women's legislative collaboration is unlikely to come to an end in the near future. Although, in some circumstances, women have begun to gain access to powerful leadership posts, women continue to face marginalization. Gains in women's numeric representation and women's increased access to formal and informal political power are the product of a long and slow process. Thus, unfortunately, women's marginalization is unlikely to come to an end in the short term. That said, even if women attain equal political power, there is room for thinking about collaboration beyond women's marginalization. There are multiple reasons to believe that collaboration – like other legislative norms – will become institutionalized and transcend women's marginalization: 1) as more women gain access to leadership posts, they will likely employ leadership styles that promote collaboration; 2) institutions that are in place to facilitate collaboration will endure; and 3) norms of collaboration will continue to be transmitted to new cohorts of women – and perhaps even men. In the following section, I discuss women's continued marginalization, and then explain how each of these factors will contribute to enduring collaboration among women.

Women Continue to Face Marginalization

Unfortunately, women continue to experience marginalization in legislatures worldwide; this does not appear to be changing in a rapid fashion. Thus, it is likely that norms of collaboration will become institutionalized long before women's marginalization ceases. Consider the Argentine provinces as an example of this trend. The adoption of gender quotas began in the early 1990s. Women have held a sizable (although still minority) proportion of seats in most of the chambers for almost two decades now. But, as I demonstrated in Chapter 4, women still have not been proportionally incorporated into formal positions of power. Only recently have we started to see women rise in the ranks and assume leadership positions in some legislatures in Argentina. The U.S. Senate presents a similar scenario. Women made major strides in increasing their numeric representation in the early 1990s; but more than twenty years later, women still hold minority status in the Senate, and they still have not gained a proportional share of powerful leadership positions. In fact, under some circumstances, increases in women's numeric representation have resulted in backlash, further limiting women's access to political power (Barnes 2014; Heath, Schwindt-Bayer, and Taylor-Robinson 2005; Kathlene 1994). This is not unique to Argentina or the U.S. Congress. Women still lag behind men in attaining leadership posts in most legislatures throughout the world (e.g., CAWP 2013; Christensen 2013; Krook and O'Brien 2012; O'Brien 2015), evidenced also by the fact that any time a women assumes a powerful position in a parliament, it still makes headline news.

When women do make it to the top, they are often outliers who are not representative of women's status more generally, and they face a number of informal barriers that prevent them from exerting similar levels of influence in parliaments as their male counterparts. In the case of Linda Suarez, the vice president of a province in Argentina, she noted that as a female leader in the legislature she is held to different standards than men. She explained that the opposition party behaves differently when she presides over the Senate – interrupting during debates and not maintaining order in the chamber. She maintained that this disrespectful behavior "does not happen when the vice-governor (a man) is presiding over the chamber."[1] Her attempts to place limits on this type of disrespectful behavior sometimes meet with hostile responses. For example, she noted: "They have said to me before, 'Okay, don't yell at me.' That is the biggest difference; if men yell, it is because they are machos, but if I yell, I'm hysterical or crazy." Other female leaders, in different regions of the world, encounter similar situations. Consider the recent experience of former Prime Minister Julia Gillard in Australia. During her time in office, she was subject to continued sexism that made international headline news. She reports that her experiences were not unique to her or to Australia. For instance, when interacting with other female heads of state, she noted: "You'll gather and chat about common experiences, where there's never-ending focus on appearance."[2] She acknowledged that it will take time before women overcome these obstacles: "I think it's all part of a journey, where we will over time be treating women and men far more equally in politics."[3] It is not surprising that the process of incorporating women into positions of political power is slow. Given that institutions are put in place to benefit the people in power (North 1990), it is not unexpected that those in power would endeavor to retain the status quo.

The Norm of Collaboration Will Become Institutionalized

Institutions and social norms are "sticky" – they are slow to change and endure over time. As such, the norm of women's marginalization is difficult to overcome. Nonetheless, the same logic applies to the norm of women's legislative collaboration. When women establish norms of collaboration in an effort to overcome their marginalization, these collaborative norms have the capacity to become sticky and institutionalized – enduring beyond women's marginalization. The case of the U.S. Senate exemplifies this concept. Senator Barbara Mikulski became secretary of the Senate Democratic Caucus in 1995. As she sees it, her position of power does not give her a reason to stop hosting her monthly dinners and power coffees for female legislators. Instead, her leadership post better positions her to mentor female legislators

---

[1] Interview with female legislator. Her name was changed to protect her anonymity. I do not provide information about her province or political party because so few women have held the top-ranking legislative position in their provinces.
[2] Interview with former Prime Minister of Australia Julia Gillard, cited in Franks (2014).
[3] Ibid.

and teach them how to obtain power in the U.S. Senate (Boxer, Collins, and Feinstein 2001). Informal meetings have become institutionalized norms among women in the Senate. Thus, as women's marginalization becomes less pronounced and women gain more political power, norms of collaboration will continue.

By the same token, women's access to leadership positions may also serve to institutionalize collaboration. As women often do not have the same experiences in leadership that men have, women must work to navigate structural barriers once in leadership. As I explained in Chapter 2, women are socially penalized for employing traditional – masculine – leadership tactics (Heilman and Okimoto 2007; Ridgeway 2001). Instead, women are expected to take a more cooperative and collaborative approach to leadership and are typically more influential when they conform to these gendered expectations (Eagly and Carli 2007; Meeker and Weitzel-O'Neill 1977; Ridgeway 1982; Shackelford, Wood, and Worchel 1996). Further, research on women in political leadership positions indicates that women are more likely than men to employ an integrative leadership style in which they emphasize "problem solving and collaborative win-win strategies" (Holman 2014; Rosenthal 1998, 19). Accordingly, as women continue to rise to top-ranking political posts they will likely continue to use leadership styles that promote collaboration.

The presence of formal institutions that advance women's collaboration reinforces the institutionalization of collaborative norms. In particular, women's caucuses and women's issues committees are unlikely to be disbanded when women begin gaining access to more formal positions of power. In the case of the Mendoza Senate in Argentina, for example, a woman has finally been appointed to the highest leadership position in the Senate, and women in the Senate are currently mobilizing in an effort to create a women's issues committee. Women in the Mendoza Senate recognize that even though one woman has made it to the top, there is still work to be done in terms of women's rights policies and in terms of women's status in the legislature. In Rwanda, women now comprise more than 50 percent of the Chamber of Deputies. Here too, female members of the parliament still see a clear need for a women's caucus. The Forum of Women Parliamentarians is still going strong; its members recently prepared a new strategic plan for the 2013–2018 period. These examples each suggest that women's caucuses and women's issues committees will continue to play an important role in facilitating collaboration among women in legislatures around the globe even as women make strides in improving their status within the chambers.

Although some of the regional assemblies in Argentina have women's issues committees and women's caucuses, they are more common among national parliaments; thirty-eight national parliaments have a formal women's caucus, and an additional forty-eight parliaments have an informal women's caucus (or a women's caucus for which the IPU lacks specific information regarding the status), meaning that eighty-six parliaments have some form of women's

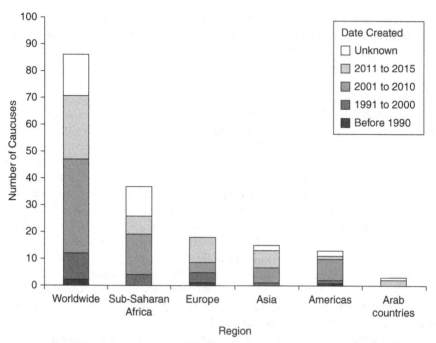

FIGURE 8.1. Women's caucuses worldwide.
Figure 8.1 graphs the number of women's caucuses on the y-axis and the region on the x-axis. Different shades indicate the period during which the caucuses were created. Data was collected from the IPU Database on Women's Caucuses (2015).

caucus (IPU 2015).[4] Figure 8.1 graphs the distribution of women's caucuses by regions and over time. It illustrates that the vast majority of women's caucuses were created since 2001, and Sub-Saharan Africa is the region with the most women's caucuses. The prevalence of women's caucuses in combination with the enduring nature of institutions implies that where institutions are permissive of collaboration, women's caucuses and women's issues committees will continue to facilitate collaboration among women chamber-wide – even as women and men move toward equality in numerical representation.

Finally, women's collaboration is unlikely to come to an end because norms and benefits of collaboration are likely to be transmitted to new cohorts of women. For example, in the U.S. Senate, Barbara Mikulski's tradition of taking newcomers under her wing, hosting an informal women's caucus, and establishing networks among women illustrates how women's seniority status can be useful for solidifying norms in the institution by passing them on to newcomers. In institutions where legislators have a higher probability of standing

[4] This does not take into account the existence of women's issues committees for which the IPU does not have systematic data.

for and winning reelection, these norms are more likely to get handed down to new cohorts of female legislators. However even in chambers that have low reelection rates, it is possible that partial renovation of the chamber can help to institutionalize collaboration. When only half of the chamber is elected at one time, experienced legislators have the opportunity to influence newcomers and share knowledge and strategies for succeeding in the legislature. In the same way that other legislative rules and norms are transmitted to newcomers, the norm of collaboration can be diffused among women. Moreover, these norms may eventually be transmitted to men. Indeed, women's collaboration is not entirely limited to collaboration with women. Instead, women often seek out male collaborators. There is empirical evidence to suggest that over time, men move away from stereotypically masculine behaviors (such as prioritizing competition) when more women are participating in an institution (Karpowitz and Mendelberg 2014). This suggests that as women's numeric representation becomes institutionalized in legislatures, collaboration may also become more common among men.

In sum, even as women continue to make gains in legislatures, it is unlikely that they will cease to collaborate. More likely is that as women's representation becomes institutionalized, their way of doing politics will change legislative norms. Consequently, to the extent that women do have incentives to behave differently in politics from men, increased women's representation has the potential to change the nature of policy making and partisan competition around the world.

POLICY IMPLICATIONS: WOMEN'S RIGHTS LEGISLATION

In addition to contributing to our understanding of women's legislative behavior, my research has broad implications for how we think about both the passage and substance of women's rights legislation. Specifically, it has implications for how champions of women's rights legislation can effectively work within different types of legislatures to get women's rights on the agenda and see them through the policy-making process. Moreover, this research has clear implications for the quality of women's rights legislation that is likely to be passed in different types of legislative environments. Indeed, the structure of some institutions reduces the probability that women's rights legislation will be passed and compromises the quality of legislation that is passed into law. This further underscores the need for external pressures from autonomous women's movements to potentially offset negative consequences fostered by some political institutions (Htun and Weldon 2012).

Getting Women's Rights on the Agenda

Although there is a strong normative concern for electing representatives who reflect the demographics of a constituency, demands for increases in women's presence in the legislature extend far beyond the debate of equitable numeric representation. Campaigns to promote women's numeric representation are often justified by the claim that increases in women's presence in the legislature will result in more attention to women's issues (Holman 2014; Karam and Lovenduski 2005; Krook 2009; Sawer 2000). There are many reasons to believe that increases in the number of representatives of historically marginalized groups will lead to increases in substantive representation of those groups (Mansbridge 1999; Phillips 1995; Weldon 2002; Williams 1998; Young 1990), yet research that systematically examines this relationship often leads to inconsistent findings. Some research finds strong support for the hypothesis that increases in women's presence in the legislature leads to increased attention to women's issues (Kittilson 2008), whereas other studies do not support this hypothesis (Weldon 2002).

One reason for these inconsistent findings is that different institutions provide different incentives that shape legislators' behavior. Some institutions create incentives for legislators to toe the party line and promote the party agenda and disincentivize legislators from pursuing interests beyond the party platform. For example, in the case of South Africa, strong party discipline prohibited women from working together to advance a women's rights agenda. In the case of Uruguay, women who broke with the party line to support women's rights were sanctioned and prohibited from running for reelection. Other legislative institutions are far more permissive of legislative behavior that is not in lockstep with the party. This autonomy provides representatives with the opportunity to represent constituents independently of the political party and to pursue independent policy agendas. For instance, in the case of Rwanda, party leaders exercise far less control over women's political careers.[5] As a result, women were more willing to break with party rank and work with women from all political parties to develop, cosponsor, and pass legislation prohibiting and punishing violence against women. Similarly, in the U.S. Senate, party leaders exercise relatively weak party constraints and women worked together across a large number of issues to advance their agendas.

It is necessary to consider the institutional context in which legislators govern in order to understand when women will have an opportunity to advocate women's rights agendas and their probability of successfully knitting together coalitions of support. On the one hand, women who are elected in chambers that discourage legislators from pursuing an independent political agenda may be far less likely to promote women's rights for fear of ending their political careers. The female deputy from Salta summarizes this point nicely: "Not all women are willing to advance. Maybe out of fear of losing their positions, their

---

[5] Recall, in the case of Rwanda, party leaders have high control over the careers of members elected from closed lists, but little control over the legislative careers of women elected to reserved seats in women-only elections.

job. Maybe they say I can't go against this government, or against my party's president. It is not easy; these battles are tough."[6] On the other hand, women who have more flexibility and autonomy may be able to promote women's rights with relatively few restrictions.

The Quality of Women's Rights Legislation

Even in chambers that I have described as potentially inhospitable to the advancement of women's rights, there are a number of circumstances that may ultimately lead to the adoption of women's rights legislation. For example, international pressures (Bush 2011) and the election of "women friendly" political parties (Kittilson 2008) may promote the advancement of women's rights legislation. Still, for a number of reasons, institutions that permit party leaders to exercise strong partisan constraints and discourage women's legislative collaboration may compromise the quality of legislation that is passed in these institutions by precluding the consideration of diverse perspectives and experiences.

Indeed, women's rights legislation is uniquely positioned to benefit from collaboration above and beyond the benefits realized by other types of legislation. If women's rights legislation is developed in isolation (e.g., only one political party or only one legislator), the quality of the legislation is likely to be compromised because of a limited range of perspectives. Women belong to all different groups in society as gender cuts across a broad number of both marginalized and privileged cleavages (Cassese, Barnes, and Branton 2015; Crenshaw 1993; Htun 2004, 2014; Weldon 2006). In other words, women have a number of *intersecting* identities that influence their policy needs and concerns. Although the majority of women face some shared structural disadvantages, each woman experiences these disadvantages in different ways, resulting in different perspectives on different experiences with a broad set of issues (Brown 2014a; Minta and Brown 2014; Phillips 1995; Simien and Hancock 2011; Strolovitch 2007). Collaboration among women who represent different groups is essential to better represent these diversities among women. Additionally, minority women's vast underrepresentation in national legislatures (Hughes 2011, 2013) further underscores the need for women to collaborate with colleagues both inside and outside of the legislature. In Rwanda, for example, developing successful gender-based violence legislation required female legislators to collaborate not only across party lines but also with civil society, constituents, and experts. Women's rights legislation that neglects to incorporate different perspectives and concerns may result in policy failures for some women (Bassel and Emejulu 2010; Crenshaw 1991; Hancock 2007a, 2007b; Harris-Perry 2011). For this reason, the quality of legislation developed in institutions that discourage collaboration may be inadequate.

[6] Interview with female deputy from Salta, Partido Justicialista, July 10, 2013.

Gendering Legislative Behavior

Autonomous Women's Movements

Autonomous women's movements and other external groups able to pressure governments can help to compensate for the policy deficiencies that result from a lack of collaboration. When female legislators cannot work within the system to promote women's rights and collaborate on women's rights legislation, it is all the more important that interest groups and advocacy groups apply pressure directly to the government to represent women's rights. Under these circumstances, it may not be sufficient to lobby women or other rank-and-file legislators. Instead, advocates of women's rights may benefit more from targeting party bosses and party platforms.

In the case of South Africa, for example, where strong party discipline prohibited the development of a multiparty women's rights agenda, some progress on women's rights legislation still occurred. Advancements in women's rights were a product of explicit pressure from groups outside of the government (Goetz and Hassim 2002). Similarly, other scholars have recognized the necessary role that autonomous women's movements play in expanding women's rights (Drysdale Walsh 2008; Htun and Weldon 2012; Paxton, Hughes, and Green 2006). My research suggests that autonomous women's movements and other external forces are even more critical when political parties exert considerable constraint over legislators' behavior. Finally, even if a legislature successfully passes women's rights legislation, as previously noted, the quality of legislation developed in institutions that discourage collaboration may be inadequate because it is less likely to incorporate the concerns and perspectives of women affected by the legislation. This further underscores the need for outside organizations and autonomous women's movements to articulate and represent women's concerns (Drysdale Walsh and Xydias 2014; Htun and Weldon 2012; Weldon 2002, 2011). External pressure of this nature is most important when institutions constrain women's ability to make changes from within the legislature.

WOMEN'S REPRESENTATION AND ELECTORAL SYSTEM DESIGN

The findings from this research have interesting implications for how scholars think about institutional designs that maximize women's representation. Although we have developed a clear understanding of how institutions can maximize women's descriptive representation, we know less about the institutional designs that maximize women's substantive representation. This research contributes to our understanding of how institutional design influences women's legislative behavior, which has clear implications for how and when women will represent women's interests. *But these findings imply that the institutional mechanisms that are best for increasing women's descriptive representation are not completely compatible with the goal of maximizing women's substantive representation.* This is because the implementation of gender quotas is the most immediate way to increase descriptive representation of women (Htun and Jones 2002; Kittilson 2005; Matland 1998; Matland and Studlar 1998; Norris 2004; Tripp and Kang 2008), but quotas are most effective when they combine placement mandates and closed-list proportional representation systems with large district magnitudes (Caul 1999, 2001; Jones 2009; Larserud and Taphorn 2007; Schwindt-Bayer 2009).[7] That said, these types of electoral institutions foster strong party constraints.

My research demonstrates that strong party constrains limit women's legislative behaviors by restricting their ability to forge cross-partisan alliances and exert their influence on the policy-making process. As I explained earlier in this chapter, these limitations have serious implications for both the adoption and quality of women's rights legislation. Beyond this, existing studies suggest that electoral rules that foster strong party constraints are more likely to result in the marginalization of women (Britton 2005; Goetz and Hassim 2003; Schwindt-Bayer 2010; Tinker 2004; Tripp 2006; Vincent 2004).

The results in this book demonstrate that women elected in legislative districts with weak party constraints are likely to work with female colleagues to exert their influence in the legislature. Female legislators in these circumstances have more autonomy from their political parties. I also demonstrate that women are likely to take advantage of this autonomy by forging cross-party alliances, and this autonomy leads to the development of successful women's rights legislation. These findings imply that women who face weak party constraints have more freedom to pursue a women's rights agenda and may be more likely to engage their colleagues in doing so. In addition to the implications from my research, there are other reasons to think that women may fare better in districts with weak party constraints. Schwindt-Bayer (2010), for example, argues that women are less likely to climb party ranks into leadership positions in systems that permit strong party constraints. The findings from this book, together with findings from extant research, indicate that *institutions that foster strong party constraints stifle women's voices.*

With few exceptions, however, women are woefully under-elected in legislatures with weak party constraints in comparison to those that promote party constraints (Thames and Williams 2013; Valdini 2012, 2013). This implies that electoral systems that promote the descriptive representation of women do not promote the substantive representation of women. At first glance, there appears to be a direct trade-off between institutions that facilitate the election of women to office, and those that stimulate collaboration among women (and potentially other positive legislative behavior).

I argue that this trade-off – between institutions that promote women's numeric representation and those that permit women's collaboration – is not

---

[7] See Wylie and Dos Santos (forthcoming), Wylie (2015b), and Wylie, Marcelino, and Dos Santos (2015) for a discussion of the challenges associated with electing women in open-list electoral systems.

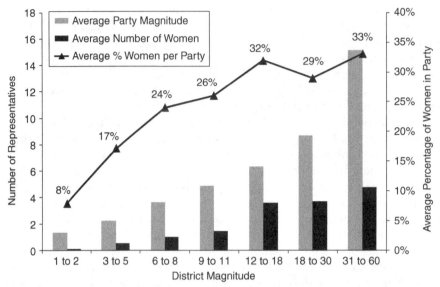

FIGURE 8.2. District magnitude, party magnitude, and the election of women.
Figure 8.2 graphs the district magnitude on the x-axis, number of representatives (full party and women in the party) on the left y-axis, and the percentage of women in a political party on the right y-axis. The figure illustrates the relationship between district magnitude, the number of representatives, and the election of women to office. Data are taken from the sample of legislators used in Chapter 5 and only include legislative sessions for which a quota was in place for two or more legislative sessions.

clear-cut. Rather, the findings from this book suggest that there may be a sweet spot – some combination of electoral systems that is conducive to both women's numeric representation and women's collaboration. That is, in closed-list systems, an optimal district magnitude exists where the district is large enough to still elect a large proportion of women, but small enough to limit party constraints.

I have already made the case that small and medium-sized districts (magnitude from 1 to 8) are small enough to limit partisan pressures. This idea is articulated in previous research (e.g., Carey and Hix 2011; Shugart, Valdini, and Suominen 2005), and corroborated by the findings I present in this book. Still, the question remains: Are these districts large enough to advance the election of women?

Figure 8.2 illustrates how increases in the average district magnitude are related to: 1) increases in the average party magnitude (i.e., the number of seats in a given district held by the same party); and 2) increases in the average percentage of women elected into systems with a closed list and a 30 percent gender quota.

First, Figure 8.2 illustrates that as the district magnitude increases, so does the average party magnitude. Party magnitude is important for determining women's numeric representation (Jones 2009; Matland 1993; Matland and Taylor 1997). Gender quotas often include placement mandates that demand women be placed on the electoral list in a certain order. Most Argentine provinces employ a placement mandate that requires women occupy at least one of every three positions on the ballot. Yet it is extremely rare that political parties exceed the minimum quota or place women in better positions than those necessary to comply with the law. As a result, the number of seats that an individual party wins has extremely important consequences for women's numeric representation. If a party is required to place a woman in one of every three positions on the ballot, and it chooses to place a woman in the third and sixth positions on the ballot, the same number of women will advance to office if the party wins three, four, or five seats. Only if the party wins six seats will it increase the number of women who win a seat in office.

Figure 8.2 illustrates that in districts with a magnitude between 6 and 8, the party magnitude is on average 4.5. Similarly, in larger districts with a magnitude between 9 and 11, the average party magnitude is 5.3. As a result, on average, women do not fare much better in districts with a magnitude of 9 to 11 than they do in systems with slightly smaller districts with a magnitude of 6 to 8. Data from Argentina show that women hold about 24 percent of seats won by each party in districts with a magnitude between 6 and 8 and about 26 percent of seats won by each party in districts with a magnitude between 9 and 11 – a difference of only 2 percent. This difference is much smaller than the increase in women's numeric representation that is achieved by moving from a district with a magnitude of 3 to 5 to a district with a magnitude of 6 to 8.

This pattern is consistent with the expectations developed in the literature. The logic advanced by Jones (2009; see also Jones, Alles, and Tchintian 2012) implies that the optimum party magnitude for women in systems in which gender quotas mandate that women must occupy one of every three positions on the party list is a multiple of three. This is because when the party magnitude is three (or 6 or 9...), the minimum percentage of seats a woman can occupy is 30 percent. If the party magnitude is less than three, there is some likelihood that women will not occupy any seats in the legislature. But once the party magnitude is 4 or 5, women can potentially occupy as few as 25 or 20 percent of the seats in the legislature, respectively. Given this logic, it is evident that the proportion of women elected in a district is not likely to increase if the district moves from an average party magnitude of 3 to a party magnitude of 9. Moreover, the figure illustrates that as district sizes increase past a district magnitude of 9, the probability of electing more women to office increases at a decreasing rate. This implies that medium-sized districts are large enough to facilitate the election of women.

Taken together, these findings suggest that medium-sized districts with closed-list ballots are optimal for *both* advancing women's descriptive representation *and* facilitating women's collaboration. This is because they are large enough to promote the election of women but small enough to foster relatively weak party constraints.

It is important to acknowledge that women are not as well represented in districts ranging from 6 to 11 as they are in larger districts. Figure 8.2 indicates that moving from a district sized 9 to 11 to one sized 12 to 18 results in a 6 percent increase in women's numeric representation. This is not trivial. Still, one possible solution to this in medium-sized districts is stricter placement mandate language. In the case of the Argentine National Congress, the placement mandate stipulates that female candidates must be placed in electable positions. For political parties who failed to win more than two seats in the previous election, parties are required to reserve one of the top two positions on the list for a female candidate. This is because the interpretation of the placement mandate used in the Argentine Congress suggests that the third place on the list is not an "electable" position if a party is not capable of winning more than two seats. A more rigid placement mandate such as this one would undoubtedly lead to increases in women's numeric representation in small and medium districts. Thus, this combination of electoral rules represents a sweet spot, one that maximizes the election of women to office and is conducive to women's collaboration.

COLLABORATION AND OTHER HISTORICALLY MARGINALIZED GROUPS

My theory is also generalizable to other marginalized groups. In legislatures, a number of different groups are in positions of institutional weakness. In Chapter 2, I explained that members of the opposition, legislators from the minority parties, and women are institutionally disadvantaged and thus have incentives to collaborate in an effort to exert more influence in the policy-making process. Other historically excluded groups can also benefit from collaboration. In particular, ethnic, religious, national, and racial minorities have historically been excluded from government decision-making bodies across the globe. This is particularly true for members of numerically small groups whose limited constituent numbers mean they cannot viably compete for legislative seats in elections. In recent years, however, a number of electoral rules such as reserved legislative seats, electoral quotas, and majority-minority districts have been designed to increase their numeric representation and to guarantee legislators from historically excluded groups a place in parliaments (Bird 2014; Grofman and Davidson 1992; Tan 2014).

Unlike for women, increased representation of ethnic, religious, national, and racial minority groups typically does not occur through established political parties. As gender identities tend to cut across partisan cleavages, policies designed to increase women's numeric representation usually entail legislative gender quotas that apply to all political parties and incorporate women directly into those parties (Htun 2004). By contrast, minority identities tend to coincide with party cleavages, thus policies designed to increase the numeric representation of other marginalized groups in society are different: in the most common scenarios, countries have adopted legislative reservations – or reserved seats in parliaments – to ensure the representation of marginalized groups who are not otherwise competitive in legislative elections (Htun 2004; Lijphart 1984; Reynolds 2005). These policies reserve seats in the chamber for which non-minority legislators are ineligible to contest (Htun 2004, 2015). In Colombia, for example, the constitution establishes that 5 of the 166 seats in the lower chamber (and 2 of the 102 seats in the upper chamber) are reserved for Afro-descendants, indigenous people, and other political minorities (Htun 2004). Five percent of seats (7 of 120) in the New Zealand unicameral chamber is reserved for Māori ethnic minorities, and almost 10 percent (8 of 83) of seats in the unicameral chamber of Niger is reserved for Tuareg national minorities. Reservations in Lebanon guarantee the representation of eleven different religious groups. In all, approximately forty countries have adopted electoral rules to improve the numeric representation of religious minorities, ethnic minorities, or other historically marginalized groups (Krook and O'Brien 2010; Protsyk 2010).

Reserved seats are successful at increasing the numeric representation of minority groups in parliaments. Yet reserved seats do not ensure that political parties incorporate representatives of marginalized groups. Exclusion from political parties limits their ability to exert influence in the policy-making process and motivates collaboration. At the same time, independence from established political parties means that minority legislators are not subject to strong partisan constraints (Htun and Ossa 2013). For this reason, my theory implies that minority legislators elected via reserved seats have both the incentives and opportunities to work collaboratively.

Incentives for Legislators from Reserved Seats to Collaborate

Minority groups have a strong incentive to collaborate. Representatives of marginalized groups are rarely incorporated directly into political parties. As a result, they lack institutional power within legislatures and have limited ability to exert influence in the policy-making process. Given that minority legislators are both marginalized in the chamber and excluded from political parties, they may have an even stronger incentive than women to collaborate in an effort to attain political power.

Indeed, despite the efforts to increase the numeric representation of minority groups in decision-making bodies, substantial evidence suggests that minority legislators continue to have limited access to power. Cross-national survey data from parliamentary groups show that minorities are often excluded from decision-making structures within the parliament (Protsyk 2010). Although there are a number of challenges associated with studying the representation of minority legislators (Bloemraad 2013; Hughes 2013), and more work needs to be done in this area to better understand how minorities access political power within legislatures, evidence from case studies further illustrates minorities' marginalized status within legislatures. In the case of Estonia, for example, Estonians dominate leadership positions in the Riigikogu (i.e., the national parliament), and national minorities remain virtually absent from these influential posts (Crowther and Matonyte 2007). Instead, they rarely attain formal and informal positions of power within the legislature and have a limited ability to exert their influence in the chamber. When minorities lack access to formal positions of power within the legislature, it is difficult for them to wield influence over policy outcomes (Browning, Marshall, and Tabb 1984; Haynie 2001; Nelson 1991; Preuhs 2006).

Further, just as women experience informal exclusion from power, minority legislators may also be sidelined from the benefits of informal political incorporation such as unofficial meetings, important leadership discussions, and powerful policy-making networks (Browning et al. 1984; Haynie 2001). For example, in Chapter 2, I explained that, in Salta, women report that "men are the ones in control; they leave you out for being a woman."[8] Informal exclusion limits legislators' ability to shape legislation during important stages of the policy-making process and incentivizes Salteña women to collaborate. They report that they must work together if they want to have an influence on the policy-making process: "In the issues of gender, [we] women unite; if not, we do not accomplish anything."[9] Given that electoral rules designed to improve minority representation give minority groups access to national legislatures, but not political parties, it may be even more difficult for minority legislators to gain access to elite political networks than it is for women.

As with women, these formal and informal barriers to power compromise minority legislators' ability to exert influence in the legislative process. Given their position of institutional weakness, they too would have incentives to work within the system to identify alternative strategies to accomplish their goals. In sum, my theory implies that legislators from minority groups have a strong motivation to collaborate as a means of attaining influence in the policy-making process.

Opportunities for Legislators from Reserved Seats to Collaborate

Minority legislators elected to parliaments through reserved seats operate within institutional contexts that are favorable to collaboration. Reserved seats enable marginalized groups to gain access to the legislature independent of political parties (Htun 2004), and subsequently they are subject to little or no partisan constraints (Htun and Ossa 2013). My theory posits that when legislators face weak party constraints, collaboration is more likely to unfold.

[8] Interview with female deputy, from Salta, Partido Renovador de Salta, July 10, 2013.
[9] Interview with female deputy from Salta, Partido Justicialista, July 10, 2013.

As with female legislators from Rwanda – who are also selected via reserved seats (see Chapter 7) – political parties do not control nominations to reserved seats. Minority legislators' political careers are not directly tied to the success of the political party, and their behavior is not restricted or sanctioned by political parties. Consequently, where minority legislators have a strong incentive to collaborate, they are unlikely to be inhibited by political party leaders. Additionally, as they do not owe any allegiance to political parties for their election to office, minority legislators elected in reserved seats are likely to develop loyalty toward their constituents and to feel a responsibility to promote minority rights. In the case of Rwanda, for example, in Chapter 7, I explained that female legislators elected through reserved seats reported a greater sense of loyalty to the female constituents who elected them and a stronger obligation to represent women's rights as compared to female legislators elected from the party candidate lists.

Exclusion from established political parties also means that minorities are not divided between political parties. For this reason, they may find it easier to foster collaboration across a broad range of minority legislators. Recall that in the case of Rwanda, female legislators elected through reserved seats worked with colleagues from across the spectrum to develop women's rights legislation. Unlike Argentine women from large legislative districts who are often pressured to demonstrate their party loyalty, Rwandan women were not constrained by political parties. Thus, minority representatives, unconstrained by party loyalty, may collaborate more.

Alternative Institutional Arrangements, Minority Representation, and Collaboration

Whereas the vast majority of countries use a reserved seat system to increase the numerical representation of minorities, a few cases use alternative strategies. For example, in the United States, minority legislators are elected to office through majority-minority districts. These alternative institutional arrangements have important implications for minority legislators. In such circumstances, minorities are incorporated into parliaments via political parties or routine electoral arrangements. They may, therefore, face different incentives and opportunities to collaborate than those incorporated into parliaments independent of political parties. The majority-minority districts in the United States, for example, are geographical electoral seats designed to increase the proportion of racial and/or ethnic minority constituents in an electoral district with the goal of increasing the probability of electing minority members to Congress (Grofman and Davidson 1992; Lublin 1997). Minority candidates competing in these districts are typically affiliated with one of the two established political parties. Similarly, a few countries, including Brazil and Singapore, use electoral quotas to increase the numeric representation of minority legislators. Like gender quotas, they require political parties to reserve space on their candidate lists for nominees from historically marginalized groups.

Legislators incorporated into parliaments through established political parties may have more opportunities to gain formal and informal access to power. Empirical research on this issue is mixed. On one hand, research from the United States finds evidence that African Americans advance to leadership positions in subcommittees more quickly than their white and Latino counterparts (Rocca, Sanchez, and Morin 2011; also see Button and Hedge 1996; Canon 1999; Haynie 2001). Similarly, minority Congress members secure party leadership positions at the same rate as their white Democratic counterparts (Tate 2003). If it is the case that minority legislators incorporated into established political parties have access to formal and informal channels of political power, then they may have fewer incentives to collaborate than minority legislators excluded from established political parties.

On the other hand, some research finds that even when legislators are brought to power via established political parties, they still have limited access to power (Hawkesworth 2003; McClain 1993; Orey et al. 2007). As with women in Argentina (see Chapter 4), in the United States, African Americans' equitable leadership positions can largely be explained by the fact that they are more likely to serve on lower-prestige and less powerful committees where leadership posts are less influential (Rocca et al. 2011). Thus, even where minorities are incorporated into political parties, they may still face challenges in accessing political power and thus have strong incentives to collaborate (Browning et al. 1984; Haynie 2001; Nelson 1991; Preuhs 2006). In such circumstances, collaboration provides an important alternative means by which these representatives can obtain power (Rocca and Sanchez 2008). In all, more work needs to be done to understand how and when minority legislators have access to power, as this clearly structures legislators' incentives to collaborate.

Minority legislators incorporated into office via established political parties may also have different opportunities to collaborate. If members are selected via electoral quotas, party leaders have the ability to "control them through the sanctions and incentives inherent in the nomination process" (Htun and Ossa 2013, 6). My theory posits that under these circumstances – and depending on the strength of partisan pressures – legislators may have fewer opportunities to collaborate with other minority legislators and instead may be pressured to dedicate their time and energy to advancing their parties' agendas. In this way, quotas may impose partisan divisions among minority legislators from different parties and dilute their strength (Htun 2004). Indeed, I show in Chapter 5 that female legislators in Argentina elected via legislative quotas in closed-list systems with large district magnitudes face strong party constraints, which limits collaboration compared to women elected in small and medium districts.

The electoral mechanisms designed to increase minority representation have clear implications for collaboration among minority legislators. Moreover, in thinking about why and when minority legislators will collaborate, the entire institutional context shapes minority legislators' incentives and opportunities to collaborate. In Chapters 5 and 6 of this book, I demonstrated that increases in women's numeric representation have important implications for understanding when women will collaborate. When women face weak party constraints, collaboration increases as women's numeric representation increases. However, whereas gender quotas typically reserve around 30 percent of nominee positions on candidate lists for women, electoral rules frequently reserve a much smaller percentage of seats for representatives of other historically marginalized groups. Thus minority representatives have limited numeric capacity to build coalitions of support.

Beyond this, in Chapter 2 I explained that other factors that vary within legislatures, such as the content of legislation and membership on special committees or caucuses, further condition collaboration. Just as women are more likely to collaborate when working on "women's issues," minority legislators may also be more likely to collaborate when working on issues that disproportionately influence the lives of minority constituents. Constituents from historically marginalized groups often have unique political experiences (Brown 2014b; White et al. 2007, 2010). As such, members of these groups may be better positioned to represent their interests. Indeed, research shows that minority legislators are more likely to introduce legislation designed to meet the needs of minority constituents (Bratton and Haynie 1999; Brown 2011, 2013, 2014a; Brown and Banks 2014; Wallace 2014). Given that minority legislators tend to have distinct legislative priorities, they may choose to collaborate with other minority legislators when working on these issues. Additionally, specialized committees and caucuses for addressing minority issues and promoting minority rights may help solve coordination problems and foster collaboration among minority legislators (Canon 1995; Kanthak and Krause 2012; Protsyk 2010).

Minority Women and Collaboration

Finally, my theory has a variety of implications for the success of minority women in governing bodies. Although minority women's intersecting identities position them to meet the requirements necessary to benefit from *both* gender quotas and minority-reserved seats (as well as minority quotas and majority-minority districts), minority women do not typically benefit from *either* gender quotas or minority-reserved seats (Holmsten, Moser, and Slosar 2010; Hughes 2011, 2013). Instead, they are passed over for majority women when political parties fill gender quotas and minority men when they fill minority-reserved seats.[10]

---

[10] Although cross-national research finds that on average minority women are less likely to be elected than majority women or minority men (Hughes 2011, 2013), there are exceptions to this general trend. In Belgium (where gender quotas are used) and the Netherlands (where there are no quotas), for example, Celis and colleagues (2014) find that ethnic minority women are more likely to be elected than are ethnic minority men.

As is clear from the research presented in this book, institutions matter. As such, for the few minority women elected to office, it is important to consider the mechanism through which they were elected to better understand their incentives and opportunities to collaborate. If minority women come to office through mechanisms designed specifically to elect women or, alternatively, to elect minorities, they may feel like they have to choose between collaborating with women or collaborating with minority legislators. This is because working on behalf of one group may be perceived as coming at the expense of the other group (Lépinard 2013). Pressure to choose between their two identities may be exacerbated in legislative contexts that discourage collaboration. Thus, women from minority groups may be pulled in both directions and pressured to work on behalf of both women and minorities (Holman 2014; Reingold and Smith 2012).

At the same time, minority women may be uniquely positioned to promote collaboration in parliaments by building coalitions between women and minority groups. Collaboration among different minority groups may be an effective strategy that simultaneously enhances the ability of both groups to exert power in the policy-making process. Just as women form coalitions with racial and ethnic minorities in American city governments to advance their institutional status (Smith 2014), we may also expect to see collaboration across different groups to advance their legislative agendas. Minority women may also be seen as an authentic representative who can serve as a uniting actor between disparate groups. In such circumstances, legislators are more likely to craft policies that speak to the diverse needs of marginalized groups, rather than privileging one group over the other.

In sum, my theory implies that it is imperative to consider the institutional context – such as the mechanisms used to elect minority groups to office – in order to understand minority legislators' incentives and opportunities to collaborate. In general, legislators in positions of institutional weakness have a strong incentive to collaborate. Thus, where minority legislators are not incorporated into the formal and informal legislative power structure, and hence have limited opportunities to wield influence – such as legislators elected via reserved seats – my theory implies they will be motivated to collaborate. But, where minority legislators are incorporated into political parties and have equitable access to power, their incentive to collaborate more frequently than other legislators declines. Whether collaboration transpires ultimately depends on the level of party constraints and other institutional contexts that structure legislative behavior. In particular, legislators brought to power independent of established political parties face few (or no) partisan constraints and can collaborate freely. By contrast, legislators incorporated into established political parties – even if they lack equitable access to power – are likely to have fewer opportunities to collaborate. Thus, as is the case with women's legislative collaboration, institutional contexts provide crucial insights for understanding why and when minority legislators will collaborate.

CONCLUDING THOUGHTS

This book represents a call to return to some of our fundamental assumptions about democratic representation. In doing so, we must carefully discern between behavior that is structured by political institutions and behavior that is gendered. The study of institutions can and should inform our understanding of how women legislate; but also, evaluating how women legislate differently from men can inform our understanding of institutions by illuminating gendered aspects of their impact on behavior (Krook 2009, 2010; Lovenduski 2005; Mackay 2011). In particular, this research demonstrates that the adversarial nature of politics is gendered and that women pursue more collaborative approaches to democratic representation (Duerst-Lahti and Kelly 1995; Mattei 1998; Rosenthal 1998; Sapiro 1991). In addition, the findings from this book indicate that the extent to which women's numeric representation can and will change politics is conditional on their institutional opportunities and electoral incentives. Where party discipline reigns supreme, women in politics are unlikely to transform the nature of representative democracy – instead the "competitive struggle" will prevail and coordination will be limited to *strategic* efforts to enhance the efficiency of competition. But, when institutions are more permissive, the growing presence of women in politics leads to a better balance between competition and collaboration, thus transforming institutions and democratic arrangements.

References

Alcañiz, Isabella. Forthcoming. *How Skills Shape International Cooperation: Environmental and Nuclear Networks in the Global South*. New York: Cambridge University Press.

Alemán, Eduardo. 2006. "Policy Gatekeepers in Latin American Legislatures." *Latin American Politics and Society* 48: 125–155.

2008. "Policy Positions in the Chilean Senate: An Analysis of Coauthorship and Roll Call Data." *Brazilian Political Science Review* 2(2): 74–92.

Alemán, Eduardo and Ernesto Calvo. 2010. "Unified Government, Bill Approval, and the Legislative Weight of the President." *Comparative Political Studies* 43(4): 511–534.

2013. "Explaining Policy Ties in the Argentine and Chilean Congress." *Political Studies* 61(2): 356–377.

Alemán, Eduardo, Ernesto Calvo, Mark P. Jones, and Noah Kaplan. 2009. "Comparing Cosponsorship and Roll Call Ideal Points." *Legislative Studies Quarterly* 34(1): 87–116.

Alexander, Amy C. 2011. "Mayoral Selection and the Demand and Supply of Women Mayors." *The Journal of Women, Politics, and Policy* 32(2): 114–135.

2012. "Change in Women's Descriptive Representation and the Belief in Women's Ability to Govern: A Virtuous Cycle." *Politics & Gender* 8(4): 437–464.

2015. "Big Jumps in Women's Presence in Parliaments: Are these Sufficient for Improving Beliefs in Women's Ability to Govern?" *Advancing Women in Leadership* 35: 82–97.

Alexander, Amy C., Ronald Inglehart, and Christian Welzel. 2012. "Measuring Effective Democracy: A Defense." *International Political Science Review* 33(1): 41–62.

Alexander, Amy C. and Christian Welzel. 2011a. "Measuring Effective Democracy: The Human Empowerment Approach." *Comparative Politics* 43(3): 271–289.

2011b. "How Robust Is Muslim Support for Patriarchal Values? A Cross National, Multilevel Study." *International Review of Sociology* 21: 249–276.

Alexander, Deborah and Kristi Andersen. 1993. "Gender as a Factor in the Attribution of Leadership Traits." *Political Research Quarterly* 46(3): 527–545.

Alles, Santiago. 2007. "¿Hacia la consolidación política? Cambios en la 'Estructura de Oportunidades Electorales' de las Mujeres en Argentina." *América Latina, hoy* 47: 123–154.

2008. "Efectos del Sistema Electoral sobre la Representación de Mujeres. Argumentos y Evidencia a partir del caso argentino (1983–2005)." *Revista SAAP* 3(2): 313–352.

2009. "Elección de Mujeres, Sistema Electoral y Cuotas de Género en las Provincias Argentinas." *XXVIII International Congress*, LASA, Río de Janeiro: June 11–14.

2014. "Ideología Partidaria, Competencia Electoral y Elección de Legisladoras en cinco democracias latinoamericanas: Argentina, Brasil, Chile, Perú y Uruguay, 1980–2013." *América Latina, hoy* 66: 69–94.

Altman, David and Anibal Pérez-Liñán. 2002. "Assessing the Quality of Democracy: Freedom, Competitiveness and Participation in Eighteen Latin American Countries." *Democratization* 9(2): 85–100.

Ames, Barry. 1995. "Electoral Rules, Constituency Pressures, and Pork Barrel: Bases of Voting in the Brazilian Congress." *The Journal of Politics* 57(2): 324–343.

2001. *The Deadlock of Democracy in Brazil.* Ann Arbor: University of Michigan Press.

Anzia, Sarah F. and Molly C. Jackman. 2013. "Legislative Organization and the Second Face of Power: Evidence from US State Legislatures." *The Journal of Politics* 75(1): 210–224.

Archenti, Nélida and María Inés Tula. 2008. "La Ley de Cuotas en La Argentina. Un Balance Sobre Lagros y Obstáculos." In *Mujeres Y Política en America Latina Sistemas Electorales y Cuotas de Género* Nélida Archenti and María Inés Tula (eds.). Buenos Aires: Heliasta. pp. 31–54.

Archenti, Nélida and Niki Johnson. 2006. "Engendering the Legislative Agenda with and without the Quota." *Sociologia, Problemas e Práticas* 52: 133–153.

Arnold, Laura W. and Barbara M. King. 2002. "Women, Committees and Institutional Change in the Senate." In *Women: Transforming Congress.* Cindy Simon Rosenthal (ed.). Norman: University of Oklahoma Press.

Bækgaard, Martin and Ulrik Kjaer. 2012. "The Gendered Division of Labor in Assignments to Political Committees: Discrimination or Self-Selection in Danish Local Politics?" *Politics & Gender* 8(4): 465–482.

Baldez, Lisa. 2002. *Why Women Protest: Women's Movements in Chile.* New York: Cambridge University Press.

2003. "Women's Movements and Democratic Transition in Chile, Brazil, East Germany, and Poland." *Comparative Politics* 35: 253–272.

2011. "The UN Convention to Eliminate All Forms of Discrimination against Women (CEDAW): A New Way to Measure Women's Interests." *Politics & Gender* 7(3): 419–423.

Balla, Steven J., Eric D. Lawrence, Forrest Maltzman, and Lee Sigelman. 2002. "Partisanship, Blame Avoidance, and the Distribution of Legislative Pork." *American Journal of Political Science* 46(3): 515–525.

Ballington, Julie. 1999. *The Participation of Women in South African's First Democratic Elections.* Johannesburg: Electoral Institute of South Africa.

Bangi, Patience. 2012. "RWANDA: 13 Years after the Genocide, Gender-based Violence Continues behind Closed Doors." *Make Every Woman Count Blog.* Available at: www.makeeverywomancount.org/index.php?option=com_content&view=article &id=4614:rwanda-13-years-after-the-genocide-gender-based-violence-continues -behind-closed-doors&catid=70:16daysactivism&Itemid=187.

Barnes, Tiffany D. 2012a. *Gender Quotas and the Representation of Women: Empowerment, Decision-making, and Public Policy.* Doctoral Dissertation, Department of Political Science, Rice University, Houston, Texas.

    2012b. "Gender and Legislative Preferences: Evidence from the Argentine Provinces." *Politics & Gender* 8(4): 483–507.

    2014. "Women's Representation and Legislative Committee Appointments: The Case of the Argentine Provinces." *Revista Uruguaya de Ciencia Política* 23(2): 135–163.

Barnes, Tiffany D. and Emily Beaulieu. 2014. "Gender Stereotypes and Corruption: How Candidates Affect Perceptions of Election Fraud." *Politics & Gender* 10(3): 365–391.

    2015. "Unpacking the Link between Female Politicians and Reduced Suspicions of Corruption." Presented at the European Conference on Politics and Gender, Uppsala University, Sweden, June 11–13, 2015.

Barnes, Tiffany D., Emily Beaulieu, and Yanna Krupnikov. 2015. "Engaging Women: Addressing the Gender Gap in Women's Networking and Productivity." Working Paper.

Barnes, Tiffany D., Regina Branton, and Erin C. Cassese. Forthcoming. "A Re-Examination of Women's Electoral Success in Open Seat Elections: The Conditioning Effect of Electoral Competition." *Journal of Women, Politics & Policy.*

Barnes, Tiffany D. and Stephanie M. Burchard. 2013. "'Engendering' Politics: The Impact of Descriptive Representation on Women's Political Engagement in Sub-Saharan Africa." *Comparative Political Studies* 46(7): 767–790.

Barnes, Tiffany D. and Abby Córdova. Forthcoming. "Making Space for Women: Explaining Citizen Support for Legislative Gender Quotas in Latin America." *The Journal of Politics.*

Barnes, Tiffany D. and Mark P. Jones. 2011. "Latin America" In Gretchen Bauer and Manon Tremblay (eds.). *Women in Executives.* New York: Routledge.

    2015. "Women's Representation in the Argentine National and Subnational Governments." Presented at Women and Leadership in Latin America Conference, Rice University, Houston, Texas, April 10, 2015.

Barnes, Tiffany D. and Diana Z. O'Brien. 2015. "Defending the Realm: The Appointment of Female Defense Ministers Worldwide." Presented at the Annual Meeting of the American Science Association, San Francisco, California, September 3–6, 2015.

Barnes, Tiffany D. and Constanza F. Schibber. 2015. "The Political Power of Female Legislators: Committee Appointments and Institutional Design." Presented at the Annual Meeting of the American Science Association, San Francisco, California, September 3–6, 2015.

Bassel, Leah and Akwugo Emejulu. 2010. "Struggles for Institutional Space in France and the United Kingdom: Intersectionality and the Politics of Policy." *Politics & Gender* 6(4): 517–544.

Bauer, Gretchen and Hannah E. Britton (eds.). 2006. *Women in African Parliaments.* Boulder, CO: Lynne Rienner Publishers.

Bauer, Gretchen and Jennie E. Burnet. 2013. "Gender Quotas, Democracy, and Women's Representation in Africa: Some Insights from Democratic Botswana and Autocratic Rwanda." *Women's Studies International Forum* 41(P2): 103–112.

Bauer, Nichole, Laurel Harbirdge, and Yanna Krupnikov. 2015. "Who Is Punished? How Voters Evaluate Male and Female Legislators Who Do Not Compromise." Working Paper.

Beaman, Lori, Raghabendra Chattopadhyay, Esther Duflo, Rohini Pande, and Petia Topalova. 2009. "Powerful Women: Does Exposure Reduce Bias?" *Quarterly Journal of Economics* 124(4): 1497–1540.

Beckwith, Karen. 2005. "A Common Language of Gender?" *Politics & Gender* 1(1): 128–137.

2007. "Numbers and Newness: The Descriptive and Substantive Representation of Women." *Canadian Journal of Political Science* 40(1): 27–49.

2011. "Interests, Issues, and Preferences: Women's Interests and Epiphenomena of Activism." *Politics & Gender* 7(3): 424–429.

2014. "Plotting the Path from One to the Other: Women's Interests and Political Representation." In Maria C. Escobar-Lemmon and Michelle M. Taylor-Robinson (eds.). *Representation: The Case of Women.* New York: Oxford University Press, pp. 19–40.

Bernhard, William and Tracy Sulkin. 2013. "Commitment and Consequences: Reneging on Cosponsorship Pledges in the US House." *Legislative Studies Quarterly* 38(4): 461–487.

Binder Sarah A. 1999. "Dynamics of Legislative Gridlock, 1947–1996." *American Political Science Review* 93(3): 519–533.

2003. *Stalemate: Causes and Consequences of Legislative Gridlock.* Washington, DC: Brookings Institution Press.

2015. "The Dysfunctional Congress." *Annual Review of Political Science* 18: 85–101.

Bird, Karen. 2003. "Who Are the Women? Where Are the Women? And what Difference Can they Make? Effects of Gender Parity in French Municipal Elections." *French Politics* 1(1): 5–38.

2014. "Ethnic Quotas and Ethnic Representation Worldwide." *International Political Science Review* 35(55): 12–26.

Bloemraad, Irene. 2013. "Accessing the Corridors of Power: Puzzles and Pathways to Understanding Minority Representation." *West European Politics* 36(3): 652–670.

Bonder, Gloria and Nari Marcela. 1995 "The 30 Percent Quota Law: A Turning Point for Women's Political Participation in Argentina. In Alida Brill (ed.). *A Rising Public Voice: Women in Politics Worldwide.* New York: The Feminist Press.

Boulding, Carew. 2014. *NGOs, Political Protest, and Civil Society.* New York: Cambridge University Press.

Bowler, Shaun, David M. Farrell, and Richard S. Katz. 1999. "Party Cohesion, Party Discipline and Parliaments." In Shaun Bowler, David M. Farrell, and Richard S. Katz (eds.). *Party Discipline and Parliamentary Government.* Columbus: Ohio State University Press, pp. 3–22.

Boxer, Barbara, Susan Collins, Dianne Feinstein, and Whitney Catherine. 2001. *Nine and Counting: The Women of the Senate.* New York: Harper Perennial.

Brady, David W. and Craig Volden. 1998. *Revolving Gridlock: Politics and Policy from Carter to Clinton.* Boulder, CO: Westview.

Bratton, Kathleen A. 2002. "The Effects of Legislative Diversity on Agenda-Setting: Evidence from Six State Legislatures." *American Politics Research* 30(2): 115–142.

2005. "Critical Mass Theory Revisited: The Behavior and Success of Token Women in State Legislatures." *Politics & Gender* 1(1): 97–125.

Bratton, Kathleen A. and Kerry L. Haynie. 1999. "Agenda Setting and Legislative Success in State Legislatures: The Effects of Gender and Race." *Journal of Politics* 61(3): 658–679.

Britton, Hannah. 2002. "Coalition Building, Election Rules, and Party Politics: South African Women's Path to Parliament." *Africa Today* 4(49): 33–68.

2005. *Women in the South African Parliament: From Resistance to Governance.* Urbana-Champaign: University of Illinois Press.

Brown, Alice, Tahnya Barnett Donaghy, Fiona Mackay, and Elizabeth Meehan. 2002. "Women and Constitutional Change in Scotland, Wales and Northern Ireland." *Parliamentary Affairs* 55(1): 71–84.

Brown, Nadia. 2011. "Identity and the Legislative Decision Making Process: A Case Study of the Maryland State Legislature." *Ethnic Studies Review* 34(1–2): 45–68.

2013. "Employing Intersectionality: The Impact of Generation on Black Women Maryland State Legislators Views on Anti-domestic Violence Legislation." *The Journal of Race and Policy* 9(1): 47–70.

2014a. *Sisters in the Statehouse: Black Women and Legislative Decision Making.* New York: Oxford University Press.

2014b. "Political Participation of Women of Color: An Intersectional Analysis." *Journal of Women, Politics & Policy* 35(4): 315–348.

Brown, Nadia and Kira Hudson Banks. 2014. "Black Women's Agenda Setting in the Maryland State Legislature." *Journal of African American Studies* 18(2): 164–180.

Browne, William. 1985. "Multiple Sponsorship and Bill Success in the U.S. State Legislatures." *Legislative Studies Quarterly* 10(4): 483–488.

Browning, Rufus P., Dale Rogers Marshall, and David H. Tabb. 1984. *Protest Is not Enough: The Struggle of Blacks and Hispanics for Equality in Urban Politics.* Berkeley: University of California Press.

Burchard, Stephanie. 2015. *Electoral Violence in Sub-Saharan Africa: Causes and Consequences.* Boulder, CO: Lynne Rienner Publishers.

Burgess, Diana and Eugene Borgida. 1999. "Who Women Are, Who Women Should Be: Descriptive and Prescriptive Gender Stereotyping in Sex Discrimination." *Psychology, Public Policy, and Law* 5(3): 665–692.

Burns, Peter F. 2012. *Electoral Politics is Not Enough: Racial and Ethnic Minorities and Urban Politics.* Albany, NY: SUNY Press.

Burnet, Jennie E. 2008. "Gender Balance and the Meanings of Women in Governance in Post-Genocide Rwanda." *African Affairs* 107 (428): 361–386.

2011. "Women Have Found Respect: Gender Quotas, Symbolic Representation and Female Empowerment in Rwanda." *Politics & Gender* 7(3): 303–334.

2012a. *Genocide Lives in Us Women, Memory, and Silence in Rwanda.* Madison: University of Wisconsin Press.

2012b. "Women's Empowerment and Cultural Change in Rwanda." In Susan Franceschet, Mona Lena Krook, and Jennifer M. Piscopo (eds.). *The Impact of Gender Quotas.* New York: Oxford University Press.

Burrell, Barbara C. 1994. *A Woman's Place Is in the House: Campaigns for Congress in the Feminist Era.* Ann Arbor: University of Michigan Press.

Bush, Sarah. 2011. "International Politics and the Spread of Quotas for Women in Legislatures." *International Organization* 65: 103–137.

Button, James and David Hedge. 1996. "Legislative Life in the 1990s: A Comparison of Black and White State Legislators." *Legislative Studies Quarterly* 21(2): 199–218.

Cain, Bruce E., John A. Ferejohn, and Morris P. Fiorina. 1987. *The Personal Vote.* Cambridge, MA: Harvard University Press.

Calvo, Ernesto. 2007. "The Responsive Legislature: Public Opinion and Law Making in a Highly Disciplined Legislature." *British Journal of Political Science* 37(2): 263–280.

2014. *Legislative Success in Fragmented Congresses in Argentina: Plurality Cartels, Minority Presidents, and Lawmaking.* New York: Cambridge University Press.

Calvo, Ernesto and Marcelo Escolar. 2005. *La Nueva Política de Partidos en La Argentina: Crisis Política, Realineamientos Partidarios y Reforma Electoral.* Buenos Aires: Prometeo Libros.

Calvo, Ernesto and Marcelo Leiras. 2012. "The Nationalization of Legislative Collaboration." *Revista Ibero-American de Estudios Legislativo* 2: 2–19.

Calvo, Ernesto and Maria Victoria Murillo. 2004. "Who Delivers? Partisan Clients in the Argentine Electoral Market." *American Journal of Political Science* 48(4): 742–757.

Calvo, Ernesto and Iñaki Sagarzazu. 2011. "Legislator Success in Committee: Gatekeeping Authority and the Loss of Majority Control." *American Journal of Political Science* 55(1): 1–15.

Caminotti, Mariana. 2009. En el Nombre de la Democracia. La Invención del Cupo Femenino y la Difusión Subnacional de las Cuotas en Argentina. Escuela de Política y Gobierno de la Universidad Nacional de San Martín, Tesis de Doctorado.

Campbell, James. 1982. "Cosponsoring Legislation in the U.S. Congress." *Legislative Studies Quarterly* 7: 415–422.

Canon, David T. 1995. "Redistricting and the Congressional Black Caucus." *American Politics Research* 23(2): 159–189.

1999. *Race, Redistricting, and Representation: The Unintended Consequences of Black Majority Districts.* Chicago: University of Chicago Press.

Carey, John. 1996. *Term Limits and Legislative Representation.* New York: Cambridge University Press.

2009. *Legislative Voting and Accountability.* Cambridge: Cambridge University Press.

Carey, John and Simon Hix. 2011. "The Electoral Sweet Spot: Low-Magnitude Proportional Electoral Systems." *American Journal of Political Science* 55(2): 383–397.

Carey, John and Matthew Soberg Shugart. 1995. "Incentives to Cultivate a Personal Vote: Rank Ordering of Electoral Formulas." *Electoral Studies* 14(4): 417–439.

1998. *Executive Decree Authority.* New York: Cambridge University Press.

Carlson, Katie and Shirley Randell. 2013. "Gender and Development: Working with Men for Gender Equality in Rwanda." *Agenda* 27(1): 114–125.

Carlson, Margaret. 2012. "How the Senate's Women Maintain Bipartisanship and Civility." *Omaha World-Herald Bureau.* March 4, 2012. Available at: www.omaha.com/apps/pbcs.dll/article?AID=/20130113/NEWS/701139863.

Carrió, Elisa María. 2005. "Argentina: A New Look at the Challenges of Women's Participation in the Legislature." *Women in Parliament: Beyond Numbers.* Stockholm: IDEA.

Carroll, Royce and Gary W. Cox. 2007. "The Logic of Gamson's Law: Pre-election Coalitions and Portfolio Allocations." *American Journal of Political Science* 51(2): 300–313.

2012. "Shadowing Ministers Monitoring Partners in Coalition Governments." *Comparative Political Studies* 45(2): 220–236.

Carroll, Royce, Gary W. Cox, and Mónica Pachón. 2006. "How Parties Create Electoral Democracy, Chapter 2." *Legislative Studies Quarterly* 31(2): 153–174.

Carroll, Royce and Henry A. Kim. 2010. "Party Government and the 'Cohesive Power of Public Plunder.'" *American Journal of Political Science* 54(1): 34–44.

Carroll, Susan. 2008. "Committee Assignments: Discrimination or Choice?" In Beth Reingold (ed.). *Legislative Women: Getting Elected, Getting Ahead.* Boulder, CO: Lynne Rienner Publishers, pp. 135–156.

Cassese, Erin C., Tiffany D. Barnes, and Regina Branton. 2015. "Racializing Gender: Public Opinion at the Intersection." *Politics & Gender*, 11(1): 1–26.

Castellanos, Angela. 2006. "LATIN AMERICA: Women Lawmakers Find Strength in Unity." *Inter Press Service New Agency.* Available at: www.ipsnews.net/2006/09/latin-america-women-lawmakers-find-strength-in-unity/.

Caul, Miki. 1999. "Women's Representation in Parliament: The Role of Political Parties." *Party Politics* 5(1): 79–98.

2001. "Political Parties and Candidate Gender Policies: A Cross-National Study." *Journal of Politics* 63(4): 1214–1229.

Celis, Karen, Silvia Erzeel, Lisa Mügge, and Alyt Damstra. 2014. "Quotas and Intersectionality: Ethnicity and Gender in Candidate Selection." *International Political Science Review* 35(55): 55–66.

Center for American Women and Politics (CAWP). 2013. "Women in State Legislative Leadership Positions 2013." National Information Bank on Women in Public Office, Eagleton Institute of Politics, Rutgers University. New Brunswick, NJ: Center for American Women and Politics (CAWP). Available at: www.cawp.rutgers.edu/fast_facts/levels_of_office/documents/leglead.pdf.

Chama, Mónica. 2001. *Las Mujeres y el Poder.* Buenos Aires: Ciudad Argentina.

Chappell, Louis. 2006. "Comparing Political Institutions: Revealing the Gendered 'Logic of Appropriateness.'" *Politics & Gender* 2(2): 223–235.

2010. "Comparative Gender and Institutions: Directions for Research." *Perspectives on Politics* 8(1): 183–189.

Cheibub, José Antonio, Zachary Elkins, and Tom Ginsburg. 2011. "Latin American Presidentialism in Comparative and Historical Perspective." *Texas Law Review* 89(7).

Cheibub, José Antonio, Argelina Figueiredo, and Fernando Limongi. 2009. "Political Parties and Governors as Determinants of Legislative Behavior in Brazil's Chamber of Deputies, 1988–2006." *Latin American Politics and Society* 51(1): 1–30.

Cheibub, José Antonio, Jennifer Gandhi, and James Raymond Vreeland. 2010. "Democracy and Dictatorship Revisited." *Public Choice* 143(1–2): 67–101.

Christensen, Martin K. I. 2013. "Women Party Leaders." *Worldwide Guide to Women in Leadership.* Available at: www.guide2womenleaders.com/woman_party_leaders.htm.

Clark, Jennifer Hayes, Tracy Osborn, Jon Winburn, and Gerald C. Wright. 2009. "Representation in U.S. Legislatures: The Acquisition and Analysis of U.S. State Legislative Roll Call Data." *State Politics and Policy Quarterly* 9(3): 356–370.

Claveria, Sílvia. 2014. "Still a 'Male Business'?: Explaining Women's Presence in Executive Office." *West European Politics* 37(5): 1156–1176.

Clucas, Richard A. and Melody Ellis Valdini. 2015. *The Character of Democracy: How Institutions Shape Politics*. New York: Oxford University Press.

Collier, David and Steve Levitsky. 1997. "Democracy with Adjectives: Conceptual Innovation in Comparative Research." *World Politics* 49(3): 430–451.

Cox, Gary W. 1987. "Electoral Equilibrium under Alternative Voting Institutions." *American Journal of Political Science* 31(1): 82–108.

  1990. "Centripetal and Centrifugal Incentives in Electoral Systems." *American Journal of Political Science* 34(4): 903–935.

  1997. *Making Votes Count: Strategic Coordination in the World's Electoral Systems*. New York: Cambridge University Press.

Cox, Gary W. and Mathew D. McCubbins. 1993. *Legislative Leviathan: Party Government in the House*. Berkeley: University of California Press.

  2005. *Setting the Agenda: Responsible Party Government in the U.S. House of Representatives*. Cambridge and New York: Cambridge University Press.

Crenshaw, Kimberle. 1991. "Women of Color at the Center: Selections from the Third National Conference on Women of Color and the Law: Mapping the Margins: Intersectionality, Identity Politics, and Violence against Women of Color." *Stanford Law Review* 43: 1241.

  1993. "Demarginalizing the Intersection of Race and Sex: A Black Feminist Critique of Antidiscrimination Doctrine, Feminist Theory and Antiracist Politics." In D. Kelly Weisburg (ed.). *Feminist Legal Theory*. Philadelphia, PA: Temple University Press, 383–395.

Crisp, Brian, Maria C. Escobar-Lemmon, Bradford S. Jones, Mark P. Jones, and Michelle M. Taylor-Robinson. 2004a. "Vote-Seeking Incentives and Legislative Representation in Six Presidential Democracies." *The Journal of Politics* 66(3): 823–846.

Crisp, Brian and Rachael E. Ingall. 2002. "Institutional Engineering and the Nature of Representation: Mapping the Effects of Electoral Reform in Colombia." *American Journal of Political Science* 46(4): 733–748.

Crisp, Brian, Kristin Kanthak, and Jenny Leijonhufvud. 2004. "The Reputations Legislators Build: With Whom Should Representatives Collaborate?" *American Political Science Review* 98(4): 703–716.

Crisp, Brian F. and Constanza F. Schibber. 2014. "The Study of Legislatures in Latin America." In Thomas Saalfeld, Kaare Strom, and Shane Martin (eds.). *The Oxford Handbook of Legislative Studies*. New York: Oxford University Press.

Crowther, William E. and Irmina Matonyte. 2007. "Parliamentary Elites as a Democratic Thermometer: Estonia, Lithuania and Moldova Compared." *Communist and Post-Communist Studies* 40(3): 281–299.

Dahl, Robert. 1971. *Polyarchy: Participation and Opposition*. New Haven, CT: Yale University Press.

Davidson, Roger H. and Walter J. Oleszek. 2005. *Congress and Its Members*. 10th ed. Washington, DC: CQ Press.

Deal, Jennifer J. and Maura A. Stevenson. 1998. "Perceptions of Female and Male Managers in the 1990s: Plus ça Change..." *Sex Roles* 38(3): 287–300.

De Luca, Miguel de, Mark P. Jones, and Maria Ines Tula. 2002. "Back Rooms or Ballot Boxes: Candidate Nomination in Argentina." *Comparative Political Studies* 35(4): 413–436.

Delvin, Claire and Robert Elgie. 2008. "The Effect of Increased Women's Representation in Parliament: The Case of Rwanda." *Parliamentary Affairs* 61(2): 237–254.

Diekman, Amanda B., Elizabeth R. Brown, Amanda M. Johnston, and Emily K. Clark. 2010. "Seeking Congruity between Goals and Roles: A New Look at Why Women Opt out of Science, Technology, Engineering, and Mathematics Careers." *Psychological Science* 21(8): 1051–1057.

Diekman, Amanda B., Alice H. Eagly, Antonio Mladinic, and Maria Christina Ferreira. 2005. "Dynamic Stereotypes about Women and Men in Latin America and the United States." *Journal of Cross-Cultural Psychology* 36(2): 209–226.

Diekman, Amanda B. and Monica C. Schnider. 2010. "A Social Role Theory Perspective on Gender Gaps in Political Attitudes." *Psychology of Women Quarterly* 34(4): 486–497.

Dodson, Debra. 2006. *The Impact of Women in Congress.* New York: Oxford University Press.

Dolan, Kathleen and Lynne E. Ford. 1997. "Change and Continuity among Women State Legislators: Evidence from Three Decades." *Political Research Quarterly* 50(1): 137–151.

Dovi, Suzanne. 2002. "Preferable Descriptive Representatives: Will Just any Woman, Black or Latino Do?" *The American Political Science Review* 96(4): 729–743.

Downs, Anthony. 1957. *An Economic Theory of Democracy.* New York: Harper and Row.

Driscoll, Amanda and Mona Lena Krook. 2009. "Can there Be a Feminist Rational Choice Institutionalism?" *Politics & Gender* 5(2): 238–245.

Drysdale Walsh, Shannon. 2008. "Engendering Justice: Constructing Institutions to Address Violence against Women." *Studies in Social Justice* 2(1): 48–66.

Drysdale Walsh, Shannon and Christina Xydias. 2014. "Women's Organizing and Intersectional Policy-Making in Comparative Perspective: Evidence from Guatemala and Germany." *Politics, Groups, and Identities* 2(4): 549–572.

Duerst-Lahti, Georgia. 2005. "Institutional Gendering: Theoretical Insights into the Environment of Women Officeholders." In Sue Thomas and Clyde Wilcox (eds.). *Women and Elective Office: Past, Present, and Future*, 2nd ed. New York: Oxford University Press.

Duerst-Lahti, Georgia and Rita Mea Kelly. 1995. *Gender Power, Leadership, and Governance.* Ann Arbor: University of Michigan Press.

Duerst-Lahti, Georgia, and Cathy M. Johnson. 1990. Gender and Style in Bureaucracy. *Women and Politics* 10(4): 67–120.

1992. "Management Styles, Stereotypes, and Advantages." In *Women and Men of the States: Public Administrators at the State Level*, edited by Mary E. Guy (ed.). Armonk, NY: M.E. Sharpe.

Duverger, Maurice. 1954. *Political Parties.* New York: Wiley.

Eagly, Alice H. and Linda L. Carli. 2007. *Through the Labyrinth: The Truth about how Women Become Leaders.* Boston, MA: Harvard Business School Press.

Eagly, Alice H., Mary C. Johannesen-Schmidt, and Marloes L. van Engen. 2003. "Transformational, Transactional, and Laissez-faire Leadership Styles: A Meta-analysis Comparing Women and Men." *Psychological Bulletin* 129(4): 569–591.

Eagly, Alice H. and Steven J. Karau. 2002. "Role Congruity Theory of Prejudice towards Female Leaders." *Psychological Review* 109(3): 573.

Eagly, Alice H., Wendy Wood, and Amanda B. Diekman. 2000 "Social Role Theory of Sex Differences and Similarities: A Current Appraisal." In Thomas Eckes and

Hanns Martin (eds.). *The Developmental Social Psychology of Gender*. Mahwah, NJ: Erlbaum, pp. 123–174.

Eaton, B. Curtis and Richard G. Lipsey. 1975. "The Principle of Minimum Differentiation Reconsidered: Some New Developments in the Theory of Spatial Competition." *The Review of Economic Studies* 42(1): 27–49.

El Sol. 2012. "Quieren unificar cuatro proyectos de ley contra la trata en Mendoza." *El Sol, Mendoza*. Dec. 17, 2012. Available at: www.politicaspublicas.uncu.edu.ar/novedades/index/quieren-unificar-cuatro-proyectos-de-ley-contra-la-trata-en-mendoza.

Escobar-Lemmon, Maria C. and Michelle M. Taylor-Robinson. 2005. "Women Ministers in Latin American Government: When, Where, and Why?" *American Journal of Political Science* 49(4): 822–844.

2009. "Getting to the Top: Career Paths of Latin American Female Cabinet Ministers." *Political Research Quarterly* 62(4): 685–699.

2014a. "Dilemmas in the Meaning and Measurement of Representation." In Maria C. Escobar-Lemmon and Michelle M. Taylor-Robinson (eds.). *Representation: The Case of Women*. New York: Oxford University Press. pp. 1–18.

2014b. "Does Presence Produce Representation of Interests?" In Maria C. Escobar-Lemmon and Michelle M. Taylor-Robinson (eds.). *Representation: The Case of Women*. New York: Oxford University Press, pp. 247–248.

Evans, Diana. 1994. "Policy and Pork: The Use of Pork Barrel Projects to Build Policy Coalitions in the House of Representatives." *American Journal of Political Science* 38(4): 894–917.

2004. *Greasing the Wheels: The Use of Pork Barrel Projects to Build Majority Coalitions in Congress*. New York: Cambridge University Press.

Fenno, Richard F. 1978. *Home Style: House Members in Their Districts*. Boston, MA: Little, Brown.

2003. *Going Home: Black Representatives and their Constituents*. Chicago: University of Chicago Press.

Fernández Anderson, Cora. 2011. The Impact of Social Movements on State Policy: Human Rights and Women Movements in Argentina, Chile and Uruguay. Doctoral Dissertation. South Bend, Indiana: University of Notre Dame.

Figueiredo, Argelina Cheibub and Fernando Limongi. 2000. "Presidential Power, Legislative Organization, and Party Behavior in Brazil." *Comparative Politics* 32(2): 151–170.

Fiorina, Morris P. 1978. "Economic Retrospective Voting in American National Elections: A Micro-analysis." *American Journal of Political Science* 22(2): 426–443.

Fiske, Susan, Amy J. C. Cuddy, and Peter Glick. 2007. "Universal Dimensions of Social Cognition: Warmth and Competence." *Trends in Cognitive Science* 11(2): 77–83.

Folke, Olle, Lenita Freidenall, and Johanna Rickne. 2015. "Gender Quotas and Ethnic Minority Representation: Swedish Evidence from a Longitudinal Mixed Methods Study." *Politics & Gender* 11(2): 345–381.

Forret, Monica L. and Thomas W. Dougherty. 2004. "Networking Behaviors and Career Outcomes: Differences for Men and Women?" *Journal of Organizational Behavior* 25(3): 419–437.

Foschi, Martha, Kristen Sigerson, and Marie Lebesis. 1995. "The Relative Effects of Gender, Academic Record, and Decision Type." *Small Group Research* 26(3): 328–352.

Fowler, James H. 2006. "Connecting the Congress: A Study of Cosponsorship Networks." *Political Analysis* 14: 456–487.

Fox, Richard L. and Zoe M. Oxley. 2003. "Gender Stereotyping in State Executive Elections: Candidate Selection and Success." *Journal of Politics* 65(3): 833–850.

Franceschet, Susan 2011. "Gender Policy and State Architecture in Latin America." *Gender and Politics* 7(2): 273–279.

Franceschet, Susan and Jennifer Piscopo. 2008. "Gender Quotas and Women's Substantive Representation: Lessons from Argentina." *Gender and Politics* 4(3): 393–425.

 2013. "Federalism, Decentralization, and Reproductive Rights in Argentina and Chile." *Publius: The Journal of Federalism* 43(1): 129–150.

 2014. "Sustaining Gendered Practices? Power and Elite Networks in Argentina." *Comparative Political Studies* 47(1): January 2014: 86–111.

Frankovich, Kathleen A. 1977. "Sex and Voting in the U.S. House of Representatives, 1961–1975." *American Politics Quarterly* 5: 315–331.

Franks, Tim. 2014. "Has Julia Gillard's Anger Diminished?" *British Broadcasting Corporation.* Feb. 25, 2014. Available at: www.bbc.com/news/world-asia-26333568.

Freedman, Jane. 2002. "Women in the European Parliament." *Parliamentary Affairs* 55(1): 179–188.

Frisch, Scott A. and Sean Q. Kelly. 2003. "A Place at the Table: Women's Committee Requests and Women's Committee Assignments in the U.S. House." *Women & Politics* 25(3): 1–26.

Funk, Kendall D. 2015. "Gendered Governing? Women's Leadership Styles and Participatory Institutions in Brazil." *Political Research Quarterly* 68(3): 564–578.

Funk, Kendall D. and Michelle M. Taylor-Robinson. 2014. "Gender Balance in Committees and How It Impacts Participation: Evidence from Costa Rica's Legislative Assembly." *Revista Uruguaya de Ciencia Política* 23(2): 111–134.

Gallagher, Michael and Michael Marsh. 1987. *Candidate Selection in Comparative Perspective.* London: Sage.

Gelman, Andrew and Jennifer Hill. 2007. *Data Analysis Using Regression and Multilevel/Hierarchical Models.* New York: Cambridge University Press.

Gerrity, Jessica, Tracy Osborn, and Jeanette Mendez. 2007. "Women and Representation: A Different View of the District." *Politics & Gender* 3(2): 179–200.

Gibson, Edward. 2011. *Boundary Control: Making and Unmaking Subnational Authoritarianism in Democratic Countries.* New York: Cambridge University Press.

Gibson, Edward L. and Ernesto Calvo. 2000. "Federalism and Low-Maintenance Constituencies: The Territorial Dimension of Economic Reform in Argentina." *Studies in Comparative International Development* 35(5): 32–55.

Gilligan, Carol. 1982. *In a Different Voice: Psychological Theory and Women's Development.* Cambridge, MA: Harvard University Press.

Ginwala, Frene. 1991. "Women and the Elephant: The Need to Redress Gender Oppression." In Susan Bazilli (ed.). *Putting Women on the Agenda.* Johannesburg: Raven.

Goetz, Anne Marie and Shireen Hassim. 2002. "In and against the Party: Women and Constituency Building in Uganda and South Africa." In S. Razavi and M. Molyneux (eds.). *Gender Justice, Development and Rights.* Oxford: Oxford University Press.

Goetz, Anne Marie and Shireen Hassim (eds.). 2003. *No Shortcuts to Power: African Women in Politics and Policy Making.* New York: Zed Books.

Gogineni, Roopa. 2013. "Rwandan Parliament's Female Majority Focuses on Equality." *Voice of America.* Available at: www.voanews.com/content/rwandan-parliament-female-majority-targets-equality/1757899.html.

Gomez, Jessica and Carla Koppell. 2008. "Advancing Women's Caucuses in Legislatures." *The Institute for Initiative Security.* Available at: www.ndi.org/files/Advancing%20Women%27s%20Caucuses%20in%20Legislatures.pdf.

González, Diana. 2009. *Producción Legislative en Materia de Equidad de Géneo y Generaciones Durante el Período Febrero 2005–Noviembre 2009.* Montevideo, Cotidiano Mujer-UNIFEM-ICP.

Green, Eric. 2012. "Women's Caucus Boosts Uruguayan Democracy." *Global Issues: Women in the World Today.* Washington DC: United States Department of State Bureau of International Information Programs.

Grey, Sandra. 2002. "Critical Mass and New Zealand Women MPs." *Parliamentary Affairs* 55(1): 19–29.

Grofman, Bernard and Chandler Davidson. 1992. *Controversies in Minority Voting: The Voting Rights Act in Perspective.* Washington, DC: Brookings Institute Press.

Hancock, Ange-Marie. 2007a. "Intersectionality as Normative and Empirical Paradigm." *PS: Political Science & Politics* 37(1): 41–45.

2007b. "When Multiplication Doesn't Equal Quick Addition: Examining Intersectionality as a Research Paradigm." *Perspectives on Politics* 5(1): 63–79.

2014. "Intersectional Representation or Representing Intersectionality? Reshaping Empirical Analysis of Intersectionality." In Maria C. Escobar-Lemmon and Michelle M. Taylor-Robinson (eds.). *Representation: The Case of Women.* New York: Oxford University Press, pp. 41–57.

Hassim, Shireen. 2003. "Representation, Participation, and Democratic Effectiveness: Feminist Challenges to Representative Democracy in South Africa." In Anne Marie Goetz and Shireen Hassim (eds.). *No Shortcuts to Power: African Women in Politics and Policy Making.* New York: Zed Books.

Harris-Perry, Melissa V. 2011. *Sister Citizen: Shame, Stereotypes, and Black Women in America.* New Haven, CT: Yale University Press.

Harward, Brian M. and Kenneth W. Moffett. 2010. "The Calculus of Cosponsorship in the US Senate." *Legislative Studies Quarterly* 35(1): 117–143.

Hawkesworth, Mary. 2003. "Congressional Enactments of Race-Gender: Toward a Theory of Raced-Gendered Institutions" *American Political Science Review* 97(4): 529–555.

Haynie, Kerry Lee. 2001. *African American Legislators in the American States.* New York: Columbia University Press.

Heath, Roseanna Michelle, Leslie A. Schwindt-Bayer, and Michelle M. Taylor-Robinson. 2005. "Women on the Sidelines: Women's Representation on Committees in Latin American Legislatures." *American Journal of Political Science* 49(2): 420–436.

Heilman, Madeline E. and Tyler G. Okimoto. 2007. "Why Are Women Penalized for Success at Male Tasks?: The Implied Communality Deficit." *Journal of Applied Psychology* 92(1): 81–92.

Hernández, Sánchez and Ana Isabel. 2001. "Paraguay." In Manuel Alcántara Sáez and Flavia Freidenberg (eds.) *Partidos Pollíticos de América Latina: Cono Sur* [Political

Parties of Latin America: Southern Cone]. Salamanaca: Ediciones Universidad de Salamanaca, pp. 355–421.

Hicken, Allen and Heather Stoll. 2011. "Presidents and Parties: How Presidential Elections Shape Coordination in Legislative Elections." *Comparative Political Studies* 44(7): 854–883.

2013. "Are All Presidents Created Equal? Presidential Powers and the Shadow of Presidential Elections." *Comparative Political Studies* 46(3): 291–319.

Highton, Benjamin and Michael Rocca. 2005. "Beyond the Roll-call Arena: The Determinants of Position Taking in Congress." *Political Research Quarterly* 58: 303–316.

Hinojosa, Magda. 2012. *Selecting Women, Electing Women: Political Representation and Candidate Selection in Latin America*. Philadelphia, PA: Temple University Press.

Holman, Mirya R. 2013. "Sex and the City: Female Leaders and Spending on Social Welfare Programs in U.S. Municipalities." *Journal of Urban Affairs* 36(4): 701–715.

2014. *Women in Politics in the American City*. Philadelphia, PA: Temple University Press.

2015. "Gender, Political Rhetoric, and Moral Metaphors in State of the City Addresses." *Urban Affairs Review*. Online first.

Holman, Mirya R., Jennifer Merolla, and Elizabeth Zechmeister. 2011. "Sex, Stereotypes, and Security: An Experimental Study of the Effect of Crises on Assessments of Gender and Leadership." *Journal of Women, Politics, and Policy* 32(3): 173–192.

Holmsten, Stephanie S., Robert G. Moser, and Mary C. Slosar. 2010. "Do Ethnic Parties Exclude Women?" *Comparative Political Studies* 43(10): 1179–1201.

Htun, Mala. 2003. *Sex and the State: Abortion, Divorce, and the Family under Latin American Dictatorships and Democracies*. New York: Cambridge University Press.

2004. "Is Gender Like Ethnicity? The Political Representation of Identity Groups." *Perspectives on Politics* 2(3): 439–458.

2014. "Political Inclusion and Representation of Afrodescendent Women in Latin America" In Maria C. Escobar-Lemmon and Michelle M. Taylor-Robinson (eds.). *Representation: The Case of Women.* New York: Oxford University Press, pp. 118–137.

2015. *Inclusion without Representation: Gender Quotas and Ethnic Reservations in Latin America*. New York: Cambridge University Press.

Htun, Mala N., and Mark P. Jones. 2002. Engendering the right to participate in decision-making: Electoral quotas and women's leadership in Latin America. In *Gender and the politics of rights and democracy in Latin America*, ed. Nikki Craske and Maxine Molyneaux, pp. 32–56. London: Palgrave.

Htun, Mala, Marina Lacalle, and Juan Pablo Micozzi. 2013. "Does Women's Presence Change Legislative Behavior? Evidence from Argentina." *Journal of Politics in Latin America.* 2(1): 95–125.

Htun, Mala and Juan Pablo Ossa. 2013. "Political Inclusion of Marginalized Groups: Indigenous Reservations and Gender Parity in Bolivia." *Politics, Groups, and Identities* 1(1): 4–25.

Htun, Mala and Timothy J. Power. 2006. "Gender, Parties, and Support for Equal Rights in the Brazilian Congress." *Latin American Politics and Society* 48(4): 83–104.

Htun, Mala and Laural Weldon. 2012. "The Civic Origins of Progressive Policy Change: Combating Violence against Women in Global Perspective, 1975–2005." *American Political Science Review* 106(3): 548–569.

Huddy, Leonie and Nayda Terkildsen. 1993. "Gender Stereotypes and the Perception of Male and Female Candidates." *American Journal of Political Science* 37: 119–147.

Hughes, Melanie M. 2009. "Armed Conflict, International Linkages, and Women's Parliamentary Representation in Developing Nations." *Social Problems* 56(1): 174–204.

2011. "Intersectionality, Quotas, and Minority Women's Political Representation Worldwide." *American Political Science Review* 105(3): 604–620.

2013. "The Intersection of Gender and Minority Status in National Legislatures: The Minority Women Legislative Index." *Legislative Studies Quarterly* 38(4): 489–516.

Hughes, Melanie M., Mona Lena Krook, and Pamela Paxton. 2015. "Transnational Women's Activism and the Global Diffusion of Gender Quotas." *International Studies Quarterly* 59(2): 357–372.

Huntington, Samuel P. 1991. *The Third Wave: Democratization in the Late Twentieth Century*. Norman: University of Oklahoma Press.

Inter-Parliamentary Union. 2013. *Women in National Parliaments*. Available at: www.ipu.org/wmn-e/world.htm.

International Parliamentary Union (IPU). 2015. Database on Women's Caucuses. Available at: http://w3.ipu.org/en/.

Jacobson, Gary C. 2004. *The Politics of Congressional Elections*, 6th ed. New York: Pearson.

Johnson, Joel W. and Jessica S. Wallack. 2010. Database of Electoral Systems and the Personal Vote. Available at: http://polisci2.ucsd.edu/jwjohnson/espv.htm.

Johnson, Niki. 2005. *La Política de la ausencia: las elecciones uruguayas 2004–2005 y la equidad de género*. Montevideo: CNS Mujeres.

2009. "The role of cross-party parliamentary women's benches in promoting women's substantive representation: the case of the Uruguayan Bancada Bicameral Femenina." *Presented at the European Conference on Politics and Gender Universitat Pompeu Fabre, Barcelona, 21–23 March 2013*.

2013a. "The role of Cross-party Parliamentary Women's Benches in Promoting Women's Substantive Representation: The Case of the Uruguayan Bancada Bicameral Femenina." *Paper prepared for presentation at the European Conference on Politics and Gender Universitat Pompeu Fabre, Barcelona, March 21–23, 2013*.

2013b. "Opening up the 'Black Box': Candidate Selection Procedures and Gender Representation in the 2009 Uruguayan Elections." *Paper prepared for presentation at the European Conference on Politics and Gender Universitat Pompeu Fabre, Barcelona, March 21–23, 2013*.

Johnson, Niki and Verónica Pérez. 2009. *Representación (S)Electiva: Una Mirada Feminista a las Elecciones Uruguayas*. Montevideo: Contidiano Mujer.

Jones, Mark P. 1995. *Electoral Laws and the Survival of Presidential Democracies*. Notre Dame, IN: University of Notre Dame Press.

1996. "Increasing Women's Representation Via Gender Quotas: The Argentine Ley de Cupos." *Women & Politics* 6(4): 75–98.

1997. "Legislator Gender and Legislator Policy Priorities in the Argentine Chamber of Deputies and the United States House of Representatives." *Policy Studies Journal* 25(4): 613–629.

1998. "Gender Quotas, Electoral Laws, and the Election of Women." *Comparative Political Studies* 31(1): 3–21.

2002. "Explaining the High Level of Party Discipline in the Argentine Congress." In Scott Morgenstern and Benito Nacife (eds.). *Legislative Politics in Latin America*. Cambridge: Cambridge University Press.

2008. "The Recruitment and Selection of Legislative Candidates in Argentina." In Peter M. Siavelis and Scott Morgenstern (eds.). *Pathways to Power: Political Recruitment and Candidate Selection in Latin America*. University Park: Pennsylvania State University Press.

2009. "Gender Quotas, Electoral Laws, and The Election of Women: Evidence from the Latin American Vanguard." *Comparative Political Studies* 42(1): 56–81.

Jones, Mark P., Sebastian Saiegh, Pablo T. Spiller, and Mariano Tommasi. 2002 "Amateur Legislators – Professional Politicians: The Consequences of Party-Centered Electoral Rules in a Federal System." *American Journal of Political Science* 46 (3): 656–669.

Jones, Mark P., Santiago Alles, and Carolina Tchintian. 2012. "Cuotas de Género, Leyes Electorales y Elección de Legisladoras en América Latina." *Revista de Ciencia Política* 32(2): 331–357.

Jones, Mark P. and Wonjae Hwang. 2005a. "Party Government in Presidential Democracies: Extending Cartel Theory beyond the U.S. Congress." *American Journal of Political Science* 49: 267–283.

2005b. "Provincial Party Bosses: Keystone of the Argentine Congress." In Steven Levitsky and María Victoria Murillo (eds.). *The Politics of Institutional Weaknesses: Argentine Democracy*. University Park: Pennsylvania State University Press.

Jones, Mark P., Pablo Sanguinetti, and Mariano Tommasi. 2000. "Politics, Institutions, and Fiscal Performance in a Federal System: An Analysis of the Argentine Provinces." *Journal of Development Economics* 61(2): 305–333.

Julious, Stephen A. 2004. "Sample sizes for clinical trials with Normal data." *Statistics in Medicine* 23(12): 1921–1986.

Kanthak, Kristin and George A. Krause. 2012. *The Diversity Paradox: Political Parties, Legislatures, and the Organizational Foundations of Representation in America*. Oxford University Press.

Karam, Azza and Joni Lovenduski. 2005. "Women in Parliament: Making a Difference." In Julie Ballington and Azza Karam (eds.). *Women in Parliaments: Beyond Numbers*. Stockholm: International Institute for Democracy and Electoral Assistance.

Karpowitz, Christopher F. and Tali Mendelberg. 2014. *The Silent Sex: Gender, Deliberation, and Institutions*. Princeton, NJ: Princeton University Press.

Kathlene, Lyn. 1989. "Uncovering the Political Impacts of Gender: An Exploratory Study." *The Western Political Quarterly* 42(2): 397–421.

1994. "Power and Influence in State Legislative Policymaking: The Interactions of Gender and Position in Committee Hearing Debates." *American Political Science Review* 88(3): 560–576.

1995. "Position Power versus Gender Power: Who Holds the Floor." In Georgia Duerst-Lahti and Rita Mae Kelly (eds.). *Gender Power, Leadership, and Governance*. Ann Arbor: University of Michigan Press, pp. 167–194.

Kerevel, Yann and Lonna Rae Atkeson. 2013. "Explaining the Marginalization of Women in Legislative Institutions." *Journal of Politics* 74(4).

Kessler, Daniel and Keith Krehbiel. 1996. "Dynamics of Cosponsorship." *The American Political Science Review* 90(3): 555–566.

Kiewiet, D. Roderick and Mathew D. McCubbins. 1991. *The Logic of Delegation*. Chicago: University of Chicago Press.

Kim, Eun Kyung. 2013. "Record Number of Women Senators Set Tone: 'They're Able to Talk to Each Other.'" *Today News*. June 14, 2013. Available at: www.today.com/news/record-number-women-senators-set-tone-theyre-able-talk-each-6C10326404.

King, David and Richard Matland. 2003 "Sex and the Grand Old Party: An Experimental Investigation of the Effect of Candidate Sex on Support for a Republican Candidate." *American Politics Research* 31(6): 595–612.

King, Gary, Robert O. Keohane, and Sidney Verba. 1994. *Designing Social Inquiry: Scientific Inference in Qualitative Research*. Princeton, NJ: Princeton University Press.

King, Gary, Michael Tomz, and Jason Wittenberg. 2000. "Making the Most of Statistical Analyses: Improving Interpretation and Presentation." *American Journal of Political Science* 44(2): 341–355.

Kirkland, Justin H. 2011. "The Relational Determinants of Legislative Outcomes: Strong and Weak Ties between Legislators." *The Journal of Politics* 73(3): 887–898.

2012. "Multimember Districts' Effect on Collaboration between US State Legislators." *Legislative Studies Quarterly* 37(3): 329–353.

2014. "Chamber Size Effects on the Collaborative Structure of Legislatures." *Legislative Studies Quarterly* 39(2): 169–198.

Kirkland, Justin H. and R. Lucas Williams. 2014. "Partisanship and Reciprocity in Cross-Chamber Legislative Interactions." *The Journal of Politics* 76(3): 754–769.

Kittilson, Miki Caul. 2005. "In Support of Gender Quotas: Setting New Standards, Bringing Visible Gains." *Politics & Gender* 1(4): 638–645.

2006. *Challenging Parties, Changing Parliaments: Women and Elected Office in Contemporary Western Europe*. Columbus: Ohio State University Press.

2008. "Representing Women: The Adoption of Family Leave in Comparative Perspective." *Journal of Politics* 70(2): 323–334.

2011. "Women, Parties and Platforms in Post-industrial Democracies." *Party Politics* 17(1): 66–90.

Kittilson, Miki Caul and Leslie A. Schwindt-Bayer. 2012. *The Gendered Effects of Electoral Institutions: Political Engagement and Participation*. New York: Oxford University Press.

Koger, Gregory. 2003. "Position-Taking and Cosponsorship in the U.S. House." *Legislative Studies Quarterly* 28: 225–246.

Krehbiel, Keith. 1995. "Cosponsors and Waffles from A to Z." *American Journal of Political Science* 39: 906–923.

1996. "Committee Power, Leadership, and the Median Voter: Evidence from the Smoking Ban." *Journal of Law, Economics, & Organization* 12(1): 234–256.

1998. *Pivotal Politics*. Chicago: University Chicago Press.

Krehbiel, Keith, Kenneth A. Shepsle, and Barry R. Weingast. 1987. "Why Are Congressional Committees Powerful?" *American Political Science Review* 81(3): 929–945.

Krook, Mona Lena. 2006. "Reforming Representation: The Diffusion of Candidate Gender Quotas Worldwide." *Politics & Gender* 2(3): 303–327.

2009. *Quotas for Women in Politics: Gender and Candidate Selection Reform Worldwide*. Oxford University Press: New York.

2010. "Beyond Supply and Demand: A Feminist-Institutionalist Theory of Candidate Selection." *Political Research Quarterly* 63(4): 707–720.

2015. "Empowerment versus Backlash: Gender Quotas and Critical Mass Theory." *Politics Groups and Identities* 3(1): 184–188.

Krook, Mona Lena and Fiona Mackay. 2011. *Gender, Politics and Institution: Towards a Feminist Institutionalism*. Basingstoke: Palgrave Macmillan.

Krook, Mona Lena and Diana Z. O'Brien. 2010. "The Politics of Group Representation: Quotas for Women and Minorities Worldwide." *Comparative Politics* 42(3): 253–272.

2012. "All the President's Men? The Numbers and Portfolio Allocations of Female Cabinet Ministers." *Journal of Politics* 74(3): 840–855.

Krutz, Glen. 2005. "Issues and Institutions: 'Winnowing' in the U.S. Congress." *American Journal of Political Science* 49(2): 331–326.

Lang-Takac, Esther and Zahava Osterweil. 1992. "Seperateness and Connectedness: Differences between the Genders." *Sex Roles* 27(1): 277–289.

Langston, Joy. 2008. "Legislative Recruitment in Mexico." In Peter M. Siavelis and Scott Morgenstern (eds.). *Pathways to Power: Political Recruitment and Candidate Selection in Latin America*. University Park: Pennsylvania State University Press, pp. 143–164.

Larserud, Stina and Rita Taphorn. 2007. *Designing for Equality: Best-Fit, Medium-Fit, and Non-favourable Combinations of Electoral Systems and Gender Quotas*. Stockholm: International IDEA.

Laver, Michael. 1998. "Models of Government Formation." *Annual Review of Political Science* 1(1): 1–25.

Laver, Michael and Norman Schofield. 1990. *Multiparty Government: The Politics of Coalition in Europe*. Oxford: Oxford University Press.

Laver, Michael and Kenneth A. Shepsle. 1996. *Making and Breaking Governments: Cabinets and Legislatures in Parliamentary Democracies*. New York: Cambridge University Press.

Leader, Shelah G. 1977. "The Policy Impact of Elected Women Officials." In Louis Maisel and Joseph Cooper (eds.). *The Impact of the Electoral Process*. Beverly Hills, CA: Sage.

Lépinard, Eléonore. 2013. "For Women Only? Gender Quotas and Intersectionality in France." *Politics & Gender* 9(3): 276–298.

Lijphart, Arend. 1971. "Comparative Politics and the Comparative Method." *American Political Science Review* 65(3): 682–693.

1984. *Democracies: Patterns of Majoritarian and Consensus Government in Twenty-One Countries*. New Haven, CT: Yale University Press.

2012. *Patterns of Democracy: Government Forms and Performance in Thirty-Six Countries*. New Haven, CT: Yale University Press.

Linz, Juan J. and Amando de Miguel. 1966. *Within-Nation Differences and Comparisons: the Eight Spains*. New Haven, CT: Yale University Press.

Linz, Juan J. and Arturo Valenzuela. 1993. *The Failure of Presidential Democracy: The Case of Latin America*. Baltimore, MD: Johns Hopkins University Press.

Llanos, Mariana and Constanza F. Schibber. 2008. "La participacion de la Presidencia y el Senado en el nombramiento del Poder Judicial (1983–2007)." *Desarrollo Económico*, 47(188): 607–637.

Lopreite, Debora. 2012. "Travelling Ideas and Domestic Policy Change: The Transnational Politics of Reproductive Rights/Health in Argentina." *Global Social Policy* 12(2): 109–128.

2014. "Explaining Policy Outcomes in Federal Contexts: The Politics of Reproductive Rights in Argentina and Mexico." *Bulletin of Latin American Research* 33(4): 389–404.

Lovenduski, Joni. 2005. *Feminizing Politics*. Cambridge, UK: Polity Press.

Lubertino, María José. 1992. *Cuota Minimo de Participación de Mujeres: El Debate en Argentina*. Buenos Aires: Fundación Friedrich Ebert.

Lublin, David. 1997. *The Paradox of Representation: Racial Gerrymandering and Minority Interests in Congress*. Princeton, NJ: Princeton University Press.

Mackay, Fiona. 2008. "'Thick' Conceptions of Substantive Representation: Women, Gender, and Political Institutions." *Representation* 44(2): 125–140.

2011. "Conclusions: Towards a Feminist Institutionalism." In Mona Lena Krook and Fiona Mackay (eds.). *Gender, Politics, and Institutions: Towards a Feminist Institutionalism*. Basingstoke: Palgrave Macmillan, pp. 181–196.

Mackay, Fiona, Meryl Kenny, and Louise Chappell. 2010. "New Institutionalism through a Gender Lens: Towards a Feminist Institutionalism?" *International Political Science Review* 31(5): 573–588.

Mackay, Fiona and Mona Lena Krook. 2011. "Introduction: Gender, Politics, and Institutions: Setting the Agenda." In Mona Lena Krook and Fiona Mackay (eds.). *Gender, Politics, and Institutions: Towards a Feminist Institutionalism*. Basingstoke: Palgrave Macmillan, pp. 1–21.

Mainwaring, Scott P. 1999. *Rethinking Party Systems in the Third Wave of Democratization: The Case of Brazil*. Stanford, CA: Stanford University Press.

Mainwaring, Scott, Daniel Brinks, and Anibal Pérez-Liñán. 2001. "Classifying Political Regimes in Latin America." *Studies in Comparative International Development* 36(1): 37–65.

2007. "Classifying Political Regimes in Latin America, 1945–2004." In Gerardo L. Munck (ed.). *Regimes and Democracy in Latin America: Theories and Methods*. New York: Oxford University Press.

Mainwaring, Scott and Anibal Pérez-Liñán. 1997. "Party Discipline in the Brazilian Constitutional Congress." *Legislative Studies Quarterly* 22(4): 453–483.

2013. "Democratic Breakdown and Survival." *Journal of Democracy* 24(2): 123–137.

2014. *Democracies and Dictatorships in Latin America: Emergence, Survival, and Fall*. New York: Cambridge University Press.

Mainwaring, Scott and Matthew S. Shugart. 1997. *Presidentialism and Democracy in Latin America*. New York: Cambridge University Press.

Mansbridge, Jane. 1999. "Should Blacks Represent Blacks and Women Represent Women? A Contingent 'Yes.'" *Journal of Politics* 61(3): 628–657.

2005. "Quota Problems: Combating the Dangers of Essentialism." *Politics & Gender* 1(4): 622–638.

Manuel, Tiffany, Susan Shefte, and Deborah Swiss. 1999. *Suiting Themselves: Women's Leadership Styles in Today's Workplace*. Cambridge, MA: Radcliffe Public Policy Institute and the Boston Club.

March, James G. and Johan P. Olsen. 2010. *Rediscovering Institutions: The Organizational Bias of Institutions*. New York: Simon and Schuster.

Marshall, Monty G and Ted Robert Gurr. 2013. Polity IV Project: Political Regime Characteristics and Transitions, 1800–2013.

Martin, Lanny W. and Randolph T. Stevenson. 2001. "Government Formation in Parliamentary Democracies." *American Journal of Political Science* 45(1): 33–50.

Martin, Lanny W. and Georg Vanberg. 2005. "Coalition Policymaking and Legislative Review." *American Political Science Review* 99(1): 93–106.

Matland, Richard E. 1993. "Institutional Variables Affecting Female Representation in National Legislatures: The Case of Norway." *Journal of Politics* 55(3): 737–755.

1994. "Putting Scandinavian Equality to the Test: An Experimental Evaluation of Gender Stereotyping of Political Candidates in a Sample of Norwegian Voters." *British Journal of Political Science* 24(2): 273–292.

1998. "Women's Representation in National Legislatures: Developed and Developing Countries." *Legislative Studies Quarterly* 23(1): 109–125.

2002. Enhancing Women's Political Participation: Legislative Recruitment and Electoral Systems. In *Women in Parliament: Beyond Numbers*. Available at: http://archive.idea.int/women/parl/toc.htm.

2006. "Electoral Quotas: Frequency and Effectiveness." In D. Dahlerup (ed.). *Women, Quotas and Politics*. New York: Routledge, pp. 275–292.

Matland, Richard E. and Donley T. Studlar. 1998. "The Contagion of Women Candidates in Single-Member District and Proportional Representation Electoral Systems: Canada and Norway." *The Journal of Politics* 58(3): 707–733.

Matland, Richard E. and Michelle Taylor. 1997. "Electoral System Effects on Women's Representation Theoretical Arguments and Evidence from Costa Rica." *Comparative Political Studies* 30(2): 186–210.

Mattei, Laura R. Winsky. 1998. "Gender and Power in American Legislative Discourse." *The Journal of Politics* 60 (2): 440–461.

Mattes, Robert B. 2002. "South Africa: Democracy without the People?" *Journal of Democracy* 13(1): 22–36.

Mayhew, David R. 1974. *Congress: The Electoral Connection*. New Haven, CT: Yale University Press.

2011. *Partisan Balance*. Princeton, NJ: Princeton University Press.

McAllister, Ian. 2007. "The Personalization of Politics." In Russell J. Dalton and Hans-Dieter Klingemann (eds.). *The Oxford Handbook of Political Behavior*. Oxford: Oxford University Press, pp. 571–588.

McClain, Paula D. 1993. *Minority Group Influence: Agenda Setting, Formulation, and Public Policy*. Westport, CT: Greenwood.

Meeker, Barbara, F. and Patricia A. Weitzel-O'Neill. 1977. "Sex Roles and Interpersonal Behavior in Task-Oriented Groups." *American Sociological Review* 42(1): 92–105.

Meintjes, Sheila. 2001. "War and Post-war Shifts in Gender Relations." In Sheila Meintjes, Meredeth Turshen, and Anu Pillay (eds.). *The Aftermath: Women in Post-Conflict Transformation*. Scottsville: University of KwaZulu-Natal Press.

Micozzi, Juan Pablo. 2013. "Does Electoral Accountability Make a Difference? Direct Elections, Career Ambition and Legislative Performance in the Argentine Senate." *Journal of Politics* 75(1): 137–149.

2014a. "Alliances for Progress? Multi-level Ambition and Patterns of Cosponsorship in the Argentine House." *Comparative Political Studies* 47(12): 1187–1208.

2014b. "From House to Home: Linking Multi-level Ambition and Legislative Performance in Argentina." *Journal of Legislative Studies* 20(3): 265–284.

Minta, Michael and Nadia Brown. 2014. "Intersecting Interests: Gender, Race and Congressional Attention to Women's Issues." *Du Bois Review* 1(2): 1–29.

Morgan, Jana and Melissa Buice. 2013. "Latin American Attitudes toward Women in Politics: The Influence of Elite Cues, Female Advancement, and Individual Characteristics." *American Political Science Review* 107 (4): 644–662.

Morgenstern, Scott. 2001. "Organized Factions and Disorganized Parties: Electoral Incentives in Uruguay." *Party Politics* 7(2): 235–256.

2002. "Explaining Legislative Politics in Latin America." In Scott Morgenstern and Benito Nacife (eds.). *Legislative Politics in Latin America*. New York: Cambridge University Press, pp. 413–445.

Morin, Rich. 2013. "The Most (and least) Culturally Diverse Countries in the World." *Pew Research Center*. Available at: www.pewresearch.org/fact-tank/2013/07/18/the-most-and-least-culturally-diverse-countries-in-the-world/.

Morton, Joseph. 2013. "Deb Fischer, Female Senators Hope for Bipartisan Efforts." *Omaha World-Herald Bureau*. Jan. 13, 2013. Available at: www.omaha.com/apps/pbcs.dll/article?AID=/20130113/NEWS/701139863.

Miller, Patrice M., Dorothy L. Danaher and David Forbes. 1986. "Sex-Related Strategies for Coping with Interpersonal Conflict in Children Aged Five and Seven." *Developmental Psychology* 22(4): 543–548.

Müller, Wolfgang. 2000. "Political Parties in Parliamentary Democracies: Making Delegation and Accountability Work." *European Journal of Political Research* 31(3): 309–333.

Murray, Rainbow. 2010. "Second among Unequals: A Study of Whether France's 'Quota Women' Are Up to the Job." *Politics & Gender* 6(1): 93–118.

Nelson, Albert J. 1991. *Emerging Influentials in State Legislatures: Women, Blacks, and Hispanics*. New York: Praeger.

Nielson, Daniel L. and Matthew Soberg Shugart. 1999. "Constitutional Change in Colombia Policy Adjustment through Institutional Reform." *Comparative Political Studies* 32(3): 313–341.

Norris, Jean M. and Anne M. Wylie. 1995. "Gender Stereotyping of the Managerial Role among Students in Canada and the United States." *Group and Organization Management* 20(2): 167–182.

Norris, Pippa. 2004. *Electoral Engineering: Voting Rules and Political Behavior*. New York: Cambridge University Press.

North, Douglass C. 1990. *Institutions, Institutional Change and Economic Performance*. New York: Cambridge University Press.

Norton, Noelle H. 2002. "Transforming Policy from the Inside." In Cindy Simon Rosenthal (ed.). *Women Transforming Congress*. Vol. 4. Norman, Oklahoma: University of Oklahoma Press.

O'Brien, Cheryl. 2013. *Beyond the National: Transnational Influences on (Subnational) State Policy Responsiveness to an International Norm on Violence against Women*. Doctoral Dissertation, Department of Political Science, Purdue University, West Lafayette, Indiana.

O'Brien, Diana Z. 2012a. "Gender and Select Committee Elections in the British House of Commons." *Politics & Gender* 8(2): 178–204.

2012b. "Quotas and Qualifications in Uganda." In Susan Franceschet, Mona Lena Krook, and Jennifer M. Piscopo (eds.). *The Impact of Quotas on Women's Descriptive, Substantive, and Symbolic Representation*. New York: Oxford University Press, pp. 57–71.

2015. "Rising to the Top: Gender, Political Performance, and Party Leadership in Advanced Articles Industrial Democracies." *American Journal of Political Science* 59(4): 1022–1039.

O'Brien, Diana Z., Matthew Mendez, Jordan Carr Peterson, and Jihyun Shin. 2015. "Letting Down the Ladder or Shutting the Door: Female Prime Ministers, Party Leaders, and Cabinet Ministers." *Politics & Gender* 11(4): 689–717.

O'Brien, Diana and Yael Shomer. 2013. "Legislators' Motivations, Institutional Arrangements, and Changes in Partisan Affiliation: A Cross-National Analysis of Party Switching." *Legislative Studies Quarterly* 38(1): 111–141.

O'Brien, Diana and Johanna Rickne. Forthcoming. "Gender Quotas and Women's Access to Leadership Posts." *American Political Science Review* 110(1).

Orey, Byron D'Andrá, Wendy Smooth, Kimberly S. Adams, and Kisha Harris-Clark. 2007. "Race and gender matter: Refining models of legislative policy making in state legislatures." *Journal of Women, Politics & Policy* 28(3-4): 97–119.

Osborn, Tracy. 2012. *How Women Represent Women: Political Parties, Gender, and Representation in the State Legislatures*. New York: Oxford University Press.

Osborn, Tracy and Jeanette Mendez. 2010. "Speaking as Women: Women and the Use of Floor Speeches in Congress." *Journal of Women, Politics and Policy* 31(1): 1–21.

Palmer, Barbara and Dennis Simon. 2005. "When Women Run Against Women: The Hidden Influence of Female Incumbents in Elections to the U.S. House of Representatives, 1956–2002." *Politics & Gender* 1(1): 39–63.

2006. *Breaking the Political Glass Ceiling: Women and Congressional Elections*. New York: Taylor & Francis.

Pansardi, Pamela, and Michelangelo Vercesi. Forthcoming. "Party Gate-keeping and Women's Appointment to Parliamentary Committees: Evidence from the Italian Case." *Parliamentary Affairs*.

Patty, John W., Constanza F. Schibber, Elizabeth Maggie Penn, and Brian F. Crisp. 2015. "Valence, Elections, & Legislative Institutions." Presented at the annual meeting of the American Science Association, San Francisco, California, September 3–6, 2015.

Paxton, Pamela, Jennifer Green, and Melanie Hughes. 2008. Women in Parliament, 1945–2003: Cross-National Dataset. ICPSR24340-v1. Ann Arbor, MI: Inter-university Consortium for Political and Social Research [distributor], 2008-12-22. doi:10.3886/ICPSR24340.V1.

Paxton, Pamela, Melanie M. Hughes, and Jennifer Green. 2006. "The International Women's Movement and Women's Political Representation, 1893–2003." *American Sociological Review* 71(6): 898–920.

Paxton, Pamela, Melanie M. Hughes, and Matthew Painter II. 2010. "Growth in Women's Political Representation: A Longitudinal Exploration of Democracy, Electoral System and Gender Quotas." *European Journal of Political Research* 49: 25–52.

Payne, Mark, Daniel Zovatto, and Mercedes Mateo Díaz. 2007. *Democracies in Development – Politics and Reform in Latin America*. Washington, DC: Inter-American Development Bank.

Pearson, Elizabeth. 2008. "Demonstrating Legislative Leadership: The Introduction of Rwanda's Gender-Based Violence Bill." *The Initiative for Inclusive Security*. Available at: www.inclusivesecurity.org/wp-content/uploads/2012/08/1078_rwanda_demonstrating_legislative_leadership_updated_6_20_08.pdf.

Pereira, Carlos and Marcus André Melo. 2012. "The Surprising Success of Multiparty Presidentialism." *Journal of Democracy* 23(3): 156–170.

Phillips, Anne. 1995. *The Politics of Presence.* Oxford: Clarendon Press.

Piscopo, Jennifer M. 2011. "Rethinking Descriptive Representation: Rendering Women in Legislative Debates." *Parliamentary Affairs* 11(3): 1–25.

2014a. "Female Leadership and Sexual Health Policy in Argentina." *Latin American Research Review* 49(1): 104–127.

2014b. "Inclusive Institutions versus Feminist Advocacy: Women's Legislative Committees and Caucuses in Latin America." World Congress of the International Political Science Association, Montreal, 2014.

Poguntke, Thomas and Paul D. Webb. 2005. *The Presidentialization of Politics: A Comparative Study of Modern Democracies.* Oxford: Oxford University Press.

Poole, Keith T. and Howard Rosenthal. 2001. "D-Nominate after 10 Years: A Comparative Update to Congress: A Political-Economic History of Roll-Call Voting." *Legislative Studies Quarterly* 16(1): 5–29.

Powell, Gary N. and D. Anthony Butterfield. 1989. "The 'Good Manager': Did Androgyny Fare Better in the 1980s?" *Group and Organization Studies* 14(2): 216–233.

Powley, Elizabeth. 2003. Strengthening Governance: The Role of Women in Rwanda's Transition. Washington: Hunt Alternatives Fund. Available at: www.huntalternatives.org/download/10_strengthening_governance_the_role_of_women_in_rwanda_s_transition.pdf.

2005. "Rwanda: Women Hold Up Half the Parliament." *International IDEA*, pp. 154–163. Retrieved from www.idea.int/publications/wip2/upload/Rwanda.pdf.

Powley, Elizabeth and Elizabeth Pearson. 2007. "Gender Is Society: Inclusive Lawmaking in Rwanda's Parliament." *Critical Half: Bi-annual Journal of Women for Women International* 5(1): 15–20.

Preuhs, Robert R. 2006. "The Conditional Effects of Minority Descriptive Representation: Black Legislators and Policy Influence in the American States." *Journal of Politics* 68(3): 585–599.

Propp, Kathleen. 1995. "An Experimental Examination of Biological Sex as a Status Cue in Decision Making Groups and Its Influence on Information Use." *Small Group Research* 26(4): 451–474.

Protsyk, Oleh. 2010. "Promoting Inclusive Parliaments: The Representation of Minorities and Indigenous Peoples in Parliament." Inter-Parliamentary Union and United Nations Development Programme: New York. www.ipu.org/splz-e/chiapas10/overview.pdf.

Rabe-Hesketh, Sophia and Anders Skrondal. 2005. *Multilevel and Longitudinal Modeling Using Stata.* College Station, TX: Stata Press.

Reingold, Beth. 2000. *Representing Women: Sex, Gender, and Legislative Behavior in Arizona and California.* Chapel Hill: University of North Carolina Press.

Reingold, Beth and Adrienne R. Smith. 2012. "Welfare Policymaking and Intersections of Race, Ethnicity, and Gender in U.S. State Legislatures." *American Journal of Political Science* 56(1): 131–147.

Reingold, Beth and Michele Swers. 2011. "An Endogenous Approach to Women's Interests: When Interests Are Interesting in and of Themselves." *Politics & Gender* 7(3): 429–435.

Retamero-Garcia, Rocio and Esther López-Zafra. 2009. "Causal Attributions about Feminine and Leadership Roles: A Cross-Cultural Comparison." *Journal of Cross-Cultural Psychology* 40(3): 492–509.

Reynolds, Andrew. 2005. "Reserved Seats in National Legislatures: A Research Note." *Legislative Studies Quarterly* 30(2): 301–310.

Ridgeway, Cecilia L. 1982. "Status in Groups: The Importance of Motivation." *American Sociological Review* 47(1): 76–88.

2001. "Gender, Status, and Leadership." *Journal of Social Issues* 57(4): 637–655.

Riker, William H. 1962. *The Theory of Political Coalitions*. New Haven, CT: Yale University Press.

Rocca, Michael S. and Gabriel Sanchez. 2008. "The Effect of Race and Ethnicity on Bill Sponsorship and Cosponsorship in Congress." *American Politics Research* 36: 130–152.

Rocca, Michael S, Gabriel Sanchez, and Jason Morin. 2011. "The Institutional Mobility of Minorities in Congress." *Political Research Quarterly* 64 (4): 897–909.

Rodriguez, Victoria E. 2003. *Women in Contemporary Mexican Politics*. Austin: University of Texas Press.

Rosenthal, Cindy Simon. 1998. *When Women Lead*. New York: Oxford University Press.

Ross, Karen. 2002. "Women's Place in 'Male' Space: Gender and Effect in Parliamentary Contexts." *Parliamentary Affairs* 55(2002): 189–201.

Samules, David. 1999. "Incentives to Cultivate a Party Vote in Candidate-centric Electoral Systems." *Comparative Political Studies* 32(4): 487–518.

2002a. "Progressive Ambition, Federalism, and Pork-Barreling in Brazil." In Scott Morgenstern and Benito Nacife (eds.). *Legislative Politics in Latin America*. Cambridge: Cambridge University Press.

2002b. "Pork Barreling Is Not Credit Claiming or Advertising: Campaign Finance and the Sources of the Personal Vote in Brazil." *The Journal of Politics* 64(3): 845–863.

2003. *Ambition, Federalism, and Legislative Politics in Brazil*. New York: Cambridge University Press.

Sapiro, Virginia. 1983. *The Political Integration of Women*. Urbana: University of Illinois Press.

1991. "Gender Politics, Gendered Politics: The State of the Field." In *Political Science, Looking to the Future*, ed. William Crotty. Evanston, IL: Northwestern University Press.

Sawer, Marian. 2000. "Parliamentary Representation of Women: From Discourses of Justice to Strategies of Accountability." *International Political Science Review* 21(4): 361–381.

Schein, Virginia E. 1973. "The Relationship between Sex Role Stereotypes and Requisite Management Characteristics." *Journal of Applied Psychology* 57(2): 95–100.

1975. "Relationships between Sex Role Stereotypes and Requisite Management Characteristics among Female Managers." *Journal of Applied Psychology* 60(3): 340–344.

Schein, Virginia E. and Ruediger Mueller. 1992. "Sex-Role Stereotyping and Requisite Management Characteristics: A Cross-cultural Look." *Journal of Organizational Behavior* 13(5): 439–447.

Schein, Virginia E., Ruediger Mueller, Terry Lituchy, and Jiang Liu. 1996. "Think Manager – Think Male: A Global Phenomenon?" *Journal of Organizational Behavior* 17(1): 33–41.

Schibber, Constanza F. 2012. "Vetos e Insistencias como mecanismos de negociación entre el Ejecutivo y el Legislativo." In Ana Mara Mustapic, Alejandro Bonvecchi, and Javier Zelaznik (eds.). *Los legisladores en el Congreso Argentina. Practicas y Estrategias*. Buenos Aires: Instituto Torcuato Di Tella.

Schneider, Monica C., Mirya R. Holman, Amanda B. Diekman, and Thomas McAndrew. Forthcoming. "Power, Conflict, and Community: How Gendered Views of Political Power Influence Women's Political Ambition." *Political Psychology.*

Schumpeter, Joseph. 1942. *Capitalism, Socialism, and Democracy.* Whitefish, MT: Kessinger Publishing.

Schwartz, Helle. 2004. *Women's Representation in the Rwandan Parliament – An Analysis of Variations in the Representation of Women's Interests Caused by Gender and Quota.* Gothenberg, Sweden: Gothenburg University, p. 71.

Schwindt-Bayer, Leslie A. 2006. "Still Supermadres? Gender and the Policy Priorities of Latin American Legislators." *American Journal of Political Science* 50(3): 570–585.
  2009. "Making Quotas Work: The Effect of Gender Quota Laws on the Election of Women." *Legislative Studies Quarterly* 34(1): 5–28.
  2010. *Political Power and Women's Representation in Latin America.* New York: Oxford University Press.

Schwindt-Bayer, Leslie A. and Michelle M. Taylor-Robinson. 2011. "The Meaning and Measurement of Women's Interests: Introduction." *Politics & Gender* 7(3): 417–418.

Shackelford, Susan, Windy Wood, and Stephen Worchel. 1996. "Behavioral Styles and the Influence of Women in Mixed-sex Groups." *Social Psychology Quarterly* 59: 284–293.

Shepsle, Kenneth A. 1978. *The Giant Jigsaw Puzzle: Democratic Committee Assignments in the Modern House.* Chicago: University of Chicago Press.

Shepsle, Kenneth A., Robert P. van Houweling, Samuel J. Abrams, and Peter C. Hanson. 2009. "The Senate Electoral Cycle and Bicameral Appropriations Politics." *American Journal of Political Science* 53(2): 343–359.

Shepsle, Kenneth A. and Barry R. Weingast. 1994. "Positive Theories of Congressional Institutions." *Legislative Studies Quarterly* 19(2): 149–179.

Shugart, Matthew Soberg. 2001. "'Extreme' Electoral Systems and the Appeal of the Mixed-Member Alternative." In Matthew Soberg Shugart and Martin P. Wattenberg (eds.). *Mixed Member Electoral Systems: The Best of Both Worlds?* New York: Oxford University Press, pp. 25–53.

Shugart, Matthew Soberg and John M. Carey. 1992. *Presidents and Assemblies: Constitutional Design and Electoral Dynamics.* New York: Cambridge University Press.

Shugart, Matthew Soberg, Melody Ellis Valdini, and Kati Suominen. 2005. "Looking for Locals: Voter Information Demands and Personal Vote-Earning Attributes of Legislators under Proportional Representation." *American Journal of Political Science* 49(2): 437–449.

Silveira, Silvana. 2010. Women Join Forces in the Parliamentary Trenches. *Inter Press Service* July 1, 2010. URL: www.ipsnews.net/2010/07/uruguay-women-join-forces -in-the-parliamentary-trenches/.

Simien, Evelyn M. and Ange-Marie Hancock. 2011. "Mini-Symposium: Intersectionali ty Research." *Political Research Quarterly* 64(1): 185–186.

Sinclair, Barbara. 1988. "The Distribution of Committee Positions in the U.S. Senate: Explaining Institutional Change." *American Journal of Political Science.* 32(2): 276–301.

Smith, Adrienne R. 2014. "Cities Where Women Rule: Female Political Incorporation and the Al- location of Community Development Block Grant Funding." *Politics & Gender* 10(3): 313–340.

Smooth, Wendy. 2011. "Standing for Women? Which Women? The Substantive Representation of Women's Interest and the Research Imperative of Intersectionality." *Politics & Gender* 7(3): 436–441.

Snyder, Richard. 2001. "Scaling Down: The Subnational Comparative Method." *Studies in Comparative International Development* 36(1): 93–110.

Steinhauer, Jennifer. 2013. "Once Few, Women Hold More Power in Senate." *New York Times*. March 21, 2013. Available at: www.nytimes.com/2013/03/22/us/politics/women-make-new-gains-in-the-senate.html?pagewanted=all&_r=0.

Streb, Matthew J. and Brian Frederick. 2009. "Conditions for Competition in Low-Information Judicial Elections: The Case of Intermediate Appellate Court Elections." *Political Research Quarterly* 62(3): 523–537.

Strolovitch, Dara Z. 2007. *Affirmative Advocacy: Race, Class and Gender in Interest Group Politics*. Chicago: University of Chicago Press.

Swers, Michele L. 1998. "Are Women More Likely to Vote for Women's Issue Bills than Their Male Colleagues?" *Legislative Studies Quarterly* 23(3): 435–448.

2002. *The Difference Women Make*. Chicago: University of Chicago Press.

2005. "Connecting Descriptive and Substantive Representation: An Analysis of Sex Differences in Cosponsorship Activity." *Legislative Studies Quarterly* 30(3): 407–433.

2013. *Women in the Club: Gender and Policy Making in the Senate*. Chicago: University of Chicago Press.

Tam Cho, Wendy K. and James H. Fowler. 2010. "Legislative Success in a Small World: Social Network Analysis and the Dynamics of Congressional Legislation." *The Journal of Politics* 72(1): 124–135.

Tan, Netina. 2014. "Ethnic Quotas and Unintended Effects on Women's Political Representation in Singapore." *International Political Science Review* 35(55): 55–66.

Tate, Katherine. 2003. *Black Faces in the Mirror: African Americans and Their Representatives in the U.S. Congress*. Princeton, NJ: Princeton University Press.

Taylor, Michelle M. 1992. "Formal versus Informal Incentive Structures and Legislator Behavior: Evidence from Costa Rica." *The Journal of Politics* 54(4): 1053–1071.

Taylor-Robinson, Michelle M. 2010. *Do the Poor Count? Democratic Institutions and Accountability in the Context of Poverty*. University Park: Pennsylvania State Press.

Taylor-Robinson, Michelle M. and Roseanna Michelle Heath. 2003. "Do Women Legislators Have Different Policy Priorities than Their Male Colleagues?" *Women & Politics* 24(4): 77–101.

Thames, Frank C. and Margaret S. Williams. 2013. *Contagious Representation: Women's Political Representation in Democracies around the World*. New York: New York University Press.

Theriault, Sean. 2005. *Power of the People: Congressional Competition, Public Attention, and Voter Retribution*. Columbus: Ohio State University Press.

Thomas, Sue and Susan Welch. 1991. "The Impact of Gender on Activities and Priorities of State Legislators." *Western Political Quarterly* 44(2): 445–456.

Thomas, Sue. 1994. *How Women Legislate*. Oxford: Oxford University Press.

Thomas-Hunt, Melissa C. and Katherine W. Phillips. 2004. "When What You Know Is Not Enough: Expertise and Gender Dynamics in Task Groups." *Personality and Social Psychology Bulletin* 30(12): 1585–1598.

Tilly, Louise A. and Patricia Gurin. 1992. *Women, Politics and Change*. New York: Russell Sage Foundation.

Timberlake, Sharon. 2005. "Social Capital and Gender in the Workplace." *Journal of Management and Development* 24(1): 34–33.

Tinker, Irene. 2004. "Quotas for Women in Elected Legislatures: Do They Really Empower Women?" *Women's Studies International Forum* 27: 531–546.

Towns, Ann. 2003. "Understanding the Effects of Larger Ratios of Women in National Legislatures: Proportions and Gender Differentiation in Sweden and Norway." *Women & Politics* 25(1): 1–29.

Tremblay, Manon and Réjean Pelletier. 2000. "More Feminists or More Women? Descriptive and Substantive Representation of Women in the 1997 Canadian Federal Elections." *International Political Science Review* 21(4): 381–405.

Tripp, Aili Mari. 2000. "Rethinking Differences: Comparative Perspectives from Africa." *Signs* 25(3): 649–675.

  2006. "Uganda: Agents of Change for Women's Advancement?" In Gretchen Bauer and Hannah Britton (eds.). *Women in African Parliaments*. Boulder, CO: Lynne Rienner Publishers.

Tripp, Aili Mari and Alice Kang. 2008. "The Global Impact of Quotas on the Fast Track to Increased Female Legislative Representation." *Comparative Political Studies* 41(3): 338–361.

United Nations Development Program. 2012. Rwanda: Women Helping Lead Country's Transformation. Available at: www.undp.org/content/undp/en/home/presscenter/articles/2012/07/12/rwanda-women-helping-lead-country-s-transformation/.

Valdini, Melody Ellis. 2012. "A Deterrent to Diversity: The Conditional Effect of Electoral Rules on the Nomination of Women Candidates." *Electoral Studies* 31(4): 740–749.

  2013. "Electoral Institutions and the Manifestation of Bias: The Effect of the Personal Vote on the Representation of Women." *Gender and Politics* 9(1): 76–92.

Vickers, Jill. 2011. "Gender and State Architectures: The Impact of Governance Structures on Women's Politics." *Politics & Gender* 7(2): 273–279.

Vincent, Louise. 2004. "Quotas: Changing the Way Things Look without Changing the Way Things Are." *Journal of Legislative Studies* 10(1): 71–96.

Volden, Craig, Alan Wiseman, and Dana Wittmer. 2013. "When Are Women More Effective Lawmakers than Men?" *American Journal of Political Science* 57(2): 326–341.

Vos, Suzanne. 1999. "Women in Parliament: A Personal Perspective." In Sonja Boezak (ed.). *Redefining Politics: South African Women and Democracy*. Johannesburg: CGE.

Wängnerud, Lena. 2015. *The Principles of Gender-Sensitive Parliaments*. New York: Routledge.

Wallace, Sophia J. 2014. "Representing Latinos Examining Descriptive and Substantive Representation in Congress." *Political Research Quarterly* 67(4): 917–929.

Wawro, Gregory. 2001. *Legislative Entrepreneurship in the U.S. House of Representatives*. Ann Arbor: University of Michigan Press.

Waylen, Georgina. 2007. *Engendering Transitions: Women's Mobilization, Institutions, and Gender Outcomes*. New York: Oxford University Press.

Weaver, R. Kent. 1986. "The Politics of Blame Avoidance." *Journal of Public Policy* 6(4): 371–398.

Weingast, Barry. 1989. "Floor Behavior in the U.S. Congress: Committee Power under the Open Rule." *American Political Science Review* 83(3): 795–815.

Weisman, Jonathan and Jennifer Steinhauer. 2013. "Senate Women Lead in Efforts to Find Accord." *The New York Times*. October 14, 2013. URL: www.nytimes.com/2013/10/15/us/senate-women-lead-in-effort-to-find-accord.html?_r=0.

Weldon, S. Laurel. 2002. "Beyond Bodies: Institutional Sources of Representation for Women in Democratic Policymaking." *Journal of Political* 64(4): 1153–1174.

2006. "The Structure of Intersectionality: A Comparative Politics of Gender." *Politics & Gender:* 2(2): 235–248.

2011. *When Protest Makes Policy: How Social Movements Represent Disadvantaged Groups.* Ann Arbor: University of Michigan Press.

White, Ismail K., Tasha S. Philpot, Kristin Wylie, and Ernest B. McGowan. 2007. "Feeling the Pain of My People: Hurricane Katrina, Racial Inequality, and the Psyche of Black America." *Journal of Black Studies* 37(4): 523–538.

2010. "Feeling Different: Racial Group–Based Emotional Response to Political Events." In Tasha S. Philpot and Ismail K. White (eds.). *African-American Political Psychology: Identity, Opinion, and Action in the Post–Civil Rights Era.* New York: Palgrave Macmillan.

Wilber, Roxane. 2011. "Lessons from Rwanda: How Women Transform Governance." *Solutions* 2(2): 1–8. Available at: www.thesolutionsjournal.com/node/887.

Wilde, Annett and Amanda B. Diekman. 2005. "Cross-cultural Similarities and Differences in Dynamic Stereotypes: A Comparison Between Germany and the United States." *Psychology of Women Quarterly* 29(2): 188–196.

Williams, Melissa S. 1998. *Voice, Trust, and Memory: Marginalized Groups and the Failings of Liberal Representation.* Princeton, NJ: Princeton University Press.

Wilson, Rick K. and Cheryl D. Young. 1997. "Cosponsorship in the United States Congress." *Legislative Studies Quarterly* 22(1): 24–43.

Winckler, Edwin A. 1999. "Electoral Equilibria in Taiwan." In Bernard Grofman, Sung-Chull Lee, Edwin A. Winckler, and Brian Woodall (eds.).*Elections in Japan, Korea, and Taiwan under the Single Non-transferable Vote: The Comparative Study of an Embedded Institution.* Ann Arbor: University of Michigan Press, pp. 266–286.

Wolbrecht, Christina. 2002. "Female Legislators and the Women's Rights Agenda: From Feminine Mystique to Feminist Era." In Cindy Simon Rosenthal (ed.). *Women Transforming Congress.* Norman: University of Oklahoma Press, pp 170–197.

Wright, Gerald C. and Nathaniel Birkhead. 2014. "The Macro Sort of the State Electorates." *Political Research Quarterly* 67(2): 426–439.

Wylie, Kristin N. 2015a. "Strong Women, Weak Parties, and Critical Actors in Brazil's Crisis of Representation." Presented at the European Conference on Politics and Gender, Uppsala University, Sweden, June 11–13, 2015.

2015b. "Electoral Rules, Party Support, and Women's Unexpected Successes in Elections to the Brazilian Senate." Presented at the annual meeting of the Latin American Studies Association, San Juan, Puerto Rico, May 27–30, 2015.

Wylie, Kristin N. and Pedro dos Santos. Forthcoming. "A Law on Paper Only: Electoral Rules, Parties, and the Persistent Underrepresentation of Women in Brazilian Legislatures." *Politics & Gender.*

Wylie, Kristin N. Daniel Marcelino, and Pedro dos Santos. 2015. "Extreme Nonviable Candidates and the Dynamics of Legislative Elections in Brazil." Presented at the annual meeting of the American Political Science Association, San Francisco, California, September 3–6, 2015.

Yoder, Janice D. 2001. "Making Leadership Work More Effectively for Women." *Journal of Social Issues* 57(4): 815–828.

Young, Iris Marion. 1990. *Justice and the Politics of Difference*. Princeton, NJ: Princeton University Press.

Zetterberg, Pär. 2008. "The Down Side of Gender Quotas? Institutional Constraints on Women in the Mexican State Legislatures." *Parliamentary Affairs* 61(3): 442–460.

Index